SAMUEL JOHNSON

Samuel Johnson

The Life of an Author

LAWRENCE LIPKING

HARVARD UNIVERSITY PRESS

Cambridge, Massachusetts, and London, England 1998

38874405
DLC

5-8-99

Copyright © 1998 by the President and Fellows of Harvard College
All rights reserved
Printed in the United States of America

Library of Congress Cataloging-in-Publication Data

Lipking, Lawrence I., 1934–
Samuel Johnson : the life of an author / Lawrence Lipking.
p.   cm.
Includes bibliographical references (p.   ) and index.
ISBN 0–674–78777–3 (alk. paper)
1. Johnson, Samuel, 1709–1784—Biography.   2. Great Britain—
Intellectual life—18th century.   3. Authors, English—18th
century—Biography.   4. Lexicographers—Great Britain—Biography.
5. Critics—Great Britain—Biography.   I. Title.
PR3533.L56   1998
828' .609—dc21
[b]   98–18526

IN MEMORY OF JEAN HAGSTRUM

ACKNOWLEDGMENTS

The life of any author depends, at last, upon readers—not only the real-life readers, present and future, who hold the fate of the work in their hands, but also the ideal imagined readers who fill the author's mind at the moment of writing. Both kinds of readers play a part in this book. From one point of view, the story of Johnson's career is a long struggle to find an audience he eventually helped to create: the English common reader. But he also kept company in his mind with the great authors of Europe, living and dead. The effort to bring such real and imagined readers together shaped all his work. Reconceiving the public for whom he wrote, in turn he became the model reader whom others imagined.

I too have had model readers. My principal debt is to the colleague and friend to whom this book is dedicated, the late Jean Hagstrum, whose goodness and good counsel have not left my mind as I finished a work he did so much to encourage. W. R. Keast first taught me that Johnson could repay a lifetime of reading. Only a few of the host of other scholars who helped form this book can be mentioned here, but special thanks go to M. H. Abrams, W. Jackson Bate, Wayne C. Booth, Helen Deutsch, Robert Folkenflik, A. Walton Litz, Hugh Ormsby-Lennon, Pat Rogers, Nicola Watson, and Richard Wendorf. Carol Bastian read the first chapter at a moment when her sharp eye was especially needed. Joanna Lipking provided unending comfort and aid. The notes to this book record many other debts, but they hardly do justice to the colleagues and students who have given so much to me over the years of writing.

This project has also received a wealth of institutional support, for which I am very grateful, from Northwestern University and the National Endowment for the Humanities; and the Woodrow Wilson International Center for Scholars and the National Humanities Center both provided ideal conditions for work and exhilarating intellectual communities. The opportunity to share my ideas with others in lectures and seminars as well as in the give and take of conversation has been important at every stage. Johnson scholars have been especially welcoming, but people who might find a kindred spirit in Johnson, if only they knew him better, have always been the audience I have had in mind. More than one chapter of this book changed radically as the result of a question I could not answer or an idea I needed to make my own. I thank both friends and strangers for their questions.

Chapter 1 of this book draws on a piece published in *Writing the Lives of Writers,* ed. Warwick Gould and Tom Staley (London: Macmillan, 1998); Chapter 2, on a piece in *Domestick Privacies: Samuel Johnson and the Art of Biography,* ed. David Wheeler (Lexington: University Press of Kentucky, 1987); Chapter 11, on a piece from *Wilson Quarterly,* later revised in *Re-Viewing Samuel Johnson,* ed. Nalini Jain (Bombay: Popular Prakasham, 1991).

CONTENTS

SAMUEL JOHNSON

Introduction

An *Author?* 'tis a Venerable Name!
How few deserve it, and what numbers claim?

T HIS IS A BOOK about the life of an author—not the life of a man but the life that he put in his work, a life to be found not by going outside his writings but by going more deeply inside them. It begins with his first compositions, not with his birth, and ends not with his death but with the close—and afterlife—of his career. In this respect it is the opposite of most recent biographies of authors, which comb through the private life of the person but often fail to satisfy the kind of reader who cares about authors because of what they have written. By contrast, this book passes over details that do not shed light on the work. It assumes that the crucial part of an author's life is what has gone into his writing, and it tries to bring out the powers of mind and feeling that keep that writing alive.

Any author might be the subject of such a book. Perhaps no author offers more of a challenge, however, than Samuel Johnson. For most of the last two centuries, Johnson's personality—or what Bertrand Bronson more accurately called his "folk-image"[1]—has tended to be far better known than his writings. This image was born in his own time, when he became not only a famous writer but a *celebrity* to a public that hungered for stories about him. Immediately after his death, a series of biographies, capped by Boswell's pivotal *Life of Johnson* (1791), ensured that curiosity would never die. The image even has its own name, *Dr.* Johnson (a title he seldom if ever used). Nor has the fascination faded. One good anthol-

1

ogy of Johnson's prose and poetry begins by cautioning that "no one should read even a selection from his writings who is not already familiar with the man. Boswell should come first"—since to read the writings without knowing the man "is to miss the vivifying power of his personality" and "unless you know him much of his writing is dead as well as dull."[2] Surely this is an extraordinary recommendation, advising the reader to close the book and pick up another. Can any way of "knowing" a writer be better than knowing his work? Yet reading Johnson continues to be less popular than reading about him. He shines like a star, or rather a constellation—Ursa Major—so vast that watchers can piece him together only with inklings about who he once was. The author trails behind these marks on the air.

There is no doubt that Samuel Johnson has been a prize biographical subject. He fanned the interest first with his own writings, which drop faint personal hints that have proved more intriguing than many bold confessions. Once he was gone, the trickle of anecdotes swelled into a flood. Boswell's *Journal of a Tour to the Hebrides, with Samuel Johnson, LL.D.* (1785), a companion to Johnson's own *Journey to the Western Islands of Scotland* (1775), altered the landscape that Johnson had seen by casting his giant shadow over it. Within a few years, Hester Lynch Piozzi's informal *Anecdotes of the Late Samuel Johnson* (1786) and Sir John Hawkins' imperious *Life of Samuel Johnson* (1787) showed that the life was rich enough to sustain two radically different perspectives. Boswell then cornered the market with a *Life* that, however often it may be accused of filtering Johnson through a personal strainer, still holds its place as the best-known and best-loved biography in English. But many other fine biographies were to follow, right up to the present. In the twentieth century a very short list would have to include the wealth of new information in A. L. Reade's *Johnsonian Gleanings* (11 vols., 1909–1952), the broad canvas of Joseph Wood Krutch's *Samuel Johnson* (1944), the good sense and scholarship of James L. Clifford's *Young Sam Johnson* (1955) and *Dictionary Johnson* (1979), the lively human interest of John Wain's *Samuel Johnson* (1974), and the psychological depth of W. Jackson Bate's *Samuel Johnson* (1977). More recently, Robert DeMaria Jr., in *The Life of Samuel Johnson* (1993), has surveyed the literary career of a Renaissance man. These biographers are also discerning critics, and all their Johnsons and more repay our interest. Nor is this focus on the life at all unsuited to a writer who, as Boswell said, "excelled all mankind in writing the lives of others."[3] The effort to think oneself into the frame of mind and the motives of someone else helps to define a moral being, according to Johnson, and many readers have testified that Johnson's example has helped them to live. The art of biography has grown from the spark that he kindled; that is not the least of his accomplishments.

What Johnson most excelled at, however, was writing the life of an *author*—someone whose life has gone into creating a body of work. That part of his example has not borne much fruit. These days not many biographies seem comfortable with the process of writing. Often, in fact, that lonely time when the author reflects, or talks to himself, or tries out rhymes or sentences, or reads, or takes up his pen, without any witness or partner in conversation, appears to be a distraction from the main business of life, which consists of doing things that involve other people, allowing them to build a critical mass of anecdotes and sketches. Some modern biographers seem to resent the artist's hermetic preoccupation with art. Johnson has quite a different point of view: the test of a poet's life, he suggests, ought to be the poems that he makes. This book tries to see his life in the same way. It is less concerned with his personality, or even his self, than with his identity as an author, the result of some deliberate choices of life. Johnson was not born an author. Almost unknown until his forties, he gradually made himself into a writer—and more than a writer, an author—who dominated his age. How this happened, and how it makes his writings what they are, is the story this book has to tell.

Yet that sort of story can hardly be taken for granted. Few words provoke more distrust or muddle, in current literary studies, than the label "author." In the 1960s, when Roland Barthes announced "The Death of the Author" and Michel Foucault impatiently raised the question "What Is an Author?", they took delight in challenging orthodox views.[4] Today that orthodoxy no longer recruits many scholars and critics, and a new anti-authorial consensus has largely replaced it. The reasons for this change are very complex. It seems unlikely that the arguments of Barthes and Foucault themselves carried the day, since those arguments, however suggestive, do not hold up against a searching logical or historical analysis.[5] Yet a powerful convergence of associations, especially important in those unsettled years and in their aftermath, worked to foment suspicion of the author. The first is the morphology that links, or "imbricates," authors with "authorize," "authoritative," "authoritarian," and above all "authority." On the face of it, the relation between authors and authorities, particularly those authorities who have power to make and enforce the law, seems tenuous at best. Are poets really the legislators of the world? No one has ever acknowledged that except other poets. The power of authors depends on what their readers are willing to give them, and resistance to the authority of authorities has helped to define a good many modern authors from Mailer to Solzhenitsyn. But doubts about the legitimacy of vested power have become so acute, in times of national crisis, that even the touch of privilege distinguishing authors from writers has seemed evidence of an authoritarian strain. The doubts have not melted away. Some critics now seem to assume that authorship implies an insistent claim to authority, and therefore an unavoidable anxiety and guilt on the part of authors.[6] Improbable as it may be, this association has stained the name of the author.

Another association may well have been still more important. Paradoxically, the same rebellion against authority that led to suspicion of authors has also resulted in distrust of the rebel. Romantic individualism has gone out of date—at least in academic circles. Not only have the rebels failed to change the world; they have also failed to understand their own complicity with the forces of oppression. At a minimum, this line of thought attacks the self-absorption of righteous men who do not notice the damage they cause to women, minorities, and the underclass, and who erect a barricade of authorship in order to keep other people out. At an extreme, the line of thought aims at exploding humanism itself: that is, the illusion that people can master the world and the language they use. The contempt for humanist ideals that once was reserved to a handful of philosophers, mostly in Europe, has now spread abroad. Nothing could be more absurd, from

4

this point of view, than the belief of individuals that they make themselves. That belief itself is produced by the machinery of mass society, which conditions its charges to define a tiny space for themselves by selecting personal items from a menu or shopping mall of characteristics, thus cooperating decisively with the system; the rebel too follows a script. Human beings, in antihumanist eyes, belong to the structures of thought that mold them or to the languages within which they are imprisoned, and persons are not agents or subjects but subject-positions. Hence the name of an "author" has no meaning, according to Foucault, except as an abbreviation for "author-function," a feature of texts or discourse in the age of print culture, and doubtless soon to be lost. There is something pathetic or comic or mystified now about the older meaning attached to "author," the "genius" or "subject" whose unique talents originate and authorize the work. Such emphasis on individual will perpetuates at best a pleasing myth if not a tyrannical lie.

Whether or not one agrees with this critique, one can hardly deny the modern travail of the author. In current usage the word "author" itself seems not only slightly archaic but self-contradictory. The scandal goes back at least as far as the series of definitions in Johnson's own *Dictionary* (1755):

1. The first beginner or mover of any thing; he to whom any thing owes its original.
2. The efficient; he that effects or produces any thing.
3. The first writer of any thing; distinct from the *translator* or *compiler.*
4. A writer in general.

A dramatic slippage seems to take place in this series. The first sense implies a Godlike power of creation, confirmed by the first illustration, from Hooker: "That law, the *author* and observer whereof is one only God, to be blessed for ever." But the second sense retreats to a mere producer, not blessed with any particular originality; one illustration, from Dryden, refers to a warrior as the author of a wound. Then, when the definitions narrow to writing, a similar falling off occurs between the third sense, which stresses priority, and the fourth, which admits that sometimes "author" only means "writer." At times the word presupposes a special advantage—"An *author* has the choice of his own thoughts and words, which a translator has not" (Dryden). At times it does not.

The uncertainty extends to another difficult question: just what does an author create? "Any thing" does not seem very specific. A "beginner or mover" can, presumably, originate "things," as God provides the first cause of either objects or events. But "the first writer of any thing" might be inventing a literary form, as Homer wrote the first epic, or only manufacturing one further instance, as Blackmore wrote a thing called *King Arthur.* Such distinctions matter greatly to Johnson the critic, who holds that "the highest praise of genius is original invention" and that *Paradise Lost* "is not the greatest of heroick poems, only because it is not the first."[7] Yet the *Dictionary* refuses to discriminate the work of authors from the work of writers in general. The inclusiveness of "any thing" evades sensitive issues, the criteria by which some kinds of writing accredit authorship and others seem irrelevant. Did the *Dictionary* establish Johnson himself as an author? From one point of view, it seems the work of a compiler; from another, a new sort of "thing" that made its author's name. Other criteria might include the excellence of the work, the individuality of the writing it contains, and its place in the writer's work as a whole. The more one examines these standards, the more they seem to shift. Can it be that the same set of words—for instance, a series of definitions—might be mere writing, if attributed to an anonymous scribe, but deeply personal, if signed by an author?

The metaphysical quandaries raised by such questions have not been resolved. Yet metaphysics itself may cause the confusion. To expect a word like "author" to be grounded in a single, essential meaning, rather than in what Wittgenstein called a family of meanings, is surely unreasonable. In practice, different contexts prompt the word to function differently. Sometimes "author" responds to the will to prize some sorts of writing more highly than others, sometimes to an interest in individuality or genius, sometimes to the search for a guarantee of validity in interpretation, sometimes to a harking back to origins, sometimes to the effort to sanction writing as a profession, and sometimes to nothing more than a recognition that some writers are very persistent. Contradictions occur when these situations cross. Nor can such tensions be resolved by clearer thinking. At bottom, doubts as to whether the author is a first mover or an imitator seem rooted in the double nature of language itself, where any saying or scribble might be analyzed either as the product of a system of signs *(langue)* or as a fresh combination *(parole)*. Authors themselves may share these doubts, experiencing the process of writing at one moment as following a beaten track, at another as an overflow of ideas that spill from the air. No single moment can encompass all of authorship.

Nor does the meaning of "author" remain constant over time. During the past few decades, an impressive amount of scholarly attention has been focused on the historical conditions that are supposed to have led to the birth—and death—of the author. Impatient with metaphysics, many scholars have sought the explanation of authorship in the material circumstances of particular cultural constructions. A consensus now holds that the author is a modern invention, called into being by the needs of those in power for ways of understanding and regulating writing. The consensus soon breaks down, however, when scholars try to identify the precise time and conditions that formed the author. Though the eighteenth century offers a popular setting for the rise of authorship, almost every period since the fifteenth century has also been nominated. But far more remarkable are the variety and ingenuity of material explanations for the author's birth. Money deserves to come first; authors are one effect, it is frequently said, of the commodification and commercialization of culture. But currency is vastly outnumbered by other candidates: the printing press; the growth of literacy; the discovery of the Americas; the codification of gender; censorship by the state; the rise of nationalism; copyright law; and, of course, the police.

None of these hypothetical causes of modern authorship lacks force. Insofar as culture defines the author, each element of culture might well play a part, and scholars who investigate the trail of money that keeps authors alive, for instance, are surely telling literary critics something they need to know. Yet material causes cannot complete the definition. "Author" is not, in fact, a recent word. In ancient times, the Latin *auctor* already indicated one sort of respected and sanctioned writer, and by the fourteenth century English writers like Chaucer had domesticated the term.[8] Did it mean exactly what it means today (whatever that might be)? Of course not; no word controls the changing contexts in which it is used. Yet the persistence of its use, predating all the circumstances that are supposed to explain it, seems to refute the notion that the author is a modern invention (except in the circular sense that the modern conditions and connotations of authorship—for instance, the way that copyright laws define an author as an owner—are incontestably modern).[9] Clearly, the word has been adaptable. Like authors themselves, it has survived in hostile times; and despite all rumors of the death of the author and the coming of hypertext, only a very dogmatic theorist would predict that readers will not pay homage to authors a hundred years from now.

Three aspects of authorship, in particular, have preoccupied readers almost as long as writing has existed. The first is the sense that writers, or certain writers, bring something new into being. "Beginners" and "movers," they duplicate or parody at one remove the power of creation that first made the world. Thus Homer is the author of the Greeks, in more ways than one. Whatever he or she or they may really have been, the epic creator serves as fountainhead, the source from which the culture of writing flows. Second, the notion of authorship implies that some writers are better than others. What flows from Homer is not only the form and content of epic but a hierarchy of poets in which he and the epic are paramount; priority and superiority go together.[10] But a less original writer, like Virgil, also qualifies as an author, so long as readers will acknowledge that he is deserving. In this respect, the name of author makes public the sense of writing as a performance or competition, which only the most worthy will survive. Finally, however, an author seems to be recognized not by individual works but by some sense of the work or career as a whole. An uneasy consciousness that "Marx" does not stand for particular writings but for a "totality of thought" or mode of discourse is what drove Foucault to ask, "What is an Author?" In spite of his effort to find other ways of speaking, the problem persists. An author, from a reader's point of view, may be seen as a continuity among texts, or what the writer might rather view as a project that makes his writings more than the sum of their parts. "That which is creative must create itself," in Keats's famous surmise,[11] and what authors create includes themselves as authors.

All three of these qualifications depend on varying standards of taste and judgment and imagination. However contingent on material circumstances, they cannot be reduced to a calculus or formula; what one age perceives as originality, superiority, or totality might always be perceived by another age as incidental. Hence the ways in which authors prove themselves continually change. That is one reason why becoming an author is such an uncertain and controversial calling or choice of life; sometimes the goal veers away just as the runner begins to approach it. The same reason may clarify why issues of authorship can be so interesting. In the making of every author, acts of imagination collide with the realities of what a market or culture will accept, and perennial aspects of writing adjust to the fashions of a specific time and place. A look at authorial self-definition can also help to illuminate definitions of culture.

Historically, Johnson seems to occupy a crucial position. Whether or not it is true that the modern author was born exactly when Johnson was, and was nurtured as he was by a rapid growth in the book trade, it is certainly true that contracts between writers, patrons, and the public were renegotiated in his time and with his help. No writer did more to set in motion that growth of literacy and widespread engagement with cultural issues that Raymond Williams calls "the long revolution."[12] Moreover, Johnson's career represents a challenge to older traditions of authorship. Was he an author at all? Not everyone has found his writings original or exceptional or unified. Even by his own standards, a dictionary seems a drudging sort of work to make an author's name, and the best of his poems were, as he called them, "imitations." No previous author, or at any rate no celebrated author, can be so firmly associated with hackwork. Hence if Johnson is indeed a great author—as I believe—he became one by breaking the mold. In this way he offers a perfect case for testing assumptions about what an author must be.

The case might also be posed in Johnsonian terms. The principle that "human nature is always the same,"[13] no matter how customs and manners may change, informs all his work. "There is such an uniformity in the state of man, considered apart from adventitious and separable decorations and disguises, that there is scarce any possibility of good or ill, but is common to human kind."[14] Thus the biographer weighs each life against the motives and passions that influence every life; the moralist recognizes enduring patterns of thought and behavior in each new dilemma; the literary critic sifts out the inessential circumstances of a piece of writing in order to estimate its kernel of genius and truth. Similarly, in Johnson's terms, knowing an author requires some study of the historical context, not in order to merge the author with his background but precisely in order to determine what powers are his own. These discriminations call for delicate judgment. Inevitably each author lives through a conflict, striving to adapt to whatever sort of writing is allowed or welcomed at the time, but simultaneously in league with authors through the ages. Johnson's own career plays out this conflict. As much as he participates in the publishing schemes and ventures of the moment—the first magazines, the English dictionary, editions of the best-selling national poets, or anything else for which money is offered—he thinks of himself as a scholar and poet as well, in some ways closer to the ancients or to the Renaissance humanists than to most contemporaries. The author that he creates in his mind is partly a hack yet also partly an eternal ideal. The tension or balance between these two accounts for much of the interest of his writing. It also carries the burden of this book.

Above all, however, this book tries to see the life of an author through Johnson's eyes. What did being a writer mean to him? How did he understand his own career? In what ways does his writing reflect or resist the definitions of authorship that he inherited? Is there anything new in his sense of a profession? How can he help us think about the life of an author? Each of these questions leads us back to the particulars of Johnson's work, the place where the general problems of authorship must be resolved in practice. And finally the answer that this book gives to the question "What is an author?" is "Samuel Johnson"—not a paragon or an abstraction, but one oppressed, ambitious writer, forging his own identity in difficult times.

1

The Birth of the Author:
The Letter to Chesterfield

A letter always arrives at its destination.

ON THURSDAY, November 28, 1754, a fashionable London periodical called *The World* published an essay recommending a forthcoming English dictionary. Although the essayist has not yet seen this "great and desirable" work, he expresses the obligation of the republic of letters to the author, one Mr. Johnson. "Perfection is not to be expected from man; but if we are to judge by the various works of Mr. Johnson, already published, we have good reason to believe that he will bring this as near to perfection as any one man could do." The English language has fallen into a state of anarchy that only a dictator can bring to order, "and I hereby declare that I make a total surrender of all my rights and privileges in the English language, as a free-born British subject, to the said Mr. Johnson, during the term of his dictatorship." Yet however desperate the situation, the writer goes on to advise his dictator to spare "the genteeler part of our language, which owes both its rise and progress to my fair countrywomen, whose natural turn is more to the copiousness, than to the correction of diction"; a future paper will give hints of how to please the ladies. Finally, in a postscript, he denies that anyone has paid him for this puff: "neither Mr. Johnson, nor any person employed by him, nor any bookseller or booksellers concerned in the success of it, have ever offered me the usual compliment of a pair of gloves or a bottle of wine."[1]

This essayist is anonymous, yet he conveys a powerful sense of self. The essay begins with a personal reference—"I heard the other day with great pleasure from my worthy friend Mr. Dodsley" (the publisher of *The World*)—and is never shy about showing off the first person. Moreover, the writer flourishes his pedigree. Witty, knowing, and confident, he represents the *beau monde,* the only world that matters in *The World.*[2] Only someone convinced that language belongs to people of his sort would strike such a pose of surrendering his rights. Mr. Johnson, he makes clear, is dictator only by courtesy or condescension. Indeed, the essayist has "a greater opinion of his impartiality and severity as a judge, than of his gallantry as a fine gentleman," and places him among the *pedantic* rather than the *polite.*[3] No one could doubt that a very polite fine gentleman wrote the paper. Any devotee of *The World* would be familiar with that air of superiority, able to condescend with equal grace to scholars and ladies, and sure that all the world will bow to such elegantly expressed opinions. Doubtless many recognized at once the hand of the Earl of Chesterfield, perhaps the most notable aristocratic man of letters and patron of letters in England. Soon everyone would know.

A few months passed with no reply. Then one Friday, February 7, 1755, Johnson wrote a letter to Chesterfield. No manuscript of the original survives, nor was it published at the time. Yet it quickly became the talk of the town, and people have never stopped talking about it. Years later, Johnson dictated versions to Giuseppe Baretti and James Boswell. This is Baretti's text.

February 1755
My Lord:
   I have been lately informed by the Proprietor of The World that two Papers in which my Dictionary is recommended to the Public were written by your Lordship. To be so distinguished is an honour which, being very little accustomed to favours from the Great, I know not well how to receive, or in what terms to acknowledge.
   When upon some slight encouragment I first visited your Lordship I was overpowered like the rest of Mankind by the enchantment of your adress, and could not forbear to wish that I might

boast myself Le Vainqueur du Vainqueur de la Terre, that I might obtain that regard for which I saw the world contending, but I found my attendance so little incouraged, that neither pride nor modesty would suffer me to continue it. When I had once adressed your Lordship in public, I had exhausted all the Art of pleasing which a retired and uncourtly Scholar can possess. I had done all that I could, and no Man is well pleased to have his all neglected, be it ever so little.

Seven years, My lord have now past since I waited in your outward Rooms or was repulsed from your Door, during which time I have been pushing on my work through difficulties of which it is useless to complain, and have brought it at last to the verge of Publication without one Act of assistance, one word of encouragement, or one smile of favour. Such treatment I did not expect, for I never had a Patron before.

The Shepherd in Virgil grew at last acquainted with Love, and found him a Native of the Rocks. Is not a Patron, My Lord, one who looks with unconcern on a Man struggling for Life in the water and when he has reached ground encumbers him with help. The notice which you have been pleased to take of my Labours, had it been early, had been kind; but it has been delayed till I am indifferent and cannot enjoy it, till I am solitary and cannot impart it, till I am known and do not want it.

I hope it is no very cinical asperity not to confess obligation where no benefit has been received, or to be unwilling that the Public should consider me as owing that to a Patron, which Providence has enabled me to do for myself.

Having carried on my work thus far with so little obligation to any favourer of Learning I shall not be disappointed though I should conclude it, if less be possible, with less, for I have been long wakened from that Dream of hope, in which I once boasted myself with so much exultation, My lord, Your Lordship's Most humble, most obedient Servant,

SAMUEL JOHNSON[4]

The signature applies the finishing touch to Chesterfield and his pretensions. Yet even more, it seems to announce the coming of age of a writer who will never again allow himself to be ignored. Johnson awakes and tells the world to take notice. In fact the stir would make him a celebrity; few previous writers had ever whetted such an appetite for inside information about their lives. Thirty-five years later, when curiosity was still alive, Boswell paved the way for his *Life of Johnson* by publishing the letter for the first time, with notes, in four quarto pages for half a guinea.[5] How had a private message become so famous? Only two people could have been responsible, at least in the beginning. First, Johnson "entertaind" some friends with it.[6] He had an interest in letting the public know that he was repudiating the puff, which was most offensive, after all, just because it *was* public. Robert Dodsley, the intermediary who appears in the first sentence of both Chesterfield's paper and Johnson's reply, regretted the falling-out, which he thought bad for business.[7] But Johnson's instinct for business may have been sounder. By spreading the word, if not the text, he set off a public buzz that would sell many books. Yet Chesterfield also helped. He left the letter out on his table, read it to Dodsley, "said, 'this man has great powers,' pointed out the severest passages, and observed how well they were expressed."[8] Perhaps he even savored the challenge to his *savoir-faire*. A master at putting on a good face, he did not mind being the center of public attention.

The letter would not have become so famous, however, had it not represented something more than a personal quarrel. Generations of readers have found it not only moving but deeply symbolic. One era seems to clash against another. Thomas Carlyle heard in the letter a "Blast of Doom, proclaiming into the ear of Lord Chesterfield, and, through him, of the listening world, that patronage should be no more!" (the clamorous imagery, converting marks on a page into ear-splitting sounds, heralds a prophet as well as a hero—Joshua Johnson).[9] More recently, Alvin Kernan has called the whole affair "a great event in the history of letters and of print, the scene in which not just Samuel Johnson but *the author*, after centuries of subservience to the aristocracy, declares his democratic independence of patronage"; the letter "still stands as the Magna Carta of the modern author."[10] Such claims enshrine a historical landmark and hail the birth of the author.

At the same time they raise many doubts. Was Johnson's letter really so significant? By 1755 the older system of patronage had long

14

been superseded, if not eradicated, by commercial forces.[11] Alexander Pope, the great writer of Johnson's youth, had become both rich and independent by learning how to manage the literary market. Booksellers, not patrons, commissioned the *Dictionary*. When Johnson first fell into his "Dream of hope," he had already been making his living as a hack writer for ten years without any "favours from the Great." In fact he knew such dreams were laughable. An essay he wrote for *The Adventurer* in 1753, on "The Age of Authors," makes fun of any hope of patronage: "it is not to be expected, that at a time when every man writes, any man will patronize; and, accordingly, there is not one that I can recollect at present, who professes the least regard for the votaries of science, invites the addresses of learned men, or seems to hope for reputation from any pen but his own."[12] Not one genuine patron still existed. Nor was Lord Chesterfield at all an exception to the rule; he cared most of all for his own reputation. Even his joking reference to the small bribes his puff might have earned—a pair of gloves, a bottle of wine, a bit of mutton—implies a world in which writings are peddled and the noble, magnanimous patron has become as much a dream as Santa Claus. In such a world an author's declaration of independence would seem disingenuous at best.

Moreover, Johnson had not renounced the *idea* of a patron. Seven years later he had no objection to accepting a pension, however much his enemies might howl. The falsity of Chesterfield could not impugn a genuine Maecenas. At any rate, what Johnson intended to say about patronage in general was open to question.[13] Not many of his contemporaries set eyes on the letter, and those who heard about it seemed most impressed by the writer's courage in speaking up for himself: "his manly behaviour in rejecting these condescensions of Lord Chesterfield, and . . . resenting the treatment he had receivd from him with a proper spirit."[14] So far as the public was concerned, the buzz of a personal quarrel drowned out any larger issue. Carlyle might speak retrospectively of "the listening world," and Kernan of "the history of print," but during Johnson's life the absence of a printed version cast his letter into a realm of anecdote, rumor, and myth. As a matter of fact, at least one person remembered the original as different from the official copy Johnson dictated some decades later.[15] Perhaps "that celebrated letter of which so much has been said" was not at all the same in 1790 as it had been in 1755.[16] In that case readers might have to change their minds about the birth of the modern author as well as of the author Johnson. The point of any letter depends, after all, not only on what it says but on whom it addresses.

Whatever its larger significance may be, the letter makes its mark first of all as a fine piece of writing, directed to a specific occasion. Like a very resounding knock on the door, it demands that attention be paid. Hence speculations about its motives ought to defer to close reading. Until we know what the letter *does,* we will not know what it *means.* In this respect Chesterfield took it in just the right spirit, showing it off as a collector's item on which he could exercise his discrimination. The hand of the artist declares itself to a connoisseur in the smallest details. When Johnson wrote to Chesterfield, then, he had something to prove: that he could master the miniature as well as the magnum opus.

Johnson had thought a good deal about writing letters. Although he regretted that not many English "models of private correspondence" had been published,[17] and although he seems not to have written many himself, he had firm views on the principles of the form. Young people especially needed instruction in "the Importance of writing Letters with Propriety."[18] No other sort of writing so thoroughly exposed one's manners, or lack of manners. As Samuel Richardson had shown, a well-wrought series of epistles could manifest not only courtesy and social competence but also the soul of behavior, a sort of moral catechism to regulate conduct in every situation. Furthermore, letters served wonderfully well as a means of closing distances between people of different classes. A lord who might not open his door to someone shabbily dressed, or lower himself to acknowledge rebuffs from an inferior, might well be captured by graceful words on paper. As writers—and only as writers—Johnson and Chesterfield could meet on equal terms.

A private letter differs from other kinds of writing in one regard only: it aims at an audience of one.[19] "A letter," according to Johnson, "is addressed to a single mind of which the prejudices and partialities are known, and must therefore please, if not by favouring them, by forbearing to oppose them"[20]—or conversely, if it intends to displease, by knowing just what to oppose. The letter to Chesterfield perfectly understands the single mind it addresses, and it is exquisitely calculated to touch that person. First of all it draws the nobleman in. Only in retrospect does the opening paragraph unfold its irony. On a first reading, the author's apparent awkwardness about knowing how to respond to such "favours" must have seemed rather charming, a verbal tug on a forelock. The following paragraph gradually inflates this obsequious tone, which Johnson lays on thicker and thicker. "Le Vainqueur du Vainqueur de la Terre" ("the Conqueror of the Conqueror of the Earth," quoting the opening line of Georges de Scudéry's *Alaric*) reaches a height of grandiose overstatement; counting on Chesterfield's vanity to blind him, the author implicitly mocks his taste for courtly French phrases and thirst for praise.[21] Then suddenly, with "but," the flattery stops. From this point on the reader is forced to adopt the author's position. The faint foreboding of "slight" encouragement turns into the flat indignity of "so little incouraged," and for the first time the writer reveals not only his modesty but also his *pride*. The rest of the letter will have nothing to do with "the art of pleasing." Johnson assumes the character of "a retired and uncourtly Scholar," a role that Chesterfield had already assigned him in *The World,* and sets up an eternal opposition between Scholar and Patron. In this way he makes it impossible for Chesterfield to play the role he prefers—the good-natured man of letters and man of the world.[22] Pinned to the scutcheon of Patron, his lordship, as he reads, will find it very difficult to like himself.

Johnson's revenge would not succeed, however, unless he first impressed his noble foe. "To raise esteem," the Rambler had written, "we must discover abilities," and letters required particular delicacy: "the pebble must be polished with care, which hopes to be valued as a diamond."[23] It is not enough for the faithless patron to feel rebuked; he must also feel that he has made a mistake, that he was not discerning enough to see the merit he neglected. Hence Johnson needs to exhibit all his powers. The letter to Chesterfield does not conceal its own art. Rhetorically, it earns its status as a classic with majestic rhythms that work their way not only through individual periods ("a complete sentence from one full stop to another")[24] but also from sentence to sentence and from one paragraph to the next. In the second paragraph, for example, the long and elaborate first sentence is followed by two that are successively less intricate; "be it ever so little" completes the thought with little words and a deliberate trailing away. The next paragraph repeats the pattern more economically, when an ornate period that climaxes in the heavy cadence of a triplet ("one Act of assistance, one word of encouragement, or one smile of favour") yields to the brisk, sardonic anticlimax of a Patron. The rhythms of Johnson's prose rehearse his rude awakening from hope and compel the reader to undergo a similar deflation. And Chesterfield should be carried along, made aware of his lack of consideration as well as the skill of the artist he has offended. Johnson is by no means his humble, obedient servant. This author takes pride in speaking as an equal.

Indeed, the letter presumes a deeply competitive view of human relations. To "patronise" or "condescend," in eighteenth-century terms, did not yet imply the arrogance now associated with those words. "Condescension," in Johnson's *Dictionary,* remains a Christian virtue like modesty and humility. But even the definition of the word suggests a constant struggle: "Voluntary humiliation; descent from superiority; voluntary submission to equality with inferiours." To some extent that stooping seems to contradict itself; superiors, no matter how much they bend, can never sink to the level of inferiors without a strange sense of having lowered themselves, or at least without feeling humiliated. The strain is likely to bring on an involuntary recoil, like a nagging pain in the back. Johnson always perceives some tension or absurdity in "the levelling doctrine."[25] At any rate, the letter to Chesterfield cannot let go of the seesaw on which superior and inferior keep trading places. To refuse "to confess obligation" was Johnson's ostensible purpose in writing. From first word to last, from salutation to signature, the letter insists on reversing or balancing the stations of "My lord" and "Johnson." Even the repetitions of "My Lord" imply a conversation between two equals or rivals; without that rhetorical mode of address, the letter would lose its foil. Hence the epistolary form itself, borrowing some effects from a speech in a play, sets the stage for an affair of honor.[26] Having failed to conquer the conqueror of the earth by addressing him in public, Johnson strives to conquer him in private by proving himself above such condescension.

He shows most of all that he is a gentleman. Nothing that Chesterfield had written in *The World* had been more patronizing than his distrust of Johnson's "complaisance" to ladies, "because I had a greater opinion of his impartiality and severity as a judge, than of his gallantry as a fine gentleman."[27] Those words were salt on a wound. Decades later Johnson told the Rev. John Hussey that Chesterfield was the politest man he ever knew, but "indeed he did not think it worth his while to treat me like a Gentleman."[28] The letter responds by flaunting not only Johnson's politeness but also Chesterfield's discourtesy. The gallantry of the flourish in French, the courtliness with which the author admits that he is uncourtly, the punctiliousness of his language, and above all the respect of forms with which he gives offense, all speak of the utmost refinement. Good breeding has triumphed. According to Johnson, "his Lordship had returned his thanks for it and added that it was the Letter of a Scholar and a Gentleman."[29] From one point of view, in fact, the title of gentleman fit the scholar better than it did the lord. Cardinal Newman's famous precept "It is almost a definition of a gentleman to say that he is one who never inflicts pain,"[30] was corrected nicely by Oscar Wilde: "a gentleman never inflicts pain *unintentionally*." In these terms Chesterfield had failed and Johnson had won.

Yet the letter is more than a competition between two proud men. It is also a piece of autobiography, a work in which an author defines himself. A long foreground somewhere has to exist for such a piece to be written. Johnson marks out a period in his life, the seven lean years that separate what he once was from what he has become. The "retired and uncourtly Scholar" once repulsed by Chesterfield is now on the verge of publication and fame. He has carried out a great work through untold difficulties, and, what makes it still sweeter, the achievement is one "which Providence has enabled me to do for myself." Soon all the world will recognize his name.

In this respect the climactic word of the letter is *known*—"till I am known and do not want it." The rule of emphasis that Johnson followed generally put most weight on the end of a period.[31] Hence the third of three parallel clauses, completing a cadence, was meant to be very emphatic. Clearly, Johnson stresses how much he does not want Chesterfield's notice. "Want" means primarily "to be without something"; the would-be patron encumbers the writer with help he does not need. But "want" also stands for "desire," and the weight on the word conveys a great weariness, a desire to be free forever from that old yearning for favor. To be *known* is more solid than to be famous and praised; it implies an integrity that can stand out in public. Johnson no longer sues for favor or struggles for life. He is not the person whom Chesterfield thought he knew; his work will speak for itself.

The more he is known, however, the more he tempts his reader to know. By dropping hints about a troubled past, the letter kindles a spark of curiosity that the Preface to the *Dictionary* would fan into a blaze. Indifferent and solitary, the author presents himself as a resident of the rocks. He has evidently suffered irremediable losses that have left him without a companion or the capacity for joy. The death of his wife in March 1752 still preys on Johnson's mind. Yet he seems in mourning also for a younger, more innocent version of himself. Readers could hardly help asking what had happened during the last seven years.

In 1747, which Johnson apparently dates as the beginning of the end of his hopes for patronage, he had been working as a hack writer in London for ten years and had reached the age of thirty-eight without one patron or a single by-line. A line capitalized in *London* (1738), the poem that did not quite succeed in making his name, sums up and predicts his fortune: "SLOW RISES WORTH, BY POVERTY DEPREST."[32] He did manage to make a decent living, in fact, as the years went on.[33] Moreover, he showed enough abilities, in the small publishing circles that knew his work, to be entrusted with much of the editing of the *Gentleman's Magazine*, the cataloguing of the Harleian Library, and eventually the vast project of the *Dictionary* itself. Yet the public had hardly seen his name in print.[34] His works had been commissioned or written to order for others; he could scarcely consider himself an author. About the time that he left Oxford in 1729, Johnson had written a discouraging poem on "the young author panting for a name," whose first publication is hissed and damned until he flies to some retreat out of the light. This was a dismal future to expect. Yet in some ways the imaginary young author had fared much better than his creator; at least the public had noticed him, at least he had a name. When "The Young Author" eventually came out, in 1743, it was published anonymously.

Johnson's name was attached to his work for the first time at the end of his *Plan of a Dictionary of the English Language* (1747). Even then, however, what carried most weight was Lord Chesterfield's name. The *Plan* is dedicated to him; as was the custom, he gave Johnson ten pounds for the dedication. But Chesterfield dominates the body of the text as well. Its first words are

Addressed to the Right Honourable
PHILIP DORMER, Earl of CHESTERFIELD
One of His Majesty's Principal Secretaries of State

and its next are "MY LORD." The *Plan* takes the form of a public letter, which seeks the approval of the dedicatee, anticipates his wishes, and does not forget to drop the name of "My Lord" at regular intervals. Only the close reveals the author's own name:

whatever be the event of my endeavours, I shall not easily regret an attempt which has procured me the honour of appearing thus publickly,
 My Lord,
  Your Lordship's
   Most Obedient and
    Most Humble Servant,
     SAM. JOHNSON.

Clearly, a dream of hope—and money and honor and fame—inspires this peroration. In 1755 each phrase would return, ironically inverted, when Johnson parodied his old letter to Chesterfield by writing a new one. The prospective event now ripens into something achieved, the author does regret his former attempt, the public broadcast of an alliance between the illustrious lord and his humble servant grates on the ear, the exultant boast turns into a sour recantation in which every word takes back what was earlier said.[35] Johnson's letter erases the end of his *Plan*.

Above all SAM. JOHNSON meant something different in 1755. The author of the *Dictionary* had come a long way from the writer who planned it. To begin with, his circumstances had changed. An entrepreneur whom a consortium of booksellers had commissioned to produce a standard English dictionary, who had received an advance of £1,575, who had rented a three-story house as a workplace and had filled it with six amanuenses and a collection of boarders, whose work consisted largely of arranging and coordinating many thousands of scraps of paper, and who always had to keep one eye on deadlines and the other on the market, seemed more identified with management than with labor. But perhaps the change in his reputation was still more important. Early in 1749 his name first appeared on a title page; not inappropriately, for an author in his fortieth year, the work was called *The Vanity of Human Wishes*. Within a month his tragedy *Irene* opened at Drury Lane. The playwright himself attended, in a side box, and wore a scarlet waistcoat and gold-laced hat; on this occasion he may have been noticed too much. In any case he was no longer obscure. Johnson did not sign his name to *The Rambler*, whose essays began to be published the following year, yet interested readers soon found him out through the publishing grapevine as well as his style. By the time that the series ended, in 1752, some critics thought it a masterpiece of morality and high-wrought English prose. Henceforth his name would sell books.

When Chesterfield implied that "the various works of Mr. Johnson, already published," had come "near to perfection,"[36] therefore, he was commending an author who by now had made his way with a discerning public. Such praise was self-satisfied, not to say otiose. "Perfection" could hardly have been a word that Johnson wanted to hear; no one else could have been so aware of the imperfections that any keen eye would pick out when the *Dictionary* came under scrutiny. As usual, the object of Chesterfield's admiration was his own perfect taste, not any mere lexicographer. What irritated Johnson especially, however, must have been an eerie feeling of *déjà vu*. Once again the lord had patronized him; once again the great man had given a hand to his servant. Time had stood still, so far as *The World* was concerned, and the puff had blown Johnson back to the winter of his career, his long ordeal of dependency and anonymity. But more than seven years had passed, and times and he had changed. No longer a journeyman, and certainly not obedient and humble, the author refuses to retrace his steps. Psychologically, the letter to Chesterfield cancels not only a debt but also a memory that has now become shameful. The past was a dream, and, now that he is awake, Johnson knows exactly how to edit his life. It makes a very good story: The Birth of the Author.

Like any good personal story, however, Johnson's contrast of his past and present selves seems larger and neater than life. The mythical status of the letter, before and after it was published, responds to its deliberate fashioning of a myth. Author and Patron swell into allegorical figures, two individuals playing their parts in an eternal morality play. Hence the letter was always destined to be an example of something important: the fall of the patronage system, the rise of the middle class, the elevation of the man of letters to celebrity or hero, or even the commodification of personality. These sweeping issues are not irrelevant to the particular effects of the letter; they furnish a context on which Johnson seized to make a parable out of a grudge. Not even the English language was safe from his revisionary rage: the word "patron," in future, would never be the same.

Yet the myth that Johnson fashioned does not conform to the legend that later readers have woven around it. Does the letter announce the end of patronage? We have already seen some reasons for doubt. Undeniably it attacks a bad patron and expresses a disillusionment with patrons in general. No reader can miss the aim of Johnson's loaded question: "Is not a Patron, My Lord, one who looks with unconcern on a Man struggling for Life in the water and when he has reached ground encumbers him with help"—a definition so peremptory that it need not end with a question mark. And the same scorn was thrust before the public with the famous entry in the *Dic-*

tionary—"PA'TRON. One who countenances, supports or protects. Commonly a wretch who supports with insolence, and is paid with flattery"—and the famous revision in *The Vanity of Human Wishes*— "There mark what Ills the Scholar's Life assail,/Toil, Envy, Want, the Patron, and the Jail."[37] Evidently Johnson likes to ventilate his revenge. Yet his satirical hits also seem to assume that patronage remains the way of the world. In Johnson's mind, at any rate, the patron slips naturally into a sequence of ills, as inevitable in the scholar's life as any other misery and, as the fourth of five evils, very nearly the last resort of the doomed. Patrons still ambush the hopeful young writer; nothing suggests that they are out of date. On the contrary, Johnson implies that they are permanent, like vice or like the vanity of human wishes.[38]

Indeed, the letter to Chesterfield seems very nearly timeless. The two offensive essays in *The World* had been written right to the moment; Chesterfield keeps a sharp eye on the contemporary literary marketplace as well as on the slang that the smartest people are using. Johnson does not mention the market or sink to the colloquial. Instead he reduces the field to two men, each embodying his respective species of Scholar and Patron. The letter could be translated into Latin with very few footnotes. This generic quality has led Paul Fussell to cite two "paradigms" or models: "the general Ciceronian oration with the irony subtilized . . . and the Horatian satire conceived as occurring in the mode of the Horatian epistle."[39] It certainly seems to be true that Johnson's passage on "seven years" recalls and reverses Horace's *Satires* 2.6: "The seventh, nearly the eighth year now will have fled since Maecenas began to count me among his own."[40] With such a patron, Horace was "fortune's child"; presumably Chesterfield was meant to catch the allusion and note how badly he had measured up to it. But the main effect is not to assign the letter to a genre so much as to remove it from the concerns of *The World*. Johnson consciously places himself in another, immortal world, where Horace, unlike Chesterfield, lives as a presence and friend.

The brilliant sentence on Virgil increases this distance from worldly affairs. Even on many readings it gives one pause. Precisely because it interrupts the narrative of Johnson's treatment by Chesterfield, and also because its relevance takes a moment to ponder, it seems to create a private space within the letter, a silent interval for reflection (Boswell allows the sentence a separate paragraph, which puts the right artistic weight on it). Nonetheless there is something odd. The lines from Virgil's eighth Eclogue, adapted from the second Idyll of Theocritus,[41] paint a savage portrait of Love:

> Nunc scio quid sit Amor, duris in cautibus illum
> Ismarus, aut Rhodope, aut extremi Garamantes,
> Nec generis nostri puerum nec sanguinis, edunt

> Now I know what Love is, on hard stone
> Ismarus or Rhodope or remotest Garamantes
> Begot him, a child not of our race or blood.[42]

Apparently Johnson identifies with Damon, the jilted shepherd who speaks the lines. By analogy, the point seems to be that Chesterfield's coldness reveals the only "love" of which he is capable, a heartless domination that injures whomever it touches. At last the author understands his patron. The clever recasting of Damon's complaint into a tiny narrative—"The Shepherd in Virgil grew at last acquainted with Love"—sums up the story of the letter's preceding paragraphs, in which a suitor waits helplessly for the inaccessible object of his hopes. Now the cycle has ended; the suitor has found the rocks that were always his fate. Told in this way, the story associates Johnson with the pursuer of Love and Chesterfield with Love himself, the god who taught Medea to kill her children. Of course it seems absurd to think of Chesterfield as Love. But that absurdity gives the sentence its edge, a withering irony that denies that the patron can know the true meaning of love. Cupid remains unmoved by the scars he inflicts.

At the same time Johnson coaxes out another implication. He had previously condemned the lines from Virgil, not only because they sounded inappropriate or bombastic in the mouth of a shepherd but also because they seemed unnatural: "sentiments like these, as they have no ground in nature, are indeed of little value in any poem."[43] For Johnson, the "hyperbolical joy and outrageous sorrow" of lovers

25

are marks of second-rate poetry.[44] Yet the image of Love as "a Native of the Rocks" might be twisted into a far more sensible line of thought: love proves itself best in adversity, not in comfort. In the next few sentences this idea leads to a new source of grievance. Having climaxed one sequence with an allusion to Chesterfield's remoteness, Johnson uses the same words differently to begin another sequence, this time referring to Chesterfield's inability to imagine another person's troubles. True love would have been at home on the rocks. A lover, unlike a patron, could not watch a poor victim struggle without trying to help; a lover offers encouragement at the earliest, darkest moment; a lover relieves the dreariness of indifference and solitude. In all these ways Lord Chesterfield has fallen short; he has never cared to reconnoiter the rocks. Thus Johnson blames not only the patron's flinty heart but also his life of ease. The lack of assistance deserves reproach, but the lack of human sympathy is what cannot be forgiven.

The rest of the letter maintains the sense of distance from worldly considerations. No longer a disappointed suitor addressing a disappointing patron, Johnson claims to have risen above disappointment; the truth is that he has had no patron at all. What matters to him now must be the work that he is concluding, not the rewards or notice that it might bring. "Myself" is the dominant word, and Chesterfield's role in the work shrinks to less than nothing. At the end "My lord" is dismissed or reduced to a figure in an old and faded dream. As author, Johnson has the last word, and all he asks is to be left alone.

To write this way, however, he needs to predicate a special world of authorship, not subject to time or fortune—a world on which patrons and other intruders lose any right to impinge. Chesterfield has always attracted supporters to defend his conduct, and even Johnson may have suspected himself of having gone too far.[45] Perhaps his pride had made him oversensitive. But whether or not the letter exaggerates Chesterfield's faults, it certainly does exaggerate the author's independence. Johnson later acknowledged that he had received one "Act of assistance" from Chesterfield, a present of ten pounds.[46] In any case, he could hardly have begun the *Dictionary,* let alone carried it through, without plenty of help. The stark opposition of scholar and patron ignores the many other hands that contributed to the work, from the booksellers who commissioned and funded it to the copyists who wrote out the slips to the pressmen who printed the books—not to mention the earlier scholars who prepared Johnson's way or the writers who illustrated how words had been used. Surely any lexicographer has to confess obligations. From this point of view, the letter disguises the material circumstances of writing. Johnson spins a fable about the unworldly suitor and the false benefactor, and thus avoids any sordid talk about the manual labor of cobbling a dictionary. Such stories exalt a downtrodden writer in his own eyes, emboldening him to think of himself as a companion to Horace and Virgil—and equal to a lord—rather than as part of a team engaged in the business of making and selling books. Teamwork and business have no place in the letter to Chesterfield. Perhaps that absence enables Johnson to define himself so proudly as an author.

Yet Johnson's defense of authorship is far from selfish. It represents the strongest obligation he feels, his debt not to any would-be patron of learning but to "the propagators of knowledge" and "teachers of truth."[47] An author who knows his business ought always to remember where he comes from, the long line of earlier authors who have taught him how to write and think. Johnson associates his career with those of the classical poets and the great Renaissance scholars; their trials were his too. Even during his darkest years as a hack, he could no more forget the dignity of authorship than he could forget his Latin and Greek. The insult to that dignity implied by Chesterfield's condescension aroused his professional fury; all patronized authors spoke through him. Nor did he reckon the cost. As much as Johnson needs to make his living by getting along—with booksellers, collaborators, the public, and friends in high places—he needs still more to hold on to a sense of what his profession is worth.[48]

The letter reflects that loyalty to the past. In one respect, it serves as a cancelled contract: despite the expectations raised by the *Plan* as well as the puff in *The World,* Johnson apprises Chesterfield that he has no intention of dedicating the *Dictionary* to him.[49] Rather, the book will stand nobly alone, honoring only the authors cited in it. In this way the self-definition of the letter perfectly fits one model of "author" in the *Dictionary*, the boast of Coriolanus that he will "stand / As if a man was *author* of himself, / And knew no other kin."[50] No one else—at least no one alive—can claim to be a party to this work. Yet an old ideal inspires the author's pride. As much as Johnson frowns on "the patrician and military haughtiness in Coriolanus,"[51] he shares his resolve to keep faith with the dead, whatever the cost. The author may have no kin, but the spirits of other authors support him. Thus the letter alludes to the ancients as if they were compeers and sparkles with the silver ironies of Latin verse, a language endlessly drilled into British schoolboys. Seldom have the virtues of a classical education been more aggressively displayed. Summoning all the texts that have taught him to stand up for authors, Johnson authors himself.

Yet the legend that has grown around the letter to Chesterfield involves still larger issues. What seem at stake are contending visions not only of authors and patrons but also of how the nation is conceived and who is to own it. A dictionary that set a new standard would have to define not only English but England, or Great Britain, itself.[52] Almost everyone wanted something from Johnson. The first great English dictionary ought to preserve a pure native language, free from foreign encroachments; it ought to dictate proper usage; it ought to decide which words deserved to last and to be shared by every reader, and which words were merely the passing jargon or cant of one particular group. England awaited the book that would fix it in print. No wonder that, as the moment of truth approached, Johnson showed signs of feeling more and more nervous.

The papers in *The World* must have increased his apprehension. A difference with Chesterfield on the nature of English was no small matter. As the arbiter and collaborator to whom the *Plan* had been addressed, he had once personified the ideal potential audience of the *Dictionary*, its one most interested and influential reader. Yet what he wanted from the work was not at all what Johnson had done. Some of their differences resulted from different philosophies of language. The authoritarian rules and codes that the subject asked from his dictator could hardly reflect the efforts of a practical lexicographer whose first responsibility was to ascertain how English words had actually been used. Another set of differences arose from politics.[53] Chesterfield promotes a distinctly Whiggish attitude toward language. His "honest English pride, or perhaps prejudice," gives him "a sensible pleasure in reflecting upon the rapid progress which our language has lately made, and still continues to make, all over Europe." The spheres of influence that other nations must win by force of arms have been peacefully captured through the spread of English abroad: "A nobler sort of conquest, and a far more glorious triumph, since graced by none but willing captives!"[54] Johnson distrusts such expansive views, not only for their imperialism but also for the change they threaten to the insular integrity of the British people and their speech. "Commerce, however necessary, however lucrative, as it depraves the manners, corrupts the language; they that have frequent intercourse with strangers, to whom they endeavour to accommodate themselves, must in time learn a mingled dialect, like the jargon which serves the traffickers on the *Mediterranean* and *Indian* coasts."[55] English must be protected from the champions of progress and trade.

The major difference between patron and scholar, however, is marked by their radically divergent views about who owns English and the nation whose soul it represents. Chesterfield's distinction between the *pedantic* and the *polite,* "the one founded upon certain dry crabbed rules of etymology and grammar, the other singly upon the justness and delicacy of the ear," deftly catches that difference. Though in theory he approves Johnson's efforts to establish a pedantic orthography, "provided it can be quietly brought about," his heart obviously tilts toward the polite. No reader of *The World* can doubt whom English belongs to. Even the tyrant of the language serves at the grace of the best people, whose fashionable conversation expresses the spirit of the nation as it is or would like to be. The little linguistic vanities of fine ladies and polished gentlemen, opposed to the pedantic scholar, supply an affectionate running joke for Chesterfield; he ends by advising Johnson to publish, "by way of appendix to his great work, a genteel Neological dictionary, containing those polite, though perhaps not strictly grammatical words and phrases, commonly used, and sometimes understood, by the BEAU MONDE."[56] What could be more genteel, for an English lord, than a few words in French? Condescension could hardly go further. Chesterfield lightly mocks affectation but also subscribes to it. Even his style, a form of writing modeled on elegant speech, conveys his superiority to those who must follow the rules that his kind take pleasure in breaking.

Johnson's prose puts forth a different model. In every way the letter makes its case as a piece of writing, associated with the great writers of the past, the conventions of epistolary form, and cadences far too elaborate for conversation. It claims acquaintance with a society of books, with the heritage of a language written rather than spoken. The emphasis on writing comes out especially in those many moments when the letter imitates speech; for instance, in its direct appeals to "My Lord": "Is not a Patron, My Lord, one who looks with unconcern . . ." Such vocatives are purely rhetorical. The ceremonious style on which they draw resembles that of the formal oration, a mode of speech whose art depends on careful composition. Johnson had written many such orations, in the years of his parliamentary reporting (*Debates in the Senate of Magna Lilliputia,* 1740–1744), and more than one gave free renditions of what Chesterfield himself was supposed to have said.[57] The effort that Johnson put into composing those speeches prepared him for the rhetoric of the letter. Declaiming to an audience of one, he adapts a stately language, culled from Demosthenes and Cicero, to intimate ironies and delicate contempt. Thus the litotes of "I hope it is no very cinical asperity not to confess obligation where no benefit has been received," whose slowly building triple negative owes more to Latin than to English, erases not only any sense of obligation but also any accusation that the speaker might be overly harsh. Extreme indirection brings about an impression of extreme straightforwardness. No one—not even Johnson—can contrive such effects extemporaneously. Instead the letter follows a script: a writer's idea of spoken English as it might be.

Writers, as Johnson's heroes, command the language. The *Dictionary* gives priority to writing over speech, to the past over the present, and to the usage of great authors over that of ordinary writers. "From the authours which rose in the time of *Elizabeth,* a speech might be formed adequate to all the purposes of use and elegance." Thus Shakespeare sets the standard for "the diction of common life." When the Preface to the *Dictionary* reviews its choices of quotations to illustrate words, "authour" seems interchangeable with "authority": "when it happened that any authour gave a definition of a term . . . I have placed his authority as a supplement to my own."[58] The writings of such authors preserve the national genius, transmitted through language in a living tradition; every native speaker of English pays tribute to them and borrows their luster. Since "the chief glory of every people arises from its authours," the national interest demands that they be remembered, if only through loyalty to the words that they used. The "polite" do not own the language. Instead it belongs to any citizen or common reader who keeps the best writers alive in memory, on the tongue and the page. Johnson tries to represent those readers.

Hence he acts for the nation while speaking for himself. The letter to Chesterfield seems intensely proprietary, from one point of view: "*my* Dictionary," in the opening sentence, sets the tone that will climax with "enabled *me* to do for *myself.*" To its author, the *Dictionary* is nobody else's business. Yet the letter might also be read as profoundly submissive, not to Chesterfield but to the public, whose verdict means more than any notice from "the Great." In spite of his rugged independence, Johnson prides himself on being a servant of the people. No patron can come between them. Even his anger at aristocratic condescension identifies him with "the spirit of *English* liberty," or what Johnson would later call the "epidemick bravery" of the typical Englishman: "he was born without a master; and looks not on any man, however dignified by lace or titles, as deriving from Nature any claims to his respect, or inheriting any qualities superior to his own."[59] The point would not be lost on most of his readers. Perhaps the most enduring legacy of the letter to Chesterfield has been its image of Johnson as the representative Englishman, not so much an author as a man without a master, an honest working man whose self-reliance and common sense stand for a freeborn people. In this respect the *Dictionary* embodies both sides of his reputation: it is at once a heroic personal achievement and a selfless work that no one but the collective nation could ever have written.

Johnson accepted that dual role. The conflict between two visions of authorship, the hero versus the servant or the exalted genius ver-

sus the anonymous hack, oppressed many eighteenth-century writers, diminishing them in their own eyes. Yet it did not disable Johnson. More truly, in the long run it defines him. No part suits him better than that of Odysseus in rags, arrived in Ithaca to claim his
birthright after many labors, yet so disguised that the patronizing
suitors fail to recognize his strength. Someone who looks insignifi-
cant may yet be a hero. The power of the letter to Chesterfield
draws on the enduring attraction of that fable. The retired and uncourtly scholar who writes it gradually shows his hand, until from
beneath a modest outward appearance the reader perceives the
flash of fierce emotions and deadly rhetorical weapons; Odysseus
has come home. The revelation is thrilling. Had Johnson already
been famous, he could not have written the letter, nor could he have
written it without feeling that he deserved to be famous; the pain of
unjust obscurity throbs through all his protestations of indifference.
Yet just at that moment, coming into his own, he is able to prove to
the world that he is an author. The humble servant and rising hero
are one.

History itself provided his chance. From an unsympathetic point
of view, the conjunction of pride and modesty in the letter might
drop a hint of inconsistency or contradiction. From the writer's perspective, it must have seemed an opportunity to show an English author as he was, undaunted though lowly. Both pride and modesty
had roots in the national character, at least as the English liked to
see themselves—peculiarly great, peculiarly down to earth. The coupling also suited an eighteenth-century author, whose hopes to be
great would have to be validated not by a lord or coterie but by the
public alone, or by that common reader with whom Johnson identifies and to whom he submits. But finally that compound of pride and
modesty, of service and independence, was Johnson himself. His
whole career had led him to take pride in an honest day's work of
writing. Let coxcombs look down on these chores, so long as ordinary readers found their lives a little fuller, a little more easy to endure. There was satisfaction in such an ideal of duty and use, and
perhaps there would be glory as well, at least in the eyes of his
maker. Nor would a good servant repine at the script that the age

had written for him. Instead he would fit himself to the mold of an author, internally as well as in his relations with the world.

If the letter to Chesterfield does announce the birth of the author, therefore, it climaxes a process of generation that had been ripening for half a lifetime. Johnson had not created himself alone. The identity on which he put flesh had gradually formed, over more than forty years, through changes in the literary marketplace, in conceptions of authorship, and in the interests of the nation. When Johnson redefined what an author could be, he made a choice among many possible futures. The signature at the end of the letter wraps up one dream of a career and readies another; it marks the author's arrival. But to understand what Johnson was going to be, both he and the reader first had to understand where he had started.

2

First Flowers: Johnson's Beginnings

Brave Infant of *Saguntum,* clear
Thy comming forth in that great yeare,
When the Prodigious *Hannibal* did crowne
His rage, with razing your immortall Towne.
Thou, looking then about,
E're thou wert halfe got out,
Wise child, did'st hastily returne,
And mad'st thy Mothers wombe thine urne.
How summ'd a circle didst thou leave man-kind
Of deepest lore, could we the Center find!

T HE EARLIEST SURVIVING work by Johnson is a poem, written probably at fifteen, "On a Daffodill, the first Flower the Author had seen that Year." Critics have noted the influence of Herrick and amusing anticipation of Wordsworth.[1] But they have not remarked, I think, what makes these lines interesting. "On a Daffodill" is not only a beginner's poem but also a poem about beginning: the beginning of a flower, a season of life, a career.

Hail! lovely Flower, first honour of the Year,
Hail! beauteous earnest of approaching Spring;
Whose early buds unusual glories wear,
And of a fruitfull year fair omens bring.

Be thou the favourite of the indulgent Sky,
Nor feel th' inclemencies of Wintry Air,
May no rude blasts thy sacred bloom destroy;
May Storms howl gently o'er, and learn to spare.[2]

The poet goes on to entreat still greater indulgence, the smiles of such beauteous virgins as divine Cleora, whose influence might fill "ev'ry fading leaf" with new verdure. But then the poem takes a sudden turn.

> But while I sing, the nimble moments fly,
> See! Sol's bright Chariot seeks the Western Main,
> And Ah! behold the shriveling blossoms die,
> So late admir'd, and prais'd, alas! in vain.
>
> With grief this emblem of Mankind I see,
> Like one awakned from a pleasing dream,
> Cleora's self fair Flower shall fade like thee;
> Alike must fall the Poet and his Theme.

The sentiment is of course conventional. Yet it is also rather shocking in its hasty refusal of promise. Young Johnson will not even pause for the usual *carpe diem*. Committing violence against nature, he does away with the daffodil at the first nightfall, collapsing the whole season into the time it takes him to write the poem. The effect seems both self-conscious and willful. It is as if the poet had lost confidence in his verses before he came to the end, and thus slumped into an emblem that would let everyone know he was falling. Cleora will not warm him with her smile, nor will he pretend that he expects to be smiled at. At the onset of spring, this posy invokes a chill. Where can we go from here?

Any analysis of Johnson's beginnings as an author must take account of two phenomena, related yet oddly contradictory. The first is his tremendous ambition. In a Latin exercise composed about the same time as "On a Daffodill" and only recently printed, the young schoolboy responds to his Juvenalian theme by arguing that virtue thrives on fame and that great talents deserve great rewards. "An unsubdued and invincible desire of honour and praise is planted in our hearts, which I would believe wise Nature (for she does nothing in vain) has instilled in us to spur us to praiseworthy deeds."[3] Whether or not all hearts feel that desire, young Johnson's certainly did. The poem on the daffodil, for instance, heaps trophies on the meek little flower until it seems to suffocate. It is the first "honour of the Year" whose buds wear "unusual glories" and bring "fair omens"; it ought to be the "favourite" of the sky, a "sacred" bloom "impearl'd" with dew and bowed to like a deity, "admir'd and prais'd." All this honor and praise might be thought wasted on a daffodil, but surely some young person hungers for them. Johnson's first writing already aspires to glory.

The second phenomenon, bending back against the first and darkening it with irony, is a sort of preemptive dejection. The poet and his theme must fall; the young author will soon welcome oblivion; the student's life will be assailed by ills. Human wishes are vain, and the wishes of authors are most pathetic of all. The older Johnson suggests that he learned this through experience, but young Johnson seems to have known it before a trial. He cannot watch a daffodil bloom without seeing it shrivel. Hence lust for glory tends to call down immediate retribution, without so much as a middle stage of temporary success. Johnson does not seem especially interested in middles; he springs directly from rising hope to crushing defeat. Bacon's mansion *will* fall on the head of the young enthusiast, in *The Vanity of Human Wishes,* though not, as he imagines, because he is greater than Bacon.[4] Rather, the dream itself precipitates its own disenchantment; that is the common fate of every dreamer. This inexorable downfall of ambition is not without its problems for Johnson's work. In *Rasselas,* for instance, the preemptive dejection often takes effect so quickly that a reader has no time to entertain hope; each flower is nipped in the bud. Notoriously the book, though written to instruct the young, touches the old instead, who are sadder but wiser. What sort of young person could profit, at starting out, by being advised that he or she should not expect to get anywhere? Only a person who wanted to think like Johnson.

The alliance of ambition and dejection marks Johnson's beginning. What explains this odd combination? It is tempting to offer a psychological cause, to stamp these proclivities with a label like melancholy or manic-depressive or schizophrenia or repetition compulsion or anal-erotic guilt. Psychologizing Johnson has always been a popular game, and a literary critic might well find "On a Daffodil" less interesting than a psychoanalyst would. The author himself, with his usual critical acuteness, is said to have "never much lik'd" the poem, "as it was not characteristick of the Flower."[5] But in one respect the verses *are* characteristic. Botanically, the daffodil bears the formal name of *Narcissus pseudo-narcissus,* and the poem reflects a classic narcissistic pattern. Its rapture over an idolized image of the self inevitably tumbles into disillusionment if not a mock suicide. In its rise and sudden fall, the flower enacts a standard male sexual fantasy, the arc of Phaethon as well as Narcissus, an autoerotic crash. Hence ambition ends in the droop or bell jar of the blossom as it leans back toward the nothingness of unsatisfied desire. Aspiring fifteen-year-old poets tend to be well acquainted with the psychology of the narcissus.

Putting aside this temptation, an interpreter might next be tempted to explain Johnson's beginnings by stressing their roots in traditional wisdom. To idolize a daffodil or "divine" Cleora is, in fact, a mistake, as any orthodox Christian or poet would know. Those idols fade; a young man needs to stake his hopes on higher things. Johnson's harping on mortality might be precocious or abrupt, but that does not diminish its truth. At worst he is stating a platitude; at best, discovering wisdom. In an eloquent analysis of "The Young Author," W. Jackson Bate points to the value of recognizing that dreams may come to nothing. "For the moment Johnson is simply trying to drive into himself the realization of it as a fact of human existence that must be courageously and honestly faced, and assimilated as a necessary part of living . . . He did not need others to puncture his illusions about himself. He could do this on his own without help."[6] Forewarned, forearmed. This is what might be called the Mithridatic view of preemptive dejection: a dose of poison builds up one's resistance. Whether it worked that way for Johnson, however, is open to doubt. A preoccupation with the likelihood of future failure can keep a young author from seizing either the day or Cleora. Brooding wastes just as much time as dreaming, and daffodils need some sun. At any rate, there is something peculiar about Johnson's alternation of hope and discouragement that cannot be fully accounted for by traditional wisdom. Other authors, no less orthodox, wrote more encouraging fables, and Johnson's own contemporaries were struck by the strain of fatalism in his early work.[7] His ambitions were so high, his expectations so low, that even in retrospect it is hard to see how he could begin as an author. He almost did not.

What other way of reading Johnson's beginnings offers more promise? One way, in my view, has not been tried often enough. When psychology and wisdom have done their work, the literary critic and literary historian are still left with some basic questions about any young author: What was his project? What task did he think remained, in his time, for an author to do? Most students of Johnson have been peculiarly quiet on this issue. Even Bate, who as much as anyone else has taught us to ask such questions, tends to be rather diffident about venturing answers. Thus Johnson occupies an anomalous place in literary history, as if he gave the age its name but were somehow not part of it—a stranger in time, a generation of one.[8] He seems to have sprung full-blown from the head of Minerva; or, in sober Johnsonian terms, he seems hardly to have made a choice of life at all, but simply to have accepted one task after another, decade by decade, like a dutiful hack (to borrow Housman's words, he "saved the sum of things for pay").[9] This view is worth considering. Sir John Hawkins, Johnson's friend and biographer, never ceased to marvel at his want of "the impulse of genius,"[10] by which he meant that Johnson never wrote anything except under pressure and for money. Yet even a hack may be a hack of genius, and retrospectively the work of genius never looks adventitious. In some way Johnson must have chosen his life as an author. But what did he choose?

The question may be clarified by being posed in terms of Johnson's relation to his precursor. The identity of that precursor was common knowledge in the eighteenth century and dominates early criticism of Johnson's work, though modern Johnsonians seem reluctant to bring it up. I am referring, of course, to Joseph Addison. Few literary genealogies have ever been more clearly marked or more legitimate. Addison, like Johnson, had attended the Lichfield Grammar School and, on Johnson's own account, left a reputation well suited to a schoolboy hero, since he had "planned and conducted" a *barring-out,* an end-of-term mutiny in which the boys locked the master out of the school.[11] Johnson's longest juvenile poem is a translation of Addison's Latin "Battle of the Pygmies and Cranes"; and he later praised Roscommon as "perhaps the only correct writer in verse before Addison."[12] *Irene,* the tragedy on which Johnson probably expended more effort than on anything else he ever wrote, has always been recognized as an offspring of *Cato.*[13] Addison's allegorical "Visions of Mirzah" (*Spectator* 159) is by far the most important contemporary source for all Johnson's fiction, from "The Vision of Theodore" to *Rasselas.* As the logical choice to compile the first standard English dictionary, Addison is supposed to have been offered £3,000 by Tonson and actually to have begun the work.[14] Johnson defended Addison's literary criticism for awakening inquiry and expanding comprehension: "he founds art on the base of nature, and draws the principles of invention from dispositions inherent in the mind of man" (not a bad description of Johnson's own critical ideal).[15] Most important of all, as *"the Raphael of Essay Writers"*[16] Addison had set the standard against which Johnson's great work *The Rambler* deliberately measured its own achievement.[17] And one more point may be added: Addison's merit had been rewarded with the important office of Secretary of State. In that respect, at least, Johnson never succeeded in living up to the model he had chosen.

Yet Addison had also left something to do. Despite his elegance and correctness, he had not been energetic, he had not been profound. When Johnson named the great English "teachers of truth," in the Preface to the *Dictionary,* he canonized Bacon, Hooker, Milton, and Boyle. Addison had no place in that list; he had added little or nothing to the glory of literature or the store of knowledge. Though young Johnson exercised his wit on Addison's Pygmies and Cranes, the older Johnson was not sure that pygmies deserved attention in the first place. "By the sonorous magnificence of Roman syllables the writer conceals penury of thought and want of novelty, often from the reader, and often from himself."[18] The great Renaissance scholars and poets whom Johnson held so dear had made better use of their learning. Mrs. Piozzi observes that while Johnson always highly commended Addison's prose, "his praises resembled those of a man who extols the superior elegance of high painted porcelain, while he himself always chuses to eat off *plate*."[19]

Hence English prose awaited a new sort of master. Johnson took pride in refining the language by giving it weight and strength. Technically, this project might be described in three overlapping ways. First, it is possible to stress, with W. K. Wimsatt, the use of philosophic words. "When common words were less pleasing to the ear, or less distinct in their signification," Johnson writes at the end of *The Rambler,* "I have familiarized the terms of philosophy by applying them to popular ideas."[20] Here, more than ever before in English, the vocabulary of science turns inward, to the analysis of states of mind.[21] Though only a small percentage of Johnson's diction draws on this stock of words, the selection encourages a new style of thought, as if the moral universe were susceptible to the same minute and refined investigation as the world of the atom.

A second way of describing Johnson's project might view it as converting the achievements of the golden age of the heroic couplet, its precise discriminations, antitheses, and balances, into the more solid medium of English prose. "Something, perhaps, I have added to the elegance of its construction, and something to the harmony of its cadence."[22] The letter to Chesterfield displays the ear of a poet for rhythms that build a climax or spring a trap. Such hints of prosody often help shape a distinctive prose style. During the reign of Stalin, Nadezhda Mandelstam preserved the great poems of her husband in her head; for a long time her memory harbored the only surviving edition. As a result of living with those rhythms and images, as intimate and familiar as her breath, she developed her own beautiful new Russian prose style, unmatched in modern times.[23] Johnson's fabulous memory may be said to have brought about a similar transformation. He carried the English poets of the late seventeenth and early eighteenth centuries in his head, and turned them into choruses of prose.

Most of Johnson's contemporaries and successors, however, would have described his prose in a third way, as reaching after "splendor and magnificence."[24] Coleridge, a witness for the prosecution, charged that Johnson "creates an impression of cleverness by never saying any thing in a common way."[25] Testifying for the defense, Johnson himself offered this analysis of a passage from the *Journey to the Western Islands,* "We were now treading that illustrious region": "the word *illustrious,* contributes nothing to the mere narration; for the fact might be told without it: but it is not, therefore, superfluous; for it wakes the mind to peculiar attention, where something of more than usual importance is to be presented. 'Illustrious!'—for what? and then the sentence proceeds to expand the circumstances connected with Iona."[26] Both attack and defense agree on the effort of the prose to wake peculiar attention. Addison's elegant and correct style seldom calls attention to itself, but neither does it force one to take notice. "Against that inattention by which known truths are suffered to lie neglected," as Johnson said of Swift's prose, "it makes no provision; it instructs, but does not persuade."[27] Here was a project for the midcentury: to fashion a prose that would wake readers up. In this respect Johnson certainly succeeded. Though some readers were irritated at being wakened or shaken so roughly (by *"bow-wow"* sounds like a barking dog in the night), most, like Nathan Drake, applauded the effects of the heightened new style: "to clothe with fresh energy the maxims of virtue and of piety, perhaps unparalleled in the powers of impression."[28] Addison lost his sway. Johnson's prose, somewhat adulterated with sugar and water, was to become the standard prose of Victorian England.

Yet the project was not merely a matter of style. The elegance of Addison's prose meant far less to Johnson than its consistent employment in the service of virtue. "All the enchantment of fancy and all the cogency of argument are employed to recommend to the reader his real interest, the care of pleasing the Author of his being."[29] Here was a model for everyone's imitation, as Johnson advised James Woodhouse, the shoemaker poet: "Give nights and days, Sir, to the study of Addison, if you mean either to be a good writer, or what is more worth, an honest man."[30] The last words are crucial. To please the Author of his being, no author could do better, in Johnson's eyes, than to teach his readers to be good, according to the unchallengeable dictates of revelation. "I shall never envy the honours which wit and learning obtain in any other cause, if I can be numbered among the writers who have given ardour to virtue, and confidence to truth."[31] Addison deserved the highest praise as a

41

teacher of wisdom, one who had published nothing that he would have to regret in his last moments. That was Johnson's ambition as well. His duty as a guide demanded not only that his writing be useful, but that it be *faultless*. Not many ambitious young authors can ever have faced so stringent and fearful a task.

No wonder that he found it so hard to begin. He was still beginning, in fact, well into his forties. In a previous book I have argued that most great authors produce a work of initiation, which not only achieves the essential breakthrough but also explains its principles, teaching us how to read it.[32] In these terms *The Rambler* is Johnson's initiation. It begins with no fewer than five essays that discuss the problems of beginning, weigh the alternatives, and define a program for the future. The first is the well-known paper on "the difficulty of the first address on any new occasion," which explains the advantages of writing short papers without any larger commitment. The second defends the human tendency to embark on great enterprises while dreaming of future rewards, although "perhaps no class of the human species requires more to be cautioned against this anticipation of happiness, than those that aspire to the name of authors." The third considers the difficult "task of an author" by means of an allegory on Criticism, which tends "to hinder the reception of every work of learning or genius." The fourth is the famous essay on modern fiction, which in this context and the context of Johnson's own fictions might be viewed as an internal debate about whether the novel matches the moral essay as a proper medium for representing life, since almost inevitably novelists "confound the colours of right and wrong" by mixing virtue with vice. The fifth, like "On a Daffodill," ponders "the spring of the year, and the spring of life"; addressing young readers, the Rambler warns them "that a blighted spring makes a barren year, and that the vernal flowers, however beautiful and gay, are only intended by nature as preparatives to autumn fruits."[33] Is the author regretting some blight of his own, or harvesting personal fruit? Ambitious, or dejected? Perhaps he had not yet learned how to read himself.

The problem of beginning, as Johnson sees it, may be illuminated by one of his most interesting disagreements with Addison: the discussion, in *Rambler* 158, of how a poem should begin. Addison gracefully makes light of the problem: the first lines ought to be "plain, simple, and unadorned,"[34] as in the ancient epics or *Paradise Lost*. But Johnson points out the flaw in both the precept and the examples. In fact great poems open with plenty of glitter. Beginning requires a special effort, both to catch the reader and to show the author's power.

> The intent of the introduction is to raise expectation, and suspend it; something therefore must be discovered, and something concealed; and the poet, while the fertility of his invention is yet unknown, may properly recommend himself by the grace of his language.
>
> He that reveals too much, or promises too little; he that never irritates the intellectual appetite, or that immediately satiates it, equally defeats his own purpose. It is necessary to the pleasure of the reader, that the events should not be anticipated, and how then can his attention be invited, but by grandeur of expression?[35]

There is material here for a whole treatise on beginnings. But a few points seem particularly relevant to Johnson's own career. First, the issue between the Spectator and the Rambler epitomizes the difference that contemporaries observed between the styles of Addison and Johnson themselves: on the one hand, a mode "plain, simple, and unadorned," whose elegance sometimes verges on insipidity; on the other, a "grandeur of expression" piled high on the subject, not always appropriately. Significantly, each critic perceives his own principles to be exemplified by Milton. For Addison, he is striking because of the directness with which he manages his plot; for Johnson, because of his sublime grandeur of expression—"Milton's style was not modified by his subject."[36] As much as Johnson respects the truth, he does not think that a writer will succeed by revealing all at the beginning. Some glitter must first catch the eye.

The second point is Johnson's recommendation of temporary concealment, in order to *suspend* expectation as well as to raise it. The audience must be left hanging. Such suspension follows an aesthetic principle, of course, the need to engage the reader by inducing that faintly anxious attention we call suspense. But it also bears on the author's own problem at beginning, his need to show his power or "recommend himself." An ambitious writer like Johnson, proud of his abilities yet conscious that his success will depend on attracting or catering to others, may well be torn between two alternatives: defiance and seduction. Will he charm his readers, like Addison, or boldly demand their applause? It may be best for him to suspend the choice.

The first number of *The Rambler* is a fascinating study of this state of mind. "If a man could glide imperceptibly into the favour of the publick, and only proclaim his pretensions to literary honours when he is sure of not being rejected," the anonymous Johnson writes, "he might commence author with better hopes." Yet since authors are known to be both ambitious and vulnerable, it is no wonder that some "should endeavour to gain favour by bribing the judge with an appearance of respect which they do not feel," and others should try to attract regard "by a daring profession of their own deserts, and a publick challenge of honours and rewards." The dilemma is not at all hypothetical. The Rambler is obviously talking about himself, and Johnson's beginning hangs in the balance. He solves the problem only by letting it hang. "But whether my expectations are most fixed on pardon or praise, I think it not necessary to discover; for having accurately weighed the reasons for arrogance and submission, I find them so nearly equiponderant, that my impatience to try the event of my first performance will not suffer me to attend any longer the trepidations of the balance."[37] Once again he suspends expectation. Arrogance and submission must be equally concealed, or answered by the event, in a humorous blend—assertive diffidence—that leaves the reader wondering what will come next. Johnson did not resolve his opposing inclinations toward ambition and dejection. Instead he put them both to use and based his work on the conflict. That is how he managed to begin.

The conflict hangs over the fresh beginnings that the Rambler had to trot out twice every week, his weighty opening sentences: "It has been remarked, perhaps, by every writer, who has left behind him observations upon life, that no man is pleased with his present state . . ." or "That few things are so liberally bestowed, or squandered with so little effect, as good advice, has been generally observed . . ."[38]

or "It is a truth universally acknowledged . . ." Whatever truth follows, the reader eventually learns, will turn out to be not quite true. Our first impression and judgment must be suspended. The energy of Johnson's analysis is fueled by his skepticism, the restless intelligence that finds something wanting in each received opinion.[39] The very beginning of the collected *Rambler,* the motto on its title page, announces the author's freedom to think for himself: *"Nullius addictus jurare in verba magistri,/Quo me cunque rapit tempestas deferor hospes"* ("Sworn to no master's arbitrary sway,/I range where-e'er occasion points the way").[40] Horace's words give notice that these essays will be experiments in thought (the Royal Society had adopted the same motto) as well as heterogeneous in matter. But they also air a spirit of rebellion. The dicta and dogma that counterfeit wisdom will here be put to the test. Even the weight of Johnson's openings can often provoke some fidgets, if not outright contradictions. The seeming truth covers a crack, perhaps an abyss. Johnson makes room for his text by delving there.

At the same time he copes with feelings of oppression. Whatever else may be said about Johnson's beginnings, they do tend often to dampen the spirit. "No man is pleased with his present state" seems close to the sum of wisdom. When Observation surveys Mankind, at the start of *The Vanity of Human Wishes,* she immediately discerns "how Hope and Fear, Desire and Hate,/O'erspread with Snares the clouded Maze of Fate," and the first verse paragraph keeps sliding downward till it ends with Death. *The Rambler* often opens on the same low note. To generalize about human nature is to invite dejection if not despair. Not only does the collective experience of mankind attest that very few people have led happy lives; it also advises young writers that almost nothing they can say will be surprising or new. One response to this warning would take the way of piety, subduing pride and accepting the insignificance of any personal achievement. In the long run Johnson follows that way; his works conclude by bowing to God's will.[41] In the short run, however, he twists and turns the adages by which people live. A blessed state of doubt, if not a deeper wisdom, charges each commonplace with a potential for unexpected reversals. Such doubt alerts both writer and reader to the tension that always occurs when one strong mind tests what it has been taught against its own impressions. Thus a touch of parody frequently subverts the pomp of Johnson's beginnings. "It is a truth universally acknowledged, that a single man in possession of a good fortune, must be in want of a wife." Jane Austen is a fine Johnsonian—not least in knowing how to state a truth so that the reader will doubt it. Beginnings like this prepare us for many surprises.

Yet Johnson never did find it easy to begin. Throughout his career, the pleasure he took in making ambitious plans soon lapsed into a period of torpor. Nor could his best resolutions overcome this resistance to beginning; it was a part of what had made him an author. The bending back of Johnson's work against itself, the dejection that always haunted his ambition, helped form a strategy for dealing with the problem of authorship in his time. That problem came from his historical moment, as he perceived it: a sense of belatedness oppressed many writers in his generation.[42] The scholars and poets of the Renaissance had grasped the most important truths about the world and human nature; more recent critics and scholars had passed that knowledge on to a larger and larger circle of readers. Hence the problem shared by authors in Johnson's age was to reach an audience already acquainted with the broad outlines of truth, and already civilized by correct standards of art and behavior, and somehow, without departing from that truth and those standards, to delight it with an impression of something new. The prospect was intimidating; and Johnson thought that many ingenious minds of his generation had evaded rather than solved their dilemma, by chasing after untruth and incorrectness. His own solution was different. He would raise the standards higher by being satisfied with nothing less than perfection and by bringing life itself to the test of truth.

He would of course fail. Such high ambitions guarantee frustration. That failure is built into Johnson's beginnings, his discontent with the half-truths of writing even as he writes them down. Disillusionment shadows Johnson's illusions from the moment of their making; at fifteen, after the first flush, even the sight of a daffodil dejects him. Yet that too is a way to begin. The same great expectations and self-conscious doubts that made it so hard for Johnson to start would eventually prove the means of his deliverance, the talents he was born to employ. No one would ever understand dissatisfaction so well or make so much of it. He projected his life as an author from such beginnings. The problems he found there would follow him to the end.

3

Becoming an Author:
London; Life of Savage

If I were to form an adage of misery, or fix the lowest
point to which humanity could fall, I should be
tempted to name the life of an author.

JOHNSON BECAME an author against his will. Need and chance,
not destiny, were the forces that drove him to write. He would
have been a lawyer, he told Boswell, if he had had enough
money;[1] and as late as 1739, after two years of writing for hire in London, he wanted desperately to return to schoolteaching—a line of
work at which he had already failed.[2] When Johnson remarks that
the indigent Richard Savage, "having no Profession, became, by Necessity, an Author," he describes his own lot as well.[3] Necessity was
his muse. In fact Hawkins claims that "I have, more than once, heard
him assert, that he knew of no genuine motive for writing, other than
necessity."[4] Johnson dissociates himself from the sort of blockhead
who writes only for glory. However much the fever of the young Enthusiast might once have been his own, the mature author casts a
cold professional eye on amateurs who give their work away; they
cheapen the whole trade of letters, whose honor consists of supplying good copy at a good price. Want compelled Johnson to write,
and throughout his career he seldom did write except under compulsion.

Moreover, a long time passed before Johnson claimed to be an author. Insofar as the title confers some honor, he prefers to refuse it.
Anonymity suits the young Johnson. Though Pope famously pre-

48

dicted that the obscure poet of *London* "will soon be *déterré*," more than ten years went by before his name first surfaced on a title page. Nor did Johnson pretend that his early writings qualified him for authorship. According to the *Dictionary,* an "author" is "the first beginner or mover of any thing; he to whom any thing owes its original," and a hack writer does not originate his own projects. Still less could the translator of Father Lobo and parliamentary reporter fancy himself as "the first writer of any thing; distinct from the *translator* or *compiler.*"[5] Others, in retrospect, might comb the works of his youth for signs of original genius, or for the special Johnsonian stylistic signature that allows an anonymous contribution to the *Gentleman's Magazine* to be identified, in later years, for inclusion in some authoritative *Works of Samuel Johnson.* Young Johnson was more self-effacing. He trained himself, as a journeyman writer, to stay in the shade. Only in his forties, when he emerged into the light of fame as "Dictionary Johnson," did he begin, quite hesitantly, to call himself an author. Whatever his private ambitions might be, in public he wore the veil of a nameless writer.

Indeed, he took much satisfaction from the role. There is something epic in young Johnson's embrace of his status as drudge and hack. This ironic self-presentation reaches a peak in the *Dictionary*'s definition of "grubstreet": "Originally the name of a street near Moorfields in London, much inhabited by writers of small histories, dictionaries, and temporary poems; whence any mean production is called *grubstreet.*" In a burst of enthusiasm, an untranslated tag from the *Greek Anthology* then clinches the point: "Hail, Ithaca! after many labors, after bitter suffering,/gladly I touch your shore."[6] Actually Johnson never set foot on Grub Street.[7] Yet he enjoys identifying with Odysseus, the canny hero who is never more dangerous than when he masquerades as nobody. The allusion cuts two ways. On the one hand, the writer acknowledges his own insignificance, which extends not only to lexicographical drudgery but also to the histories and poems that had furnished his livelihood; grubstreet is where he belongs. On the other hand, only a sly and learned writer would be capable of the reference. In order to catch it, the reader of an English dictionary has to know Greek. This is very superior humor. Even as Johnson self-consciously claims to be nobody, he hints that the modesty of the scribbler might be as deceptive as Odysseus' shabby clothes. In a letter written just before the *Dictionary* came out, anxious about its reception, he borrowed the same identity: "I know not whether I shall find upon the coast, a Calypso that will court or a Polypheme that will eat me. But if Polypheme comes to me have at his eyes."[8] Here again the hack doubles as hero. Soon all the world will be crying up his name—as Chesterfield did in *The World.*

Such ironies of authorship seem typical of Johnson. Comparing his "bitter suffering" to that of a sailor, for instance, recalls not only William Warburton's image of English as "this wide sea of words"[9] but also the long simile that opens "The Young Author," whose hope for applause is compared to a peasant's first voyage: delightful in prospect but straightway wracked by sickening storms.[10] Johnson detested the sailor's life—"being in a ship is being in a jail, with the chance of being drowned"[11]—and evokes it whenever he wants to "fix the lowest point to which humanity could fall," short of being an author. Hack writers suffer like hands at sea; penned in galleys, they cannot steer their own course. Johnson feels the pain of slaving for pay. Yet he also keeps some distance from it, retaining the perspective of Greek or eternity even while the manacles bite into his flesh. There is dignity in looking down on one's own distress. There is dignity also in fulfilling the terms of a contract without repining. Young Johnson does not represent himself as an author *manqué.* Instead he goes about his business as a writer, with no illusions that hack work might be a high or voluntary calling. When the title of author finally comes to him, like the title of doctor, that will not be because he has begged for it.

Why was Johnson so unwilling to be an author, and why did he take so long to become one? To some extent the answer must lie in his temperament. The notorious melancholy he inherited from his father, the long periods of torpor, the self-fulfilling habit of preemptive dejection, the defensive pride would have been enough to keep most writers from ever beginning. Nor can one overlook the mournful truth he emphasized in *London:* "SLOW RISES WORTH, BY POVERTY DE-

PREST." Had Johnson been able to stay at Oxford, had his income allowed him to pursue studies and interests of his own choosing, he might well have made a name sooner. The wonder is not that his triumph came so late but that it happened at all.

Yet authors do not single-handedly create themselves. As theorists and historians have lately been insisting, the idea of authorship is a social construction, historically and culturally determined.[12] What characterizes it is not a natural condition of writers and writing in every age, but rather a hierarchy that elevates some writers over others, according to the standards of a particular time. Thus Johnson distinguishes the author from the translator or compiler, and modern dictionaries detach the editor or copyist from the true author or "composer of a literary work." These discriminations alter from one period to another. Hence scholars have reason to suspect any definition that privileges the author as original creator, the source or first cause of the work. Works can have many sources, and authors themselves are created. From this point of view, the question of how a writer becomes an author depends on the prior question of what the age considered an author to be. If Johnson found it difficult to think of himself as an author, the reason may be less personal than cultural. Perhaps his reservations and self-effacement conformed to what the age demanded. Perhaps they even represent a deliberate strategy for dealing with the problems of authorship in his time.

No career offers a better test case of the way that an author is made. Johnson's life has often been used to define what authorship means. To later generations, beginning with Boswell, he seemed the perfect model of a self-made man, "the hero as man of letters,"[13] overcoming all obstacles until he ruled the literary world by force of genius. The emblem of his fierce independence and inevitable triumph was the letter to Chesterfield. The hero had achieved his great work "without one Act of assistance, one word of encouragment, or one smile of favour," and was "unwilling that the Public should consider me as owing that to a Patron, which Providence has enabled me to do for myself." Such an author rises above the petty curbs that might throttle a lesser talent. In these terms, Johnson's career was the person himself writ large. Furthermore, his own literary biographies eventually taught the world to regard the history of poetry as a sequence of individual careers, a history to which the performance of each poet contributed a separate chapter.[14] English poetry and the lives of the poets, or their choices of life, were interleaved parts of a single book. That book itself became known as *Johnson's Lives,* just as the age became the Age of Johnson. He had shaped the profession of letters in his own image.

Yet something is wrong with that story. Appealing as it may seem to those who look backward, reading Johnson's heroic or tyrannical career from the safe harbor of the future, it does no justice to the apprehensions and hesitations of the young writer looking forward. Above all it ignores his passivity. Did Johnson make a conscious choice of life? The bulk of evidence suggests that he did not, and that he knew it. Most of his works were commissioned. The *Dictionary* may have owed little or nothing to any patron, but it owed its existence to the booksellers who gave their creature the means to carry it out and who would have found someone else had he declined. Usually Johnson considered himself a servant of the public. In this respect he seems anything but self-made; his career took shape from what people asked him to do. A case can be made (Alvin Kernan has made it) that print itself made Johnson an author.[15] "Dictionary Johnson," for instance, identifies the offspring of a publishing event, a person hatched by a folio. At any rate, he exercised little control over his development as an author. Not for him the *cursus honorum* of writers like Milton and Pope, the reaching after a whole harmonium. Johnson followed the course that his age had laid down.

The contrast between these two ways of viewing Johnson's career—between the self-made author and the passive instrument of print culture—reflects a problem in his time as well as ours. Ideas of authorship were changing.[16] Less than a year after Johnson was born, the Copyright Act of 1710 (the Statute of Anne) first granted authors some rights in literary property. This recognition might be thought decisive: "The important date for the 'invention' of authors is not some time in the Renaissance, but 1710, when they were first given legal personalities."[17] Johnson himself would take a strong interest in author's rights and copyright law. But law did not settle the touchy question of how to define an author. As Johnson's own fluctuating, sometimes contradictory statements indicate, the notion of authorship itself was contested. Extravagant praise, extravagant resentment or contempt, go along with the word and the realities behind it. Becoming an author in young Johnson's time could not have been easy; it had to be worked out by trial and chance. But just this difficulty makes his situation instructive. It shows the complexity of authorship itself, the peculiar match between some gifted individuals and a system that both rewards and punishes their efforts to make names for themselves. Johnson's career could not be taken for granted. He would have to redefine the terms of success, even as his own ambitions and identity were redefined by what his readership wanted. As times changed him, so he would change the way the British public conceived of its authors.

If Johnson became an author against his will, the reason may have less to do with temperament than with good sound logic. Why would anyone want to be an author? The question might have force at any time, but at the specific moment when Johnson came of age and looked for a profession, any intelligent young person might have quailed at the prospect. In December 1729, when Johnson left Oxford for years of vegetating at home instead of trying his hand in London, authors were in bad repute. The general causes of this stigma include the marketplace and politics of writing. As the patronage system came under attack and the booksellers gradually reorganized the trade in their own interest, writers had to adapt to new ways of making a living. Instability led to tensions.[18] The high-minded view of authors as noble benefactors of the public was balanced by the sordid myth of grubstreet slaves and toadies, and the competition for consumers of print moved writers to accuse each other of money-grubbing hypocrisy.[19] Commercially, the supply of writers exceeded the demand. At the same time, writing became increasingly politicized. Open warfare erupted between Walpole and the wits, and almost all writers enlisted in—or were bought off by—a party.[20] To choose the profession of letters meant joining the opposition and arming for battle. It did not mean a quiet and respected way of life.

There was also a far more specific cause for the low reputation of authors: in two words, Alexander Pope. The greatest poet of the age had no low opinion of his art. His standards were so high, in fact, that hardly any writer could live up to them. He towered so far above mere professional scribblers—at least in his own eyes—that they seemed an inferior species.[21] Brilliantly managing the market for writing, Pope amassed a fortune while simultaneously associating himself with Homer and Shakespeare.[22] But that monopoly did not leave room for a rival. In the 1717 preface to his *Works,* the young poet had discouraged others from following his choice of a calling. "I believe, if any one, early in his life should contemplate the dangerous fate of authors, he would scarce be of their number on any consideration. The life of a Wit is a warfare upon earth; and the present spirit of the world is such, that to attempt to serve it (any way) one must have the constancy of a martyr, and a resolution to suffer for its sake."[23] Nor did he prove reluctant to add to that suffering. The masterpiece of English poetry during Johnson's formative years, the years when he began to think about becoming an author, was a mighty satire of would-be authors, a holocaust of dunces. The first *Dunciad* (1728) and its variorum edition (1729), assisted by Richard Savage, excoriate an age when Dulness rules, the arts and learning dwindle, and commerce replaces the honor and dignity of poetry. The impression on Johnson was lasting. To be sure, he understood that only bad authors, not authors at large, were being condemned. "An author places himself uncalled before the tribunal of criticism, and solicits fame at the hazard of disgrace . . . If bad writers were to pass without reprehension what should restrain them?" In this regard the satirist qualified as "a publick benefactor."[24] But Johnson also absorbed another lesson: in choosing authorship as his profession, a young writer had to be ready for instant and violent retribution.

The example of Pope could discourage young poets in still another way. His verse was finished and brilliant; it left little room for improvement. At the end of Johnson's career, when he identified Pope with poetry itself, he regarded such perfection as a capstone or terminus in the advance of English poetic technique. "New sentiments and new images others may produce, but to attempt any further improvement of versification will be dangerous. Art and diligence have now done their best, and what shall be added will be the effort of tedious toil and needless curiosity."[25] These words must have struck the old critic who wrote them as profoundly satisfying, a confirmation of what art and diligence could accomplish and a mark of how far English verse had progressed. To many young poets they would have sounded a death knell. More than one generation of British poets elected Pope their favorite enemy, the roadblock they had to remove.[26] But Johnson, as an apprentice poet when all the dunces were being called to account, had no illusions about his ability to challenge Pope's verse. That way to authorship seemed closed to him.

One likely solution might be to select a less intimidating model. As W. H. Auden explained his choice of Thomas Hardy for a first master, "He was a good poet, perhaps a great one, but not *too* good . . . This gave me hope where a flawless poet might have made me despair."[27] Johnson did not appoint Pope as his master. Insofar as any contemporary served as an early guide, the most plausible candidate seems Edward Young. Young was a good poet, perhaps a great one, but not *too* good. His collection of satires, *Love of Fame, The Universal Passion* (1725–1728), was much admired in the late 1720s, when Johnson's own style was forming, and Johnson later called it "indeed a very great performance."[28] Some passages he could recite by heart, and the revised fourth edition of the *Dictionary* takes many examples from Young.[29] Moreover, the good humor of the satiric voice proved congenial, unlike Pope's merciless revenge on dunces. Yet Young's defects were also obvious. "He never seems to have studied prosody"; his wit was scattershot. Still worse, his satire plays "only on the surface of life; he never penetrates the recesses of the mind, and therefore the whole power of his poetry is exhausted by a single perusal."[30] An apprentice could hardly ask for a better master. Here was no flawless genius to make one despair, but an easygoing and forgettable model on which a determined student could always improve.

The young author drew on that model. Johnson's "Young Author" ("wrote in his 20th Year," according to his schoolfriend Edmund Hector) has been associated with his despondency at leaving Oxford.[31] Yet it also responds to some verses published at just the same time, Young's account of a literary wet dream.

> A Virgin-Author, recent from the Press,
> The sheets yet wet, applauds his great Success;
> Surveys them, reads them, takes their charms to bed,
> Those in his hand, and Glory in his head.
> 'Tis Joy too great, a fever of Delight!
> His heart beats thick, nor close his eyes all night,
> But rising the next morn to clasp his Fame,
> He finds, that without sleeping he cou'd dream:
> So Sparks (they say) take Goddesses to bed,
> And find next day the Devil in their stead.[32]

Writing and onanism are near allied in Young's fancy. With consistent, coy double entendre (virgin, press, wet sheets, charms, hand, etc.) he insinuates that the fledgling author has confused the self-love of poeticizing with sex and will get no satisfaction from either. Here Adam's dream is inverted; he awakes and finds it untrue.

When Johnson tells the same story, he takes out the sex. But more crucially, he tries to penetrate "the recesses of the mind" by converting the "stinging jest" into a sober reflection on the vanity of human wishes. Unlike Young's, his "young Authour, panting after fame,/And the long honours of a lasting name," is motivated by idealism as well as self-love. He scorns the "perishable prize" of wealth or title, and expects his audience to be equally generous.

> He flies to press, and hurries on his fate;
> Swiftly he sees the imagin'd laurels spread,
> And feels the unfading wreath surround his head.
> Warn'd by another's fate, vain youth, be wise,
> Those dreams were Settle's once, and Ogilby's.[33]

Elkanah Settle (1648–1724), the official city poet of London during Johnson's childhood, had "died forgotten in a hospital." Young's satire had mocked this end, and Johnson later wondered that such a laughingstock had once been considered the rival of Dryden: "Such are the revolutions of fame, or such is the prevalence of fashion."[34] But "The Young Author" is less dismissive. Settle, like Johnson, had left Oxford without a degree, and had soon made a name in London. That was a worthwhile ambition. Hence the eventual failure of his dreams serves not as a joke but as a warning.

The turn from clever, superior wit toward a compassionate moralizing, a turn that involves the author himself in the frailties he satirizes, might have pointed out a new direction to Johnson. Eventually he took it, in *The Vanity of Human Wishes* and moral essays, and left Pope as well as Young behind. Yet becoming an author would not be so easy. Young's satire of the virgin-author and Settle occurs in the first of *Two Epistles to Mr. Pope, Concerning the Authors of the Age* (1730), and it continues the savage crusade against the petty nation of writers that *The Dunciad* had aroused. A few years earlier, Young had written that "bad poets, that is, poets in general, are esteemed, and really are, the most vain, the most irritable, and most ridiculous set of men upon earth."[35] Now he carried the charge still further: "Nature's refuse, and the Dregs of men,/Compose the *black Militia* of the *Pen*."[36] How could any young author have the heart to join that militia? Johnson did not. Young's example, like Pope's, discouraged him from trying. "The Young Author" forgoes any hope for a future career and seems to announce that this writer will give up forever, even before he begins.

> The pamphlet spreads, incessant hisses rise,
> To some retreat the baffled writer flies;
> Where no sour criticks snarl, no sneers molest,
> Safe from the tart lampoon, and stinging jest;
> There begs of heaven a less distinguish'd lot,
> Glad to be hid, and proud to be forgot.

In so unforgiving an age, retreat seems the best solution. Johnson had published no verse or pamphlet as yet; the experience of the young author could not have been his own.[37] But the instinct to hide or disguise his ambitions was more than a fiction. Thirteen years passed before he published the poem—anonymously.

How did he ever emerge from this impasse? Part of the answer must be that he found the right market: the *Gentleman's Magazine,* which started in 1731 and later became the source of his bread and butter. This was no *Grub-street Journal;* it offered an air of respectability as well as steady employment.[38] Yet another part of the answer may be that he thought through his motives for becoming an author, and so redefined his understanding of authorship itself. The love of fame (as Young had painted it) could not be sufficient. Everyone wanted fame, but the quest led inevitably to delusions of grandeur and to disappointment. There was not enough fame to go around, and in any case few people deserved it. Some better motive was needed. Johnson discovered it in an ideal of service. In his most searching examination of literary fame, the magnificent *Rambler* 106, he concludes by stepping back from the pursuit of "unfading laurels, and immortal reputation," and recommending a more modest ambition. "It may, however, satisfy an honest and benevolent mind to have been useful, though less conspicuous; nor will he that extends his hope to higher rewards, be so much anxious to obtain praise, as to discharge the duty which Providence assigns him."[39] This hope is of course religious. Yet the hopeful young author will also receive a practical piece of advice: put usefulness and duty before praise. Such advice is morally improving. In addition, it may help cure writer's block.

At the same time, a commitment to service aims to restore the reputation of authors. Though Johnson never lost his youthful sense of the pride and perils of authorship—most writers, after all, would always be dunces—he spent much of his life defending the ideal. Even his hack work shines with a vision of what an author might be.

The Character of an Author must be allowed to imply in itself something amiable and great; it conveys at once the Idea of Ability and Good-nature, of Knowledge, and a Disposition to communicate it . . . When *Pythagoras* was asked How a Mortal might arrive at nearest Resemblance to the celestial Beings, he answer'd, *By Beneficence and Truth;* and surely no Man has a juster Title to these sublime Qualities than a great Genius, exhausting his Time and Health for the Service of the Publick, in discovering Truth, and recommending it, by the Ornaments of Eloquence, to the Favour of Mankind.[40]

These exalted sentiments introduce a tirade against "the abandon'd Prostitutes of the Pen" who convert every subject into party politics; but the anonymous contributor to the *Gentleman's Magazine* (January 1739) who makes the accusation might well have been accused of the same offense. Politics sold magazines, in the 1730s, and Johnson had quickly learned the tricks of the trade. Yet he never fails to distinguish the self-serving and party-serving writer from the author who devotes himself selflessly to truth and the public. In this way even his anonymity supports a claim of altruism. How can a writer prove his beneficence better than by sacrificing his name for the good of others?

Another requirement of authorship, as Johnson defined it, was learning. The ideal of the learned author, like the ideal of the author as servant of the public, did not originate with him. It represents a classical model, kept alive through the Renaissance, and most eighteenth-century authorities still paid it lip service.[41] But hardly anyone took the ideal more seriously than Johnson. At times he seems to assume that the author and scholar are one. Thus the "young Enthusiast," in *The Vanity of Human Wishes,* replays the young author's dreams of glory, though it is the *scholar's* life that captures his "letter'd Heart"; those "dedicated to the profession of literature," in Sermon 8, are men of learning; and in *Rasselas* Imlac, described as both a man of learning and a poet, equates poetry with the highest learning and the poet with a scholar beyond compare.[42] If Johnson enjoys some irony at Imlac's expense, he also agrees with him. An author is a scholar who shares his knowledge; that gift is his point of pride. Moreover, it qualifies authors for their profession.

To some extent this pride in learning must have been defensive. Johnson's college stay had lasted only a little over a year, and though he might eventually win fame as the best-read man in Europe, he was largely an autodidact. An honorary doctorate does not impress professional scholars. This was a wound. Late in his life, when Johnson reread the passage on the young Enthusiast, "in which the life of a scholar is painted, with the various obstructions thrown in his way to fortune and to fame," he could not help crying.[43] As a young man he compensated by insisting that he *was* fulfilled as a scholar, or even something better, since a writer had to put his learning to use.

Such defensiveness extended to his whole profession. *Adventurer* 115 (1753) satirically styles its age "The Age of Authors; for, perhaps, there never was a time, in which men of all degrees of ability, of every kind of education, of every profession and employment, were posting with ardour so general to the press." The word "men" is part of the satire, since the height of the calamity seems to be an invasion by women, "a generation of Amazons of the pen."[44] Johnson had always encouraged women writers. No influential author of the century gave them more practical advice or helped them more to publish.[45] Yet he cannot abide the amateur who feeds on flattery and expects to be praised for her charm instead of her labors. He especially resents these women's "claim to the regions of science." Authorship ought to require deep learning, long study of the best writers and best ideas. "The first qualification of a writer is a perfect knowledge of the subject which he[!] undertakes to treat, since we cannot teach what we do not know, nor can properly undertake to instruct others, while we are ourselves in want of instruction."[46] Few men, and very few women, command such knowledge. Thus Johnson polices the realm of letters and warns the wrong sort of people—the lazy or unlettered—to keep out.

Professional misgivings inspire this attack. Having worked to establish himself as a writer, Johnson does not want to see the field overrun. The ideal of the learned author safeguards a very peculiar profession, whose members qualify not through any certificate, apprenticeship, or examination, but simply by attracting attention. Dunces, as Pope had shown, can do that quite well. Hence Johnson tries to heighten the qualifications, to raise the repute of authors as a whole. Perhaps he succeeded, to some degree.[47] By the end of his career, and in part through his own efforts, the automatic ridicule of authors and their pretensions had abated. Wits did not cease to war, but some disarmed. *The Lives of the Poets* treats the literary squabbles of earlier generations from a certain distance, as a British historian in times of peace might look back at the civil wars. It would be too much to say that authorship had become a respectable, let alone a learned, profession. But much of the late eighteenth-century public was willing to concede that authorship *could be* a profession.[48] Johnson's own success seemed to prove it. At once a popular writer and a scholar, he had taken his place among the eminences of Britain.

To young Johnson, however, the ideal of the learned author was more than defensive. It gave him something to work toward, a goal to be achieved by training and study. Professing authorship did not have to be vainglorious; the honor could be earned. Even his years of vegetating at home, a long stretch of vast and desultory reading in every field of knowledge, assumed a retrospective purpose in this light: he had been becoming an author all along. Certainly no one could ever call him a dunce. The heterogeneous learning that, in other fields, might have seemed the mark of a dilettante, qualified him as a truly professional author. To reach the goal would demand a long course of study and much self-sacrifice. But at least the young writer knew what he had to do. He would become that ideal of a learned author.

This strategy might also be described in strict commercial terms. Learning was all that Johnson had to sell. Other young writers might know the market better, excel in the social graces, be better acquainted with literary fashions, have more powerful supporters, be versed in the language of party politics, or even hold university degrees. Johnson was learned. His interest, therefore, dictated that this one qualification for writing should precede all the rest. The priority placed on learning is Johnson's peculiar stamp as a young writer. From the first he pictures himself as "a retired and uncourtly Scholar" who lacks any other "art of pleasing." This emphasis often seems awkward if not absurd. In the world of periodicals and pamphlets, where so many writers polish the arts of pleasing, the ideal of the learned author can jangle like a sermon at a soirée. Yet Johnson does not fear to risk the incongruity. He puts himself forward, at last, as a grubstreet Odysseus, the humble hack who is also the hero as scholar. This role did not have to be feigned; it suited young Johnson's sense of himself and made a virtue of necessity. Above all, as a strategy it worked.

The strategy appears already full-fledged in the document that first announces Johnson's wish to become an author: the letter he wrote to Edward Cave, founder and editor of the *Gentleman's Magazine,* on November 25, 1734. Any reader might be amused by the young man's tactlessness. Under the archetypal alias of "S. Smith," the would-be writer commiserates with Cave on the low quality of the copy he prints and offers to help him out with poems, inscriptions, "short literary Dissertations in Latin or English, Critical Remarks on Authors Ancient or Modern, forgotten Poems that deserve Revival, or loose pieces, like Floyers [on Cold Baths] worth preserving. By this Method your Literary Article, for so it might be call'd, will, he thinks, be better recommended to the Publick, than by low Jests, awkward Buffoonery, or the dull Scurrilities of either Party."[49] Even as Johnson offers his services, he registers the superiority of his scholarship and taste to what has been common in the magazine. Yet perhaps he also implicitly flatters Cave and his public, who are assumed to hunger for more substantial fare. The commercial value of such assumptions should not be underestimated. Not all who read the magazine were gentlemen, but readers did like to be addressed as gentlefolk, acquainted with some stock of classical learning. Though the dull scurrilities of party might be in fact what interested them, a tone of being above the battle attracted the upwardly mobile public. Cave understood his audience very well.[50] He seems to have been more impressed than offended by S. Smith's letter. But he was not yet prepared to hire a learned author.

When Johnson finally did make his debut in the *Gentleman's Magazine,* more than three years later, he displayed not only his learning but also his keen appreciation of magazine politics. The Latin ode "Ad Urbanum," a panegyric to Cave (who used the pseudonym "Sylvanus Urban"), defends his principles of editing. Both the *London Magazine* and *Common Sense* had accused their rival of plagiarism and patchwork. Johnson, in turn, compares the *Gentleman's* odds and ends to a wreath twined of variegated flowers or to a wonderful rainbow. The ode is a stilted poem but a brilliant performance, a feat of which only a scholar would be capable. Its master stroke descends in the opening word.

> URBANE, nullis fesse laboribus,
> URBANE, nullis victe calumniis,
>> Cui fronte sertum in erudita
>>> Perpetuo viret et virebit

> Hail Urban! indefatigable man,
> Unwearied yet by all thy useful toil!
>> Whom num'rous slanderers assault in vain;
> Whom no base calumny can put to foil.
>> But still the laurel on thy learned brow
>> Flourishes fair, and shall for ever grow.[51]

As Johnson's friend Arthur Murphy noted, these lines recall the ode to Pope Urban VIII by the great Polish poet Casimir (Mathias Casimire Sarbiewski, 1595–1640): "URBANE, Regum Maxime, Maxime/ URBANE Vatum . . ." (Urban, of kings the greatest, greatest/Urban of seers).[52] The pope is supreme both as ruler and as farsighted patron of the arts; "Vatum" (from *vates*), the crucial compliment, stands for poet as well as prophet. A history of modern Latin poetry had been among young Johnson's abortive projects, and he seizes the chance to adapt his learning to the new dispensation of letters. One Urban blends into another. Like Casimir, Johnson praises his Urban not only for leadership but also for learning, especially in matters of poetry. The hint may have been still broader. The pope had rewarded Casimir with a gold medal and made him his laureate. Could Cave do any less?

Of course he could. Johnson's erudite flattery reached its mark, and soon he became a valued—and paid—contributor to the *Gentleman's Magazine*. But the version of patronage enshrined in the poem was a myth. As a practical man of affairs, Cave was unlikely even to notice his elegant superimposition on Urban VIII, and his employees had to please an audience larger than one. The public for learned Latin poems was limited. Indeed, there is something ridiculous about "Ad Urbanum." Its conscious archaism glosses over the distance between a style appropriate to patrons and a style befitting editors and book-sellers. Johnson drapes a businessman in the robes of a pope. He celebrates Cave as a studious friend of the muses, "unconquer'd by the rabble's venal voice," as if the "noble ends" of a magazine excluded its subscribers; and his grandiloquent language masks a polemical job application. "Ad Urbanum" asks to be parodied.

A parody appeared immediately, in fact, in the next issue of the *London Magazine,* and its author went straight for Cave's weakness.

> His rivals laugh to see him strain,
>   Flound'ring thro' thick and thin,
> Whilst Grubstreet garrets strive in vain
>   To save him, brib'd with ale and gin.

Against the myth of Cave as munificent patron, the parodist evokes a more potent myth, the mingy maestro of Grub Street. The laurel bestowed by Johnson inevitably falls under the shadow of *The Dunciad:* "Her wreath his best-lov'd goddess Dulness throws,/And all her poppies blush upon his brows."[53] Such editors feed their flock of fawning writers just enough to nurse their vices, and learning itself is debased by being sold. This Popish view of the effect of commerce on authorship may be no closer to reality than is Johnson's relic of the past. Yet it does return the dreamer to the present. Enemies lurk in wait of the learned author.

Thus Johnson's Olympian tone was brought down to earth. But that was not at all a bad result. Not only had he earned Cave's gratitude; he had shown that a dignified classicism could prove an effective weapon in the trenches. The following issue of the *Gentleman's Magazine* (May 1738) offered a loose translation of "Ad Urbanum" while assuring Cave that his rivals were beneath him. "The *London Magaziners* have, with their usual Impudence and Scurrility, ventured to publish some Lines in their last, below the most abject Production of *Grubstreet* I ever met with."[54] And so Johnson's ode was republished, allowing the unlatined reader to witness the editor's canonization. This made good copy. If magazines do not profit from learned Latin, they do thrive on wars of words, especially when they can capture the high ground. Johnson had been doubly useful; he had joined in a fight yet managed to stay above it. Much of his future work would serve the same purpose. Amidst the local brawls and political squalls, he could always maintain a learned and lofty air.

He had also found a place where he belonged. By a happy coincidence the ode "Ad Urbanum" means not only "To Urban" but "To the City," and the virtues it salutes in Cave's pages—the inexhaustible blend of the grave with the gay, of instruction with pleasure, of urbanity with all the colors and shades of life—are the charms of London too. Johnson presents his calling card to the city. Whereas Settle, the last of the city poets, had written a series of fulsome official odes to everyone in power, the new contender pays tribute to a contemporary emblem of power over authors, the bookseller. A changing system, a changing city require a different approach. Johnson would soon become a city author, as London became the home that he loved and berated. Facing the translation of "Ad Urbanum," in the same issue of the *Gentleman's Magazine,* are some extracts from his first great popular success, the poem with which the grubstreet Odysseus dropped anchor. Not surprisingly it was called *London.*[55]

The work through which Johnson made a place for himself in the London literary world is a poem that takes leave of the city. Most of the satire of *London* bursts from the mouth of indignant Thales, a disillusioned and impoverished older man who is quitting the town for the country and saying his farewells to a younger friend. His lack of success has soured his humor into bile. Thales need not be identified with any particular person. To splice him on Richard Savage, whom Johnson may not yet have met, appeals to those who relish biography more than verse, but the key that it forges does not open the poem.[56] Rather, as a *"true Briton"* the speaker seems related to the "Briton" who signs the English imitation of "Ad Urbanum"; nor is it inconceivable that that Briton was Johnson himself.[57] Thales represents a part of his author, the obscure and learned moralist who rails at the decadence of his nation and its leaders. But he does not represent all of Johnson. Those critics, including T. S. Eliot, who have suspected the poem of "falsity" because they cannot believe

65

that its author ever meant to leave London are confusing the poet with his leading character.[58] Johnson, like Thales' young friend, intends to stay. Of course he believes that the city is intolerable, an impossible place to live. But many young authors believe the same about the cities they choose to live in.

There is a better reason, I think, why *London* discomforts its readers. Despite its anger and pathos, the poem conveys a certain sense of distance. Thales looks at the town from across the river, the idealized *locus amoenus* of Greenwich, which stands apart in time as well as space.

> Struck with the Seat that gave ELIZA birth,
> We kneel, and kiss the consecrated Earth;
> In pleasing Dreams the blissful Age renew,
> And call BRITANNIA's Glories back to view.   (Lines 23–26)

He has already abandoned London for a vision of what it once was and might be again. So has the author of the poem. Here as so often elsewhere in Johnson's work (for instance, "The Young Author") a precise account of the scene defers to its psychological effect. The rhythm of hopes raised and disappointed, of pleasing dreams followed by the shock of waking, controls one verse paragraph after another. London, for Johnson, seems fundamentally a state of mind. More precisely, it manifests a young man's imagination of an older man's disenchantment. Thales imposes his vision upon the city.

> The cheated Nation's happy Fav'rites, see!
> Mark whom the Great caress, who frown on me!   (Lines 91–92)

No audience, however sympathetic, will ever see quite what he sees or share the personal slant of his humiliation. Hence the details of the poem, vivid as they are, appear to us at one or two removes. *London* is both passionate and remote. It is refracted through a screen of historical and political perspectives, fashioned less from experience than from reading. Only a learned author could have conceived it.

The main reason for *London*'s distance is its homage to a literary model, the third satire of Juvenal.[59] The modern city lies under a shadow cast from the structures of first-century Rome. As a formal imitation (a method of loose translation "in which modern examples and illustrations are used for ancient, or domestick for foreign") *London* deliberately calls attention to its ancestry.[60] Johnson insisted that Latin quotations "must be subjoined at the bottom of the Page, part of the beauty of the performance (if any beauty be allow'd it) consisting in adapting Juvenals Sentiments to modern facts and Persons."[61] Hence the reader's eye and mind should travel back and forth between the top and bottom of the page, between London and Rome. The here and now constantly waver. When Thales denounces "these degen'rate Days," he repeats a charge already seventeen centuries old, as if degeneration itself were a permanent condition. The rhyme between times is amusing; "that things go round and again go round/Has rather a classical sound."[62] But the reader who notices that sound has temporarily stopped listening to Thales.

Johnson understood this distraction quite well. Throughout his long career as a critic, he was remarkably consistent, and remarkably severe, on the disadvantages of writing imitations.[63] Perhaps no other critic has ever been so scornful of a poetic genre in which he himself excelled. "No man ever yet became great by imitation";[64] and certainly Johnson does not except himself. He points to three main defects in the imitation. First, it is too easy: the poet follows a plan already worked out by his predecessor (Johnson seems to have written *London* very rapidly). Anyone who reads Latin and lives in a city can hit upon equivalent objects of satire. Second, "such imitations cannot give pleasure to common readers. The man of learning may be sometimes surprised and delighted by an unexpected parallel; but the comparison requires knowledge of the original, which will often detect strained applications." A reader ignorant of Latin will miss part of the beauty of *London,* and a reader who knows Juvenal well will know where *London* falls short or presses too hard. Third, and most important, the parallels drawn by an imitation are never exact. "Between Roman images and English manners there will be an irreconcileable dissimilitude, and the work will be generally uncouth and party-coloured; neither original nor translated, neither ancient nor modern."[65] *London* exists in a limbo between past and present—half a translation from Latin and half an English poem.

Johnson's verses can be defended against him. Yet even defenders concede that the satire strikes several false notes. Consider, for instance, the clever early indictment of London's dangers (lines 17–18):

> Here falling Houses thunder on your Head,
> And here a female Atheist talks you dead.

The first line hardly challenges a reader. Houses did fall in ancient Rome and eighteenth-century London; they still fall in New York and Moscow. The effect of such an image depends not on statistics of pedestrian fatalities but on the reader's sense that the falling house is all too emblematic of the city—its greedy builders, weak foundations, neglectful officials, and unprotected public. Johnson translates and leaves the rest to us. But the next line seems quite different. No "female Atheist talks you dead" in Juvenal, nor does the hazard seem typical of cities. The reader, stopped cold by the spectacle of a speechless Johnson, looks in vain for a footnote. A reasonable conjecture can be offered. The equivalent line in Juvenal attacks that favorite target of Roman satirists, the poet who recites his verses in public during the hot summer days.[66] Modern English poets rarely did that. A celebrity like Pope might complain (and simultaneously boast) about the versifying dunces who pursued him everywhere—"Nay, fly to *Altars; there* they'll talk you dead;/For *Fools* rush in where *Angels* fear to tread"[67]— but ordinary Londoners were spared the ordeal of listening to poetry. When Johnson's manic friend, Christopher Smart, later accosted pedestrians with his visions, he was locked up for it. So an imitator would have to find some plausible modern substitute.

The female atheist must have seemed a godsend. First of all, she could not have been more modern. According to Edward Young's satire on women, the phenomenon was brand new: "Atheists have been but rare, since nature's birth;/'Till now, she-atheists ne'er appear'd on earth."[68] Moreover, her appearance portended an imminent apocalypse—at least in the opinion of the author of *England's Doom* (1736).[69] But what made the reference especially topical was

the recent fashion of women preachers. The novelty of such performances still dumbfounded people twenty-five years later, as in what
may have become Johnson's most quoted pronouncement: "Sir, a
woman's preaching is like a dog's walking on his hinder legs. It is not
done well; but you are surprized to find it done at all."[70] The woman
in question was a Quaker. Johnson can hardly be said to have confused Quakers with atheists; one of his first loves, Olivia Lloyd, had
been an ardent Quaker, and the days that he spent debating religious principles with her, and later with other articulate women,
may well have been among the happiest of his life.[71] They talked him
alive, not dead. Yet in the mid-1730s a female Quaker preacher had
become a *cause célèbre*. Any reader of *London* would have recalled
the spectacular May Drummond, whose poem, *The Female Speaker;*
or, the Priests in the Wrong (1735), confirmed her readiness to expose
her inner light in public, where "many Thousands flocked to hear
her."[72] Some priests thought this the devil's work. Hence the prejudices of Johnson's line are overdetermined.[73] It brings together
Pope's fearless fool at the altar, Young's apparition of the she-
atheist, the common bias against talkative, public women,[74] and
timely gossip straight from the newspapers. As poetic leeches had
been the curse of Rome, so female atheists persecuted London. The
line might have written itself.

Not all these explanations, however, can save the allusion from
self-consciousness. Johnson himself might have pointed out its
three defects. It hits too easy a target (a Punch-and-Judy show could
supply the female bully); it requires a footnote (only a learned
reader could have savored Johnson's ingenious turn on the original); and it is "uncouth" or strained (not many Londoners would
have recognized female atheists as a major urban nuisance). Once
again the effect is distancing. The line invites a reader to admire the
poet's skill at imitation, not his familiarity with the streets. *London*
cuts a figure as what Johnson called a "party-coloured" work, neither ancient nor modern. It wraps some Roman images in yester-
day's newspapers and pretends that they match.

Party also colors the poem in another respect. For all its air of
righteousness and learning, what *London* has to sell is politics. Johnson seizes each chance to blame the ills of the city on Walpole and

the court, whose venal policies have beggared Britain. Opposition slogans and charges fill each chink in Thales' jeremiad. Whether or not this partisan attack inspired Johnson to write the poem, it is surely what caught his audience's attention. The *Gentleman's Magazine* excerpted the sharpest political thrusts and omitted the rest. Readers (as Johnson himself would later complain) could scarcely be given enough abuse of Walpole to satisfy them. Hence even the most ordinary prejudices, such as distrust of foreigners, take on a special edge by being associated with dark governmental plots—appeasement of France and Spain, Hanoverian pillage. The appeal to local interests can be quite raw: "I cannot bear a *French* metropolis" (line 98). It can also employ some of Johnson's allusive finesse, as in the daring blanks of "Let——live here, for——has learn'd to live" (line 50), where anyone who remembered Boileau's version of the line would fill in "George."[75] In either case the verse strikes at specific targets, from excise taxes to the *Daily Gazetteer.* Ten years later, when *London* was republished, Johnson added some notes to explain references that were already out of date. There, at the bottom of the page, the catchwords of 1738 mingle with Juvenal's Latin.[76] Party-coloring never was plainer.

Yet even rabid partisanship works best when it puts the best color on its fury. *London* walks a fine line. Although disdain for the government lends the satire its bite, its authority stems from the moral prestige of classical virtue. Walpole must be condemned by a voice from the past; he has violated not only the purses of his enemies but also the treasury of ancient wisdom.[77] Thus Johnson mixes some Latin with his English. Though he can afford to show his anger, the satirist's prerogative, he cannot afford to use homespun language. Other translations of Juvenal, he thought, had failed to catch his dignity and grandeur;[78] *London* would remedy that. Still more, it would import the values of Rome to the shameless modern city. In this way the distance of the poem would work to its advantage. Politically, the satire seems most effective when least connected to the Ways and Means or here and now.

> Heroes, proceed! What Bounds your Pride shall hold?
> What Check restrain your Thirst of Pow'r and Gold?

> Behold rebellious Virtue quite o'erthrown,
> Behold our Fame, our Wealth, our Lives your own.   (Lines
>   61–64)

These lines refer to no specific passage in Juvenal and no specific act of government, nor would a reader know where to stand to "behold" the battle of pride against virtue. The point of view is general and lofty. Yet party rhetoric has seldom been more rousing.

The tone, moreover, is classic. Here as elsewhere, Johnson seems most comfortable when he can interpret Juvenal's busy city, crammed full of filthy details, as representative of a state of mind. Thus Greektown, a particular, noxious district in the Latin, translates into "a *French* metropolis" that exists primarily in the corrupted tastes of the English. Similarly, Juvenal's scorn for pushy slaves is redirected at another sort of slavishness, servility toward the rich. Johnson's London is not, for him, different from Rome; customs and manners have changed, but not those deep-seated human vices to which the very look of the city gives tangible form. Psychologically, the poem does not reflect an "irreconcileable dissimilitude" between times so much as an uncanny sameness. Perhaps that is not surprising. Many Londoners had always thought of themselves as living in a simulacrum of Rome, just as many architects had tried to reproduce the styles of the imperial city. Every English schoolboy grew up surrounded by Latin; it was his father tongue, his guarantee that some things never change. The learned young poet had been well schooled. Before he first walked around London, Juvenal had already taught him what he would find there.

Above all he searches for values that will last. *London* differs from most political propaganda of its time exactly because of its remoteness, its insistence on viewing the urban scene as alien and strange. Only timeless wisdom could make such a place authentic. Significantly, Johnson refuses to give his spokesman an English name. Instead he calls him "Thales," converting Juvenal's friend Umbricius into the first philosopher of Greece. To gain a true perspective on the city, one needs a very long vista. If Thales is a true British patriot, he also represents universal knowledge.[79] Johnson identifies with him.

71

There was also a more specific reason for choosing the name. According to a tradition reported by the *Gentleman's Magazine* in February 1731, "*Thales* had studied rational philosophy, the course of nature, and the influence of the heavenly bodies; but his learning was derided, because it brought him no money."[80] That anecdote gave Johnson's poem its theme. The shortsighted neglect of learning and the reduction of every value to money constitute both the political and the personal message of *London*. Its key word is "worth." Thales must leave the town, he complains, "Since Worth . . . in these degen'rate Days/Wants ev'n the cheap Reward of empty Praise" (lines 35–36), and he climaxes his indictment by returning to the same personified and slighted virtue (176–179):

> This mournful Truth is ev'ry where confest,
> Slow rises worth, by poverty deprest:
> But here more slow, where all are Slaves to Gold,
> Where Looks are Merchandise, and Smiles are sold.

Even the Latinate syntax of the truth that Thales' whole life has demonstrated shows that he does not fit in this English world. The crucial sentence deliberately drags against a fast and easy reading by reversing word order and slowing our progress. Thales and Johnson identify with "worth" and force a pause there. But the power of the word hinges on a defiant rejection of one of its meanings— "Price; value"—in favor of another: "Excellence; virtue."[81] An unrewarded, poverty-stricken worth has nothing to do with price; it cannot be sold and does not want to be. Instead it refers to an intrinsic quality, a virtue defined not by but in spite of commercial success.[82] Thales' learning brings him no money; that is at once his misfortune and his honor. So he must abandon this city of gold and look for some place where a philosopher can live (lines 174–175):

> Quick let us rise, the happy Seats explore,
> And bear Oppression's Insolence no more.

Thus Johnson collapses the many issues of British politics into the single issue of how the nation rewards its authors—at least its learned authors. By this test the nation fails; "starving Merit" finds no home in London. All Thales' complaints might be cut to one: he wants a more generous patron, who would heal the fatal breach between Worth and Gold. Nor is this view quite so limited and self-interested as it might seem. Walpole's control of the patronage system had fueled and ensured his power; no issue affected more people or had more to do with daily life in the city.[83] Official greed and contempt for learning set the social tone. As an analysis of the current political situation, therefore, *London* is far from negligible. But it offers no remedy but exile. In this respect the view from ancient Rome lacks any positive value. However much Juvenal detests his working conditions, he never tries to imagine a better system. Rather, he inveighs against the low tastes and barbarity of present-day patrons, who hand out money to Greeks and Syrians when they might be handing it to him. Johnson adopts a similar attitude. He puts no faith in a popular press or popular vote as relief for the woes of authors and the public, but pins his hopes instead on nothing but a higher class of patrons and rulers. The best of futures would reinstate the ancient patriotic good old days.

Hence *London* defends the past it imagines against the present. Even the form of the imitation serves its theme, maintaining a learned distance from the manners it skewers. Johnson's career as a hack would build on this technique. *Marmor Norfolciense* (1739), his labored and occasionally brilliant pamphlet against the king and Walpole, simulates an antiquarian commentary on a musty apocryphal fragment; the satire of political abuses combines with a learned satire of false learning.[84] The distant, scholarly tone becomes still more prominent in Johnson's main bread-and-butter assignment for the *Gentleman's Magazine,* the parliamentary debates he composed from 1741 to 1743.[85] Since parliamentary privilege banned verbatim accounts of proceedings despite intense public interest, the press devised various ciphers and subterfuges. Johnson concocted *Debates in the Senate of Lilliput,* reconstructing the speeches of thinly disguised parliamentarians ("Walelop," "Ptit") in formal, majestic oratory. An anecdote from Arthur Murphy refers to a later occasion when, after Dr. Philip Francis praised one speech by

Pitt as "the best he had ever read," Johnson shocked the company by remarking, "That speech I wrote in a garret in Exeter-street." Whatever the accuracy of the story, it bears on the style of the debates, for Francis (who had translated Demosthenes) replies, "Then, Sir, you have exceeded Demosthenes himself."[86] A halo of classicism sheds luster on the periods that Johnson wrote. To be sure, the members of Parliament themselves were schooled in classical rhetoric. But Johnson worked from scanty notes or none at all, and the theater of stately eloquence seems to have existed primarily in his imagination, where Greek and Roman orators still declaimed. His Lilliput could not have been more grand. This air of dignity suited the *Gentleman's Magazine,* which as a matter of policy favored neither party. It also suited the style of a learned author. Johnson conceives the present in terms of the past and dedicates his hack work to the ages.[87]

At the same time, he transmutes the party men of Britain into men of learning. Ancient rhetorical figures flow from their mouths. As *London* had made the treatment of authors the supreme test and emblem of the nation, much of Johnson's early political writing judges affairs of state through a sort of literary criticism—by their rhetoric ye shall know them. Statesmen, like writers, should be humble servants of the public; statesmen, like writers, should put their learning to use. Perhaps the finest moment of Johnson's *Debates* occurs right at the end (April 1743), when "Walelop" calmly defends himself against a torrent of accusations: "For my Part, that Innocence which has supported me against the Clamour of Opposition, will establish my Happiness in Obscurity, nor shall I lose by the Censure which is now threatened any other Pleasure than that of serving my Country."[88] As modern scholars have noted, this speech seems almost entirely a fiction and "probably the most dramatic thing Johnson ever wrote."[89] Consulting his own predilections, the author registers the lofty ideal of a happy author's life: obscurity and service. Thales himself could not have spoken with more detachment.

Walpole, however, had not spoken that way. The Britain young Johnson imagines, a nation informed by learning and classical models, saw the light not in Westminster but in Exeter Street. No real authors live in Johnson's *London;* or if they do, they live a fantasy in which a noble patron might arise, appreciate their worth, and save them. It would take years for Johnson to wake from that dream—at least according to his confession in the letter to Chesterfield. In the meantime he would live a contradiction. The ideal of authorship shaped by his early writings, an ideal of scholars rewarded by patrons, conflicted at every turn with his experience as a hack. Such conflicts themselves could furnish a source of interest. If Johnson's efforts to reconcile his conception of what an author should be with the reality of a writer's employment in London sometimes go to absurd lengths, they also spark his work with energy. The allegory of an author's life—its noble hopes, its comic falls—seems the story young Johnson most needs to tell. To tell it best he would require a rich example, an author whose tragicomic life brought all the contradictions of authorship forward. He found him in Richard Savage.

In 1729, just at the moment when the twenty-year-old Johnson looked out at the embattled world of letters and, like the infant of Saguntum, elected not to enter it quite yet, a pamphlet published in London described the career of "a perfect Town Author." The work seems to have left a strong impression on Johnson. He later praised its author in very high terms: "Of his exact Observations on human Life he has left a Proof, which would do Honour to the greatest Names."[90] That author was Richard Savage, then at the peak of his own career—close friend of Pope and other literary giants, poet of the recently published, much admired *The Wanderer,* and a celebrity admitted into the best houses in London. But the pamphlet admired by Johnson conveys a very different image of a literary career. It is called *An Author To be Lett,* and its title page bears the name Iscariot Hackney.

Even by the standard of the War of the Dunces, *An Author To be Lett* seems remarkably vicious—one might say savage—in its portrait of a perfect London artist. Iscariot Hackney lives up to his name. He takes as his motto the words of Satan, *"Evil be thou my Good,"* and boasts throughout of his skill at plagiarism, obscenity, blackmail, sycophancy, and libel—all the techniques a town author must master to earn a living. His "Genius for Mischief" serves no purpose but to fill his own purse and torment others: "to be a *great Wit,* is to take a Pleasure in giving every Body Pain." Hackney personifies the bad conscience of Grub Street. He begins his career when "hired by a reverend Prebend to libel Dean *Swift* for Infidelity," and crowns it with "several Treatises in Defence of *Ingratitude* . . . My private Resentment, like that of other *Great Men,* is always a publick Justice."[91] Despite what Johnson called its "Sallies of . . . sprightly Humour,"[92] *An Author To be Lett* is calculated to disenchant any would-be writer. To succeed in London, it implies, means selling one's soul.

The work is especially unsettling because it so obviously represents the view of an insider. Hackney and Savage know the world they despise like a book. They peddle anecdotes about the private lives and backgrounds of many dunces; they name names and uncover secrets of the trade. What Johnson most admired about Savage was his familiarity with all sorts of people. "He had perhaps a more numerous Acquaintance than any Man ever before attained, there being scarcely any Person eminent on any Account to whom he was not known, or whose Character he was not in some Degree able to delineate."[93] This amazing knowingness accounts for the particular virtue of *An Author To be Lett,* its "exact Observations of human Life." But the life that Savage unearths here might have crawled out from under a rock. Evidently the author has also spent time there. When Johnson later discussed Milton's Satan, the great father of Hackney, he remarked that there are thoughts "which no observation of character can justify, because no good man would willingly permit them to pass, however transiently, through his own mind."[94] By this rule Savage cannot have been a good man. He understands the inside of the devil—as well as of the professional London author.

Still more unnerving, Savage cannot be clearly distinguished from Hackney. Any acquaintance would mark the resemblance, as Johnson later did. Even the preface to the pamphlet, where Savage speaks in his own voice, includes some passages "such as *Iscariot Hackney* might himself have produced." Johnson cites the "ungenerous Reflections" on the birth, circumstances, and relatives of petty writers, as well as Savage's sneers at poverty (eventually he would suffer them himself) and betrayal of friends. Like Hackney, he was adept at "making use of the Confidence which he gained by a seeming Kindness to discover Failings and expose them"; Eliza Haywood, a former crony whose *A Wife to be Lett* prompted his title, was one such victim.[95] This behavior was bad enough. But an unfriendly reader of *An Author To be Lett* might accuse Savage of worse, since he had committed most of Hackney's crimes or, in some cases, predicted those he would later commit. No grubstreet author ought to pretend there is something he will not do.[96] In this one regard Iscariot proves more honest than his creator. "I have tried all Means (but what Fools call honest ones) for a Livelihood. I offer'd my Service for a secret Spy to the State; but had not Credit enough even for that. When it was indeed very low with me, I printed Proposals for a Subscription to my Works, received Money, and gave Receipts without any Intention of delivering the Book."[97] During the last decade of his life, Savage constantly sought subscriptions for his works; "To form Schemes for the Publication was one of his favourite Amusements." Of course the book never appeared. Unlike Hackney, Savage "really intended some time to publish," according to Johnson.[98] But this only suggests that Hackney was less self-deceived. The noble pretensions of Savage gloss over the confidence games he plays.

Such was the author whose story Johnson would tell. The *Life of Savage* is a masterpiece—*the* masterpiece—of Grub Street.[99] It offers the obituary of an aristocrat unfairly deprived of honor and riches, as well as a hero of literary history whose "intellectual Greatness" did not bring him happiness, and it draws enduring moral lessons from this turn of fortune's wheel. But it also encompasses *An Author To be Lett,* the shabby chronicle of all the means by which a grubstreet denizen tries to survive. In Johnson's story, as in Savage's mind, two opposite images of authorship compete. The first is noble and proud. In a curious way the claims of Savage to noble birth serve to legitimate the superiority of his poems. Even Johnson's diction supports the claim, as when he calls Savage "a Man whose Writings entitle him to an eminent Rank in the Classes of Learning." An author of "eminent Rank" deserves a place among the great, the same honorable and lordly place as "legislator of mankind" that Sidney and Jonson once had stood upon and that Imlac and Shelley would assert again. As nobleman and poet alike, Savage demands respect. Yet a second image subverts him: the author as parasite and mountebank, someone who grubs for a living. The *Life of Savage* tells this story too—a portrait of the artist as scrounger. It takes the reader to prisons and houses of ill fame, "sometimes in Cellars among the Riot and Filth of the meanest and most profligate of the Rabble"; and though Johnson does not insult Savage's poverty, neither does he acquit him of the stratagems and double-dealing that have made "the Name of an Author" contemptible. To put the matter nicely, Savage "had not Resolution sufficient to sacrifice the Pleasure of Affluence to that of Integrity."[100] Less nicely, he was a hireling. A grubstreet masterpiece cannot forget how authors make their money.

Thus Johnson, summing up Savage's life, was also balancing two attitudes toward the author. Undoubtedly he preferred the more dignified. Savage had been not only his friend but also his link to the great writers of the previous generation, an intimate of Steele and Pope and Thomson and Young. He was the first poet of genius whom Johnson had known, the first entrance to that larger scene of letters of which the young author had dreamed. Furthermore, Johnson took this survivor from the age of giants almost entirely at his own evaluation. Ever since Boswell, readers have been startled at how unquestioningly Johnson accepted Savage's life story: a noble if illegitimate birth, a cruel abandonment and persecution by his implacable mother. Even the full title of *An Account of the Life of Mr Richard Savage, Son of the Earl Rivers* endorses this version of events (if *not* the son of Rivers, Savage had no right to his name; he might have been Lee or Smith or Portlock). The title of Clarence Tracy's biography, *The Artificial Bastard,* expresses a more skeptical modern view. Why was Johnson so trusting? One possible answer may be that he *wanted* to believe Savage, perhaps for psychological reasons (hostility toward his own mother?) of which he was hardly aware.[101] Another answer, not to be idly discounted, may be that Johnson found Savage's story true because it *was* true; the case against it has never been proved.[102] But Johnson believed in Savage even more strongly:

he thought him among the best and most original authors of the age.[103] If not unalloyed, nevertheless this admiration does seem to have been genuine. Savage qualified as a noble author. The very terms of Johnson's praise—"elevated," "sonorous and majestick," "Dignity," "Sublimity"—suggest a poet above the crowd, a poet born to strive for greatness. Small people, like those who disregarded Savage "when his Coat was out of Fashion," might measure his height by an accident of birth.[104] But people of judgment would read his life story more deeply, as the trials of a noble mind.

The *Life of Savage* enforces such a reading. Its beginning and ending frame a "mournful Narrative" on a perennial theme: "It has been observed in all Ages, that the Advantages of Nature or of Fortune have contributed very little to the Promotion of Happiness."[105] Great expectations lead to great disappointments. Writing immediately after Savage's death (in August 1743), Johnson has no trouble placing him. The fall of greatness might seem a hackneyed plot, but the fall of Walpole had made it seem fresh again. Ironically, the minister so many wits had hated became, in his defeat, an inescapable and sympathetic literary type. Johnson fits Savage into the pattern.[106] Thus all the grievances and humiliations of the author's life, which a satirist might render as the dues that a scribbler must pay the devil, turn into dark ironies of fate. Savage's comedowns only point up his greatness. Behind the actual events of the career, Johnson imagines another, more worthy story: the man as he might have been. "On a Bulk, in a Cellar, or in a Glass-house among Thieves and Beggars, was to be found the Author of the *Wanderer,* the Man of exalted Sentiments, extensive Views and curious Observations, the Man whose Remarks on Life might have assisted the Statesman, whose Ideas of Virtue might have enlightned the Moralist, whose Eloquence might have influenced Senates, and whose Delicacy might have polished Courts."[107] The failure of such a hero to find his rightful place in life is tragic not only for him but for his nation.[108] His genius should have profited mankind.

On the other hand, Johnson knew how authors actually live, and he knew Savage. Another parable informs the *Life:* the son who squanders his talents. However much society had beaten Savage down, he also had ruined himself. The suspense of the *Life of Savage* depends less on his attempts to reclaim his patrimony than on an ever-increasing anxiety about money. Nothing stays in his hands; he keeps going down. When Johnson later paraphrased the proverb on the sluggard and the ant, he might have been remembering his friend.

> Amidst the drousy charms of dull delight,
> Year chases year, with unremitted flight,
> Till want, now following fraudulent and slow,
> Shall spring to seize thee like an ambush'd foe.[109]

Prudence, not greatness, furnishes this theme. Whether or not Savage lived a lie, he did live a dream, and authored not only his identity but also his fate. "He proceeded throughout his Life to tread the same Steps on the same Circle; always applauding his past Conduct, or at least forgetting it, to amuse himself with Phantoms of Happiness, which were dancing before him; and willingly turned his Eyes from the Light of Reason, when it would have discovered the Illusion, and shewn him, what he never wished to see, his real State."[110] No allegory typifies Johnson more; it represents his settled view of the fallacies that tempt all human beings and often destroy them. But it represents as well the particular life of an author, someone who dwells in a world of imagination. The final two words of the sentence, "real State," abruptly break the cadence; Savage would never have chosen such a harsh anticlimax. Yet authors desperately require to be shaken from their routine. Johnson insists on dispelling Savage's story.

In practical terms, this means a keen interest in pounds, shillings, and pence. Not much research went into the *Life,* and Johnson got some crucial facts and dates wrong. A grubstreet masterpiece is likely to be written fast, with very few sources. But Johnson did care about the way in which a hack makes a living. Though vague about many other details, the *Life of Savage* records the specific sums that the author was paid for his writings and by his patrons, and it takes note of every bad bargain. *The Wanderer,* for instance, brought only ten guineas, of which Savage returned two for the opportunity of correcting some faulty proofsheets, and Johnson reports this with "some Degree of Indignation and Concern." Such facts are not beneath notice, nor are they irrelevant to the life of a poet. Nor does Johnson blame the writer for selling himself and his art. Nothing could be an easier target, for example, than Savage's notorious venture as *Volunteer Laureat*—a series of uncommissioned birthday odes to Queen Caroline. The official laureate, Colley Cibber, objected not unreasonably that "he might with equal Propriety stile himself a Volunteer Lord" (as many argued Savage had done already). Johnson sees the absurdity, of course. But he addresses most of his criticism not to the volunteer but to his reception, which was "not in the highest Degree generous"—only fifty pounds a year, and even that tied to the drudgery of an annual panegyric. "It was a kind of avaricious Generosity, by which Flattery was rather purchased than Genius rewarded."[111] The pride of a hack, however deluded, deserves more consideration. A pittance that costs the patron very little may turn out to decide the poor author's life or death.

The account of how Savage made what is called his "living," therefore, includes his lifelong slide to dependency, desertion by friends, and end in a debtor's prison, where income and breath expire together. Johnson keeps tally of the debits and credits. And he does blame Savage, not for selling himself but for selling himself cheap. "He appeared to think himself born to be supported by others, and dispensed from all Necessity of providing for himself; he therefore never prosecuted any Scheme of Advantage, nor endeavoured even to secure the Profits which his Writings might have afforded him."[112] Improvidence like this injures all writers. If a poet as gifted as Savage takes less than he is worth, he drives down the whole market (young Johnson, we might remember, demanded ten guineas for *London* because "I would not take less than Paul Whitehead").[113] The *Life* refuses to forget what its subject forgot too readily, that someone must always pay. The loans that Savage put out of mind, the advances he swallowed, the promises he never kept depress the value to be placed on the word of an author. Hacks, like thieves, must obey a code of honor. In this respect Savage's pride was doubly vicious: thinking himself above the rest of his trade, he did not mind sinking lower. The closing words of the *Life* state the moral clearly: "Negligence and Irregularity, long continued, will make Knowledge useless, Wit ridiculous, and Genius contemptible."[114] Savage hurt knowledge, wit, and genius as well as himself. He was the opposite of a professional model—at least for a writer who wanted to survive.[115]

Yet Johnson puts him to use. The *Life of Savage* confronts some notions of authorship that its writer himself had rejected—the noble amateur and untrustworthy hireling—and converts them into an opportunity to show what an author can do. Johnson profits from his friend's example. He does this quite literally, first of all, by cashing in on his fame. Even in death, Savage continued to be a property of the *Gentleman's Magazine,* which had often retailed his writings and his story, and the *Life* wrings a few last drops from his remains. This was hardly an insult to Savage. The public eye had always been his element as well as his infatuation. In many ways he fed on attention; he could never "read his Verses without stealing his Eyes from the Page, to discover in the Faces of his Audience, how they were affected with any favourite Passage."[116] Most of his major writings contain advertisements for himself, a pathetic passage or two that refer to his cruel treatment by his mother and solicit the reader's sympathy—if not a donation. Savage lived off that skill. His poetic appeals connected him to the actors, literary entrepreneurs, and noble patrons who gave him support; and publicity saved his life when the interest of friends and the public gained him a royal pardon for murder. Hence, whatever else he might have thought of the *Life,* he would surely have been delighted to see his name in bold print once again. The length of an obituary measures one definition of success.

In the long run, readers would come to Savage through Johnson's fame. In 1744, however, the anonymous *Life* defers to the fame of its subject, with copious quotations from his poems (when modern editions cut these, they shift the emphasis from Savage's text to Johnson's). Earlier biographies had already capitalized on the sensational, if unfortunate, gentleman-bastard-murderer-poet.[117] Now the time had come for a cool reappraisal. Johnson accepts this responsibility and judges the reputation as well as the man. To some extent, therefore, he passes sentence on society too: its slavery to fashion, its inability to right injustice or reward a poet of genius. Even Savage's false values as an author—especially his compulsion "of drawing upon himself the Attention of Mankind"—reflect the poor estate of writing in his time. The *Life* attempts to set the record straight, deliberately underplaying the scandal in order to concentrate on the legacy of the author, who "now ceases to influence Mankind in any other Character."[118] Thus Johnson quietly substitutes one grubstreet type for another, the anonymous servant of the public for the notorious scandalmonger. He even manages to rehabilitate Savage himself as a good and faithful servant.

This ideal of service shapes the *Life* as a whole. On the face of it, few careers might seem less promising as occasions for moral instruction. Savage had done no one any good. Had he been Iscariot Hackney or Jonathan Wild, his life might at least have served as a caution to trusting souls: keep your hands in your pockets! But the essence of the life, as Johnson perceived it, was not evil but dissipation (in the eighteenth-century sense of "scattered attention"). On his deathbed, having forgotten whatever he meant to say, Savage could manage nothing but *"'Tis gone"* as his last words. This seems more pathetic than useful. Moreover, he lacked responsibility, Johnson contended, even for his misfortunes, which "were often the Consequences of the Crimes of others, rather than his own."[119] Bad luck, like the savagery of an unnatural mother, does not compose an edifying text. Nor did Savage's extraordinary background and irregular conduct qualify him as a model for any ordinary person. A reader might well regard this life as a freak.

Yet such responses are just what Johnson will not allow to happen. Against all odds, the *Life* converts a feckless social outcast into a series of lessons for everyone's profit. It moralizes every bit of Savage, paying tribute to his humanity less by excusing his actions than by imagining what it must have been like to perform them; "nor will a wise Man easily presume to say, 'Had I been in *Savage*'s Condition, I should have lived, or written, better than *Savage*.'"[120] Originally these words seem to have ended the *Life*,[121] but Johnson added one more paragraph, which points out the value of this story for fortifying the patience of those who suffer like Savage or for reminding other proud souls to regard "the common Maxims of Life." Savage's genius matters less than the instruction he offers. Johnson even attributes this good intention to Savage's own works, which, however imperfect, are at least *zealous* for virtue. In this way the hack who could not help himself becomes a source of help for future readers.

Thus Savage, a vain and self-absorbed writer, adjusts to the self-less authorial pattern that Johnson favored, "exhausting his Time and Health for the Service of the Publick"—posthumously, as it were. In order to bring about this redemption, Johnson must keep his distance. Only once in the *Life* does "the Author of this Narrative" make an appearance, and then to take leave of his friend. To be sure, some warmth and even advocacy for Savage run through the work. But Johnson's apprenticeship on Grub Street—and perhaps the counterexample of Savage himself—had taught him the value of maintaining a stately, impersonal tone. The detachment of classical wisdom wore better than confessions and fulminations, and the income that it generated was steady. The *Life of Savage* maintains an exceptional balance. Considered as an immediate response to the death of someone Johnson loved, it seems designedly dispassionate, and steers its middle course right to the end: "Such were the Life and Death of *Richard Savage,* a Man equally distinguished by his Virtues and Vices, and at once remarkable for his Weaknesses and Abilities."[122]

The achievement of the *Life* consists in preserving these distinctions. Johnson will not mix virtues and vices together or fall into Savage's habit of suppressing the faults of a friend. A moralist cannot afford to believe that good and evil are inextricable in human nature; to think that way would tempt us to cherish the vices of those we love—our own most of all. Hence Johnson persists in separating Iscariot from Thales, the dark and bright angels who fought for his friend's soul. The ledger of virtues and vices is not a reflection on Savage but Savage himself, as posterity now regards him and as God will eventually judge him. The *Life* builds a strong case for both the prosecution and the defense. Who then was Savage? The final verdict belongs to a higher court.

At the same time Johnson was finding out who he himself was and what he could do. Remaking the image of Savage the author, he confirms an ideal of humility, learning, and service. The *Life* comes to terms with Grub Street. It displays a writer confident of his powers, who can walk through the valley of the shadow of failure and fear no evil, since he relies on his ability to discriminate right from wrong and to supply good copy fast. To be sure, he is still a hack. The admonitions against "Negligence and Irregularity" with which the *Life* closes may well nag the writer himself, whose "Confidence of superior Capacities or Attainments" had not yet made him nearly so eminent as Savage. Nor did even his grubstreet masterpiece ensure that he could make a living. During the next few years Johnson's career would hardly progress. His work from 1742 to 1744, cataloguing and extracting the great Harleian Library, is best remembered because of a dispute in which he knocked down the publisher, Thomas Osborne;[123] a proposed edition of Shakespeare came to nothing; and from time to time he still looked round for some better profession. Yet by now his apprenticeship was reaching its end. He knew his own gifts as an author, and he knew what he wanted an author to be. What he had to find next was a project worthy of him.

4

Preferment's Gate:
The Vanity of Human Wishes

Unnumber'd Suppliants croud Preferment's Gate,
Athirst for Wealth, and burning to be great;
Delusive Fortune hears th' incessant Call,
They mount, they shine, evaporate, and fall.

F IREWORKS DID NOT impress Johnson. At the end of 1748, after
the treaty of Aix-la-Chapelle concluded the war of the Austrian
succession, the most expensive fireworks show in history was
planned in London. The "machine" or temple, 114 feet high and 410
feet long, took more than five months to build in Green Park; Handel
composed the music, to be accompanied by 100 brass cannon; and
the official cost eventually rose to £14,500. The London press kept
watch over every detail and, when the show itself fizzled, on the
evening of April 27, 1749, turned against the projectors.[1] But even
during the preparations some critics had deplored the waste of time
and money. Among them was Johnson. In a letter printed in the
January number of the *Gentleman's Magazine*, he threw cold water
on the pyrotechnics. "Four hours the sun will shine, and then fall
from his orb, and lose his memory and his lustre together, the
spectators will disperse as their inclinations lead them, and wonder
by what strange infatuation they have been drawn together. In this
will consist the only propriety of this transient show, that it will
resemble the war of which it celebrates the period . . . How many
widows and orphans, whom the war has ruined, might be relieved,

by the expence which is now about to evaporate in smoke."[2] Fireworks become an image for idle dreams, like those of the powers who set Europe aflame for no purpose, except that they burned to be great.

Just at that moment, on January 9, Johnson published his greatest poem, the first work ever to bear his name on its title page. *The Vanity of Human Wishes* belongs to its time. Its mood is postwar, exhausted by schemes that have vanished like smoke, among them the pathetic ambitions of "the bold *Bavarian*" (Charles VII, who had died in 1745) and Charles XII of Sweden, who may or may not recall the débacle of the '45 and Bonnie Prince Charlie.[3] The failure of great expectations provided a theme for the decade, and Johnson was not alone in wishing that politicians and warriors might try instead to be modestly useful and good. Moreover, the hour for great writing also seemed to have passed. Within a few years, the deaths of Pope (1744) and Swift (1745) along with Savage (1743), Johnson's link to that age of giants, had left no obvious candidate for monarch of letters. Night thoughts and graveyards cast shadows on English verse. And Johnson was also personally depressed. As he composed his poem, very rapidly, that autumn of 1748, in and around the small house in Hampstead where his sickly wife lodged, his hopes for comfort—and sex—in marriage had withered away, and Juvenal's disenchantments spoke strongly to him.[4]

Yet the poem also represents a strategy for dealing with the trials of a writer's life and career. As Johnson, still almost unknown to the public, neared forty, he had hardly advanced beyond preferment's gate. In the long run his tedious work on the *Dictionary,* begun two years before, would make his name. In the short run he knew better than to expect to shine. A few brief flurries—his association with Chesterfield, the success of his poem, the debut of *Irene* at Drury Lane—might spark some hope of fame. But these were fireworks, transient, not to be trusted. Nor did he trust the audience that liked and praised a gaudy public show. Three prologues he wrote for Drury Lane, to open the theater in 1747, *Irene* in 1749, and a performance of *Comus* in 1750, reflect some wariness, if not disdain, for the flighty theatergoer.

Hard is his lot, that here by Fortune plac'd,
Must watch the wild Vicissitudes of Taste;
With ev'ry Meteor of Caprice must play,
And chase the new-blown Bubbles of the Day.[5]

Vanity rules the playhouse, and a writer who hopes for more solid success must found his work on virtue and truth, not bubbles. Success like that will not come overnight.

Furthermore, Johnson's sense of an audience had changed. The poet of *London,* an eager apprentice, addresses himself to the readership of the *Gentleman's Magazine,* an urbane, well-informed crowd expected to enjoy a nicely turned bit of Latin or a cunning political gibe. The role of a scholar suits that young writer, whether assuming the air of a pedant in deciphering the "Ancient Prophetical Inscription" of *Marmor Norfolciense,* or transmuting the speeches of Parliament into something more worthy of oratory in Latin and Greek. Another habit prevails in the sagacious, middle-aged Johnson: the role of a teacher. In the works that define him in the late 1740s, he often seems to address a young and inexperienced audience that is badly in need of instruction. *The Vanity of Human Wishes* keeps asking questions and calling on its readers to "see" and "attend," as if a schoolmaster feared that his class might be falling asleep. To some extent he was in fact writing down to the young, or trying to raise them up. The entrepreneur who bought the poem (for fifteen guineas) and put the poet's name on it was Robert Dodsley, who had first asked Johnson to undertake the *Dictionary* and who employed him on *The Preceptor* (1748), a "general course of education" compiled to aid unschooled young people to grasp "the first principles of polite learning"; Johnson supplied both the preface and an instructive allegory, "The Vision of Theodore," which preaches the importance of good habits.[6] Dodsley himself had risen from a footman to a prosperous writer and publisher; he served those who wanted to climb like him. Such customers were not sophisticates. Hence Johnson adopts a particular voice, that of the tutor who guides his flock's first steps on the path of life.

The path will be long. "The Vision of Theodore" imagines a tortuous march up the Mountain of Existence, in which wandering from the straight and narrow leads to the Caverns of Despair, and *The Vanity of Human Wishes* repeatedly pictures a traveler who forges ahead but soon loses the way. No short cuts are allowed. The poem consistently rebukes enthusiasm ("a vain belief of private revelation" or "violence of passion"),[7] whose heat feeds the fire of wishes until they explode. Thus the suppliants who begin the survey of "every State" and "ev'ry Pray'r" in line 73 bring about their own doom by "burning to be great." The burning ignites them like rockets; "They mount, they shine, evaporate, and fall" (the moral and physical sequence figured in Johnson's letter on fireworks). A similar pattern, in which a metaphor for aspiration turns viciously literal and destructive, recurs throughout the poem. Wolsey's "restless Wishes tow'r" to new heights until his overbuilding on weak foundations tumbles the pile "With louder Ruin to the Gulphs below" (lines 105–128); the "young Enthusiast" catches a lifelong fever from "the strong Contagion of the Gown" (135–138); Charles of Sweden gets exactly what he asks for—"'Think Nothing gain'd, he cries, till nought remain'" (202)—and dwindles to nought. Even the evangelical turn at the end of the poem, when pious petitions and prayers relieve the dissipation of wishes, takes care to hold enthusiasm back.

> Yet when the Sense of sacred Presence fires,
> And strong Devotion to the Skies aspires,
> Pour forth thy Fervours for a healthful Mind,
> Obedient Passions, and a Will resign'd.   (357–360)

Here fires are taught to damp themselves, and aspirations work to down their own excess. The poem does not regard this as a paradox; patience and calm are Christian blessings, not the capitulation of hope. Yet prayer, unlike wishfulness, must "leave to Heav'n the Measure and the Choice" (352). In "The Vision of Theodore," those who manage to stay on the path disappear at last in the mists on top of the mountain, where only Religion can see. Johnson does not pretend he can see there himself.

He also seems to retrace his own career. Though *The Vanity of Human Wishes* includes all states and stages of life, one subtext persistently follows the life of a scholar or author (assumed to be the same). "Preferment's Gate" is crowded with scribblers. Johnson borrowed the image from some verses by Swift about the perils of clerical authors, assaulted by would-be wits—"They croud about Preferment's Gate,/And press you down with all their Weight"[8]—and the same poem sounds a warning for "The Young Author." Heroes and writers compete, in the *Vanity,* for the vainest wishes. The rivalry reaches a standoff in a devastating couplet that returns to Swift, "From *Marlb'rough*'s Eyes the Streams of Dotage flow,/And *Swift* expires a Driv'ler and a Show" (317–318), where two antagonists finally join in "Life's last Scene."[9] But much of the rest of the poem also closes the distance between those whose lives make legends and those who write about them. The triumphal progress of the young Enthusiast, burning for scholarly fame, is deliciously satirized by the mode of description, drawn from an allegory known to every fledgling scholar, "The Choice of Hercules";[10] the comparison only exposes his weakness. Johnson was clearly thinking about himself. Many years later, reading the passage aloud, "he burst into a passion of tears" until George Lewis Scott (another man of Herculean proportions) "clapped him on the back, and said, What's all this my dear Sir? Why you, and I, and *Hercules,* you know, were all troubled with *melancholy.*"[11] Scott had recognized the source, and like other contemporaries he found it easy to translate Johnson into a myth of heavy burdens and strength. But writers who identify with Hercules are bound to feel the insignificance of what they have done; no wonder they burst into tears. The situation soon reverses, however, when the titanic Charles XII is reduced to a piece of writing—*this* piece of writing: "He left the Name, at which the World grew pale,/ To point a Moral, or adorn a Tale" (221–222). The career of the hero shrivels into motifs of print—just like the career of an author.

Yet Johnson was also showing what he could do. He had outlived the young Enthusiast and turned his eyes on the passing world, where usefulness, not glory, would measure his success. *The Vanity of Human Wishes* demonstrates how far he has come. Returning to Juvenal, the partner who had backed his gambit into poetry and London, he picks another text, Satire 10, more suited to the long haul of experience. The choice must have been deliberate. At a turning point in his career, when he would have been quite justified in hoping for public acclaim, he puts himself forward as Democritus, laughing at vanity, content to spy on folly from the shade. Nor does the poem target foibles of the age. Another poet might have made more of the faddish image of fireworks, so easy to exploit for comedy and political gossip; Johnson adapts it to an eternal condition. The poem, Garrick said, "is as hard as Greek."[12] It does not strive for popularity; and though admired, it was not popular (six years passed before it was reprinted). Yet its mastery proves that Johnson's long years of honing his skills had not gone to waste. He was not famous, he did not shine; but he was a poet.

The Vanity of Human Wishes is a poet's poem. The line of major writers who have paid tribute to its power extends through Walter Scott, Byron, and Tennyson to T. S. Eliot, Ezra Pound, and Robert Lowell. One reason, I think, may be that poets understand and vibrate to one underlying theme, the pathos of a literary career. But more explicitly, they find the poem *useful*. It seems to have some quality that most verse lacks, some virtue that poets seek out and try to learn from. Scholars and critics usually read the poem for its argument, debating whether its tone is tragic or comic, and whether the wisdom it offers is still consoling. Poets are more likely to love its style. Speaking of "style of composition," Scott once said that "he had more pleasure in reading *London,* and *The Vanity of Human Wishes,* than any other poetical composition he could mention."[13] His favorite lines, on the death of Charles of Sweden, were altered (not for the better) to provide a mournful end for *Ivanhoe;*[14] and when a very young T. S. Eliot read the quotation, it impressed him so much that it stayed with him forever. Not many modern readers "appreciate poetry as poetry," Eliot wrote in 1930, but if the thirty-two lines on Charles "are not poetry, I do not know what is."[15] Such poems provide an example—something to build on.

What is this special quality? Modern poets tend to define it in terms of Johnson's precision: he knows exactly the meaning and value of each word he uses. According to Eliot, such verse has all the virtues of good prose: "It is the certainty, the ease with which he hits the bull's-eye every time, that makes Johnson a poet." And Pound, though not at all responsive to what *The Vanity* says, agrees that it "attains the apogee and top notch of that mode, being 'as good as Pope with a touch of Saml. J. into the bargain', its triumph is of the perfectly weighed and placed word."[16] These are a lexicographer's talents. While Johnson was writing *The Vanity of Human Wishes* in Hampstead, a crew of amanuenses back at Gough Square, in the house he had rented with money advanced for the *Dictionary*, was going through the alphabet and copying quotations into notebooks for him to review.[17] Words were always on his mind; he spent his days discriminating shades of meaning. But that was his passion as well as his occupation. Donald Davie rightly points out that Pound and Eliot, when they talk about Johnson, think of the lexicographer as the natural ally of the poet, someone whose "purity of diction" allows poems to function collectively as "a manual of correct usage" or even an epitome of language at its best.[18] Poets must pay attention to words, and no one sets a better example than Johnson.

Yet there is more to Johnson's poetry than style. An exclusive focus on diction, however useful to poets, distorts the work of a writer who never forgot that "words are but the signs of ideas."[19] Eliot regards the ideas of *The Vanity of Human Wishes* as so many commonplaces, and Pound says that "by and large the poem is buncombe. Human wishes are not vain in the least."[20] Such opinions tell us more about their views than about Johnson's. Moreover, they tend to miss the special mark of his contribution to language, a constant awareness of the moral or mental connotations of physical things. Consider the couplet that Eliot treasured (219–220):

> His Fall was destin'd to a barren Strand,
> A petty Fortress, and a dubious Hand.

He wrote about it on at least three occasions, praising at one time its metaphysical yoking of heterogeneous ideas, at another the "just inevitable sequence of *barren, petty,* and *dubious*," and finally the way it culminates the whole passage.[21] But none of these quite accounts for the effect. That depends instead on the double implication of the adjectives, each psychological as well as descriptive. Thus the Norwegian shore was not only bare and unfruitful but *unmeaning* (sense 4 in the *Dictionary*), the fortress was not only small but unimportant

92

and mean, and the dispute about whether Charles was shot by the enemy or by his own aide-de-camp is attached to the hand, suggesting uncertainty not only about what happened (in the eyes of the viewer) but also about the motives of the assassin (as if the hand itself felt doubt). Cumulatively, the sequence loads the historical facts with sullen moods, like the recriminations of a king; that is why it seems inevitable. The choice of words is not mere play for Johnson, and certainly not an end in itself. Rather, it shows his fitting of matter to spirit, of action to moral.

Meanwhile the hero seems to disappear. One reason that human wishes are vain, in the poem, is that humanity leaches out, absorbed by the unfeeling schemes of fate. Again and again, a passage that begins with a human being's desires and purposes will end with disembodied things or empty signs. The suppliants *become* the fireworks that express them, the statesman contracts to his image or "painted Face," and a name is all that remains of what once was Charles. Things take over the poem. When Xerxes sets out to conquer Greece, he insists on his personal agency, even to madness: "The Waves he lashes, and enchains the Wind" (232). When he escapes the battle, defeated, the waves retaliate, and no hand seems to guide the boat (239–240):

> Th' incumber'd Oar scarce leaves the dreaded Coast
> Through purple Billows and a floating Host.

Johnson is said to have preferred this to any of his other couplets.[22] Very likely the fitting of sound to sense appealed to him: the accumulation of consonants at the beginning, especially in unstressed syllables, drags the encumbered verse until it picks up speed in the second line (with only four stresses). Though Johnson did not rate such effects very high, he did have a keen ear for them.[23] But the resonance of the lines derives from something more subtle, an eerie dehumanization. Both Juvenal and earlier translators had painted a grisly picture, with a prow forcing its way through bloody waters thick with corpses ("cruentis fluctibus ac tarda per densa cadavera prora"), a vivid horror that Johnson tones down. Yet the single oar, the decorous "purple Billows" and "floating Host" serve oddly to intensify the scene by calling attention to its artificiality—its vanity.[24] Xerxes' barbarous wishes are now becalmed. As in a nightmare, he and the reader passively drift on a sea—"Th' insulted Sea"—where, in the absence of people, inanimate things take on a menacing life.

While persons drop into the background, however, personifications grow strong. A few generations later, the figure of prosopopoeia ("the change of things to persons") would be denounced as a feeble rhetorical tic. In Johnson it often conveys ferocious energy or more than human will. Eighteenth-century poets and critics regarded the power to visualize and represent abstractions or absent things as the mark of poetic genius. According to Hugh Blair, a second-rate artist "gives us words rather than ideas," whereas "a true Poet makes us imagine that we see [the object] before our eyes."[25] *The Vanity of Human Wishes* barrages the reader with moving and vital ideas, more concrete than the world of shadows where most of us wander. When the statesman sinks, it is his picture we see, cut out of its frame in disgrace.

> For now no more we trace in ev'ry Line
> Heroic Worth, Benevolence Divine:
> The Form distorted justifies the Fall,
> And Detestation rids th' indignant Wall.   (87–90)

The object of sight degenerates in the spectator's mind. Implicitly the couplets reproach the faithlessness of retinues and parasites, who justify themselves after the fall of their patron by looking askance at his portrait. "Line" packs in many meanings: not only features of the face, the painter's strokes, and a poet's flattering verses, but also genealogy. What viewers once recognized in the painted face was not mere family likeness but inherited virtues, Worth and Benevolence so unmistakable that they assumed a visible form, like members of the family. Now Britain has changed. Greed drives out respect for noble ancestry, the principle that once upheld the dignity and continuity of the nation, and only money matters. But Johnson's imagination bursts forth most in the final prosopopoeia. Here feeling, rising too high to be contained by any particular person, must be projected onto ideas and things. The personified Detestation and Wall collaborate on shedding the hated portrait, but they do not seem to like each other much. The Wall might be indignant not only about the face it has borne but also about being defaced (a touch of the Latin *indignitas,* indignity, may cling to it), and Detestation might be leaving an empty patch on the Wall as well as clearing it. At any rate, the amount of hatred seems excessive, directed at a mere form. Humanity is nowhere to be seen; and that is the point.

The diminishment of humankind, in the *Vanity,* stems from its source. Juvenal's irony belittles the tiny figures it puts on the scale or scans from a distance, and Johnson keeps returning to "the clouded Maze of Fate," "Delusive Fortune," "Chance," "the Doom of Man." Properly speaking, the Destiny that rules the poem is related not to the goddesses of classical myth but to the goddess Fortuna in Boethius' *Consolations of Philosophy.* Johnson's characters twist on Fortune's Wheel, and we are instructed to look for salvation not in Juvenal's stoic self-containment—"mens sana in corpore sano"—but in submission to a higher power.[26] Some lines translated from Boethius a few years later, as a motto to *Rambler* 7, express Johnson's essential, pious hope.

> O THOU whose pow'r o'er moving worlds presides,
> Whose voice created, and whose wisdom guides,
> On darkling man in pure effulgence shine,
> And chear the clouded mind with light divine.[27]

But most of *The Vanity of Human Wishes* remains in the clouds with Juvenal. Its structure, like that of the *Consolations,* consists of a search for a point of view. The goddess Observation who begins the poem—"Let Observation with extensive View,/Survey Mankind, from *China* to *Peru*"—sees far but not very deep, and has no power to affect what she perceives. This perspective can lead to an all-inclusive sense of frustration. The reader, looking for some way out of this maze and tempted in the dark by each new illusion, encounters one instance of failure after another. Even a blameless life, "an Age exempt from Scorn or Crime" (292), is burdened with daily sorrow. But just when the point of view seems darkest, another observer pierces the clouds with heavenly vision, and this time does affect the wretchedness she sees. Love, Patience, and Faith conclude the poem: "With these celestial Wisdom calms the Mind,/And makes the Happiness she does not find." An upscale version of Lady Philosophy, celestial Wisdom consoles as well as anyone could, after a trek through Juvenal's vanity fair.

The triumph of poetry, however, is not just seeing but seeing tenaciously through. *The Vanity of Human Wishes* strives to see beyond appearances, to view life as a whole. Perhaps none of Johnson's critical principles has been more debated—not always fairly—than his insistence that "great thoughts are always general,"[28] and therefore more poetic than particulars. "'The business of a poet,' said Imlac, 'is to examine, not the individual, but the species; to remark general properties and large appearances: he does not number the streaks of the tulip.'"[29] Whatever the merits of this rule, considered abstractly, the *Vanity* makes a brilliant case for it. More precisely, it seizes on the general *within* particulars. A characteristic kind of Johnsonian wit refers at once to specific figures and to the larger ideas they represent: "Now kindred Merit fills the sable Bier,/Now lacerated Friendship claims a Tear" (303–304). In the first line a relative dies, in the next a friend is rent by violence or disease. Yet the personifications imply as well that the good old woman is mourning the passing of goodness like her own (kindred *Merit*), or a broken friendship. What makes old age painful is not only the weakness of flesh but an awareness that values and sympathies may also be dying. One cannot call this play on words a pun. Rather, it typifies a state of mind in which life assumes the form of a perpetual allegory and some abiding truth shines through each circumstance and moment as it passes. The particular is always already the general, in Johnson's best verse.

That vision is his business as a poet. When other poets praise the rightness of his choice of words, they are responding to his spirit as well. The *Vanity* teaches writers and readers that language can do justice to human affairs, precisely because it bundles specific perceptions within the generalities or common understandings that enable us to speak to one another. Few poems have ever worked so hard to be inclusive. Its subject is not an individual but Man—and

96

Woman too, whose various missteps, in lines 319–342, conclude the long parade of vanity. But even a single character would illustrate the way in which the frustrated wishes of one life act out the misfortunes of all. By inclination and experience, Johnson identifies with unfulfillment. The preemptive dejection of his youth, his postponement of a choice of life in young manhood, and the slow progress of his adult career had all prepared him for *The Vanity of Human Wishes.* Yet they also kept him from thinking that he stood out. Juvenal's wit and Johnson's compassion for others join in a general, all-encompassing vision, a poem that makes sense of something as idle as wishes. It seems a poem he was born to write.

Johnson's accomplishment as a poet can also be put in historical terms. In the 1740s, verse and other kinds of writing were changing, perhaps as rapidly as in any decade of English history.[30] Eventually the experimentation would be sorted out, especially when readers took to what Johnson called "the modern form of romances," or novels. But in the meantime poets struggled to find a new style. Polemically, the struggle revolved around a posthumous dethroning of Pope, a famous shift in poetic and critical taste that began immediately after his death, with Joseph and Thomas Warton, and lasted well into the next century.[31] Despite or perhaps because of these assaults, Pope's dominance lingered, not least in an obsession with throwing off his influence, as candidates to be the next great poet mounted, shone, and fell. Yet even without that competition, poetry would have changed. A growing audience, often alienated from the intrigues and partisanship that had stung so many court poets into satire, turned to a verse more fashioned to its own immediate interests, hopes, and fears. Just as novels appealed to common readers by welcoming people like them into the story, so poems courted friendship. A new "controlling attitude," which Eric Rothstein defines as "one of sympathy, a call for fellow-feeling," became the norm in verse.[32] *The Vanity of Human Wishes* reaches out to its readers.

In other ways it resists its age, however. Contemporary polemics, elaborated most fully by Joseph Warton's *Essay on the Genius and Writings of Pope* (1756–1782), focused on poetic genres and schools.

Pope's works were largely "of the *didactic, moral,* and *satyric* kind; and consequently, not of the most *poetic* species of *poetry*," Warton pronounced,[33] and the artificial wit of the School of Pope must yield to the children schooled by Nature and Fancy: Spenser, Shakespeare, and Milton. Such categories offended Johnson's principles as well as his tastes. Though deeply versed in traditional genres, like any good critic of his time, he considered them means to an end—the power of the writer to teach and delight—and not an end in themselves.[34] Hence Warton's demotion of Pope, on the grounds of the genres he used, could only show "the pedantry of a narrow mind."[35] An Ode to Fancy was by no means more inherently poetic than an imitation of Horace or Juvenal.

Nor did one become more poetic by joining a school. As much as Johnson admires the best of Spenser and Milton, the effort to write in their style strikes him as hopelessly anachronistic, as well as affected: "life is surely given us for higher purposes than to gather what our ancestors have wisely thrown away."[36] Even Shakespeare, the great master of "the diction of common life," "wrote at a time when our poetical language was yet unformed," and thus embarrasses modern readers "with obsoleteness and innovation."[37] Art and judgment complement Nature; they do not oppose it. Therefore poets need to select the word that is most precise, not the word that fashion or nostalgia suggests. The true poetic school consists of every writer who has used English well; it makes a style in which no word goes to waste. That was what Pope had done and what Johnson wanted to do.

The standard histories tell us they lost the battle. The Preromantics, as everyone knows, prepared the way for a still more radical change, and the Romantics came to regard the verse of Pope and Johnson as an abyss or obstruction in poetry's progress, a prose in masquerade. From this extremely Whiggish point of view, Johnson's poems, like his politics, seem reactionary to the core. Clinging to the Anglo-Latin tradition, to an outmoded poetic diction, and to a suspicion of liberty as well as of imagination, he belongs to the past already in his own time and would molder away in the future.[38] But there are other ways to tell the story, of course. The history of poetry adapts to the needs of each new generation, which revives or discards any style that matches or repels contemporary tastes. On the face of it, the

Romantic period cannot have been entirely hostile to Johnson's verse, since Scott and Byron (as popular as any poets of the age) so warmly embraced it. And later, when Eliot and others intervened on behalf of Johnson, they were deliberately rewriting history, raising him up in order to bring down Milton and the Romantics (the plot succeeded for a time). Perhaps a simple pattern of Before and After cannot account for shifting tides of taste. Perhaps the stir of the 1740s has not ended yet.

How did Johnson himself view his place in the verse of his time? Clearly, he thought his work part of a long reformation in poetry—not backward but forward looking. After centuries of progress, the improvement and refinement of versification had reached a grand climax in Pope: "By perusing the works of Dryden he discovered the most perfect fabrick of English verse, and habituated himself to that only which he found the best."[39] Nor was it only versification that had grown better. Since "poetry is the art of uniting pleasure with truth, by calling imagination to the help of reason," modern advances in truth and reason would necessarily foster a poetry more worthy of intellectual respect, just as Christianity had elevated its moral sentiments.[40] Here Pope himself might be improved. His most ambitious foray into "metaphysical morality," the *Essay on Man,* had decorated "penury of knowledge and vulgarity of sentiment."[41] In 1738–39 Johnson translated and annotated Jean Pierre de Crousaz' *Commentary on Mr. Pope's Principles of Morality, or Essay on Man,* and though most of his notes defend the English poet against French mistranslations and misconstructions, he also takes care to distance himself from the *Essay's* "Leibnitian reasoning." At best, Pope's love of wit had disguised his meaning; at worst, he had stumbled into sophistries that might bewilder or corrupt the innocent reader.[42] In either case truth needed an unambiguous and vigilant champion. That was a task for the next generation of poets.

The Vanity of Human Wishes assumes that task. Its versification resembles Dryden's and Pope's, with the addition of a "declamatory grandeur" that Johnson thought previous versions of Juvenal (including Dryden's) had neglected, and that surpasses Juvenal as well as Pope in "stateliness"—a compressed, slow-moving, sometimes clotted line that cannot be read without pausing for breath and thought

("See nations slowly wise, and meanly just,/To buried Merit raise the tardy Bust"; 161–162).[43] Still more, the replacement of pagan Stoicism by faith confirms the truth of the poem for a Christian reader. To translate Juvenal too literally would be to "submit to the servility of imitation only to copy that of which the writer, if he was to live now, would often be ashamed,"[44] and Johnson corrects the past while he transmits it. To be sure, he knows that poetry can do more. No imitation, however fine, can rival the power of an original invention, drawn from nature and fulfilled by art. "To strike out the first hints of a new fable" and to carry it through "so as to delight the imagination without shocking the judgment of a reader," he wrote, "is the utmost effort of the human mind."[45] In that respect the ancients had yet to be bettered; nor, for that matter, did any living poet match the genius of Milton, Dryden, or Pope. Johnson had not come up to that standard. Nevertheless, he had added something to English verse: new gravity to the heroic couplet, a new precision of language. These were small steps, but they made poetry better.

He also had very strong views on what was *not* progressive. Poetry would *not* advance, he was sure, by reviving old genres like the ballad or the pastoral elegy, "in which all is unnatural, and yet nothing is new."[46] Improvement was *not* to be found in a strained poetic diction that chased after archaisms and neologisms in a desperate attempt to swerve from the language of the age or the language of prose. For similar reasons, versification would *not* be enhanced by the absence of rhyme; to avoid monotony or prose, blank verse routinely fell into "artifices of disgust."[47] Modern poetry could *not* abide mythology and pagan gods, whose absurdity and puerility put an intelligent reader to sleep. Nor would a pious Christian verse serve better: "Contemplative piety, or the intercourse between God and the human soul, *cannot* be poetical . . . Poetry loses its lustre and its power, because it is applied to the decoration of something more excellent than itself."[48] The supernatural, or "flights of imagination which pass the bounds of nature," would *not* survive in an enlightened age. All these attempts to break from the line of Dryden and Pope might seem temporarily novel, but reason did not support them, and they would not last.

Hence Johnson took the negative way as poet and critic. He tended to oppose, on principle, the most ambitious poets of his time, such as

Akenside and Gray. His friendship with the Wartons could not survive their differences of taste, nor did he much value the verse of his young friends Collins and Smart. And he paid a heavy forfeit for his principles: he did not belong to a school, and those who did considered him an enemy of progress. Many Romantic poets grew up with the bogy of Johnson, a symbol of resistance to experiments in verse. The standard histories still reflect their views.

Yet the negative way can also have its attractions. It certainly did for Samuel Beckett, whose first attempt at a play was called *Human Wishes*. "They can put me wherever they want," he told Deirdre Bair, "but it's Johnson, always Johnson, who is with me. And if I follow any tradition, it is his."[49] Though literary histories largely ignore it, Johnson's resistance to fashion proved influential. In every later age of English poetry, some poets have taken pride in writing verse that works within traditional forms, that prefers precision to innovation in language, that follows no false gods, that tries to tell the truth, and that always keeps in mind the vanity of human wishes. A line of influence might be drawn from Johnson through Goldsmith and Crabbe (whose work he helped revise), through Scott and Byron and Landor, through Housman and Hardy, through Eliot, Auden, and Beckett, through Davie, Wain, and Larkin, and down to the present. But that list is eclectic. More accurately, the principles that Johnson helped to formulate have never died; they remain a permanent alternative within poetic traditions. Despite their harsh words about his taste, for instance, both Wordsworth and Coleridge incorporate a Johnsonian strain in their verse.[50] Right at the heart of Romantic poetry—the contradictory pictures of the Child in stanzas 7 and 8 of the "Intimations Ode," or the marginal gloss attached to "The Ancient Mariner"—lies a tension between an unbounded imagination and progressive eighteenth-century views of human nature and truth. The history of English poetry is shaped by that tension. Hence Johnson's voice, however small and still, remains a sort of poetic conscience—nagging and not to be quelled.

Nor would his poetry lack disciples. In a curious way, the relative unpopularity of Johnson's verse, as well as its reputation for going against the grain of taste, only confirmed his stature. They were the proof of his integrity. "He that writes upon general principles, or delivers universal truths," he wrote in *Idler* 59, cannot expect his work "to be received with eagerness, or to spread with rapidity, because desire can have no particular stimulation; that which is to be loved long must be loved with reason rather than with passion."[51] Fireworks would be greeted with more applause, and disappear quickly. But *The Vanity of Human Wishes* would last as long as its theme. A peculiar kind of negative glamour shields those writers who resist their time. Crabbe's devotees, for instance, seem to prize him just *because* he is so little read:

> Give him the darkest inch your shelf allows,
> Hide him in lonely garrets, if you will,—
> But his hard, human pulse is throbbing still
> With the sure strength that fearless truth endows.[52]

A similar resistance to fashion probably spurred Eliot to edit Johnson's poems (Pound thought the edition a rebuke to his own "slapdash" call to Make It New).[53] Every age can use reminders of the style it chooses to ignore.

Yet Johnson would not devote the rest of his life to writing verse. He could not afford to do it; fifteen pounds was the most he would ever receive for a poem, and booksellers did not come calling for his rhymes. Nor did he feel that poetry would be his way to fame. *The Vanity of Human Wishes* offers a less than promising subject, after all, for any poet who might hope to rise. Perhaps he also agreed, at least in part, with the friends who thought that he lacked a specifically poetic imagination—"he had no eye that could be said to roll or glance."[54] At any rate he knew his limitations. From time to time, in the years to come, an occasion would move him to verse—a scene or book revisited, the death of a friend—and he never lost that remarkable talent for hitting precisely the general truth within the particular image. But preferment now lay in another direction, in the mundane grind of Gough Square. It was time to leave wishes behind and to shoulder the work that would make him or break him.

5

Man of Letters:
A Dictionary of the English Language

> This same Man-of-Letters Hero must be regarded as
> our most important modern person. He, such as he
> may be, is the soul of all.

I N THE LATE 1740s a new word begins to be prominent in Johnson's writing. The word is "I." Johnson had used it often before, of
course—especially in letters. But his early publications tend to
reflect a discomfort with the first person, or to treat it as a satiric
mask behind which the real author can keep his distance. Thrust
forward, "I" and "my" hint at a dangerous prevalence of ego. Thus
Marmor Norfolciense and *A Compleat Vindication of the Licensers of
the Stage* (1739) both reek of the first person, brandished by imaginary speakers whose fatuous politics and bad scholarship are
equaled only by their self-importance. "It is therefore with the utmost satisfaction of mind, that I reflect how often I have employ'd
my pen in vindication of the present ministry," writes the "Impartial
Hand" that smugly blots out freedom of the stage; and the projector
of *Marmor,* putting forward "my scheme" to fund his pet Society of
Commentators with government money, has the gall to pose as a
disinterested public servant: "I intreat all sects, factions, and distinctions of men among us . . . to sacrifice every private interest to the
advantage of their country"—an advantage that just happens to co-
incide with his own.[1] No good can come of such an "I" and "my";
they warn of pride, hypocrisy, and self-deception or of persons who
put themselves first. The warning peaks at the end of the *Life of Savage,* which tempts self-satisfied readers to feel superior and then re-

bukes them for it: "nor will a wise Man easily presume to say, 'Had I been in *Savage*'s Condition, I should have lived, or written, better than *Savage.*'"[2] Even the grammar, promoting "I" to a hypothetical subject, participates in the moral. Wise people refuse to speak such sentences. Hence young Johnson reserves his first person for special occasions. Even when deeply, personally involved, as in the *Life of Savage,* he passes as "the Author of this Narrative," not "I." A servant of the public ought to know his place, and that place is the background.

The new Johnsonian "I" first comes to the foreground in 1747, in *The Plan of a Dictionary of the English Language.* A second person empowered it. Johnson's "Short Scheme" for a dictionary, written the previous year while he was working out the project with a group of booksellers, had opened with a brief self-reference: "When I first conceived the design of compiling a new Dictionary . . ."[3] But the *Plan* expands this remark into a structural principle, sketching the development of the dictionary as a series of events in the author's mind—his musings, hopes, and fears. Prospectus joins with autobiography. The reason is largely a matter of genre. Between the "Scheme" and the *Plan,* Johnson had been persuaded to address his proposal to Chesterfield, who was not only a wealthy patron of letters but also "One of His Majesty's Principal Secretaries of State" and therefore a channel to potential government backing.[4] Hence the *Plan* takes the form of a letter, written by one particular person to another. If "I" is a character, so is "My Lord." Indeed, the two collaborate in laying down rules to follow. "With regard to questions of purity, or propriety, I was once in doubt whether I should not attribute too much to myself in attempting to decide them . . . but I have been since determined by your Lordship's opinion, to interpose my own judgment."[5] Here Chesterfield serves to bring Johnson out, enjoining the lexicographer to declare himself and settle hard issues boldly, in his own voice. "I" comes to the fore; the second person authorizes the first.

The climax of this dialogue arrives, as we have seen, at the end of the *Plan,* when Johnson signs his name for the first time in print. To attract the attention of Chesterfield, to play a scene with him, however brief, was to enter the public eye.[6] Yet the letter writer was not so sure that he liked it. The *Plan* itself recoils from being distinguished by such a lord. "Its first effect has been to make me anxious lest it should fix the attention of the public too much upon me"; and Johnson claims that he is bringing his scheme forward not "to raise expectation, but to repress it."[7] More is at stake here than false modesty or a latent suspicion of the word of patrons. Johnson's predicament involves the very "I" that he had been building for more than a decade, his self-definition as an author. Obscurity, learning, and service had brought him a station in life—not "splendid," as he confessed, but anyhow "safe." Henceforth he would be watched. The high hopes Chesterfield had raised might prove as ephemeral as his patronage, and public interest might well lead to disappointment. Johnson had spent too long in the shade to enjoy the sudden glare that exposed him. The doubts and fears expressed by much of the *Plan,* its gingerly circumspection, reveal the fallible first person who gives them voice. No longer would anonymity and impersonality protect his authority. From now on he would have to take the blame along with the credit.

Thus the contract for the *Dictionary* helped forge him a new identity as an author. Long before the public christened him "Dictionary Johnson," he had learned to think of himself as wrapped up in the book, its agent and bondsman.[8] The scope of the project demanded a total investment. When the booksellers commissioned the magnum opus, they gave Johnson a steady income, a means of making his name, and a set of duties and occupations from which he would not be free for nearly a decade. Moreover, they altered his professional standing. Instead of the hack or craftsman who furnished various pieces of copy on request, he had now developed into a sort of small factory owner, leasing a house in Gough Square, hiring assistants, marking up books to be processed, managing a production line, negotiating with his backers and the pressmen, and finally delivering the goods. A one-man dictionary is possible only when a large community stands behind it. Hence Johnson modified his way of life and his sense of himself. The crowded household in Gough Square, with copyists in the attic, servants, visitors, and an increasing number of lodgers, hardly resembles the lonely garret of the mythical hack. Johnson may not have been a very efficient business-man, but many people depended on him as he assembled—and only occasionally *wrote*—the book that dominated his existence. This was not the life of a poet. He would have to grow into his task, sub-jecting himself to a work that would always be bigger than he was.

He became, in short, a lexicographer: "a writer of dictionaries, a harmless drudge," according to the *Dictionary* itself. That identity would stick to him for a long time to come. Sometimes he found the work congenial, sometimes a trial. But for a literary man or learned author, the great advantage of assuming the identity was that it was so well defined. Everyone understood the role of a lexicographer; it attracted no envy, it put on no airs. There is security in following such a routine, especially when an income goes with it. A writer of dictionaries knows just what he is supposed to do and be.

In fact Johnson played the role to the hilt, even or perhaps most of all when he complained about it. *The Plan of a Dictionary* composes a personal drama in which "I" communicates both his superiority to the lowly status of "the unhappy lexicographer" and his intention humbly to submit. Even Johnson's description of the dreary voca-tion he has chosen seems to enjoy the prospect of such a fine oppor-tunity for self-abasement. "MY LORD, When first I undertook to write an English Dictionary," without expecting a patron, "I knew, that the work in which I engaged is generally considered as drudgery for the blind, as the proper toil of artless industry, a task that requires nei-ther the light of learning, nor the activity of genius, but may be suc-cessfully performed without any higher quality than that of bearing burthens with dull patience, and beating the track of the alphabet with sluggish resolution." Only a very gifted and self-conscious writer could degrade his own profession with so much relish, reduc-ing the mental activities of lexicography to plodding physical labor—"bearing burthens," "beating the track." Nor does Johnson go on to dispute this vulgar conception. Is it true that the laurel will never grow in these barren regions of learning? "Neither vanity nor interest incited me to enquire."[9] Johnson draws the identity around his shoulders like a shabby but cozy shawl.

Yet warning signs appear on the horizon of the *Plan*. In retrospect, the conflict with Chesterfield may be anticipated right at the beginning, as soon as "I" expresses his wonder, surprise, and anxiety at having attracted a patron. Johnson insists that he cannot believe his good fortune, and he tempts the reader not to believe it either. Some scholars discern a proleptic irony or underlying antipathy in the whole relation between "I" and the lord he solicits for aid and advice.[10] The two men had little in common except pride, and Johnson did not sue with a very good grace. Nor did the two agree at all, in the long run, on matters of language.[11] Perhaps a personal dislike accounts for the undercurrent of tension. But another explanation might be a double edge in Johnson's role. On the one hand, we have seen, he defines the lexicographer as harmless drudge, the lowest grub in the field where nearsighted writers ply their tedious trade. On the other hand, he knows that the task is heroic, pitting one scholar against the combined forces of foreign academies in a contest for the honor of his nation. If humility is one note of the *Plan,* the vaulting ambition—almost the megalomania—of a lexicographer is another. "When I survey the Plan which I have laid before you, I cannot, my Lord, but confess, that I am frighted at its extent, and, like the soldiers of Caesar, look on Britain as a new world, which it is almost madness to invade."[12] The conquest of a language calls for a great adventurer, the arm of Caesar if not Caesar himself. The scholar who rules the words of his country also controls its history and spirit. Hence Johnson plays the role of a budding hero.

Tradition authorized this mixed identity. Ever since the Renaissance, it had been conventional for great scholars to lament the lowly tasks on which their powers were engaged—a complaint that was also a boast. Johnson adopts this mode as his second nature. Despite his bantering homage to Grub Street, he identifies far more with the giants of Renaissance philology, those heroes who had claimed the science and history of language as a new world.[13] Such scholars were what he might have been; what he still might be. The young Enthusiast of *The Vanity of Human Wishes,* who dreams of filling up the Bodleian and topping Roger Bacon, is obviously a portrait of the author as a young man. Nor did the dream fade. The most personally revealing poem that Johnson ever wrote, the Latin verses on the theme of *Gnōthi seauton,* "Know thyself," that followed his revision of the *Dictionary* in 1773, opens with a long, depressed comparison of himself with the great Joseph Scaliger—another suffering lexicographer.[14] It weighs on Johnson that he does not measure up. Yet even to venture the comparison, while imitating Scaliger's own verse, shows powerful, tacit ambitions. He knows that he was made for something better.

The thought of patronage especially rouses the dream of a Renaissance scholar. As Johnson ponders the implications of Chesterfield's support, in the *Plan,* he drifts into a different age of authorship. "I had read indeed of times, in which princes and statesmen thought it part of their honour to promote the improvement of their native tongues, and in which dictionaries were written under the protection of greatness." But he had supposed that those times were past and that acts of bounty to scholars were "prodigies," almost too wonderful to credit.[15] In fact great scholars had never been able to count on the goodwill of patrons. Johnson was well acquainted with the vicious rivalries of Renaissance philologists, their untrustworthy alliances and internecine feuds. In every respect great scholarship is expensive. It demands long years of unrelenting, obsessive labor, which brings no certain profit in the end and will never pay for itself, and even in an age of patronage there are never enough patrons to go around. That had been Scaliger's world—dedicated and cutthroat.[16] When Johnson pictures himself in it, he feels a well-justified apprehension. The competitiveness and defensiveness of the Renaissance scholar, along with his heroism, carry over to the self-portrait in the Preface to the *English Dictionary* (1755), where the author expresses both pride and sorrow at having performed "a task, which *Scaliger* compares to the labours of the anvil and the mine."[17] Nor has his patron been faithful. In that regard also the lexicographer follows a well-worn tradition.

Hence the final quarrel with Chesterfield seems thoroughly predetermined. As Johnson's first person grew, it needed another person to strive against, to test its strength. No reader of the *Plan* could overlook the presence of its author, defining himself in the act of imagining future travail. Already he lays the ground for a clash of two contestants: the great but obscure scholar, the "great" but petty lord. To anyone versed in the classics, the rest of the story could almost be taken for granted. Johnson's career would go on to write and rewrite it. Psychologically, the effort to adapt the role of a Renaissance scholar to changing times and patrons would set the terms on which he made his living. Despite his pride in writing only for money, he did not bargain well.[18] Income seemed always more welcome when it appeared as a sort of largesse, the tribute of one benefactor of the public to another. Thus it is only appropriate that he should call Andrew Millar, the bookseller who advanced him funds for the *Dictionary,* "the Maecenas of the age";[19] nor is it surprising that by the time the book was published he had already spent the whole sum agreed on and then some.[20] Scaliger would not have haggled or counted the pennies. One patron had failed, as patrons always did, but the booksellers were generous men and knew how to take care of authors. They had replaced the noble patrons of old.

In 1747, however, the *Dictionary* still had to be written. The new authorial identity that Johnson was shaping would help him, up to a point. He needed the confidence that a strong first person would give him, the sense of professional power to carry him through, as well as the sense of a role that he could master. The "I," in years to come, would grow and grow. But a lexicographer also had to keep it in check. Neither humility nor ambition would solve the problems of compiling a dictionary, the exhausting process in which first principles and practical realities would have to be aligned day after day, year after year. He lost himself in the work. At the end of the road lay the figure of an author barely glimpsed before, a comprehensive national man of letters. But first came the alphabet.

Everything about *A Dictionary of the English Language* is exaggerated. The size of the book, the tremendous store of knowledge that it contains, the speed with which one man produced it, the legendary definitions, the praise and blame it has always received, and the reputation as the ultimate authority on English usage that it wielded for more than a century: all seem blown out of proportion. But most of all, exaggeration begins on the spine, with the customary short title: *Johnson's Dictionary.* The name mounts a claim of ownership, as if one man commanded the language. Nor is that label merely a trademark, like *Webster's*. Almost alone among works of its kind, *Johnson's Dictionary* conjures up the image of its author. Not just a book of words, it represents a personal vision of language, an English on which the author has put his stamp.

Yet Johnson would have been the first to ridicule such overstatement. Neither the dictionary nor its words belonged to him; the booksellers owned the first and all literate English men and women the second. Any authority he exerted was strictly conditional, good only by suffrage. Even equivocal uses of words would have to be admitted, a confusion "not to be imputed to me, who do not form, but register the language; who do not teach men how they should think, but relate how they have hitherto expressed their thoughts" (paragraph 75). Johnson compiled the book; he did not compose it.

Nor was he convinced that any lexicographer could qualify as an author. The "harmless drudge, that busies himself in tracing the original, and detailing the signification of words," is always aware that he originates nothing.[21] Hence the making of a dictionary mocks the standard conception or ideal of authorship, which assumes that one person can make a difference. The lexicographer effaces himself in order to serve as the passive instrument of all the people who have molded English in the past and will use it in the future. No longer an individual but rather a scribe who registers the accidents of history, he vanishes into communal, collective language. That is the condition of a word-book's success. Only by courtesy can *Johnson's Dictionary* be taken for Johnson's.

The process of making the book spells out this exigent self-effacement. At every stage the work resisted its agent's will. Significantly, Johnson's first statement about the project, when Robert Dodsley suggested that "a Dictionary of the english language would be a work which would be well received by the Publick," is reported to have been "I believe I shan't undertake it." Poverty and the booksellers changed his mind. Yet both the *Plan* and the Preface testify to his low expectations of "any other advantage than the price of my labour."[22] Nor did he admit that he later warmed to the task. According to Johnson's account, his designs for the work were consistently frustrated by the strenuous reality of executing it. At the end of the three years first allotted, he seems to have gone through a crisis, scrapped the method he had fixed on as well as much of the copy prepared for the printers, and started again.[23] His early resolve "to leave neither words nor things unexamined" soon faded: "these were the dreams of a poet doomed at last to wake a lexicographer" (par. 72). The work that he tried to shape would at last shape him.

In practice the *Dictionary* had to be patched together from other books. The preliminary list of words was gleaned from Nathan Bailey's *Dictionarium Britannicum* (1721), a predecessor and rival; the etymologies from Junius, Skinner, and others; the grammar and history of the language from standard sources such as Wallis and Hickes.[24] And even the conception of lexicography draws on the preface to Ephraim Chambers' *Cyclopaedia* (1728), which also furnished a model for the personal tone of Johnson's Preface.[25] Moreover, the character of the *Dictionary*—as well as its bulk—depends on the omnibus illustrative quotations that Johnson combed from what he considered the golden age of English (Sidney to Locke, with some silver additions such as Pope), as he collected passages and underlined words for his amanuenses to transcribe. In this respect the book is literally patchwork. It devours and digests other books, which Johnson's rough handling often turned into mincemeat. One might argue that he left a personal imprint by choosing sources that reveal his own mind as well as the authorities who formed it. Yet even that way of characterizing the author implies that his identity converged with the library he owned and borrowed. He did not coin a single word or idea. Indeed, the only room for originality lay in occasional blunders ("Pastern: the knee of an horse"). A dictionary takes a leaf from the language already recorded by other books; its art is based on knowing what to copy.

Yet every text incorporates other texts. From one point of view, the dictionary might be considered the exemplary text, precisely because it exposes the web of borrowed words in which all texts are wound, and does not pretend to break free. Similarly, the author of a dictionary might be considered the archetypal author—someone who arranges words and meanings he did not invent. Many theorists would welcome that view. In recent decades, a revulsion against the fictions of autonomous individualism and original genius—the single, separate, creative figure who owes nothing to anyone else—has provoked the counterfiction of the death or disappearance of the author. And even if that obituary seems premature, challenges to a traditional idea of the author, as the transcendent subject who originates and guarantees all meaning, continue to spread.[26] What is an author? Recent scholarship offers a host of views that do not leave the lexicographer out.

The seeds of this dispute were planted in the eighteenth century. Johnson himself gives grounds for contrary views of authorship. Sometimes he contrasts the honorific author with the mere writer; sometimes he does not. Hence the second paragraph of the Preface to the *Dictionary* begins with that unhappy mortal, "the writer"—not author—"of dictionaries"; but the following sentence, "Every other authour may aspire to praise; the lexicographer can only hope to escape reproach," implicitly concedes that the writer of dictionaries, however lowly, qualifies as an author among others. The same oscillation runs through Johnson's career. The author as original mover vies with the author as efficient producer, and Johnson can take pride in either role.

He may have learned this method of self-presentation from Ephraim Chambers. The preface to the *Cyclopaedia* combines an ostentatious modesty with latent megalomania, a hint that it knows everything worth knowing. Even the long subtitle of the work—*an Universal Dictionary of Arts and Sciences; . . . the whole intended as a Course of ancient and modern Learning, Extracted from the best Authors*—suggests its ambition to provide the one indispensable book. Nor does Chambers hesitate to call himself an author. Whether the lexicographer descends from "some little grammarian" or from the high priest who first explained language, he seems entrusted with the power to collect and analyze the whole world of knowledge.[27] Chambers concedes his dependence on other writers. A work like the *Cyclopaedia* is "not the produce of one man's wit . . . but of a whole commonwealth."[28] But the well-being of a commonwealth depends on someone's preserving its constitution—its history and principles of organization—and Chambers elects himself to that office. Not only an author, he acts as the epitome of authors: the arts and sciences distilled to their essence. Despite the fashion for be-

112

littling lexicography, a quirk that Chambers blames on Scaliger and other pedantic polymaths, the maker of a dictionary contributes to the public good and ought to be acknowledged as an artist.[29] That is one lesson that Chambers taught Johnson.

In what sense does the lexicographer qualify as an author? One answer to the question might draw on a comparison with another art, the art of music. Ever since the eighteenth century, the composer has served as a model of inspiration, the creator who plucks melodies from the air. Even as Johnson labored on the *Dictionary,* Rousseau's articles for the *Encyclopédie* were insisting that melody was the heart of music, unique in its ability to communicate passion.[30] Learning, craft, the rules of harmony could hardly signify without the gift of song. Nor could that gift be taught. Eventually this stress on the power of natural passion led to the deification of the composer, just as Rousseau himself—the author who spoke soul to soul—became an idol to many sensitive readers.[31] But no one expects a lexicographer to be inspired, or even to carry a tune. A more plausible analogue might be the conductor of an orchestra or chorus. In addition to having a good memory and a talent for organization and coordination, above all a conductor must know how to *listen.* Such listening is constructive; the effect of the music depends on how well it has been received and transmitted. And writers, too, conduct as well as compose. In this regard the author of a dictionary needs most of all to be a master reader. Like a conductor, he proves himself by the quality of his attention, not by inventing; the score or text must come first. Thus no matter how famous such authors become, they always aim to minister to the language, the work, and the public. Johnson reads on behalf of everyone else.[32]

Yet Johnson was by no means a typical reader. A virtuoso at ripping the kernel out of a book, he made his name by gobbling up whole libraries.[33] Nor did he read only in private. His feats went the rounds; as soon as the *Dictionary* appeared, the public sought out its author. Chambers had not created such a stir. Evidently the nature of authorship itself was rapidly changing. No less than a poet, a lexicographer could now fill the role of a hero, as Carlyle would proclaim: "Had Johnson left nothing but his *Dictionary,* one might have traced there a great intellect, a genuine man."[34] Somewhere within

113

the alphabet, a man of letters proved to be hiding, and ever since then a faithful readership has tried to bring him out. However an author might be defined in theory, no one who looked at the book seemed able to keep from wondering what sort of person had put it together. This effect—this "author-function"—is part of the *Dictionary* itself: the book as a whole reflects the life of its author. But what does that mean?

One reason that almost every reader of the *Dictionary* constructs an image of its author is that Johnson compelled it. In the last three paragraphs of the Preface, the discreet authorial "I" abruptly thrusts itself forward and measures the book on the scale of the person who wrote it: "In hope of giving longevity to that which its own nature forbids to be immortal, I have devoted this book, the labour of years, to the honour of my country" (par. 92). The first clause seems ambiguous. Though presumably "that which its own nature forbids to be immortal" is "our *language,*" a reader might be excused for taking the author's own work as the object of hope. The struggle against mortality preoccupies Johnson. Much of the Preface plays variations on the theme of the vanity of human wishes; a living language can be fixed no more than the wind or the tide. Yet reminders of how much has not been accomplished also remind the author of what he has done. The book has given meaning to his life, and in the future it will always be part of his story.

The final paragraph of the Preface carries the story further. "The *English Dictionary*"—already referred to here as a standard work, *the* dictionary—"was written with little assistance of the learned, and without any patronage of the great; not in the soft obscurities of retirement, or under the shelter of academick bowers, but amid inconvenience and distraction, in sickness and in sorrow . . . I have protracted my work till most of those whom I wished to please have sunk into the grave, and success and miscarriage are empty sounds." A portrait of the author momentarily displaces the book. Johnson surely exaggerated his "gloom of solitude" and indifference to censure or praise. Yet the mixture of dignified unconcern and self-revelation turned out to be irresistible. Not even Horne Tooke, a relentless critic of the *Dictionary,* could refrain from shedding tears over these words.[35] The hinted story soon acquired a life of its own. From the moment that Johnson completed the Preface, involving the reception of the *Dictionary* with the fate of its human and fallible maker, someone was going to have to write his life. Virtually every reader of that final page has felt a tiny Boswell stir within, the prick of curiosity that wants to be acquainted with this man. What patrons spurned him, what friends had he lost, what brought about his "frigid tranquillity"? The half-discerned author teases us into thought.

Doubtless a strong psychological need accounts for this personal touch. Johnson was looking back at eight years of work, and could hardly resist the chance to take leave not only of the project but also of the person who had executed it. Not for the first time, he said goodbye to his youth and its dreams. Few moments ever satisfied him more than those in which he confided his disillusionment. Even the preemptive dejection with which the author awaits the verdict of the public rehearses the lesson that he had been reading all his life. Johnson had spent a long time practicing this signature.

At the same time, however, the authorial image inscribed in the Preface seems part of a comprehensive and canny marketing strategy. This *Dictionary,* unlike most others, abounds in human interest. Even before publication, the quarrel with Chesterfield had stirred more desire to see the book than Chesterfield's praise alone could have whetted. Now readers would remember the author forever. Johnson's anger and sorrow, however sincere, were calculated to put the audience in the right frame of mind to appreciate his achievement. Similarly, he gave the public an English hero to stimulate the national pride that regarded support for an English dictionary as a patriotic duty—he "has beat forty French, and will beat forty more!"[36] A competitive feat as well as a work of honest domestic manufacture, the book spread the word of its author's striving, his trials and triumphs.

The author's authority was also in question. What makes one dictionary more valuable than another? Part of the answer might be the credentials of the person responsible for it. Chambers' name, on the title page of the *Cyclopaedia,* is followed by "F.R.S."; the Royal Society stands behind him. During the months before the *Dictionary* was published, much of Johnson's energy went into securing a degree from Oxford.[37] The honor rewarded him for the "labour and judgement" the great work had required. But it also served to promote the book. Johnson kept back the title page in order to insert, when at last it was printed, the letters he had been wanting most of his life: "By SAMUEL JOHNSON, A.M." Here personal gratification blends with a useful commercial message: a scholarly somebody endorses this work.

Yet a name on the title page did not guarantee the authority of the book. Neither did Chesterfield's puff, though it might lend the imprimatur of a national figure as well as a touch of noblesse oblige. High titles alone, despite their charm, will not secure buyers for a costly reference work. Instead an English dictionary had to invent the terms of its own authority, since no predecessor had set the standard. This point is worth dwelling on. Most scholarship, in the mid-eighteenth century, still relied heavily on citing approved texts by approved authors. Scholars raised on a limited canon of Greek and Latin classics, or on the unchallengeable witness of the Bible, could hardly oppose their own opinions to the weight of the past. On the title page of his pioneering *Dictionarium Britannicum*—an English dictionary with a Latin name—Nathan Bailey dubs himself *philologer,* in Greek. Even the Moderns, when they fought the Ancients, fought them with ancient weapons, claiming to be *more* faithful to the oldest texts.[38] Similarly, the originality of Renaissance scholars had depended on adapting classical ideas and languages to present purposes. Sometimes this led to contortions. Franciscus Junius, the great humanist scholar whose *Etymologicon Anglicanum* (1743) furnishes many of Johnson's etymologies, so reverences the ancients that he manages to trace a remarkable number of plain Anglo-Saxon words to fanciful strains of Greek; for instance, as Johnson points out, he derives "*dream* from *drama,* because *life is a drama, and a drama is a dream*" (par. 25).[39] Evidence always weighs more for such a philologist when it stems from a learned language. But a vernacular lexicon must look for other principles. The Greek and Latin and Hebrew authorities shared just one fault, through no fault of their own: they did not speak good English.

Johnson's solution is clear. The *Dictionary* achieves its authority through a massive embrace of the honorary English "classics," the writers whose pure and venerable language had forged an equivalent to ancient precedents. This is Johnson's master stroke, and it is momentous; it changes the nature of authority itself.[40] Henceforth good English will be not merely a set of conventions but an object of reverence. Sidney, Shakespeare, Hooker, Raleigh, Bacon, Dryden, Locke, Addison, and Pope, along with the King James Bible and those divines who built on its vocabulary, validate their native language as well as the book that contains it. Virtually every word is propped up by a tiny history of usage by worthies; the *Dictionary* incorporates 116,000 quotations, a golden treasury of national wisdom. Collectively, these examples are supposed to provide "the solution of all difficulties, and the supply of all defects" (par. 56). Practically, however, they absolve the faults of the *Dictionary* with a sort of blessing, ablution from *"the wells of English undefiled"* (par. 61). The great writers of England stand behind Johnson's work, recommending it through their unimpeachable presence. Such a book is authoritative because authorities compose it, chapter and verse.

Yet authorities can be mistaken, as Johnson well knows. Despite its author's "zeal for antiquity" and veneration of the past, the *Dictionary* reserves the right of final judgment to itself. More than one illustration of the word "authority" casts doubt on the wisdom of submitting to it: "We urge *authorities* in things that need not, and introduce the testimony of ancient writers, to confirm things evidently believed." The example comes from Sir Thomas Browne's *Vulgar Errours (Pseudodoxia Epidemica,* 1646), a favorite work of Johnson and one he was tempted to bring up to date;[41] and a skeptical attitude toward fallacies about things might easily extend to mistakes about words. Not even the best authority could justify the abuse of language. "Although their intention be sincere, yet doth it notoriously strengthen vulgar errour, and *authorize* opinions injurious to truth," Browne had complained, and he was seconded by Robert South: "Be a person in vogue with the multitude, he shall *authorize* any nonsense." These two examples of sense 5, "to give credit to any person or thing," put the reader on guard against authorizations.[42] Page by page the *Dictionary* asserts its independence—if not from great writers, at least from the vulgar and those to whom they give credit.

In a peculiar way, a refusal to bow to authority might even be viewed as essential to any dictionary that claimed to be English. The spirit of England, after all, was free. At several moments in the Preface, the author breathes defiance. He will not surrender to the forces of decay, the vulgar, the canters, the critics, the academicians. Above all he will not surrender to the French. Preserving English from a century-long swerve "towards a *Gallick* structure and phraseology" (even the *k* in "Gallick" signifies Teutonick resistance to French spelling), Johnson identifies his love of language with love of country. He plays here to the patriotic crowd. "If an academy should be established for the cultivation of our stile, which I, who can never wish to see dependance multiplied, hope the spirit of *English* liberty will hinder or destroy, let them, instead of compiling grammars and dictionaries, endeavour, with all their influence, to stop the licence of translatours, whose idleness and ignorance, if it be suffered to proceed, will reduce us to babble a dialect of *France*" (par. 90).[43]

Whatever the justification for this defense of linguistic borders (perhaps the advent of Franglais confirms the danger of traffic across the Channel), it neatly juggles two loaded terms: English *liberty* must put a stop to French *licence*. Johnson had learned to use this language as soon as he wrote for pay, and mastered it in *London*. Its sources probably lie in the British dissenting tradition. But politics, especially the patriotic rhetoric developed by the opposition to Walpole, offers a more immediate context.[44] Long after Walpole fell, the wits who had come of age at the time of his supremacy still practiced the grand old tirades against corruption. The vocabulary of Johnson's attack recalls their stock phrases, here adapted to a new enemy—not Spanish picaroons but French translators. If "liberty" is the key term,[45] "dependance" equally sets the tone. Walpole had been notorious for governing through placemen and hangers-on. The *Dictionary* defines "pensioner" first as "a dependant" and next as "a slave of state hired by a stipend to obey his master" (a coda to the famous definition of "pension": "In England it is generally understood to mean pay given to a state hireling for treason to his country").[46] Johnson aligns himself with the opposition. Academies are not only alien imports, in this view, but also threats to liberty, like a standing army. At worst they might function as language-police to tyrannize over independent, uncorrupted, native-born dictionaries; at best they might prevent a Whiggish free trade in language. But an English lexicographer disdains such authorities.[47] He will make his way, without assistance from the learned or the great, through the strength bred in him by his country.

Hence the *Dictionary* had to reconcile two opposite roles, combining a selfless devotion to the language already preserved by the best English writers with a single, vigorous, self-reliant voice. A true authority called for both, and so did the public. When Johnson slipped the first person into his work, he was certainly taking a risk. In the future, readers would always know too much about him; they would judge what he wrote in terms of a prior impression. This could be dangerous. A dictionary tries to offer *the* definition, not *Johnson's* definition, and thoughts of the author detract from the sense of impartiality and impersonality that reference books prefer to convey. Individuals have opinions; opinions prompt disagreements; disagreements reduce confidence in the neutrality of the arbiter. To a critic like Coleridge, the figure of Johnson loomed so large as to eclipse his work. The *Dictionary* might be "a most instructive and entertaining *book*," but no "philosophic and thorough scholar" would praise it "as a *dictionary*."[48] Johnson lacks authority, according to Coleridge, precisely because of his visibility as an author. Yet even this admonition pays tribute to the power of Johnson's reputation, a power that Coleridge must challenge, again and again, in order to urge his own superior learning. A thorough fusion of writer and text comes naturally to the author of *Biographia Literaria*. It came less naturally, however, to Johnson; his kind of author still needed to be invented. The "I" of the *Dictionary* remains experimental, exposing the mere humanity of the book yet also drawing the reader into its web.

What is the evidence that any dictionary has an author? The title page and the preface furnish some clues, as do occasional first-person pronouns. But many of Johnson's readers have wanted more. Some readers have even made their own book by culling the most notorious or amusing definitions.[49] Their evidence consists of words, the hoard or stock of language on which the author has put his stamp. Some turns of phrase, some twists of diction will always evoke the writer who has used them most memorably, as Johnson made "cant" his own. Like handwriting, the use of language is always distinctive; "every man whatever has a peculiar style, which may be discovered by nice examination and comparison with others."[50] Similarly, each lexicographer has a peculiar vocabulary; no two word-hoards are exactly alike.[51] In this respect the *Dictionary* seems "a wonderful intellectual autobiography written in terms of the atoms of meaning, i.e. the words Johnson himself acknowledged and used."[52] But a popular dictionary cannot afford too much peculiarity. Rather than pick and choose among words, it tries to include whatever a reader might need, and the author's handwriting blends with copy from many hired hands. Nor are most of Johnson's definitions eccentric; later dictionaries often borrowed them word for word. Here the author vanishes into a common text, where personality and style are rubbed to a uniform blandness.

Anyone who reads the *Dictionary* from beginning to end, however, will not accuse it of lacking character. If a true image of Johnson cannot be found in an anthology of oddities, he does preside over the full ensemble. Thus the place to look for evidence of authorship is the work as a whole. The principles that shape the book can furnish an entrance into the mind of its author.

There are two main ways of describing those principles. Roughly speaking, they correspond to process and product, the difference between viewing the *Dictionary* as an enterprise that follows a plan or plans, evolving through several editions toward an end it can never quite reach, and viewing it as something accomplished, an artifact, each part complete despite its imperfections. I will call these the difference between an author's *design* and an author's *intention*. The distinction was common in eighteenth-century theology, where evidence for an Author of the universe might be sought in His design—the guiding principles that inform every created thing, as a watch manifests the watchmaker's calculations—or in His intention—the ever-present spirit that communicates its purpose directly, like a voice heard in the wind or in the conscience. For the deist, religion rested on Nature; for traditionalists, on Revelation or Truth.[53] And so with the dictionary, that world in miniature. Some readers might take it as odds and ends, one item after another. But the book, like the world, makes sense when we see it as the result of someone's plan or as charged with someone's meanings. Even an unbeliever in gods or authors is likely to resort to these lines of argument when confronted with something apparently senseless. I design and intend to consider them in turn.

A scheme, a plan, a preface, the book itself, the book revised—Johnson made no secret of his designs. Yet his continuing effort to explain what he was doing might well be the sign of an author's dissatisfaction. The scheme, the plan, and the preface are not consistent, nor do they always clarify the book. The writer appears most comfortable, it seems, when he is explaining why his earlier plan could not be carried out. Hence each successive stage of making the *Dictionary* seems to represent a falling away. What begins in the "Scheme" as a mental activity—"When I first conceived the design of compiling a new Dictionary..."—becomes a practical job of work in the *Plan*—"When first I undertook to write an English Dictionary..."—and a tentative experiment in the Preface—"I have, notwithstanding this discouragement, attempted a dictionary . . ." (par. 3). To conceive a design was easier than to execute it. Johnson's first method did not work, in fact. At the end of 1749 he seems to have discarded much of his manuscript and recommenced on a new plan. The notebooks he had previously used, organizing a fixed sequence of words in alphabetical order, were replaced by loose sheets of paper on which an indefinite number of slips could be pasted.[54] No calculation could predict how much room the language might need. With or without its author's will, the design had to change.

A technical necessity drove the change. As examples of usage multiplied, squeezed into the prearranged notebooks, the pages must have become impossibly clotted. But the lexicographer was changing as well. To put it simply, the work turned Johnson from an Ancient into a Modern. He began with a firm idea of what the dictionary should be: "The chief intent of it is to preserve the purity and ascertain the meaning of our English idiom"[55] (instead of ascertaining the meaning, the "Scheme" had suggested "fixing the use"). Such ideas point backward, toward the root meaning or pure primal stem of each word. Older texts, not yet corrupted, ought to be best. "By tracing in this manner every word to its original, and not admitting, but with great caution, any of which no original can be found, we shall secure our language from being over-run with *cant,* from being crouded with low terms, the spawn of folly or affectation, which arise from no just principles of speech, and of which therefore no legitimate derivation can be shewn."[56] This is the creed of an Ancient, like Sir William Temple or his successor (Johnson may once have hoped) Lord Chesterfield. These patrons of scholarship believe in the timeless truths of experience, embodied in a few exemplary books (to know a great many books would be pedantic). Ancients seldom require a large vocabulary. The supply of wisdom is limited, and our ancestors managed quite well with fewer words. The purpose of any dictionary, for an Ancient, ought to be to restore a simpler, Adamic language, with unblemished etymologies, stable spellings, correct pronunciations, and firm definitions. That was the commission that Johnson accepted.[57]

He could not discharge it. The very process of collecting examples of usage from the best English writers broke down any hope of fixing a timeless language. As soon as they were examined, those quotations revealed a language in flux, with each word capable of endless nuances and fine discriminations.[58] Often the original meaning seemed lost in time. Slowly, as Johnson fought his own battle of the books, he metamorphosed into a Modern. The day-to-day cut-and-paste work of a dictionary maker recreated the historical turn from humanism to the new scholarly techniques of the Enlightenment. Like the great Pierre Bayle, whose *Dictionnaire historique et critique* (1697) replaced approved traditions with a skeptical analysis of all the texts on which traditions were founded, Johnson began to review the wandering history of meaning.[59] Words had to be sorted, anatomized, and put into sequence; the right place had to be found for each quotation. This process was not mechanical. At each point someone had to decide whether the example repeated the meaning of another or introduced some delicate new shade. Any lapse in vigilance could prove costly, as in Johnson's disastrous lumping together of "coco-nut" and "cacao" under "cocoa," a blunder whose confusions endure to the present day (when we still pronounce both words "coco").[60] Pure English or not, words registered changes in knowledge and thought. A lexicographer would have to record those changes.

Moreover, the juxtaposition of quotations from authorities separated in time often set up a little debate among them, provoking basic doubts about which to rely on. For example, "authority," in its first sense of "legal power," is somewhat undermined when two neutral instances from Shakespeare are followed by Temple's distinction between "Power arising from strength" and "*authority* arising from opinion," and then by Locke's suggestion that Adam's authority could not have been inherited by his children. Some readers might be led to question authority. Misgivings such as these arose from history, not from Johnson; after the British civil war, the meaning of authority would never again be quite the same. Thus the *Dictionary,* whatever its author's opinions, supplies materials for a modern point of view, in which particular contexts modify univocal truths. The book both chronicles and represents an explosion of meaning.

The new design cost Johnson plenty of work. In opening his stock of words to variations over time, he was forced to let in some very impure strains, as well as an indefinite number of quotations. Logically, hardly any example could be discounted; comparison with other uses might always detect some faint refinement. Sometimes illustrations threaten to run away with the book. For sense 20 of "to give"—"to addict; to apply"—Johnson includes no fewer than fifteen examples, at least ten of which seem superfluous. Here the manual labor of lexicography plies a shovel instead of a sieve. On the other hand, some words lack good references. Not even Johnson's prodigious memory, as he marked passages for use, could ensure that he would remember everything; in the Preface he notes that his first collection overlooked "sea" (par. 81). In addition, the *Dictionary* omits a surprising number of words, including some of its author's own favorites. For instance, although it lists no fewer than eleven derivatives of "lapis" (stone) such as "lapicide" and "lapidifick," it passes over the adjective "lapidary," which Johnson used often in referring to a poetic style.[61] At other times the absence of illustration provokes a comment. No recent writer attests to "hell," and Johnson inserts his own dry observation: "It is used in composition by the old writers more than by the modern."

But the main burden he had to shoulder was intellectual. Not only by sifting quotations, but by perpetual, painstaking attention to meanings that might be overlooked, the lexicographer needed to recognize and distinguish the many layers of sense that could be compressed into any one word. Here Johnson shines. The powers of mind required to write a dictionary are finical, exact, and unimposing; they seldom catch the notice of a reader. Yet little things reveal intelligence. In this respect the *Dictionary* rewards close reading.

Consider that unpromising adjective, "dull." One well-known entry (sense 8) exposes the author: "Not exhilaterating [*sic*]; not delightful; as, *to make dictionaries is* dull *work*." A momentary spark of personality relieves the dullness. But a more solid, if less showy, wit also informs sense 1, where Johnson confronts the basic problem of defining a simple Anglo-Saxon word ("To explain, requires the use of terms less abstruse than that which is to be explained, and such terms cannot always be found").[62] Modern dictionaries resort to circularity, as in defining "dull" as "lacking brightness of mind." Johnson does better: "stupid; doltish; blockish; unapprehensive; indocile; slow of understanding." The succession of adjectives, beginning with terms of abuse, gradually expands the sense into something more dignified, descriptive, Latinate, potentially even "philosophical"—dull people do not catch a point ("unapprehensive"), they are hard to teach ("indocile"), they are slow to understand but perhaps not hopeless. The way is thus prepared for a quotation from Dryden: "Every man, even the *dullest,* is thinking more than the most eloquent can teach him how to utter." Johnson provides alternative ways of analyzing dullness. Though he has not solved the problem of reducing a simple idea to something more simple (the entry might suit a thesaurus better than a lexicon), he does seem to have thought the word through. Another mark of alertness fills a gap between sense 4—"hebetated; not quick"—and sense 6—"sluggish; heavy; slow of motion." Here Johnson, without a quotation to prompt him, supplies the missing term: "sad; melancholy." Characteristically, this definition adapts the physical conditions of hebetude and sluggishness to a mental or psychological state—a state, one might add, with which the writer was well acquainted. Another lexicographer might not have noticed the gap. The train of thought anticipates Johnson's later remark on the first line of *The Traveller,* "Remote, unfriended, melancholy, slow," when he corrected Goldsmith's own interpretation of "slow": "No, Sir; you do not mean tardiness of locomotion; you mean, that sluggishness of mind which comes upon a man in solitude."[63] Johnson understands such states of mind. But his recognition of sense 5 is not merely personal. It is intelligent, the opposite of dull.

Page by page and letter after letter, the *Dictionary* gradually unfolds its design, as the pattern of etymology, definition, and examples continually repeats. Small variations and habits of mind hint at the author in the background. So do accidents. For instance, fish seem to mystify Johnson. Dependent on his sources, he often fails to distinguish one kind from another. The glamour of salmon and notoriety of pike, well celebrated in literature, come out in fine quotations; but hake and halibut remain no more than "a kind of fish" or "a sort of fish," and even "dolphin" is shrunk to "the name of a fish." The lexicographer wants a taxonomy and an index, or at least a more efficient method for storing and sorting his items.[64] Ideally, all the sea creatures strewn through the book, from minnows to whales, would be caught in a single taxonomic net, the comprehensive superclass of "fish." But Johnson lacks that device. His classifications are usually tactical, or improvised in response to some particular problem. The same might be said of the design of the book as a whole. It rides on the intelligence, and occasional failings, of its author. The world of knowledge that it holds obeys no master plan—or none that Johnson ever spells out for us.

Yet what did he *intend?* In one regard the question is easy to answer. "When I had thus enquired into the original of words, I resolved to show likewise my attention to things; to pierce deep into every science, to enquire the nature of every substance of which I inserted the name, to limit every idea by a definition strictly logical, and exhibit every production of art or nature in an accurate description, that my book might be in place of all other dictionaries whether appellative or technical." In short, he intended to make a book of books, an encyclopedia where every library would be distilled. He would do this by choosing the very best quotations. The intention was vain, of course.

When Johnson writes sentences of such presumption, we always know he is heading for a fall. "Thus to persue perfection, was, like the first inhabitants of Arcadia, to chace the sun, which, when they had reached the hill where he seemed to rest, was still beheld at the same distance from them" (par. 72). As usual, the high ambitions sink to a long, detailed explanation of why they could not be fulfilled in practice. But Johnson's disclaimers might also be seen as a challenge. The *Dictionary* does contain a vast amount of learning, scattered arbitrarily throughout. Hence it poses a basic problem of information retrieval. Properly stored and indexed, the materials of the book might be reassembled in any number of meaningful discourses and juxtapositions. At one time the tools for such work were memory and desire: what a reader remembered best or cared most about. Today a computer can simplify the process. Perhaps the touch of a key might recover the author's intentions.

The exercise can certainly be instructive. In *Johnson's Dictionary and the Language of Learning,* Robert DeMaria has organized the field of knowledge collected by the *Dictionary* into ten categories, from "Knowledge" itself to "Happiness."[65] Replacing the mechanical sequence of the alphabet with an imaginative cross-index, he converts the book into a small encyclopedia of learning (cross-references, Diderot thought, were what held the learning of his own *Encyclopédie* together).[66] In one respect this distinctly improves on Johnson; it retrieves not merely scattered information but a coherent moral world, the world that Johnson shares with his authorities. More problematically, it also assumes that Johnson *intended* that world—that is, that each time he selected a quotation or juxtaposed it with another he put his own seal on its meaning, as if he were its author. Such an assumption can hardly be taken for granted. Johnson himself warned that he sometimes "mutilated" quotations in cutting them down to size—"the divine may desert his tenets, or the philosopher his system" (par. 58). Moreover, the need to illustrate words came first, and no one can tell how thoughtfully the lexicographer read or absorbed the passages he marked, or how carefully he noted possible conflicts among them. Like an anthologist, he did not deserve all the blame or credit for the "sentiments or doctrine" that came to hand, sometimes by choice and sometimes, doubtless, by chance. Johnson made, and intended to make, a dictionary. The encyclopedia found within it will depend on a reader's own sense of what is important or of what discourse to retrieve. Responsible readers create hypothetical authors, or what phenomenologists call intentional objects. Johnson's intentions, in short, will be what we make them.

Most readers, however, want something far more specific. The identity of Johnson as author of the *Dictionary,* and the question of what he intended, seem to revolve around his conception of language. What principles did he follow? That is the issue to which scholars keep returning, the issue capable of turning a book of disconnected words into a landmark of linguistic thought. To be sure, a consistent theory can hardly be expected.[67] A dictionary is strung together from hundreds of thousands of tiny decisions, interminable and opportunistic, and collectively such a flood of detail will sap the best-laid foundations. Certainly Johnson thought so. On his own testimony, he no sooner began the work than he started revising his sense of the language it would inscribe. Yet work could not proceed without some policies or assumptions to govern his choices. Gradually, after one or two false starts, his notes and premises came together and a view of language evolved—workable, if not wholly consistent. In one way this view is less than a theory, since it accepts principles as arbitrary and contingent as *ABC*. In another way it is more, since it takes account not only of ideas but of the history that modifies them.[68] The principles implicit in the *Dictionary* seem more complex, and perhaps more adequate, than any that Johnson or his contemporaries could have stated explicitly. The book knows language better than it knows.

Etymology provides a handy example. In theory the chore of "tracing the original" of words should have been all-important. Like most linguists of his time, Johnson believed in the authority of genesis. His reverence for origins goes deep. It draws on the doctrine of original sin, which frequently interpreted the story of Babel as a fall from the innocent state of a crystal-clear, universal language, as well as on arguments for political and national stability.[69] "Tongues, like governments, have a natural tendency to degeneration," according to the Preface; "we have long preserved our constitution, let us make some struggles for our language" (par. 91). The earliest meaning ought to be the best. Even the definition of "etymology" reflects this zeal for sources and roots. Modern dictionaries define the word as "the study of historical linguistic change, esp. as applied to individual words." But Johnson, whose *Plan* had maintained that "all change is of itself an evil," values the immaculate word from which all changes lapse. "ETYMO'LOGY: The descent or derivation of a word from its original; the deduction of formations from the radical word; the analysis of compound words into primitives."[70] Moreover, the etymology of "etymology"—*etymon,* "origin; primitive word," + *logia,* "study of"—supports this analysis. A radical etymology might insist on pursuing this Latin hybrid to its Greek stems, *etymos* and *logos,* which yields "the true word" if not the Heideggerian "Word of word." Original, radical, primitive—these are the words on which a language is founded, the words that sustain the inviolate essence of language.

Yet Johnson's practice smudges such purity. The retreat from a backward-looking, change-resisting notion of etymology is already foreshadowed by two ironic citations: "When words are restrained, by common usage, to a particular sense, to run up to *etymology,* and construe them by dictionary, is wretchedly ridiculous" *(Collier's View of the Stage);* and "If the meaning of a word could be learned by its derivation or *etymology,* yet the original derivation of words is oftentimes very dark" *(Watts's Logick).* However desirable a pristine language might be, the dictionary records something else, a language in which usage and time supplant the root. In fact Johnson's etymologies are indifferent; he had neither the will nor the tools (knowledge of German, for instance) to improve on Skinner.[71] Even the arrangement of the *Dictionary* undermines the authority of origins. After the etymology comes the definition, and after the definition the illustrations; each stage tends to qualify the previous one. The definitions explain what the word has meant through history, not only at the beginning of time, and the illustrations endorse seventeenth-century, not archaic, English. Thus the typical entry conveys a mixed message: etymology for origins, definition for standard usage, quotation for practical examples as well as contexts and anomalies. The search for an ultimate source is not Johnson's fetish.

Nor is his view of "genuine diction" consistent. One crucial eighteenth-century debate on language addressed the question of where words came from: how did they first arise? what was their relation to ideas? did one simple meaning underlie all the others? A popular school of thought, developed from hints by Locke, traced every word to a specific material cause or sensory impression (what Locke calls "sensible *Ideas*"); complex words combined those clear, distinct ideas, often obscuring them in the process. Hence the task of a student of words involved, first, finding the primitive sense—"*Spirit, in its primary signification, is Breath*"[72]—then showing how other senses attached to or fell away from it. Johnson was influenced by this school; the first of the nineteen senses he gives for "spirit" is "breath; wind in motion." In the Preface, he insists that the "primitive ideas" of words must be set first, so that "the figurative senses may be commodiously deduced," as with "ardour" from "material heat" (par. 52). Yet often he forgoes that principle.[73] Other linguists might track the "soul" to something the senses can apprehend, its etymological origin in the "sea," but Johnson sets first "the immaterial and immortal spirit of man." Hence a later generation of etymologists would accuse him of succumbing to mere usage, allowing the contexts and histories of words to distract him from their intrinsic and invariable meanings.

Johnson's search for the "radical" meanings of words does not follow any one system.[74] Sometimes a sense of history governs his choice. The first definition of "Nature," for instance, ignores the stem (*natura,* "birth") in favor of an old personification: "An imaginary being supposed to preside over the material and animal world" ("Thou, *nature,* art my goddess"). Why should this meaning come first? The answer seems determined less by chronology (other senses of the word are illustrated from the same text, *King Lear*) than by the author's own judgment about historical progress. To begin with the pagan goddess and end with "11. Physics; the science which teaches the qualities of things" (exemplified by Pope's epitaph on Newton)[75] arranges a very satisfying sequence, a triumph of human knowledge in which Nature and nature's laws do move, as

129

Pope had deemed, from night to light. Superstition has yielded to truth, with some help from Johnson. Such entries exhibit the lexicographer's art—as well as the author's.

They also show his turn for metaphor. As W. K. Wimsatt argued long ago, the metaphor between matter and spirit engrosses Johnson, so that he habitually applies the language of science ("philosophic words") to moral and psychological states. The result of this tendency is not to reduce the life of the spirit to material explanations, however, but greatly to expand and refine the vocabulary available for describing nuances of spirit.[76] An acquaintance with the physical basis of "subtilty" ("thinness; fineness; exility of parts") prepares the reader to guard against "too much acuteness" and "cunning; artifice; slyness" when the term refers to a quality of mind. Similarly, Descartes seems discredited when his scientific theory— "Deny Des Cart his *subtile* matter,/You leave him neither fire nor water"[77]—leaks into other senses of the word: "deceitful"; "acute beyond exactness." Johnson's eye for the radical implications of metaphor distinguishes him from other lexicographers. The *OED* delivers a vast, impersonal, chronological repository of words, but the *Dictionary* handles each word—or at least a great many—with attention to the good it might do in the world. This writer does not forget "that *words are the daughters of earth, and that things are the sons of heaven*" (par. 17), yet he hopes to join them as God would join matter and spirit. The presence of a guiding hand reveals the figure cloaked beneath the letters. Johnson makes words his own, and comes out an author.

Yet he also was making his nation. If lexicography gave Johnson the means to bring himself before the public and write his name into history, it appealed still more to his ideal of service. England itself was in need. The *Dictionary* fulfills a contract not only with booksellers but also tacitly with the people of Britain, so long deprived of the reputation that their language and learning deserve. Johnson appoints himself the champion of national glory. At the climax of the Preface, he proudly raises two banners together: first person singular and first person plural.

130

I have devoted this book, the labour of years, to the honour of my country, that we may no longer yield the palm of philology without a contest to the nations of the continent. The chief glory of every people arises from its authours: whether I shall add any thing by my own writings to the reputation of *English* literature, must be left to time ... but I shall not think my employment useless or ignoble, if by my assistance foreign nations, and distant ages, gain access to the propagators of knowledge, and understand the teachers of truth; if my labours afford light to the repositories of science, and add celebrity to *Bacon,* to *Hooker,* to *Milton,* and to *Boyle.*   (Par. 92)

Here self-aggrandizement and self-effacement perfectly suit each other. The writer enters no claim—at present—of authorship, but identifies himself with the national interest. Johnson's whole career as hack had prepared him for this moment. The quiet sense of heroism that he had harbored so long behind the anonymous mask of a grubstreet Odysseus, the scholarly gifts he had spent without recognition, come out of the shadows and put forward a new model of what a writer might be: a national man of letters. From one point of view, of course, he is waving the flag. Yet Johnson does not rely on the patriotic claptrap that had been so popular in his youth.[78] Instead he provides a way of reading the *Dictionary* that redefines what the English people ought to take pride in: their language; their authors. The man of letters wraps himself in the knowledge and truth that belong to his book and his country, and he does not distinguish their glory from his own. Hence what he is as an author depends on how well he has represented the nation. No writer can monopolize *A Dictionary of the English Language.* He holds it in trust; and what he may claim is measured by what he has given.

If Johnson thought of the *Dictionary* as one with the nation, however, whom did he imagine that nation to be? One answer is stated quite forthrightly in the preface he supplied for the abridged edition of 1756. "Having been long employed in the study and cultivation of the English language, I lately published a Dictionary like those compiled by the academies of Italy and France, for the use of such as aspire to exactness of criticism, or elegance of style." The greater number of readers, he concedes, "seldom intending to write or presuming to judge," have little need for such a book; all they want is some help with spelling and hard words, which the abridgement will give them.[79] Yet this concession to "common readers" also reveals the uncommon audience at which Johnson first aimed: a readership of writers and critics. Clearly, such readers compose no more than an educated minority of English speakers. Nevertheless, for Johnson they represent the essential spirit of Great Britain, the heritage that distinguishes her from other nations. The unabridged *Dictionary,* with its wealth of quotations from the best English writers, responds to the needs of writers and critics and at the same time endeavors to swell their numbers by teaching them a more exact and elegant language.[80] Eighty years later, when Robert Browning decided on literature as his profession, "he qualified himself for it by reading and digesting the whole of Johnson's Dictionary."[81] In this respect he was just the reader whom Johnson had in mind, a reader who would absorb what his nation stood for and add to its glory.

Furthermore, Johnson had poets in mind. The epigraph to the *Dictionary* illustrates this program: on the title page, nine lines of untranslated Latin poetry introduce English readers to the sort of tutor they can expect. Inscribing himself in the words of a classic, the lexicographer explains and justifies his mission.

> Cum tabulis animum censoris sumet honesti:
> Audebit quaecunque parum splendoris habebunt,
> Et sine pondere erunt, et honore indigna ferentur.
> Verba movere loco; quamvis invita recedant,
> Et versentur adhuc intra penetralia Vestae:
> Obscurata diu populo bonus eruet, atque
> Proferet in lucem speciosa vocabula rerum,
> Quae priscis memorata Catonibus atque Cethegis,
> Nunc situs informis premit et deserta vetustas.[82]

> (With his tablets he will take the spirit of an honest censor:
> He will dare, if they have too little distinction,
> Or shall be without weight, or be held unworthy of esteem,
> To remove words from their place; though they retire
>   unwillingly,

And linger still within Vesta's sanctuary:
Those long lost to people's sight the good man will unearth, and
Bring to light splendid terms for things,
Which though uttered in olden times by Cato and Cethegus,
Are now pressed down by formless decay and desolate old age.)

The lines from Horace are brilliantly chosen. Johnson portrays himself in classical terms as the ultimate judge and policeman of words, stringent but reverent too. The passage reeks of authority, and promises the learned—those who can understand the Latin—the linguistic tyrant they had called on to set the limits of proper English. At the same time it is masterfully cropped. Had it not been cut, the line that precedes the quotation would have clarified that poetry, not lexicography, is the subject: "at qui legitimum cupiet fecisse poema" (but he who wishes to make a legitimate poem). Horace describes tasteful poetic diction, not diction in general, and the "good man" *(bonus)* actually refers to the good poet. Thus Johnson steals the rod of a poet and critic, as if the finesse of an artist—and the decrees of a Roman censor—could furnish norms of correctness for any writer. Surreptitiously, this dictionary is designed for poets. Nor does the cropping end there. At the end of the passage, Horace adds one line: "Adsciscet nova, quae genitor produxerit usus" (He will adopt new ones, which father Usage has brought forth). The poet opens his verse to newborn terms, to whatever he wants and needs. But Johnson draws the line. More classic than the classics, this lexicographer will close the book to unauthorized, modish words. Latitude, even when Horace's, has to be censored.

The two missing lines reveal what Johnson thought he owed his public. A dictionary that served the nation well would have to accept two obligations. The first was to preserve an elegant written language. Whether voluntarily or not, speakers of English would now be held to the standard of poets and critics. The *Dictionary* anticipates Mallarmé's rule for a Poe or poet: it tries to give a purer sense to the words of the tribe.[83] Second, it strives to protect the language from change. *Usus,* the word that Horace had employed to justify a newer, richer Latin diction, properly means "need" as well as "use"; language adapts to the needs of each generation, with usage as guide. Johnson resists that logic. The public had asked him to settle issues of language, not merely report them, and stability, not flexibility, was what the nation needed. Hence the *Dictionary* wages a rearguard action, by modern standards, against the encroachments of usage.

It could hardly have done anything else. Without a demand for linguistic authority, Johnson would not have been hired, and he knew what his readers wanted. For instance, they urgently wanted standardized spelling. When Johnson wrote that anomalies of language "must be tolerated among the imperfections of human things . . . but every language has likewise its improprieties and absurdities, which it is the duty of the lexicographer to correct or proscribe" (par. 6), he spoke for public opinion. Even today, few linguists would argue against the advantages of a fixed orthography, a protocol that allows words to be looked up in a dictionary.[84] Accepting the lexicographer's fiat is so convenient that it goes without saying. Johnson's audience felt the same way about usage. For most of his readers, a dictionary could never be too prescriptive. "Those who have been persuaded to think well of my design, require that it should fix our language, and put a stop to those alterations which time and chance have hitherto been suffered to make in it without opposition" (par. 84). Johnson knew that this requirement was unrealistic. Yet he would have to indulge it as best he could.

The desire for a purer language was rooted in language itself. When eighteenth-century writers discuss the causes of linguistic change, the word they use most often is "corruption." Other favorites include "barbarous" and "cant" (which Johnson defines as "1. A corrupt dialect used by beggars and vagabonds. 2. A particular form of speaking peculiar to some certain class or body of men. 3. A whining pretension to goodness, in formal and affected terms. 4. Barbarous jargon"). "Refinement" and "polite" describe more positive developments, though often with a hint of irony; "Improvement in elegance or purity" points out one sense of "refinement," but "Affectation of elegant improvement" points out another. The words *not* available to Johnson may be still more significant. "Slang" appears in the *Dictionary* only as "The preterite of *sling.*" "Unconventional" and "colloquial" are also absent, though in the Preface Johnson had referred to "colloquial licentiousness." The illustrative quotation for "idiomatick" (whose final *k* Johnson's authority failed to establish) dooms its acceptance: "Since phrases used in conversation contract meanness by passing through the mouths of the vulgar, a poet should guard himself against *idiomatick* ways of speaking" *(Spectator)*. Nor is "usage" permitted to govern the current state of English. Johnson defines it as "custom; practice long continued," and illustrates it with Hooker's "long *usage* is a law sufficient," where "long" counts as much as the noun it modifies. *Recent* usage would be no law at all. Hence the *Dictionary* lacks any terms that might describe linguistic changes or regional variations without prejudging them.[85] Quite literally, such words are not in its vocabulary.

This poverty of terms affects Johnson's view of the language his nation needs. A model of purity achieved and then corrupted recurs throughout the book. Two of the three examples of "corruption," in the sense of "the means by which any thing is vitiated; depravation," refer to language. English seems hopelessly fallen, like man, his history, and all his works. To be sure, such terminology oversimplifies Johnson's own historical understanding. He quotes few authorities on English so often or densely as Swift's *Proposal for Correcting, Improving and Ascertaining the English Tongue* (1712), for instance, but belittles the pamphlet for its rigid sense of history and language. Swift had proposed an academy to ensure that no good English word would ever be "antiquated and exploded," a notion that Johnson considers absurd: "what makes a word obsolete, more than general agreement to forbear it? and how shall it be continued . . . when it has once by disuse become unfamiliar, and by unfamiliarity unpleasing?" (par. 88). Academies would only provoke the disobedience they meant to forestall. Johnson ridicules Swift's amateurish linguistic zeal for "the certainty and stability which, contrary to all experience, he thinks attainable."[86] No lexicographer would be so naive.

In one important respect, however, Johnson and Swift agree. Both think of the English language, in its least corrupt state, as essentially a product of writing. When Swift proposes to correct the English *tongue,* he commissions writing to hold speech in check. The tongue and its works are suspect—out of control.[87] Though more tolerant of speech, Johnson too puts his faith in the written word. The *Dictionary* announces this bent at the start. "When I took the first survey of my undertaking, I found our speech copious without order, and energetick without rules: wherever I turned my view, there was perplexity to be disentangled, and confusion to be regulated." Worse yet, this wanton speech had to be tamed "without the suffrages of any writers of classical reputation or acknowledged authority" (par. 4). But the problems that had proliferated through a language "merely oral" could be solved through attention to fixed and visible signs. "Having therefore no assistance but from general grammar, I applied myself to the perusal of our writers; and noting whatever might be of use to ascertain or illustrate any word or phrase, accumulated in time the materials of a dictionary, which, by degrees, I reduced to method" (par. 5). Writing alone could stabilize the vagaries of speech. This principle applies most obviously to spelling, which reduces to homogeneity the "wild and barbarous jargon" of innumerable dialects and accents. Yet it also bears on language as a whole. The *Dictionary* puts English into the custody of writers, and grants them power not only over the written word but over speech.

Writers had long campaigned for such a privilege. From the time of Dryden, the impermanence of English, its rapid and restless mutations, had been deplored as a national scandal. The archaism that had already overtaken Chaucer and had begun to threaten Shakespeare would soon overwhelm all authors.[88] Self-interest clearly motivates Swift's *Proposal.* How can any author work "with Spirit and Chearfulness," he asks, "when he considers, that he will be read with Pleasure but a very few Years, and in an Age or two shall hardly be understood without an Interpreter?" A deep distrust of fashions and "false Refinements" of style impels him to recommend a radical simplicity, a language so plain and well preserved that it might last as long as Greek or Latin. Swift appoints himself an Ancient. In defending simplicity, moreover, he also associates his style with that of the King James Bible and Book of Common Prayer, works that "have proved a Kind of Standard for Language, especially to the common People."[89] Their style should endure for all time. As *A Tale of a Tub* had satirized the fashionable mutilation and catachresis of "the Father's Will" (or New Testament), so the *Proposal* derides the misbegotten English hatched

136

by "illiterate Court-Fops, half-witted Poets, and University-Boys." Language must be saved from these infidels for the sake of Scripture as well as the fate of the writer. Swift could not take the issue more personally.[90] This was the only publication to which he ever put his name.

Permanence matters greatly to Johnson as well. Like Swift, he considers writers the guardians of ancient wisdom and religion against the whirligig of fads in thought and speech. Moreover, like Swift he regards linguistic change as culpably Whiggish, the consequence of freethinking and courtly affectations. Class hostility also plays its part. When Chesterfield teasingly proposed a "genteel Neological" appendix, to contain "the fashionable words of the most fashionable people"—"flirtation," "to fuzz," and "vastly"—the joke did not strike Johnson as funny. He admitted none of Chesterfield's neologisms nor, for that matter, "neological" itself.[91] Such terms, as both men understood, functioned as passwords or code, designed to distinguish those in the know from those whose learning came only from books or, as Chesterfield explained, "polite" from "pedantic" language. Johnson was assigned the pedantic, "provided it can be quietly brought about"—without interrupting genteel conversation. He accepted the charge with a vengeance. The *Dictionary* bans every word that cannot be found in a book, and it snubs the *beau monde.* Instead it guides its readers to well-aged English, a language not to be picked up in the drawing room or the street.

Yet Johnson's view of language is also progressive. It aims at a wide diffusion of learning, or a nation that every reader can join by mastering the book of words on which all great English writers have collaborated. Politically, this inclusiveness is decisive.[92] In an interesting discussion of Johnson's effort to establish "custom as the law of language," John Barrell has stressed the political ideal implicit in the *Dictionary:* a nation in which "the increasingly differentiated society of Britain" might still be imagined as unified. Much of this argument rings true. But Barrell badly misrepresents Johnson as someone who believes that the *polite* are "guardians" of custom. "The stability of the language of the *polite,* and the stability of their constitution, are alike threatened by the mutability of the people, who properly considered, have no interest in either matter. They are no part of the true language community, which is now a closed circle of the polite whose language is now presented as durable and permanent."[93] Such deference to the polite seems foreign to Johnson (who tends to think of "politeness" as suspiciously French). Two weeks after Chesterfield patronized the *Dictionary* in *The World,* Horace Walpole advanced the startling thesis that "we are the most polite nation in Europe; and that France must yield to us in the extreme delicacy of our refinements." His explanation was calculated to horrify Johnson. "It is not virtue that constitutes the politeness of a nation, but the art of reducing vice to a system that does not shock society. POLITENESS (as I understand the word) *is an universal desire of pleasing others (that are not too much below one) in trifles, for a little time; and of making one's intercourse with them agreeable to both parties, by civility without ceremony, by ease without brutality, by complaisance without flattery, by acquiescence without sincerity."*[94] In Walpole's national ideal, facetiousness confederates with fashionable vice. That nation could never be Johnson's.

By contrast, his native language is built on a bedrock of candor. The "Preface to Shakespeare" insists that "a stile which never becomes obsolete" is "to be sought in the common intercourse of life, among those who speak only to be understood," while "the polite are always catching modish innovations."[95] The *Dictionary* avoids any mention of *the* polite (in the sense of a class of people), and its definition of "polite" leans on the scientific meaning, "Glossy; smooth," as in the polite surface of glass—not a quality that appeals much to Johnson. Nor do polished manners like Chesterfield's or Walpole's imply any durable language. On the contrary, "no such constancy can be expected in a people polished by arts" (par. 87), with leisure to think and speculate. Whatever "the true language community" may be, for Johnson, it is certainly not the polite.

The issue is more than verbal. It involves Johnson's sense of history as well as politics, and his vision of both the past and the future of Britain. For the unity of the nation had been threatened before. The very period that grounds the word-list of the *Dictionary,* its golden age of English, had witnessed a civil war in which language and language communities had been trampled like so many battle-

138

fields. "It is scarcely possible, in the regularity and composure of the present time, to image the tumult of absurdity and clamour of contradiction which perplexed doctrine, disordered practice, and disturbed both publick and private quiet in that age, when subordination was broken and awe was hissed away."[96] In mid-seventeenth-century Britain, any accent or prose style could stir up instant hatred.[97] Puritans and royalists, and many sects beside, despised each other's ways of talking and writing, and no vocabulary was neutral; even quoting the Book of Common Prayer could be fatal, in the wrong surroundings.[98] Hence Johnson's decision to model English diction on seventeenth-century usage implies a compromise between warring parties, if not a restoration. The *Dictionary* forces a truce in which *Eikon Basilike* and *Paradise Lost* must lie down together. To be sure, not all texts are equally welcome; there is no place for the "atheist" Hobbes at the table.[99] Yet Johnson largely ignores the old battles over the fate of the nation. Good English, the diction of the best writers, supplies the *Dictionary* with a standard behind which every citizen can rally, a genuine good old cause. The language that once divided the country will now become the instrument of its healing.[100]

At the same time, however, Johnson's embrace of the past does tend to slight the present state of the nation and its language. For a reader who looks for signs of the times, the *Dictionary* can seem purposely frustrating. It will not acknowledge neologisms like Chesterfield's, we have seen, nor the class assumptions that breed them. Worse yet, it refuses to touch almost all the terms on which modern historians of ideas prefer to focus, the terms whose shifting meanings characterize the age and provide the major evidence for Lovejoy's *unit-ideas,* Foucault's *epistemes,* or Raymond Williams' *keywords*—terms such as "culture," "literature," "class," and "sentimental." The last of these does not appear at all, despite the currency that led Lady Bradshaigh in 1749 to ask Richardson (whom Johnson considered the expert on *sentiments*), "what, in your opinion, is the meaning of the word *sentimental,* so much in vogue among the polite?"[101] The *Dictionary* would not answer her question. Nor would it satisfy later students of linguistic fashions. At a time when all received ideas began to come under siege, when (according to many scholars) human nature itself was changing, Johnson records a language already passé and sustains the before in spite of the after.

This preference for old terms over new was anything but accidental. When Johnson undertook a major revision of the *Dictionary* for its fourth edition (1773), he managed to make it *more* backward-looking. Few new words were added, and the large supplement of illustrative quotations tended to reinforce the Established Church and its authority, both political and theological.[102] To lend weight to this conservative polemic, Johnson rummaged forgotten seventeenth-century divines, especially nonjurors who had defended the Stuarts. Even in poetry the didactic strain increased, and older poets were preferred to new—more Cowley, less Thomson.[103] The fourth edition is retrograde in many respects. It mounts a defense of orthodoxy in thought, not only in language, and responds to innovation with disregard or active defiance. Not all these attitudes should be read back into the first edition. Johnson's world had changed by the 1770s—not least, he was himself a pensioner—and the duty he once had felt toward the national language had hardened into outrage at those who defined the nation differently. Yet the two editions do have much in common. In each the English language reminds its congregation of what they have been, not of how much they have altered.

Nevertheless, the *Dictionary* leaves room for growth. The writers and critics at whom it aims are given a language whose possibilities remain to be explored. This point emerges clearly from comparisons with Swift, whose ideal reader would require no dictionary at all. "The peruser of Swift wants little previous knowledge; it will be sufficient that he is acquainted with common words and common things." Such plain style has its virtues, as Johnson concedes, but it is not suited to "nice disquisitions" or "far-sought learning."[104] The *Dictionary* offers a more ambitious vocabulary, a language prepared for ornament, philosophy, and persuasion. The reader or writer who uses it will find a treasure-house of metaphor, adaptable to whatever new worlds of thought the future may bring. Such readers and writers will be many, Johnson implies. Instead of the ancients imagined by Swift, a few skilled authors fiercely committed to holding the line of the past against an invasion of pagans and barbarians, Johnson imagines a large middle class of students, a nation in which learning builds on learning. This audience deserves uncommon instruction. Accumulating knowledge from every sphere—moral, scientific, and practical—it will continually convert writing into more writing and spread literacy abroad. Potentially a dictionary is the most democratic of institutions, a public place where low and high words mingle. Johnson gives his readers the means to write an accurate and classless English.

From this point of view, the crucial word not to be found in the *Dictionary* may well be "literary." This seems a remarkable omission. Johnson's first letter to Edward Cave, in 1734, had offered "short literary Dissertations" to improve "your Literary Article, for so it might be call'd," and otherwise to aid his "Literary projects."[105] Chambers had edited the *Literary Magazine* in 1735 and had written at length on "*Literary* CRITICISM," which discerns "the real works of an author, the real author of a work, the genuine reading of a text," and so on.[106] Johnson helped found a new *Literary Magazine,* which began publishing in 1756; he later belonged to the famous Literary Club; and the word appears regularly in his conversation and writing (though he did not add it to the *Dictionary* in 1773). One of the books he cites most often, *Pseudodoxia Epidemica,* had used "literary" as early as 1646, and many others had used it since. The meaning of the word was still in flux. Originally it referred strictly to "letters"—either the alphabet or epistles. Yet Johnson's own use of the word in his letter to Cave seems to stretch the meaning; evidently he wants to specify writing that displays some learning or formal distinction, not mere information. The "Literary Article" would continue to grow. Thus the *Literary Magazine, or Universal Review,* whose preliminary address "To the Public" was written by Johnson, explicitly promises to examine "all the productions of Science" or any writing worthy of attention.[107] It seems that all the books that Johnson cares about are classified as "literary."

How then can he have forgotten the word in 1755? Aside from a slip of the hand or mind, perhaps its absence marks the insignificance of another distinction, that between demotic and literary language. For Johnson, literary English represents English itself, the store of words available to anyone who has properly learned to read and write. To some extent, therefore, the particular word is redundant; a dictionary consists of literary language and nothing else. Just as the spoken language, as Johnson conceives it, defers to the written, or departs from it only as a symptom of corruption, so *non*literary language (if there could be such a thing) would represent an adulteration of meaning—the fall of learning, the death of the word.

A similar implication might be read into the absence of "literate." Here Johnson surely did blunder, for he includes "illiterate" and defines "lettered" as "Literate; educated to learning." To repair the fault, one might construct a definition by crossing out "illiterate" prefixes: "xxlettered; xxtaught; xxlearned; xxenlightened by science." Literacy, for Johnson, implies not merely the ability to read and write but also acquaintance with learning in general. It therefore admits of degrees; a well-read person is by definition more literate, or less illiterate, than an ignoramus ("a vain uninstructed pretender"). In fact, the most dangerous abusers of language, according to the Preface, are precisely those who read and write without learning: "illiterate writers will at one time or other, by publick infatuation, rise into renown, who, not knowing the original import of words, will use them with colloquial licentiousness, confound distinction, and forget propriety" (par. 88). Such illiterates write as they talk. The *Dictionary* aims at another standard, by teaching the public to use words with the care and fidelity of the best English authors. Johnson had trained himself to talk as he wrote, with scrupulous attention to what he was saying, and he hoped to raise up a literate nation.

Above all he wants to further the cause of English literature—that is, to "add celebrity to *Bacon,* to *Hooker,* to *Milton,* and to *Boyle.*"[108] Great writers preserve the honor of Britain. As the examples indicate, "literature" did not yet distinguish the art of writing from scholarly writing. The *Dictionary* defines it simply as "Learning; skill in letters." In 1778, when Johnson told William Seward, "Were I to make a new edition of my *Dictionary,* I would adopt several of Mr. Horne's [Horne Tooke's] etymologies," he added, "I hope they did not put the dog in the pillory for his libel; he has too much literature for that."[109] Clearly, literature, in the sense of wide reading, is exactly what a lexicographer needs, and Johnson is fond of people who have it. But *skill* in letters implies something more. The two illustrative quotations in the *Dictionary* suggest that learning alone will not make literature. "This kingdom hath been famous for good *literature;* and if preferment attend deservers, there will not want supplies," according to Bacon, stressing the public service performed by writers. And Addison shows the gradation from learning to true skill in letters: "When men of learning are acted by a knowledge of the world, they give a reputation to *literature,* and convince the world of its usefulness." Evidently one cannot have literature without men of letters, those who adapt their learning to do some good by promoting the stock of the nation. Bacon and Addison spoke for a cause that Johnson struggled to follow.[110] They called on him to put his talents to use, to be more than a scholar and more than a hack—in short, to become an author.

The first writer to use "literature" in its modern sense of "the activity or profession of a man of letters," according to the *OED*, was Johnson himself.[111] Appropriately, the innovation occurs in the first sentence of the first of the *Lives of the Poets,* which praises Thomas Sprat as "an author whose pregnancy of imagination and elegance of language have deservedly set him high in the ranks of literature."[112] The final word closes the cadence on a note of accomplishment that goes beyond learning and opens the way to imagination and style—a distinction that, during the next century, would come to separate literature from other sorts of writing. But Johnson had sounded the same high note before. In the most ambitious sentence of the Preface to the *Dictionary,* which had asserted that "The chief glory of every people arises from its authours" and had aspired to add "to the reputation of *English* literature," the later sense of literature as "writing regarded as having permanent worth" already begins to flourish. Johnson puts tremendous weight on the word. It does not mean mere belles lettres (defined by the *Dictionary* as "polite literature"), for the adjective limits the noun to a consequence of good manners or polished surfaces, rather than intelligence or depth; and even the fact that the French term has no English equivalent suggests that it remains a foreign import, suited to a people who excel at the arts of pleasing but not to the best that a proud free people can do. Johnson expects more from literature: not only learning and polish but glory.

Only the context of the nation, however, allows the man of letters to come into his own. If fame is the spur, it properly belongs to the honor of the country, not to any one writer. Learning passes through many hands, like a dictionary, and when Johnson identified literature and letters with learning, he never forgot the collaborative process integral to any work that contributes to the store of knowledge. The difference between a hack and an author was not, in the long run, so great. It consisted of one main point: the hack serves anyone who hires him, the author serves his people as a whole. Henceforth a part of Johnson's soul would always belong to the public. Much of his subsequent work—the edition of Shakespeare, the surveys of politics and the law, the *Lives of the English Poets*—builds on his character as the national man of letters. In defining himself as an author, he would also define the reputation of English literature until eventually, in the eyes of many readers, the two would seem the same. Johnson's first person had grown; more than a laureate, the lexicographer now stood for the pride of his nation. He was, after all, despite his disclaimers, an author, "the first beginner or mover of any thing; he to whom any thing owes its original," and what he had invented was a new sense of the author as a representative of his people. He would have to live with that burden the rest of his life.

6

The Living World:
The Rambler

> The task of our present writers is very different; it
> requires, together with that learning which is to be
> gained from books, that experience which can never
> be attained by solitary diligence, but must arise
> from general converse, and accurate observation of
> the living world.

HE WRITER WHO finished the *Dictionary* was not the writer who
had started it. If the contract for the work, in 1746, marks the
end of Johnson's apprenticeship, its publication in 1755 confirms that he is a master—officially "A.M." on the title page. Johnson
had grown into a man of letters; his signature counted for something,
and even a lord would have reason to fear the needle of his first person
singular. Part of the change had been brought about by the pressure
of the *Dictionary* itself. A work of such size demanded a writer who was
able to be not only a scholar and businessman but also a public figure,
and Johnson obliged by becoming a giant of industry as well as a national hero. Yet the change also depended on Johnson's new sense of
himself as an author. During his years of trial by lexicography he had
produced some writing that pleased his harshest audience, himself:
"The Vision of Theodore," *The Vanity of Human Wishes,* and scraps at
least of *Irene*. But above all he had defined himself as an author through
a work that represented not only what he could do but also who he
could be. In *The Rambler* the essential Johnson came of age, and those
who look for him still find him there.

145

It began, like virtually all his work, as an occasion to make some money. We do not know whether the idea for a series of periodical essays came first from Johnson or from someone else, perhaps the bookseller John Payne.[1] In any case it required no long-term commitment. Each Tuesday and Saturday, from March 20, 1750, a single essay would appear, for which the writer would receive two guineas. Some small forethought might be needed to supply an advance copy of the Latin or Greek motto that served as an advertisement for each essay as well as a preview of its theme. Otherwise Johnson wrote to the moment, one piece at a time. Each Monday and Friday night, according to contemporary reports, he would finish his draft while the printer's boy waited.[2] Another writer might have found this harrowing; for Johnson it seems to have been a comfortable, if mildly anxious, routine. Nor does he seem to have worried much about building an audience. The sales of *The Rambler* were modest, but its author takes some pride in not soliciting popularity. Instead he writes for himself and posterity, or for his "future life"[3] (in context this refers to hopes of salvation, but Johnson lived to see the collected *Rambler* prosper through ten editions). It suits him not to be a favorite of the public. Begun without fanfare, the series ended abruptly, after two full years or 208 essays, with little warning except, in the penultimate number, one general observation: "He that is himself weary will soon weary the public" (*Works* 5: 315). Mr. Rambler will not stoop to asking his readers to ask him to continue; enough is enough. Even his pen name suggests a readiness to move on to something else.

Yet the seeming casualness of the form does not mean that the author took his work lightly. Each essay might be "A loose sally of the mind; an irregular indigested piece; not a regular and orderly composition," according to the *Dictionary;* but both illustrations of this definition point to larger possibilities: "My *essays,* of all my other works, have been most current" (Bacon), and "Yet modestly he does his work survey,/And calls his finish'd poem an *essay*" (Dryden).[4] Modesty does not preclude ambition. Johnson regards Roscommon's *Essay on Translated Verse* as "his great work," and *Rambler* 106 remarks that Bacon expected his essays, "which come home to mens business and bosoms," to "live as long as books last."[5] Indeed,

146

the very ease of these "petty compositions" (5: 201) may serve to ingratiate them with readers, who need to pause only a moment for timeless wisdom. Such moments have the potential to change a life. Nor does the author's brief investment of time imply that what he says does not matter to him. The opposite might be true. Johnson's ability to write his essays at the very last minute might argue that, far from spontaneous and improvised, they flowed from a brimming, ready store of mind.[6] Perhaps he had been waiting his whole life to write them.

For the first time in his career, in fact, he was free to write what he chose. The duty of a hack, hired to satisfy someone else's commission, or of a translator, the servant of someone else's text, or of a would-be playwright, having to please a fickle crowd or the manager of the theater, could now be put aside. So could the drudgery of servicing the alphabet—at least for two nights a week. Those nights belonged to him. Hawkins, who was particularly well acquainted with Johnson during this period, stresses the voluntary nature of *The Rambler,* a "relief from the fatigue" of dictionary-making. "The truth is, that not having now for a considerable space committed to writing aught but words and their significations, his mind was become tumid, and laboured to be delivered of those many and great conceptions, which for years it had been forming. The study of human life and manners, had been the chief employment of his thoughts, and to a knowledge of these, all his reading, all his conversation, and all his meditations tended."[7] At this crucial moment, "teeming with new ideas" he found the outlet he needed. The metaphor of birth seems too extravagant. None of Johnson's biographers is more uneasy than Hawkins with the financial aspect of writing, as if payment might taint an author with the wages of trade, and no biographer is more hopeful that his author's motives might have been love and virtue rather than money. Yet whatever motives inspired the work, an air of independence does characterize *The Rambler.* Even Johnson's indifference to courting the public helps make him his own man, the lord of the essay. If one did not know better, at times one might think that this essayist actually enjoys the process of writing.

To enter *The Rambler* is thus to enter Johnson's world—not only the social world of eighteenth-century London but also the mental world inhabited by one of its strongest-minded citizens. Here the proprietor seems almost jealous of his ownership. Despite his awareness that the periodical writer "who endeavours to gain many readers, must try various arts of invitation, essay every avenue of pleasure, and make frequent changes in his methods of approach" (3: 129), Johnson seldom varies his style, even when impersonating a correspondent. The frivolous Euphelia, who cannot manage to read through an essay by Mr. Rambler, nonetheless adopts his tone when she complains to him: "I had not in myself any fund of satisfaction with which I could supply the loss of my customary amusements" (3: 230). Nor was the Rambler willing to share his chore with other contributors. Of the 208 essays, only 4 (as well as parts of 3 others) can be assigned to someone other than Johnson, and he seems to have received no help at all during the second year. This Addison would make his way without a Steele; readers who asked for more variety or sent their own submissions were ignored or quietly discouraged. The integrity of *The Rambler* depends on remaining true to what it knows best: "an author has a rule of choice peculiar to himself; and selects those subjects which he is best qualified to treat, by the course of his studies, or the accidents of his life" (3: 129). Its sphere will be the world according to Johnson.

Hence the series is internally consistent. Although, by his own account, the Rambler writes four different sorts of paper—in ascending order of importance, "excursions of fancy," "disquisitions of criticism," "pictures of life," and "essays professedly serious" (5: 319–320)—all feed into the same recurring moral preoccupations. The stories reported by imaginary correspondents (pictures of life) could readily turn into allegorical fables (excursions of fancy), with the addition of a few capital letters for Vanity and Providence, and so could many of the critical essays (*Rambler* 3 presents an allegory of Criticism as the daughter of Labour and Truth). Johnson does not mind repeating himself. The consistency of the essays comes especially into focus on those few occasions when another writer takes over. In No. 30, Catherine Talbot's ingenious riddle on "Sunday" ("My elder brother was a Jew" is one of the clues) has nothing in common with Mr. Rambler's manner; and Samuel Richardson's offering, No. 97, which outsold all others, is palpably a throwback to *The Spectator* and its fashions.[8] No reader would or did mistake them for Johnson's. However broad his range, however playful his sallies, he does not stray far from his "principal design to inculcate wisdom or piety" (5: 319), nor will he leave the moral world in which he feels at home.

Indeed, the self-enclosure of the Rambler's world becomes a sort of unifying thread if not a running joke. Many "correspondents" object to his stern philosophy and offer to put him in touch with real life as they know it. Nor can the author resist self-parody. The more that readers protest hard words, the more he relies on adscititious diction.[9] Even the persona invented for the work has a comical aspect, since—insofar as Mr. Rambler does describe himself—the adventurous wanderer one might expect gives way to a sedentary old philosopher. Johnson both admits and makes fun of his own somber cast of thought.

At one point he uses it for an especially clever finesse on his reputation. In the famous No. 59 on Suspirius the screech-owl, Mr. Rambler deplores that "species of beings in human form" who are "born for no other purpose than to disturb the happiness of others" with complaints and woeful predictions. This writer, unlike the screech-owl, claims to be free from all superstitions but one: a greeting by Suspirius will guarantee an unhappy day. "I have now known Suspirius fifty-eight years and four months, and have never yet passed an hour with him in which he has not made some attack upon my quiet" (3: 315). Clearly, Johnson (forty-one at the time) has put on the mask of a much older man. But why should he be so specific about the date when the Rambler met the screech-owl? The reason, I think, must be that *The Rambler* itself, one-third into its fifty-ninth number, has reached an age, fifty-eight issues and four paragraphs, exactly equivalent to its acquaintance with Suspirius (each essay corresponding to a year). It seems unlikely that this perfect match can be a coincidence. Rather, Johnson is playing with the Rambler's own affinity for "mournful meditations," as if each new number measured out a certain quota of squawks. The charge of gloominess may be unfair—the essayist specifically *denies* that he is a screech-owl—but even the author has to concede that he is no stranger to the prophet of doom; "neglect of merit," for instance, is a favorite topic of both. The moralist associates with the killjoy. Johnson's distinction between them reinforces his own resolve to offer better hopes. Yet he also knows the value of preying on his readers' minds, like an uneasy conscience, during the hours they pass with their guide. The spirit of Suspirius sighs through the essays and darkens their world.

At the same time, however, the world of *The Rambler* obeys the dictates of its author, who fashions it according to his taste and his experience of life. Few literary forms allow so many options. In the eighteenth century, before the novel achieved its later popularity, many readers looked to periodical essays for pictures of what Johnson called "the living world," or "life in its true state, diversified only by accidents that daily happen in the world, and influenced by passions and qualities which are really to be found in conversing with mankind" (3: 19). *Rambler* 4, where these words appear, offers a tribute to the power of the new fiction to capture that sense of life, as well as a warning against the abuse of that power by novelists who promiscuously mingle virtue with vice. This essay has always been viewed as a recommendation of Richardson over Fielding and Smollett.[10] It might also serve as a defense of the periodical essay itself, whose leading practitioner, Addison, "as a describer of life and manners . . . must be allowed to stand perhaps the first of the first rank," and who yielded to none as "a teacher of wisdom."[11] *The Spectator*—if not *The Rambler*—rewards its readers with many of the pleasures of fiction: accurate observation of the world, an easy style, human interest, moral improvement, and above all that variety in which all pleasure consists.[12] In many respects, moreover, a series of essays has advantages over a novel. It need not involve its characters in long plots, or apologize for digressions, or concentrate on only one part of the world, or avoid direct instruction, or camouflage its truth in invented finery. Instead it takes the whole world for its province. Its only disadvantage is a lack of sustained suspense; its only constraint is an obligation to turn out fresh copy two days a week. Sooner or later, whatever the author sees and feels can find room in an essay.

Hence *The Rambler* draws on all of Johnson's resources. The Latin and Greek tags display his familiarity with the classics, and frequent errors in these quotations prove not only that he was quoting from memory but also that, in his internal commonplace book, he had made them part of his own way of thinking. His choice of words, as many scholars have noted, reflects his long immersion in the *Dictionary;* no earlier essayist had used such philosophic language or had been so attentive to fine distinctions of meaning. The cadences of his prose express his devotion to seventeenth-century divines and the English heroic couplet.[13] Nor is his mental world composed of writing alone. Though the scenes from high society in *The Rambler* seem to owe more to traditions of satire than to personal knowledge, the accounts of provincial boredom and insolvency in London can strike too near his own estate for comfort. One specialty of the "pictures of life" is some correspondent's sad tale of a fall from early prosperity to hardship or the Fleet, and clearly Johnson knows what he is talking about.

Yet the bulk of the essays inhabit a different space, amidst the furniture of his mind. Like every imaginative writer, Johnson employs a stock of recurrent patterns and images—the circus animals, in Yeats's phrase, that he puts through their paces. The Rambler's inventory includes the journey through life, phantoms in the mist, the choice between incompatible desires or designs, the painful awakening from a dream, and always and everywhere an underlying pit of emptiness. A similar list had occurred a few years before, in the opening paragraph of *The Vanity of Human Wishes,* where the picture of a rambling "wav'ring Man" anticipates the Rambler himself. These well-worn images suggest a mind too passive to escape from reveries, like Thomson's ironic self-portrait in *The Castle of Indolence* (1748). But Johnson's repertoire does not exhaust his resources. Instead it is where he begins, or the means through which he thinks. In just the same way, the moral vocabulary that readers sometimes mistake, at a glance, for platitudinous, eventually proves, to those who read on, the vehicle of a remarkably agile intelligence.[14] Johnson's turns of thought follow a settled track of images and principles, yet they are far from predictable. *The Rambler* arranges its furniture in surprising new combinations.

Nevertheless, the control that the essayist enjoys in his own small world can tempt him, like the astronomer in *Rasselas,* to use himself as the measure of all things. Even when he feels doubtful, he himself writes the letters that question him. *Rambler* 193, an amusing analysis of the universal hunger for praise, carries this autarchy to its logical conclusion: periodical writers can always manufacture their own panegyrics.

> When we think our excellencies overlooked by the world, or desire to recall the attention of the publick to some particular performance, we sit down with great composure and write a letter to ourselves. The correspondent, whose character we assume, always addresses us with the deference due to a superior intelligence; proposes his doubts with a proper sense of his own inability; offers an objection with trembling diffidence; and at last has no other pretensions to our notice than his profundity of respect, and sincerity of admiration, his submission to our dictates, and zeal for our success.   (5: 247)

Despite its irony, this model of self-flattery does catch some of the real opportunities of the periodical form, the author's freedom to take both sides in a debate, to pose as his own audience, and even to applaud what he has written. No one else can tell him what to do.

The end of *Rambler* 193, however, springs a surprise. As the writer peruses his tribute to himself, "I was so much delighted with the passages in which mention was made of—universal learning—unbounded genius—soul of Homer, Pythagoras, and Plato—solidity of thought—accuracy of distinction—elegance of combination—vigour of fancy—strength of reason—and regularity of composition—that I had once determined to lay it before the publick." But at the last minute he changes his mind: "reflecting that I was about to waste panegyricks on myself, which might be more profitably reserved for my patron, I locked it up for a better hour, in compliance with the farmer's principle, who never eats at home what he can carry to the market" (5: 247). However much the writer longs for flattery, he knows that his bread-and-butter depends on flattering a patron. At first sight the joke seems to belong to some other time and genre— perhaps to one of Martial's epigrams. Mr. Rambler has not previously been characterized as a sycophant, and the classical coupling

152

of host and parasite does not fit the mold of an independent British professional. Yet the intrusion of this foreign toadying into the Rambler's world does serve a purpose. It reminds the reader of the one surveillance the author can never escape, the reader's own sharp eye. The mental world so painfully constructed by the writer can always be destroyed by the readership's disapproval, or even its mere indifference. In this regard his freedom, no less than the props to his vanity, seems an illusion. But more than that, the game that Johnson plays with his persona suggests the vulnerability of the writer to the very follies he laughs at. If the subject of *The Rambler* as a whole is life, its main example is the life of an author. Thus Johnson makes his private world a gift to the public.

If *The Spectator* were a novel, it would tell a story about the members of a club and their adventures in society; the social impulse takes its form from Addison's and Steele's own partnership. If *The Rambler* were a novel, it would tell a story about the author and his choices—or misadventures—of life. Interior monologue would have to be its mode. The first essay begins not with the writer's introduction of himself but rather with his effort to decide *how* he should introduce himself. More precisely, it begins with some general reflections on beginning—"The difficulty of the first address on any new occasion, is felt by every man in his transactions with the world"— and only gradually fixes on the author as an instance of that difficulty. *Rambler* 2 adopts the same procedure: the pursuit of "schemes of felicity" by "the mind of man" occupies the first part, and only the second half of the essay reveals that it has been talking about the malady of a writer. Many later essays—*Rambler* 193, for example—arrange a similar swerve. Apparently the author's story, as well as a story about how it should be told, is seldom far from Johnson's mind.

One reason for this preoccupation must be the truism that a writer ought to write about whatever he or she knows best. Johnson knew the literary world both inside and out. He had grown up in a bookshop, spent years dreaming about the projects that would bring him fame, consorted with other dreamers, apprenticed as a hack, helped edit a magazine, attended the opening of his own play, laboriously patched together a dictionary, and fantasized about finding a patron. Moreover, he always insisted that any life, well examined, would supply all the materials that a moralist needs: "there is such an uniformity in the state of man, considered apart from adventitious and separable decorations and disguises, that there is scarce any possibility of good or ill, but is common to human kind" (3: 320). The life of a writer, therefore, could serve as well as any other to measure the balance of good and ill. When the Rambler went looking for parables of ordinary human motives and their consequences, he could usually find an instance close to home.

Yet a better reason supports the prominence of writers in *The Rambler*. Not only do they share the common lot and common obsessions; they also expose them with naked clarity. All people are possessed by fantasies, according to Johnson, but writers make fantasies into a living. They refer to absent things as if they were present, they imagine impossibilities, they talk with the dead and those yet unborn. If "no human mind is in its right state," according to Imlac (that enthusiast for poetry), then the minds of writers must be constitutionally out of order.[15] Nor does that make them atypical. On the contrary, the writer represents human instability—the tendency to ramble, one might say—at its most characteristic. Everyone feeds on false hopes, but "perhaps no class of the human species requires more to be cautioned against this anticipation of happiness, than those that aspire to the name of authors" (3: 12). Johnson's careful phrasing enforces the point. As a "class of the human species" rather than members of a labor force or profession, writers seem designed to exemplify a general truth about the species; and since they only "aspire to the name of authors," they may well be condemned to a life in limbo, identified by a hope and not an achievement. In this respect authorship seems an emblem for all who live on promises, if not for the fate of all human beings. "Every man, like an author, believes himself to merit more than he obtains, and solaces the present with the prospect of the future."[16] Johnson examines the human species with sorrow and pity. He also knows that he himself is a writer.

154

The emphasis on writers in *The Rambler* affects its view of life in many ways. One important consequence is a tendency to think of each person as struggling in solitude, or choosing a moral path in the mind as one might choose a topic or a word. The Rambler himself seems lonely. Some people, then and now, may think of a text as intrinsically social, composed of a web of language and activities that binds all writers and readers together in one long collaboration. Johnson does not. Despite his recognition that English belongs to all who use it, despite his moral imperative to improve the lives of his readers, he thinks of a text as an individual performance, a test of powers not unlike the test of souls by which a higher power will eventually judge the sum of each human life. Every writer has personal talents and private tasks. Hence even the correspondents of *The Rambler* seem isolated, or infected by their creator's isolation; as they review their instructive but singular stories, the act of writing removes them from the social backgrounds they describe. "Learn from my fate," each letter advises, shrinking a life to its emblematic core or the fictitious signature—Pertinax, Quisquilius, Myrtylla, Captator—that sums it up.[17] Lives so compacted tend to be antisocial. Often they culminate in a retreat from society, so that the writer may learn self-knowledge or take the time to write.

As an example to others, moreover, the life of an author figures forth not only loneliness but disappointment. Johnson tells one story again and again, sometimes in parables, sometimes in poems, sometimes in biographies, sometimes in personal confessions: the story of a young writer whose dreams of fame are crushed by his reception. "No place affords a more striking conviction of the vanity of human hopes, than a publick library," where "innumerable authors whose performances are thus treasured up in magnificent obscurity" sink, sooner or later, into oblivion (4: 200–201). *The Rambler* plays many variations on this dejecting theme. A particularly sly twist occurs in No. 16. As a result of the flattery of his sponging friends and his own narcissism, Misellus persuades himself that everyone recognizes the greatness of his work. Yet praise brings him no satisfaction: "I am now, Mr. Rambler, known to be an author, and am condemned, irreversibly condemned, to all the miseries of high reputation." Harassed by publicity seekers and shunned by his former acquaintances, who fear to beard such a lion, "I live, in consequence of having given too great proofs of a predominant genius, in the solitude of a hermit, with the anxiety of a miser, and the caution of an outlaw" (3: 88, 91). Genius, no less than dullness, is a curse. To be sure, the misfortunes of this "wretch" (whose namesake Misella, in Nos. 170 and 171, suffers the genuine wretchedness of prostitution) are all in his head. But the better part of any author's life goes on in the head, where dreams are born and die.

Most of *The Rambler* treats this theme with deadly seriousness. Johnson's preemptive dejection will barely pause to acknowledge the possibility of making dreams come true. In this respect the series foreshadows the aftereffect of the *Dictionary,* when his gratification at having carried the work through and made his name would quickly yield to feelings of desolation.[18] Johnson was not prepared, in his heart, to regard his career or that of any author as a success. Private losses, especially the deaths of his wife and Hill Boothby, the woman he may have wanted for a wife, contributed to this malaise. But he also endured a melancholy that he associated with his profession. "If I were to form an adage of misery, or fix the lowest point to which humanity could fall, I should be tempted to name the life of an author."[19] Nothing in *The Rambler* sinks quite so low. Yet the use of writing as an emblem of life does lead to grave thoughts. If most careers resemble those of the author, humanity had better not expect to be happy.

Nor are loneliness and disappointment all that a writer has to fear. Perhaps the strongest impression that authorship gives rise to, in *The Rambler,* is a sense of being embattled. Johnson seems to stand against the world or in the arena. Defending the right of a critic to be severe, in No. 93, he looks at every author as fair game: "he that writes may be considered as a kind of general challenger, whom every one has a right to attack; since he quits the common rank of life, steps forward beyond the lists, and offers his merit to the publick judgment. To commence author is to claim praise, and no man can justly aspire to honour, but at the hazard of disgrace" (4: 133–134). The codes of chivalry supply the basic imagery here: the author jousts for a prize like a knight and had better wear armor.

Yet everyone, not only other knights, has a right to attack him. The idea seems nearer to Hobbes than to Spenser—a war of all against all. Other essays present a more benevolent view of authorship. Nevertheless, the image of a challenger does permeate *The Rambler*. Even before the series got under way, a motto from Juvenal's first satire declared that it was entering a competition ("Why to expatiate in this beaten field,/Why arms, oft us'd in vain, I mean to wield," in Elphinston's translation);[20] and later, when the writer launches his "publick challenge of honours and rewards," a quotation from Horace's first satire clinches the belligerent mood: "The battle join, and, in a moment's flight,/Death, or a joyful conquest, ends the fight."[21] Significantly, Johnson's choices of classical tags associate his project with those of the great classical satirists, who are willing to wage war with their society in order to reform it. Mr. Spectator had begun with a more ingratiating Horace, bringing light and amusement.[22] Mr. Rambler throws down a gauntlet.

The same competitive strain returns whenever Johnson contemplates a typical author's career. A sequence of essays that includes Nos. 21, 22, and 23, for instance, moves from one skirmish to another. Number 21 argues that authors are no less anxious and embattled than statesmen or warriors: "The garlands gained by the heroes of literature must be gathered from summits equally difficult to climb with those that bear the civic or triumphal wreaths, they must be worn with equal envy, and guarded with equal care from those hands that are always employed in efforts to tear them away" (3: 117). Number 22 allegorizes the war between Learning and Wit, whose son Satyr shoots poisoned arrows at Learning; antagonism ceases only when the two rivals marry, in a utopian demobilization. Number 23 reports Mr. Rambler's own experience. Battered on all sides by a "tumult of criticism," he determines to keep his own course, "held upright by the contrariety of the assailants, and secured, in some measure, by multiplicity of distress" (3: 130). Despite their differences, these essays share a common ground: the cutthroat battlefield where literary honors must be seized and defended.[23]

Nor will an author's victories be justly rewarded. In the long run, the problem is simply that the stock of literary fame is in short supply and reserved for only a few: "most are forgotten, because they never deserved to be remembered" (4: 201). In the short run, every hero must stand against a swarm of enemies, not only rivals but those who feel diminished by anyone else's success. "Such is the state of the world, that no sooner can any man emerge from the crowd, and fix the eyes of the publick upon him, than he stands as a mark to the arrows of lurking calumny, and receives, in the tumult of hostility, from distant and from nameless hands, wounds not always easy to be cured" (5: 4). Malice like this, sprung from original sin, is damaging enough. But the author's enemies endanger him less than his supposed friends. *The Rambler* fumes with resentment of patrons. At times this hostility flares to the surface, as in No. 91, an allegory in which celestial Patronage descends to earth, degenerates, consorts with Pride, and eventually shunts her vassals "into the habitations of Disease, and Shame, and Poverty, and Despair, where they passed the rest of their lives in narratives of promises and breaches of faith, of joys and sorrows, of hopes and disappointments" (4: 120)—the typical fate of an author. Other essays relate specific stories of authors betrayed by patrons. In No. 27, Eubulus pursues "the favour of the great" until he loses "the dignity of virtue" (3: 150); in No. 163 Liberalis, ironically named the "freeborn," is tortured like Tantalus by "the standing patron of merit" who gradually fixes "the shackles of patronage" on him (5: 103, 105). It has been calculated that no fewer than 42 *Rambler* essays refer to patronage.[24] No ill or grievance seems more real to Johnson.

Obviously a personal grievance sparks this smoldering anger. Had Lord Chesterfield read *The Rambler* carefully, he would certainly have known what to expect a few years later. Whatever had passed between him and Johnson had already achieved a mythic aura, at least in the lexicographer's mind, by the early 1750s.[25] In retrospect, no reader could miss the autobiographical implications. When Liberalis describes his own seduction by an eminent hypocrite, "the standing patron of merit," he draws on memories of hope and mortification. "If you, Mr. Rambler, have ever ventured your philosophy within the attraction of greatness, you know the force of such language introduced with a smile of gracious tenderness, and impressed at the conclusion with an air of solemn sincerity" (5: 104). At last, like Johnson himself, he remembers that he is freeborn: "I turned away with that contempt with which I shall never want spirit to treat the wretch who can outgo the guilt of a robber without the temptation of his profit, and who lures the credulous and thoughtless to maintain the show of his levee, and the mirth of his table, at the expence of honour, happiness, and life" (5: 106). Nor would Johnson want spirit to publish his contempt. "PA'TRON. 1. One who countenances, supports or protects. Commonly a wretch who supports with insolence, and is paid with flattery."[26]

Cumulatively, however, the Rambler seems concerned with patronage not as an injury to be avenged but as a way of life. Authors are not the only ones who spend their days waiting for crumbs to spill from opulent tables. Many correspondents, perhaps a majority, pin their hopes for fortune on some superior—the nod of a functionary, the death of an uncle, or someone's hand in marriage. Johnson's business as a moralist is to deride such frail hopes and to recommend honest labor and self-reliance. Yet the society that he records has not yet reached that state of independence. A patronage system still rules the country, one might conclude, and placemen divide the spoils with the great. The Age of Walpole—and Pope's Dunces—had fixed that system in the minds of writers, including Johnson's as he came of age,[27] nor had he yet forgotten Thales' jeremiad in *London.* Psychologically the author of *The Rambler* acknowledges the power of patrons even as he bridles at them; they are part of his dreams as well as his nightmares. Whether or not he likes the system, and whether or not it corresponds to the real economics of authorship in his time, he continues to think of it as the scaffold that every ambitious young person must climb to reach rewards—or to dangle hopelessly forever.

One reason for Johnson's obsession with patronage must be that it epitomizes his sense of the ills that assail a scholar or author. A patron is the human agent who lures the young enthusiast into the Toil, Envy, Want, and Jail of a routine career. Patrons embody dreams of success as well as the bitterness of waking to the truth.[28] In this respect Lord Chesterfield filled a role that Johnson had been scripting all his life, more deeply with every slight and disappointment. But the classic simplicity of the plot should not be allowed to hide its complications. First of all, Johnson does recognize that authors are not always right or patrons always wrong. *The Rambler,* like the *Life of Savage,* helps its readers to balance the inflated wishful thinking of writers against the limited ability of patrons to satisfy unlimited demands. Not all writers merit support, and not all patrons deserve ingratitude. In No. 190, the generous Abouzaid heaps gifts on artists, "but in a short time they forgot the distress from which they had been rescued, and began to consider their deliverer as a wretch of narrow capacity, who was growing great by works which he could not perform, and whom they overpaid by condescending to accept his bounties" (5: 232–233). He soon learns to try to please the only Being whom one can trust.

The word "condescending" raises another complication. In Johnson's *Dictionary,* condescension—"Voluntary humiliation; descent from superiority; voluntary submission to equality with inferiours"—signifies a Christian virtue, illustrated approvingly by divines.[29] The ironic reversal in *Rambler* 190, however, shows Johnson's uneasiness with his own definition. Number 172 describes the mood of someone who meets a newly rich friend: "if he is treated with familiarity, he concludes himself insulted by condescensions" (5: 147); and No. 200, often read as Johnson's portrait of Garrick as parvenu, takes umbrage at "my old friend receiving me with all the insolence of condescension at the top of the stairs."[30] Here the later history of the word, used almost exclusively for self-conscious, disdainful stooping (or "putting down"), seems already implied. And "patronise" goes through a similar transformation: Johnson does not record the offensive modern meaning, but after his treatment of patrons no one could ever again use the word without being aware of some negative connotations. A wounded author might attribute the fraying of the old positive meanings to the bad behavior of those who condescended and patronized. Perhaps more decisive, however, is the presumption of superiority and inferiority built into the words, which never escape the ups and downs of competitive pride. As surely as a cat may look at a king, an author may condescend to those who pay him. No one has ever been more sensitive than Johnson to the pulse of competition that throbs, however faintly, beneath every exchange between human beings. Indeed, it is possible to analyze most of his thought (as Isobel Grundy has done) in terms of "the scale of greatness," or constant shifts in perspective in which superior and inferior trade places.[31] Even the writer potentially strives with the reader, as one or the other assumes the position of master or servant. Hence the tension in patronage reflects a larger, inescapable tension, the conflict of class with class and person with person.

One final complication modifies Johnson's views. Who are the patrons of modern writers? Once again the history of the word supplies an answer: in later dictionaries than Johnson's, a patron is a customer, someone who pays, who patronizes certain shops or writers, who offers patronage where value is received. That low commercial meaning had not yet penetrated eighteenth-century sensibilities, which still gave lip service to an ideal of the patron as guardian or protector, as in a patron saint. In practice, however, writers knew that saints were not the audience they had to please. A new book trade had redefined the market, and sellers and buyers of books provided the livings of those who produced them. Thus the notion of patronage shaded into more ambiguous transactions.[32] A wealthy subscriber, for instance, who paid a handsome sum in advance for a book that might or might not appear, and who also lent a prestigious name to the list, might well regard this support as patronage rather than trade. But the life of Savage demonstrates how many misunderstandings could arise from such confusions of philanthropy with business; author and purchaser might blame each other for failing to live up to their obligations. A similar gray area surrounds the stage. "The Drama's Laws the Drama's Patrons give," Johnson wrote in the "Drury-Lane Prologue," conceding that the customer was always puissant if not right.[33] The arbiters of fashion could protect or ruin a play, defray the playwright's "benefit," and welcome a star into the best drawing rooms in London. Like other patrons, moreover, they demanded a tribute of flattery, not least in the prologues and epilogues that addressed them directly. Yet an author who counted on their noblesse oblige would soon find how quickly they could turn. Modern patrons did not defend their protégés from the world; they *were* the world.

To view the Rambler as rejecting the old system of patronage and selling his wares straightforwardly to the public, therefore, would oversimplify his attitudes. The Rambler aspires to "honours and rewards," to praise and favor, not only to a healthy balance sheet; while he speaks to the public, he speaks to them as if they were patrons. One might regard this as anachronistic, to be sure. Johnson prefers the older meanings in the *Dictionary* and uses the language of patronage to mask the different commercial rules by which he lives. But more than vocabulary seems at issue. When the writer puts the public in the chair of the judge or patron, he also defines his own relation to those whom he must please in order to live. That relation is not at all simple. Its central term, for Johnson, remains independence. Just as a patron like Chesterfield might forfeit his standing by humiliating the author he had pledged to support, so the public might grant its favor on conditions that no author of integrity could accept. Johnson demands equality with his patrons, if not the right to talk down to them. Hence the tone of the Rambler sounds haughty or defensive, at times, as if he were about to write his public a letter like the one to Chesterfield. To read him at all, they must take him on his own terms. Only then will he condescend to sue for their favor.

The final essay confirms the author's pride in having shifted for himself. One likely way to end such a series would be to take leave nostalgically, as the writer and reader part company after their long ramble together. Johnson is not so friendly. He will not pretend that he will be missed or that he will miss his employment. "I have never been much a favourite of the publick, nor can boast that, in the progress of my undertaking, I have been animated by the rewards of the liberal, the caresses of the great, or the praises of the eminent" (5: 316). Once again the public merges into the patronage system, and both are found wanting. Nor does the Rambler "think it reasonable to complain of neglect from those whose regard I never solicited." Proud to the last, he takes satisfaction from tallying all the means of currying favor that he has not used. This author renews his "publick challenge" right to the end. Unlike *The Spectator,* which prefixed a different dedication to each of the eight volumes of its first collected edition, *The Rambler* spurns any nod to a patron. "Having laboured to maintain the dignity of virtue, I will not now degrade it by the meanness of dedication" (5: 317). No name, not even the author's own, will be allowed to paper over the truth.

Johnson's pride in resisting corruption extends to language, which he has labored to clear "from colloquial barbarisms, licentious idioms, and irregular combinations" (5: 319) like those which Chesterfield would later recommend in *The World.* Here too the desire to please must submit to uncompromising standards, "grammatical purity" and an English unadulterated by foreign expressions. But the last words of *The Rambler* appeal to a still higher authority: "Celestial pow'rs! that piety regard,/From you my labours wait their last reward." The tag from Greek, translated by Johnson himself, offers a softer version of the defiant Greek motto that Johnson had put at the beginning of No. 208.

> Be gone, ye blockheads, Heraclitus cries,
> And leave my labours to the learn'd and wise:
> By wit, by knowledge, studious to be read,
> I scorn the multitude, alive and dead.[34]

The author bids no farewell but rather good riddance. He would rather be in a better place—somewhere more pure.

Few candidates for favor can ever have been more patronizing to almost any potential audience or patron. Johnson goes over the heads of his readers to aim at a readership that is highly elite—in the last analysis, more than human. Nor would a faithful reader have been surprised. The coda of *Rambler* 208 repeats the usual practice of its author, not only in its rejection of patronage but also in the turn of its moral from earth to heaven. After all the advice he provides on how to live, Johnson believes that nothing is certain but death, and all that reason can say must give way to religion. Hence wisdom consists in knowing when to retreat from the world. In this regard the final essay epitomizes the series as a whole. Before he began *The Rambler,* Johnson prayed "that in this my undertaking thy Holy Spirit may not be witheld from me, but that I may promote thy glory, and the Salvation both of myself and others."[35] The end of the work completes a pious circle and dedicates its offering to the only patron who matters.

From a less exalted perspective, however, the author might be viewed not as looking down on his readers but as trying to raise them up. When the blockheads have gone, the learned and wise remain. Johnson pays his readers the compliment of assuming that their moral seriousness might match his own and that, like him, they genuinely aspire to be better. Evidently the strategy worked; not many moralists have reached a wider audience in the past few centuries, and probably none at all has communicated a more vivid sense of the motives that writer and reader share. Somehow the Rambler's refusal to be ingratiating eventually proved as congenial as the Spectator's charm, and easier to identify with. Perhaps this effect is Johnson's main contribution to the periodical essay: he renegotiated the implicit contract between author and audience. Anonymous, unpopular, and armored in the dignity of virtue, the Rambler was no more easy to forget than a pang of conscience. His life had been written into the lives of his readers; his story became their stories.

What is the secret of Johnson's hold on his readers? He himself might have answered that he told them the truth. "The mind can only repose on the stability of truth," he wrote in explaining why Shakespeare had lasted, and many Johnsonians—most notably Walter Jackson Bate—have explained the endurance of Johnson in similar terms.[36] Customs and manners may change, but the principles of human nature remain the same, and every great writer keeps returning to them; they are the truth that every age and people have recognized and recognize still. Johnson says this so firmly, and so often, that only a very willful critic could ignore it. Moreover, the experience of many readers seems to endorse it. Much of *The Rambler,* when shorn of its eighteenth-century contexts, is strangely familiar or (to coin a phrase, as is the habit of truth) fresh as today's newspaper. As I write this, today's newspaper carries stories and editorials on crime bills that propose harsher, mandatory penalties for repeat offenders; virtually every line of argument is anticipated by *Rambler* 114 ("The necessity of proportioning punishments to crimes"), which contends that such penalties fail to take account of human nature. Tomorrow will bring another echo of another truth. If "literature is news that STAYS news," as Ezra Pound would have it, then *The Rambler* certainly qualifies as literature.[37] Readers return to Johnson for news that does not date, especially the truth about themselves.

Yet though truth may be stable, the meaning of truth is not. Few statements of Johnson provoke more incredulity, or are more likely to be ignored or explained away, than his boast in the final *Rambler* of "establishing all my principles of judgment on unalterable and evident truth" (5: 319). Surely that claim is dated. And a similar skepticism must temper Johnson's assertion, in the "Life of Cowley," that "Truth indeed is always truth, and reason is always reason; they have an intrinsick and unalterable value; and constitute that intellectual gold which defies destruction."[38] As any modern student might note, the value of gold is *not* intrinsic or unalterable, and what is accepted as truth and reason varies from place to place and time to time. That variability constitutes truth for scholars today, if anything does. Even the self-interest of recent scholarship prescribes a dramatic disjunction between historical periods or between one people and others. It is precisely because no common principles of human "nature" can be defined, and no permanent truth established, that scholars can always mine the past for new insights to publish; each special period or group offers a frame of reference that differs from any other and needs specialists to explain it. Johnson's own attitude toward truths of human nature might be considered a good example, intelligible only in the context of his times.[39] In that case none but a scholar ought to be trusted to interpret his meaning.

Scholars have not been slow to take up the burden. Most modern studies of Johnson absolve him from the charge of believing in unalterable truth.[40] His skeptical cast of mind and his gift for looking at life from many perspectives ally him with the fox, not the hedgehog, and even within a single essay he is quite capable of taking both sides of the argument.[41] Nor are his explicit statements about truth so unequivocal. If "the stability of truth" accounts for Shakespeare's endurance, nevertheless the excellence of his works "is not absolute and definite, but gradual and comparative," like that of any work "not raised upon principles demonstrative and scientifick, but appealing wholly to observation and experience." If truth has "an intrinsick and unalterable value," nevertheless truth and gold "may be so buried in impurities as not to pay the cost of their extraction."[42] In *Rambler* 96, an allegory on Truth, Falsehood, and Fiction, the goddess Truth can make no headway among mankind, who frequently mistake Falsehood for her, until she wears the captivating robe of Fiction. Each of these instances suggests that truth, however stable in the abstract, can hardly be recognized, let alone followed, in the shifting currents of human affairs.

The structure of a typical *Rambler* essay exemplifies the practical difficulty of arriving at truth. As many readers have noticed, each essay tends to move from an opening truism or piece of received wisdom through a series of skeptical qualifications to a moral that concludes the debate not by resolving it but by showing how the insights we gain from it might be put to use.[43] Sometimes Johnson seems to reverse his opinion in mid course, and he has often been accused of carelessness or self-contradiction. But this is superficial. "Inconsistencies," Imlac tells Rasselas, "cannot both be right, but, imputed to man, they may both be true,"[44] and the issues the Rambler considers usually lead to forking paths in human behavior. The truth of inconsistency is one of his major themes.

Rambler 14 may serve as a model both of Johnson's method and of the sort of truth he expects from authors. It begins with a truism about a contradiction. "Among the many inconsistencies which folly produces, or infirmity suffers in the human mind, there has often been observed a manifest and striking contrariety between the life of an author and his writings." The Rambler does not deny that writers frequently disappoint those readers who seek them out: "the bubble that sparkled before them has become common water at the touch; the phantom of perfection has vanished when they wished to press it to their bosom." But the problem may have more to do with those who expect perfection than with those who fall short of it. In life, if not in mathematics, "many impediments obstruct our practice, which very easily give way to theory," and people naturally write better than they live. Therefore "Nothing is more unjust, however common, than to charge with hypocrisy him that expresses zeal for those virtues, which he neglects to practise; since he may be sincerely convinced of the advantages of conquering his passions, without having yet obtained the victory." The mere humanity of a writer cannot invalidate good moral arguments. Moreover, "the interest which the corrupt part of mankind have in hardening themselves against every motive to amendment, has disposed them to give to these contradictions, when they can be produced against the cause of virtue, that weight which they will not allow them in any other case." Nor can writers fairly be expected to converse as well as they write. "A man of letters for the most part spends, in the privacies of study, that season of life in which the manners are to be softened into ease, and polished into elegance." The essay concludes by circling back to its starting point, this time in the form not of a precept but of a lengthy simile. "A transition from an author's books to his conversation, is too often like an entrance into a large city, after a distant prospect. Remotely, we see nothing but spires of temples, and turrets of palaces, and imagine it the residence of splendor, grandeur, and magnificence; but, when we have passed the gates, we find it perplexed with narrow passages, disgraced with despicable cottages, embarrassed with obstructions, and clouded with smoke" (3: 74–80). London cannot compare to the vision its name conjures up, and neither can the author of "Ad Urbanum," who so identifies with London.

Such disappointment is not, however, the fault of the city. It results instead from the limitations of a human perspective, our inability to take in the long view and short view at once. If authors, in person, are not what readers expect, perhaps the lesson is to beware of approaching too close. A reader who went back to the opening sentence of *Rambler* 14 might find a new implication: the "folly" and "infirmity" that produce inconsistencies may well pertain more to readers and their fantasies than to authors. Johnson does not deny the inconsistency of authors' lives with their writings. What he does take a stand against, however, is the cynical fallacy such contradictions might foster. Readers who have "felt themselves less inclined to toil up the steeps of virtue, when they observe those who seem best able to point the way, loitering below" (3: 74), ought to blame their own inflated ideas of perfection and learn to take responsibility for their own missteps. Nor should a virtuous author forget his duty to readers: "Thus much at least may be required of him, that he shall not act worse than others because he writes better, nor imagine that, by the merit of his genius, he may claim indulgence beyond mortals of the lower classes" (3: 77). If the search for "positive and absolute excellence" cannot be satisfied on earth, it can always lead to the way station of "humbler virtue." Readers and writers collaborate in creating an image of "how far humanity may be exalted."

167

The gradual entanglement of author with reader, until it becomes impossible to tell which one the essay has more in mind, reveals how Johnson manages to draw the reader in. So does the seeming distance that he keeps. Even while the essay cautions readers to restrain their curiosity about who writers are when they are at home, it tempts us all to speculate. According to Edward Cave, *Rambler* 14 may have intended to offer "a kind of excuse" to the courtier (and well-known patron) Bubb Dodington, who had sent a letter inviting the Rambler to his house.[45] Johnson declines on general principles: "it may be prudent for a writer, who apprehends that he shall not enforce his own maxims by his domestic character, to conceal his name that he may not injure them." At this early stage of *The Rambler,* when only a few people knew his identity, Johnson holds on to anonymity like a shield. Perhaps he relies on it for authority; perhaps he genuinely doubts his social skills, since a man of letters "is diffident and bashful, from the knowledge of his defects; or if he was born with spirit and resolution, he is ferocious and arrogant from the consciousness of his merit" (3: 78, 79). Or perhaps, having had enough of patrons, he cannot abide the thought of Dodington. Whatever his personal reasons for staying in the shade, at any rate, his guardedness serves the author extremely well. An air of mystery surrounds the Rambler. Though hardly confiding, he drops so many clues about his own experience that readers cannot help but pick them up. Even the motto of No. 14, from Horace, "Nil fuit unquam/ Sic dispar sibi" (No one was ever/so unlike himself),[46] teases us to wonder about the relation between the Rambler and the person concealed behind his mask. Can it be that this high-minded moralist really has something to hide? A reader who asks that question has already been snared by the curiosity against which the essay warns.

Most of Johnson's ways of drawing us in work still more subtly. One strategy on which he prided himself was the deliberate rationing of "novelty or surprize" in the pictures of life. Departures from reality might subvert the lesson: "The mind of the reader is carried away from the contemplation of his own manners; he finds in himself no likeness to the phantom before him; and though he laughs or rages, is not reformed" (5: 320). The Rambler would rather be mundane than uninstructive. But his most important way of involving the reader consists in the author's quiet but steady acknowledgment that he himself is susceptible to the vice and folly he puts on trial. Johnson seldom writes satire. *Rambler* 14, for instance, fails to exploit the rich comic potential of a meeting between a starry-eyed reader and an obnoxious author. Instead, as Bate has suggested, Johnson writes satire *manqué,* "a kind of double action in which a strong satiric blow is about to strike home unerringly when another arm at once reaches out and deflects or rather lifts it."[47] Again and again an essay that seems designed to ridicule some foible turns gently away at the end; even the broadest butt is safe from a flaying. No. 145 puts in a good word for that beau ideal of the Dunce, the hack writer: "the common interest of learning requires that her sons should cease from intestine hostilities, and instead of sacrificing each other to malice and contempt, endeavour to avert persecution from the meanest of their fraternity" (5: 12). One might argue, of course, that Johnson is only defending himself, the drudging lexicographer behind the scenes. But that is just the point: the Rambler never assumes any air of superiority to human failings. From this point of view the famous self-referring essay on procrastination, No. 134, exemplifies the series as a whole by taking itself to task; and it also holds out appropriate hope, since the procrastinator has managed, despite his faults, to carry it through.

Thus the reader learns to consider the Rambler a fellow traveler through the morass as well as a guide. In such a journey, as in a long ride in a stagecoach (*Adventurer* 84), no one gains by pretending to be better than anyone else, because the true state of affairs will always come out in the fullness of time. Each private reader might as well confess that the vices on the page are not unfamiliar. Moreover, each of us is encouraged to make a clean breast when the Rambler not only exposes his own involvement but also assures us that "the depravity of mankind is so easily discoverable, that nothing but the desert or the cell can exclude it from notice. The knowledge of crimes intrudes uncalled and undesired . . . Even he who ventures not into the world, may learn its corruption in his closet" (5: 160). Moralists and historians can help the innocent to see the reign of wickedness, but few of us need look outside ourselves. *The Rambler* often assumes the worst about human nature. Some of Johnson's own contemporaries complained about the gloomy misanthropy of his views, which might persuade an impressionable young mind that humankind is "an undistinguished mass of fraud, perfidy, and deceit," and that this life is "a monstrous association of all possible evils."[48] But in fact the essays do not seem to have this effect. Amid the dark places, a keen-eyed reader will find many glimmers of light. One strong consolation follows from probing the sinful thoughts and deeds that other people keep secret: none of us is alone or unique in guilt. Nor does any mortal have much reason to envy another. "One of the great arts of escaping superfluous uneasiness, is to free our minds from the habit of comparing our condition with that of others on whom the blessings of life are more bountifully bestowed, or with imaginary states of delight and security, perhaps unattainable by mortals" (5: 211). The false fronts worn in public, where each person puts on a show of self-satisfaction and virtue, fall apart beneath the moralist's ruthless gaze, which pierces to the fester of a smothered, universal discontent. Reading *The Spectator,* each of us feels momentarily more civilized, perhaps at the cost of a few qualms about whether that club would accept us. Reading *The Rambler,* each of us feels more able to see through the veneer of society, perhaps at the cost of misgivings about our own goodwill. At any rate we are no worse than others. This thought is undeniably reassuring.

Moreover, *The Rambler* implicitly flatters its readers by taking them into its confidence. Each time that Johnson vouches for his lack of popularity, he confirms the superiority of those who remain with him—clearly a group who are not only intelligent and discriminating but also secure enough to face the truth. Even his unwillingness to woo the reader becomes a mark of mutual respect. Rhetorically, the Rambler asks his audience to meet him more than halfway. He begins with his own predicament at beginning, and ends by weighing his own accomplishment without regrets. The reader is free to nod assent or, unaffected, to keep the writer and his problems safely at a distance. No tears will be shed at parting. Instead, if the essays have done their work, they will gradually be absorbed into a habit of moral awareness or an attitude that measures the little daily triumphs and pains of life against a steady mindfulness of its end. Ideally readers will fill their few moments of empty time, each Tuesday and Saturday, with musings of their own.

Johnson himself could not easily break the habit. Within a year of ending *The Rambler,* he became a secret contributor to John Hawkesworth's *Adventurer,* eventually supplying 29 of its 140 essays.[49] Cumulatively these articles lack the strong character of the earlier series, if only because they complement someone else's plan and hence cannot develop a sustained relationship with readers. Nor is this member of the *Adventurer* crew very adventurous; marked only as "T," he hardly establishes a distinct persona. Yet Johnson's essays do confirm his mastery of his new role as an author. Even when less than fully engaged, this writer knows exactly what he is doing.

First of all, he comes to terms with his readers. The strain that the younger Johnson sometimes betrays in stretching his learning to suit the general public—the strain that shows in the first word he published in the *Gentleman's Magazine*—is relaxed in the tractable form of occasional essays. This author does not need to prove himself. In *Adventurer* 137, whose motto, just before the close of the series, asks the most basic of questions, "What have I been doing?",[50] the answer seems self-assured if not complacent. Johnson does not take the world on his shoulders, but suggests that his labors have modestly added to the stock of pleasure and virtue. "The progress of reformation" depends on many gradual and imperceptible causes. "The business of life is carried on by a general co-operation; in which the part of any single man can be no more distinguished, than the effect of a particular drop when the meadows are floated by a summer shower: yet every drop increases the inundation, and every hand adds to the happiness or misery of mankind." The sentence exemplifies its own point, the mingling of the one in the many, since Johnson is speaking not only for himself but for all the contributors to the *Adventurer;* his "I" or "T" implies "we." Nor does he assume any uniformity or unanimity in his readers. A succession of paragraphs explores the many motives that tempt people to look, or not look, into a book—"spite, vanity, and curiosity," or simply cheap amusement—and the writer concedes his lack of control over how he will be read. Yet Johnson will not be discouraged. "[I] am willing to think, that many have been affected by sin-

171

gle sentiments, of which it is their business to renew the impression; that many have caught hints of truth, which it is now their duty to persue; and that those who have received no improvement, have wanted not opportunity but intention to improve."[51] The author has done his duty, and now responsibility rests with the readers. Johnson seems quite content.

His whole career had brought him to that moment of satisfaction. From the beginning, a humble ideal of service had blanketed his restless ambition. Now, in the periodical essay, he was able to balance submission and restlessness, achieving selfless self-sufficiency and anonymous greatness. No form had fewer pretensions than these exercises, each written at a single sitting, with the regularity and devotion of a sermon or prayer. Yet drop by drop they flowed into a body of work that would still be refreshing long after most epics had shriveled. An immense if quiet pride suffuses the Rambler's farewell. "I shall never envy the honours which wit and learning obtain in any other cause, if I can be numbered among the writers who have given ardour to virtue, and confidence to truth" (5: 320). Perhaps this is Johnson's happiest moment as an author. Enlisted among the writers he most admires, he can enjoy the glow of a public benefactor without the guilt of competitiveness or envy. Whether or not his talents are honored by notice, he sees what he has accomplished and finds it good. Misery might still haunt the lives of most authors; but, after all, he had made a principled choice of life.

7

Reclaiming Imagination:
Rasselas

The moving accident is not my trade.

I N THE LATE 1740s, as one struggling author labored inch by inch to make his name, others devised a new sort of writing that took the public by storm. The rise of the novel and the rise of Johnson happened at the same time. With the publication of *Clarissa* (1747–48), *Roderick Random* (1748), and *Tom Jones* (1749), Richardson, Smollett, and Fielding not only won unprecedented popularity but also helped to change the market for writing; booksellers competed for their works. Sir John Hawkins, in his biography of Johnson, distinguishes between ordinary "authors by profession," the scholars and hacks who "were, in fact, pensioners of the booksellers," and the new class of writers of fiction, who "vended their compositions" to the highest bidder.[1] Johnson was not prepared to enter that class. Despite the talent for narrative displayed in the *Life of Savage,* he lacked the interest in manners, the easy prose style, and above all the dramatic flair or gift for inventing memorable *scenes* that all best-selling writers of fiction shared. He was always better at telling than showing, even when he tried to write a play. Nor would he ever stop viewing himself as a scholar. However high his fame might rise, it would not rise overnight.

Yet the popular and commercial success of the genre that came to be known as the novel did compel Johnson to think. Pleasing the public mattered greatly to him, even if giving it what it truly needed

173

mattered still more. The Rambler who agonized about the best way of addressing the public, in his first number, could hardly forget how quickly some other writers had wooed and won; nor would he be surprised when Richardson's one contribution to *The Rambler* outsold every other. Was Johnson jealous of novelists? Hawkins, who took a dim view of the tribe, implies that he was, and certainly the acclaim for such "blockheads" as Fielding and Sterne aroused some competitive disdain.[2] But more important was the challenge they posed to his self-definition as author. A writer might owe his first duty to truth, but truth became most irresistible when robed in fiction,[3] and Johnson could not deny his weakness for a good fable. Judging the new style of fiction, he would also be comparing it with his own attempts to catch the living world.[4]

He judged it first and best in *Rambler* 4. That essay itself might be considered a bid for attention; as early as its second week, the series turns to the writing then most in vogue. But Johnson also managed, as usual, to take a long view. The previous essay, an allegory on the progress of Criticism, had concluded by breaking the scepter of Justice and leaving all power to Time. Doubtless the Rambler is comforting himself; rather than "dread the united attacks of this virulent generation" of critics, he waits for a fairer test.[5] Yet he states a general principle as well: this critic will not bow to popularity or the tastes of the moment. *Rambler* 4 lives up to this principle.[6] In spite of Arthur Murphy's hint that Johnson meant to contrast Smollett and Fielding unfavorably with Richardson,[7] the essay does not in fact mention a single current writer or work of fiction, nor does it flirt with any such term as "the novel" (the word, for Johnson, still meant "a small tale, generally of love"). Instead it surveys "The works of fiction, with which the present generation seems more particularly delighted," from a dignified distance, comparing the form with older heroic romances and defining it quite classically (like Fielding himself in the preface to *Joseph Andrews*) as "the comedy of romance," hence subject to "the rules of comic poetry." What interests the Rambler seems to be not one sort of fiction so much as the effects of fiction in general—its pleasures and obligations.

Above all he holds writers to account for the lessons they bring home to readers. The first part of the essay affirms the advantages of the new fiction: unlike heroic romances, these works "exhibit life in its true state, diversified only by accidents that daily happen in the world, and influenced by passions and qualities which are really to be found in conversing with mankind." Here fiction strives to imitate the goings-on that pedestrians stumble across in the street, and writers, "engaged in portraits of which every one knows the original," expose how much they do or do not know to "every common reader." As every reader qualifies as a critic, in this singularly involving form, so every reader can recognize the adventures and passions on the page. All this Johnson approves. Yet the new works also entail a new sort of danger. Just because these imitations resemble real life so closely, readers may well identify with the protagonists and take them for models of how to live; "the power of example is so great, as to take possession of the memory by a kind of violence, and produce effects almost without the intervention of the will." Such spellbinding may be almost unprecedented in fiction, and the control it exerts can offer enormous potential for evil as well as for good.

The rest of the essay weighs the consequences of that power. Two special preoccupations thread through all Johnson's remarks. First, he assumes that the audience for fiction consists of inexperienced and impressionable readers. "These books are written chiefly to the young, the ignorant, and the idle, to whom they serve as lectures of conduct, and introductions into life." Johnson himself had aimed squarely at that same audience. Not long before, his allegorical picture of life, "The Vision of Theodore, the Hermit of Teneriffe, Found in his Cell" (1748), had counseled unschooled youths to watch their habits; years later, he would still regard it as "the best thing he ever wrote."[8] Fiction, for Johnson, often seems to amount to a mode of teaching, sweetened by fancy for easy digestion. Even *Rasselas* implicitly lectures young dreamers, those "who expect that age will perform the promises of youth" The school-age audience always comes first in Johnson's view of the novel. When he summarizes an ideal type of narrative, a type perhaps embodied by *Clarissa,* he conceives "a perfect idea of virtue . . . the highest and purest that humanity can reach, which, exercised in such trials as the various revolutions of things shall bring upon it, may, by conquering some

175

calamities, and enduring others, teach us what we may hope, and what we may perform." The plot of this narrative relates *Clarissa* to the contemporaneous "Vision of Theodore," another set of instructions in virtuous living and dying. All stories tutor the student for the same ultimate test. As a writer and critic of fiction, Johnson follows the straight and narrow; youth must not be led astray.

Yet the morals of fiction are often mixed and sometimes corrupt. That is the second preoccupation of *Rambler* 4, which seems less concerned with the art of the new kind of writing than with its tendency to blur distinctions between right and wrong. The bulk of the essay insists on poetic justice. Virtue and vice must not be confused with each other, and the new fiction, "which is likely to operate so strongly" through the power of its lifelike examples, "should not be mischievous or uncertain in its effects." Johnson will not allow any exceptions. Elsewhere in his writing, as in the life of Savage, "a Man equally distinguished by his Virtues and Vices," he is ready to concede that a character whose actions are often immoral, if not worse, may yet deserve admiration. The Rambler makes no such concession. "Many writers, for the sake of following nature, so mingle good and bad qualities in their principal personages, that they are both equally conspicuous; and as we accompany them through their adventures with delight, and are led by degrees to interest ourselves in their favour, we lose the abhorrence of their faults, because they do not hinder our pleasure." Such writers poison the minds of the young and show how treacherous a novel can be.

Are Johnson's concerns at all valid? The didactic and moralistic tone of *Rambler* 4 seems so at odds with later criticism of the novel, or so near to the accusatory tone of people who do not know how to read fiction, that it has provoked some aggravated replies. Very likely Coleridge had Johnson in mind when he noted that "no young man who consulted his heart & Conscience only, without adverting to *what the World* would say—could rise from the perusal of Fielding's Tom Jones . . . without feeling himself a better man—at least, without an intense conviction that he *could* not be guilty of a *base* Act."[9] These words are quoted several times by Sheldon Sacks in one of the best books on eighteenth-century fiction, which goes on to applaud the sentiment. "Fielding, who had asserted that his 'sincere endeavor' in

Tom Jones was 'to recommend goodness and innocence,' would certainly have been pleased to learn that so sensitive and intelligent a
critic had testified to the success with which he had embodied his
moral purpose."[10] The air of sound morality, as well as of goodwill,
seems palpable as it passes from Fielding to Coleridge to the modern
critic. Who could disagree? Yet Johnson, or a reader trained by Johnson, would surely have noticed a damaging, ironic equivocation. A
young man who rises from a novel convinced that "he *could* not be
guilty of a *base* Act" testifies mainly how well it has flattered him into
the delusion that he is immune to original sin. In fact we all can be
guilty. To be sure, no one identifies with Blifil rather than Tom, but
that does not mean that no one *acts* like Blifil. Young men are all too
ready to assume the purity of their own motives; that is just why they
need to be taught to distrust themselves. Similarly, a sterner moralist
might well compare Fielding's "recommendation" of goodness and innocence to one of those letters that warmly praise someone whom the
writer himself would never think of employing. Johnson cares about
what characters *do,* not what they *are.*[11]

In issuing warnings about the power of fiction, however, Johnson
must have been thinking also about himself. The old chivalric romances had cast a spell over him in his boyhood, a charm he never
wholly escaped. Thomas Percy "heard him attribute to these extravagant fictions that unsettled turn of mind which prevented his ever fixing in any profession."[12] As a creator as well as a critic of fiction, Johnson could not forget that he had first been its victim. Nor did the new
genres of less extravagant fiction leave minds any less unsettled. If
anything, their violent domination of the memory and will was capable of enslaving a whole generation, persuading young people that
their dreams might be not only fetching but true. Even as he succumbs
to the charm, therefore, the critic strives to dispel it. Johnson is
poised between dreaming and waking, like someone in bed at day-
break who clings to the warmth of his fantasy while consciously struggling toward the harsh but redemptive light. After all, he wrote fiction
himself.

He wrote it, as a result, on very hard terms. Though Johnson often
cautioned others against taking vows, which would inevitably be broken—"a vow is a horrible thing, it is a snare for sin"[13]—he did take a

177

sort of vow as an author of fiction, a pledge not to mislead the young or "confound the colours of right and wrong." Imagination could not be allowed to prevail. In 1760, on his fifty-first birthday, Johnson drew up a list of resolutions that included "To reclaim imagination."[14] Very likely he had sexual fantasies in mind. Yet the full force of "reclaim," which includes not only "to reform; to correct" and "to reduce to the state desired" but also "to tame," suggests the same long-standing mental hazard that he had analyzed, the year before, in chapter 44 of *Rasselas,* as "the dangerous prevalence of imagination": "to indulge the power of fiction" until the mind riots in "unattainable dominion." The underlying metaphors of this chapter return, almost compulsively, to visions of power and control; even sex represents a way of subjugating reality to desire. Such fantasies acquire a life of their own, like characters in the new realistic novel.

In this respect, the absolute sway that a libertine such as Lovelace desires at any cost, and that Rasselas also dreams about, reflects the enslaving violence of fiction itself: "By degrees the reign of fancy is confirmed; she grows first imperious, and in time despotick."[15] Free will, and even basic decency, depend on throwing off those mind-forged chains. Like the "Habits" in "The Vision of Theodore," who at first seem quite weak and benign but ultimately bind their victims in unbreakable links, fiction gradually steals away the will. Nor is anyone more susceptible than writers of fiction; the dreams they master eventually master them. That is the challenge that Johnson faces whenever his imagination comes into play. Somehow he must control a faculty that overrides all restraints and turns the mind into its own betrayer. At their best, the examples of the new fiction "may perhaps be made of greater use than the solemnities of professed morality, and convey the knowledge of vice and virtue with more efficacy than axioms and definitions." Yet first they must be tamed.

How did the Rambler guard against the dangers he saw? Practically speaking, three main tactics come up again and again in Johnson's own fiction. The first is explicitness—an effort to spell out each moral, leaving as little as possible to imagination. Whether or not young people want to read Johnson, they are the audience he keeps

resolutely in mind. The attempt to control every implication becomes especially clear in the Rambler's favorite modes of fiction, his
allegories, oriental tales, and cautionary autobiographies in letters;
almost all might be grouped in the category of apologue, "a work organized as a fictional example of the truth of a formulable statement
or a series of such statements."[16] Johnson stays close to "the truth."
When he writes allegories, for instance, he takes great care to limit
the character and action of each personification—the Reason and
Labour and Justice who carry the moral—to a few unequivocal
points, or what he calls "their natural office."[17] Labour works hard
and does very little else; otherwise the connotations would always
threaten to get out of hand. Though the Rambler considers allegory
"one of the most pleasing vehicles of instruction,"[18] he also knows its
potential for shifting into elaborate and deceiving fancies. Even the
definition in the *Dictionary* exposes a strain: "A figurative discourse,
in which something other is intended, than is contained in the words
literally taken; as, *wealth is the daughter of diligence, and the parent
of authority.*" The gap between figurative and literal meaning, which
constitutes the form, can never be wholly filled. Thus the example itself might provoke many doubts about what is intended; the notion
that Wealth is the parent of Authority ("legal power"; "influence";
"credibility") will strike some readers as too reverent toward wealth,
and ripe with opportunities for satire.[19] "Absurdity" is the word that
occurs to Johnson himself, whenever he comments on extended allegories.[20] As a writer of fiction, he tries not to be absurd.

Therefore he finds many ways to rein meaning in. A perfect, self-
referring example of this effort is delivered by *Rambler* 96, an allegory of the long struggle between Truth and Falsehood.[21] Johnson
does not launch into his fable at once. Instead he prepares it with
seven paragraphs of explicit moral instruction, distinguishing the
virtue of truth from the vice and guilt of lying. Youth must be taught
to speak truth, despite the many incitements to forsake it. But how
is this to be done? "Truth is, indeed, not often welcome for its own
sake; it is generally unpleasing because contrary to our wishes and
opposite to our practice." Hence arts are invented to make truth
palatable, "that mankind may be bribed by pleasure to escape destruction." Only now, with the moral firmly in place, does the story

179

begin. "While the world was yet in its infancy, Truth came among mortals from above, and Falsehood from below." The encounters between these goddesses—one attended only by Reason, the other supported by legions of Appetites and Passions as well as by Fraud, Impudence, Sophistry, Vanity, Obstinacy, Suspicion, and Prejudice—act out a military plot, in which the straightforward advances of Truth are often frustrated by Falsehood's quick retreats and shifting of ground. At length the Muses weave "a loose and changeable robe, like that in which Falsehood captivated her admirers; with this they invested Truth, and named her Fiction. She now went out again to conquer with more success." And so the story ends—not with a final victory but with Truth in ascendance, thanks to Fiction's aid.

No story could be more explicit. Nevertheless, some holes might be poked in the fable. In her final maneuvers, Truth actually *impersonates* Falsehood, disguising herself in order to conquer the Passions; surely this requires some stretching of truth. Similarly, the late introduction of Fiction evades the hardest question about the story, the extent to which a fuller picture of fiction might reveal it as the natural ally of falsehood rather than truth. Sophisticated readers raise questions like this, and so do some clever children. Johnson does his best to make the moral plain. At the close of the allegory, for instance, Truth disrobes and "shone out, in her original form, with native effulgence and resistless dignity"; virtue fights fair against vice. Nor does the storyteller complicate his lesson, as Spenser might have done, by inventing a scene in which a naive reader might mistake Falsehood for Truth. Yet the search for truth cannot allow an easy resolution. No matter how much Johnson favors the triumph of plain dealing, he knows that readers prefer "the enchantment of fancy";[22] fiction itself must be employed to warn against fiction.

As *Rambler* 96 makes clear, however, the dangers of fiction may also be the moral the story preaches. That is Johnson's second tactic for safeguarding the reader. Not only does he spell out each lesson, he also keeps telling versions of a single tale: the tyranny of wishes. No theme inspires him to more eloquence, or more repetition. Each story—and almost every paragraph of each story—begins with a hope or fancy and ends with its deflation. Thus even the victory of Truth over Falsehood must move from a false surmise to a cold look at things as they are. "Truth, who, when she first descended from the heavenly palaces, expected to have been received by universal acclamation, cherished with kindness, heard with obedience, and invited to spread her influence from province to province, now found that, wherever she came, she must force her passage." A similar plot underlies the majority of fictional autobiographies by the Rambler's supposed correspondents. "Deluded by projects of honour and distinction," which "always recover their dominion by force or stratagem," Misocapelus, the would-be gentleman of *Ramblers* 116 and 123, writes "a history of disappointed expectations" that ends only when he learns to "hope to secure esteem by honesty and truth."[23] The false dreams of fiction never quite quit their hold. Even after his disillusionment, Misocapelus still can "hope," in his final sentence, for esteem he may never secure. Yet Johnson's next story is sure to resume the warning: fiction deceives.

This is, to be sure, a paradoxical theme. A fiction that constantly inculcates the danger of fiction runs the risk of self-cancellation and self-contradiction—not to mention monotony. Yet if inconsistencies "cannot both be right," in Imlac's words, "imputed to man, they may both be true." No matter how often a writer and reader may burst the bubble of imagination, it always pops up again, for "some desire is necessary to keep life in motion, and he, whose real wants are supplied, must admit those of fancy" (chap. 8). From this point of view, a self-repudiating fiction seems the one inexhaustible form; its contradictions reflect the mixed motives, both toward and away from truth, that lead the writer to write and the reader to read. The stories that Johnson tells allow just enough appeal to imagination to stir a faint regret at its collapse. One might consider this effect a deliberate turning away from the pleasures of fiction. But one also might consider it a model of how fiction works in general: a dream that rides on its own vanishing.

Thus even a fairy tale, in Johnson's hands, may subtly warn its readers against the charm of its own make-believe. On the surface, "The Fountains: A Fairy Tale," which he wrote to help fill up the *Miscellanies* (1766) of Anna Williams, observes the classic features of the genre. A grateful fairy rewards the young heroine, Floretta, by giving her access to two fountains: the sweet Spring of Joy, whose waters grant any wish, and the bitter Spring of Sorrow, whose waters undo it. Successively Floretta drinks in beauty, a lover, "a spirit to do her own way," riches, wit, and long life. But none of these leads to happiness, and, each time, she drinks her disappointment bitterly away—with the sole exception of wit, which she cannot bear to give up.[24] At last she renounces a too prolonged old age and resigns herself "to the course of Nature." In Johnson no one lives happily ever after.

Yet the moral is still more sober. Though wish-fulfillment and its risks account for the allure of this fairy tale, like so many others, "The Fountains" differs in one key detail: Floretta's power to take her wishes back and wish again. This one condition changes everything. In place of the heady but frightening thrill of wish-fulfillment, with its fear that the hero or heroine might choose wrong and lose her magic powers or be reduced to something merely human, Johnson removes the suspense as well as the glory of wishes. Floretta cannot go very far wrong or right. Each wish entails another set of frustrations—the envy caused by beauty, the unpopularity caused by wit. No choice avoids the ordinary dissatisfactions of life. Hence Johnson annuls the most basic spell of the fairy tale, its privilege of shaping the world according to desire and making dreams come true. "The Fountains" insists on the impotence of even the most entrancing fairy to alter the fated human cycle of time and death. Elizabeth Carter complained about the melancholy impression left by the story, and found the idea of Floretta "finally sinking under the miserable consequences" of her wishes to be "inexpressibly painful."[25] But the source of that pain is nothing other than "the course of Nature" itself, which wishing cannot affect for good or ill. A few lines from Boethius provide the epigraph, and perhaps the starting point, of "The Fountains": "Felix qui potuit boni/Fontem visere lucidum"—in Johnson's own translation, "Happy he whose Eyes have view'd/The transparent Fount of Good."[26] These verses cast an unearthly, ironic light on wishful thinking. The fountain of Joy may promise happiness in this world, but the only true happiness comes from leaving the world behind and adoring the source that never fails, the indivisible Fount of Good.

Once again a fanciful story tells readers not to put their faith in fanciful stories. The full effect of the tale, however, hinges not only on what it says but also on how it undermines the comfort of readers. Disenchantment inheres in the form itself. That is Johnson's third tactic for warning against the dangers of fiction. A degree of self-consciousness almost always troubles the stream of his stories, deterring the reader from being too easily carried along. These fictions find ways to remind us not to surrender, not to mistake their artifice for anything real. It is not accidental that Johnson's stories so often end as the storyteller wakes up. His favorite allegory, *The Pilgrim's Progress,* is "Delivered under the Similitude of a DREAM," as its title page declares; and the close of part one, "So I awoke, and behold it was a Dream," is followed by verses that warn the reader to

> take heed
> Of mis-interpreting: for that, instead
> Of doing good, will but thy self abuse:
> By mis-interpreting evil insues.[27]

Bunyan, like Johnson, clearly wants to keep fiction under control, so that its inventions consist of all pith and no husk. The story must always yield to a moment of reckoning, when truth blazes out without any disguise. Johnson tends to use more subtle framing devices; he writes with young people, but not with children, in mind. Yet he too refuses to linger in Vanity Fair, where human wishes furnish the trade of fiction, and he too takes the role of a pilgrim whom pleasure can hardly tempt. One mark of his integrity, in fact, is that his stories should never be too absorbing. Whenever the narrative threatens to hold us spellbound, the narrator is certain to awake.

Such endings also suggest a lack of closure. The dream is over as the sleeper wakes, but the day is only beginning. Hence Bunyan felt free to resume his dream, in part two of *The Pilgrim's Progress.* Johnson's first major piece of fiction is built on the frame of an extended dream-vision, in which a superhuman "protector" reveals the human pageant on the "Mountain of Existence" to the narrator, the hermit Theodore, who has been climbing Teneriffe. At the end, as the hermit muses on the scene, his protector calls out a warning. "'Remember, Theodore, and be wise, and let not Habit prevail against thee.' I started, and beheld myself surrounded by the rocks of Teneriffe; the birds of light were singing in the trees, and the glances of the morning darted upon me."[28] Did the narrator profit from his vision? There is no way of knowing; he pauses at a resting place, nor do we know whether his next steps will go up or down. Real life rushes back with dazzling force as Theodore returns to himself and the rocks around him, and his journey has yet to find a path, let alone to finish. Conclusions of this sort typify Johnson. In the absence of any firm resolution, the story recoils on the reader, who presumably stares around like Theodore, baffled and yet with a sense of possibilities dawning. Even the diction implies a drastic change of perspective. The speaker now beholds himself as if from outside; the "birds of light," evidently those who sing at the rising sun, also seem to *embody* light, as if the speaker could not tell singing from shining; and though "glance" means "a sudden shoot of light or splendour" (*Dictionary* 1), it also hints at "a stroke or dart of the beam of sight" (*Dictionary* 2), as if a personified Morning were glancing at Theodore to see what he might do. These glimmerings unsettle the steady allegorical point of view; now the beholder may be beheld and the reader be read. Meanwhile the story dissolves and refuses to close.

The uncertainty takes its pattern from life itself. In one of Johnson's most explicit allegories, *Rambler* 102, the familiar image of life as a voyage is given a special grim twist by the lack of any haven or destination: "all that Hope ventured to promise, even to those whom she favoured most, was, not that they should escape, but that they should sink last." Predictably, the vision does not conclude so much as collapse, when "some unknown Power" admonishes the dreamer not to gaze "idly upon others when thou thyself art sinking," so that "I looked, and seeing the Gulph of Intemperance before me, started and awaked." Once again the narrator is implicated in the vice he warns against, and fiction itself, an intemperate dream, seems part of that vice. The story must be shaken off so that its lesson may take

184

hold. Hence a peculiar sense of inauthenticity infects the narrative, preventing the reader from being caught up in its plot, and inducing a perpetual sinking feeling. No human being knows for certain how the story will end, and fiction teaches the futility of fiction. Meanwhile we are all at sea.[29]

Nor do we ever touch shore in Johnson's fables. All his techniques for insuring that fiction will do no harm—the explicitness, the cautionary morals, the disenchanting of fictional form—work against the spell that novelists had learned to cast so well, the spell that makes readers lose themselves in another world. No one could be corrupted by any story the Rambler tells. Instead, he inoculates readers against the disease of wishing by giving them a small dose of homeopathic or deadened imagination, calculated to dull any craving. From one point of view, therefore, he voids the pleasure of fiction, or replaces it with self-conscious mortification. The sense of superiority that the heroes of novels communicate to many young people, who vicariously triumph over fortune, is never allowed to the Johnsonian hero, whose best efforts fall short of success. Exhilaration dissipates, sobriety lingers. This writer ends where epics begin, *in medias res.*

Yet another claim still needs to be made for Johnson's mode of narrative or antinovel. Deliberately not novel in any way, it reasserts the traditional role of fiction as the first nurse or minister of education. The world of fantasy, from this perspective, needs no encouragement; it needs to be reclaimed. This turn of imagination against itself might be considered reactionary, at least by novelists. Yet it also might be considered a return to the primal cause or origin of fiction, the struggle of the mind against its own propensity for self-deception. That is the only story Johnson ever tells. But what other story needs to be told more often, or tells us more about the nature of stories? Johnson writes a thinking person's fiction, a fiction that takes thought itself as its object. If the novel had set out to "exhibit life in its true state," another sort of tale might go still further, by showing life in the process of being shaped by the mind. Such a story will never provide a refuge from the uncertainties of every person's individual struggle. Yet perhaps it might help some readers to face their weaknesses more honestly, especially their weakness for incontinent dreams. It might even help them to think again about their choices of life.

Early in 1759, when Johnson wrote his greatest work of fiction, he seems to have been at loose ends. Money was part of the problem. Without a regular source of income, he composed *Rasselas* "in the evenings of one week," by his own account, in order to pay for his mother's funeral and debts.[30] But the sense of being unsettled went deeper. Several months earlier he had lost his lease in Gough Square, and the household of dependents over which he had presided since 1747 soon scattered. Nor did he feel professionally well grounded. About this time, according to Hawkins, Bennet Langton's father offered Johnson a good living as a country clergyman; and though the offer was declined—"'I have not,' said he, 'the requisites for the office, and I cannot, in my conscience, shear that flock which I am unable to feed'"[31]—his career as an author does not seem to have kept him from looking for something better to do. "I go on as I formerly did," he wrote young Langton on January 9, "designing to be some time or other both rich and wise, and yet cultivate neither mind nor fortune. Do you take notice of my example, and learn the danger of delay. When I was as you are now, towering in the confidence of twenty one little did I suspect that I should be at forty nine what I now am."[32] Time passed as Johnson drifted. In less than two weeks his mother would die; and just at that moment he thought of a story about a man searching for some way to live.

Rasselas is a masterpiece of loose ends. It starts and finishes with characters as unsettled as their author, and years of experience outside the Happy Valley get them nowhere at all. Certainly no one fixes on a profession. Rasselas never arrives at a choice of life, let alone a line of work, and though Imlac is first introduced as a poet whose enthusiasm for the "illustrious fraternity" of writers leads him "to aggrandize his own profession" (chap. 11), we never thereafter observe him composing a single word; instead he fills the role of a generic sage. Even the process of growing up is prolonged out of recognition. "In the twenty-sixth year of his age" when the book begins (rather old for a model "youth"), Rasselas seems about thirty when he escapes the Valley,[33] and many more years go by before he reaches his inconclusive conclusion. All this while he neglects to live, as Imlac points out. Whether or not the work means to warn its young readers of "the danger of delay," it leaves its hero on the brink of middle age, still dreaming about a future that he might not live to see.

A similar postponement marks the book as a whole; unfulfilled or disappointed expectations drive the plot. Even the opening paragraph is likely to raise an expectation that will not be fulfilled. "Ye who listen with credulity to the whispers of fancy, and pursue with eagerness the phantoms of hope; who expect that age will perform the promises of youth, and that the deficiencies of the present day will be supplied by the morrow; attend to the history of Rasselas prince of Abissinia." This story clearly aims to dash our hopes. Yet the doom that such an opening seems to announce—the blighting of wishes, the fall of a prince—at long last never comes down. *Rasselas* is not a tragedy, and hardly even a satire. An optimistic reader might point out that some plans do meet with success, that the hero does realize his hope of leaving the Valley and seeing the world, and that a sequel could always retain the option of a happy ending, with the prince as a ruler who lived up to the promise of his youth.[34] Johnson himself would surely never have written that sequel. Yet neither did he have the heart to punish his hero for dreaming. At most the reader is given a gentle shake.

To expect some more violent action, however, would be to misunderstand what the book proposes. The history of Rasselas is not designed to show changes in fortune or the failure of youth to realize its hopes, but rather to challenge a reader's habits of thinking—above all, the tendency to look ahead. The wise man, according to *Rambler* 29, "is not surprised because he is not disappointed, and he escapes disappointment because he never forms any expectations." That is the lesson absorbed at the end of *Rasselas* by Imlac and the astronomer, who "were contented to be driven along the stream of life without directing their course to any particular port," although, since they are human, "Of these wishes that they had formed they well knew that none could be obtained."[35] As the irony of this anticlimax reminds us, not even the wisest person can avoid pursuing some phantom of hope. Nevertheless, a thoughtful reader can be trained not to turn the pages too fast, corrupted by "dull Suspence."

Rasselas deliberately slows the pace and frustrates guesswork. Those who attend to it learn gradually not to put too much faith in stories.

Even the genre of the story enforces this lesson. Conjuring up a vision of exotica—the magic carpet ride of the *Arabian Nights*—the oriental tale is supposed to transport us to the realm of Otherness. The Edenic, idealized Happy Valley seems a good place from which to take off. But within a few pages we are brought down to earth. This place is just as dull as home, and its routine is as monotonous as dripping water. Romance cannot survive in Johnson's world. The later "adventures" of Pekuah, abducted by a dashing Arab, replay a familiar erotic fantasy, but this Arab is no son of the sheik; despite being tempted by Pekuah's superior conversation, he respects her chastity and at last agrees to ransom her, "like a man delivered from the pain of an intestine conflict" (chap. 39). No British shopkeeper could count the balance better. Hence the genre of the oriental tale, in Johnson's hands, constantly bows to the hard cash of reality, which converts the Other into one more proxy of daily life. Here Boredom, not Death, inscribes its eternal presence: "et in Arcadia ego." Fiction undermines fiction.[36]

Much of *Rasselas,* in fact, is not based on fiction at all. For the Abyssinian background, Johnson drew not only on Lobo's *Voyage to Abyssinia,* which he had translated by 1735, but on a variety of other historical sources, and his reading also furnished many accurate details about Egypt.[37] The scholarly outweighs the fabulous. Modern readers, accustomed to freedom of travel as well as to travel writing that relishes oddities, the more outlandish the better, can easily overlook the care that Johnson takes to set his scene. His travelers may not evoke the Great Pyramid at all picturesquely, but they do appreciate its principles of construction and measure all its dimensions. Contemporary readers tended to praise the "rich and luxuriant" descriptions of *Rasselas* as well as its learning, even when the story did not entertain them. Here was instruction, no mere make-believe.[38]

Yet the truth of the story hangs on its pictures of mental states, not on the external world. Very few works of fiction pay less attention to what the characters look like or what distinguishes them from one another. In this Abyssinia, race does not matter; black and white are equally invisible. We do not know if Rasselas is tall or short, if Nekayah is pretty, whether they are full or half brother and sister, whether they have any sense of humor, or whom they might love. Johnson's indifference to the normal curiosity of novel readers could hardly go further. Nor does he prefer the individual to the species. If multiplicity of voices or heteroglossia defines the novel, as in Bakhtin's famous formulation, then *Rasselas* must be the diametric opposite of a novel;[39] one voice keeps resounding, with few variations, through dialogue and description alike. Perhaps no writer of fiction ever kept his personages less distinct from one another; all of them share the same tone.[40] This is no way to write a novel. Yet implicitly the single voice suggests what Imlac explicitly teaches, that human nature is everywhere much the same. At the beginning of *Rasselas,* the discontent of the hero in the Happy Valley seems to distinguish him from all his companions, so that the "singularity of his humour" allows him "to feel some complacence in his own perspicacity" (chap. 2). But gradually he learns that his unhappiness with what Nekayah calls "this tasteless tranquility" (chap. 14) is quite common—ordinary at best, and perhaps universal. This revelation holds for the book as a whole. Even the most remarkable and troubled person forms "only one atom of the mass of humanity" (chap. 46), and the prevailing state of mind is that "no human mind is in its right state" (chap. 44). In our thoughts, no matter how isolated or unhinged we may be, we are never entirely alone. That is the truth and the consolation offered by Johnson.

The focus on states of mind supplies the plot as well. Like almost all of Johnson's extended pieces of fiction, *Rasselas* composes a thought experiment, exploring the consequences of one proposition. Its closest counterpart, the tale of Seged, lord of Ethiopia, in *Ramblers* 204 and 205, had raised the question of whether an absolute monarch could ensure some days of happiness by excluding all trouble from his house and his thoughts. Of course he fails. His demand for perfect happiness intimidates and depresses all his subjects, and unforeseen events and vexing thoughts keep breaking in. Each day he tests a new formula for felicity; each day it miscarries. "This narrative he has bequeathed to future generations, that no man hereafter may presume to say, 'This day shall be a day of happiness.'"[41] That moral sets the terms of the story. In order for the test to be fair, Seged must have total control—of all that a human being can control. The narrative allows no other source of interest to sidetrack its experiment. A logic of thought must chart the sequence of events, discarding each piece of wishful thinking until nothing remains but hard-bought, hopeless wisdom. Hence a new disappointment arrives each day, as regular as the mail. How can such a plot avoid a tedious predictability? First of all, it had better be brief, and some variety will help. But in practice the writer must manage a balance between two forces, the momentum of ingenious tests of the project from moment to moment and the inertia of an inevitable end. We cannot ask for suspense. What we can ask from this process of thought, however, is some sign that the writer is thinking.

Rasselas observes the laws of its form. Johnson began with a proposition, not with a character or story. His first written mention of the "thing" says that its title will be

The choice of Life

or

The History of ——— Prince of Abissinia,[42]

and though the first phrase dropped from the printed title page, it always dominates the text as well as the mind of the prince: "Whatever be the consequence of my experiment, I am resolved to judge with my own eyes of the various conditions of men, and then to make deliberately my *choice of life*" (chap. 12). Rasselas never deviates; even digressions bear on the one main point of how to live, an experiment carried out in the characters' actions and Johnson's thoughts.

The phrase does not explain itself, to be sure. What exactly does Rasselas want to choose? Though his statements clearly refer to a definition of "life" as "condition; manner of living with respect to happiness and misery," he is far from indifferent to an alternative definition,

190

"conduct; manner of living with respect to virtue or vice,"[43] and his growing awareness that no condition can guarantee happiness tends to turn his attention toward matters of conduct. Nor are such words as "condition" and "happiness" free from ambiguous possibilities. In the beginning, Rasselas pins his hopes on a change of scene; once out of the Valley, he is absorbed by the notion that someone might possess a secret, some philosophy or pursuit from which happiness follows; for a while, he and his sister debate whether public or private stations will suit them better; and in the penultimate chapter, when they visit the catacombs, both of them gain some distance from their "present state": "'To me,' said the princess, 'the choice of life is become less important; I hope hereafter to think only on the choice of eternity'" (chap. 48). Perspectives continually vary. In this respect the progress of the book, for Johnson if not for his hero, might be said to consist of playing with terms, just as a lexicographer will find fifteen different ways to view the meaning of life.

The quest itself may also be in question. From Rasselas' point of view, the problem is always, What is the best choice of life? But his creator often seems to be asking, Is this a reasonable question to ask? Only the latter problem explains how the book can afford so much satisfaction to readers, even while it frustrates the hero's search for an answer. Johnson italicizes the *choice of life,* as if to reduce it to a motto, detached from the living stream. Meanwhile a pageant of failed and amusing choices keeps passing by. A reader who shares the hunger of Rasselas will surely notice how little it has been slaked, but the reader who stops expecting any solution is in position to enjoy whatever comes—inquisitive, not inquisitional. Expecting too much, in this book, is forever mistaken; that is the point of the book.

The spirit of the thought experiment in *Rasselas* materializes in its structure. However full of loose ends the story may be, the sequence of ideas is tied in tight double knots. Each possible answer to the choice of life leads first to disillusionment and then to an alternative or opposite answer. Hence an elaborate binary system frames the work as a whole as well as each of its sections. A partial and schematic diagram might trace the following:

191

Happy Valley/World Outside

The Young/The Old

The City/The Country

The Country as Pastoral/Country Prosperity/The Country as
  Solitude

High Stations/Private Life

Being Married/Being Single

The Present State of Things/Remains of History

Life in a Seraglio/A Life of Learning

The Perils of Madness/The Vacancy of Reason

The Choice of Life/The Choice of Eternity

As soon as the insufficiencies of one mode of life have been exposed, a rigorous logic produces some counterbalancing extreme. For example, once Pekuah has experienced the weariness of living imprisoned among childish, uneducated women, "while my intellectual faculties were flown to Cairo" (chap. 39), the next chapter, back in Cairo, introduces the astronomer, whose intellectual abstraction has bound him in another sort of prison, the dungeon of madness. If absence of mind confines the soul—the women in the Arab's fortress "ran from room to room as a bird hops from wire to wire in his cage" (chap. 39)—then so does a hypertrophy of imagination, as the reign of fancy "grows first imperious, and in time despotick" (chap. 44). The two conditions reverse and mirror each other. Thought can find no escape; each way out runs up against another cul-de-sac, until all likely avenues have been exhausted. Then the journey circles back toward its starting place.

The balance of the structure is also thematic. If any one paragraph can be said to sum up the wisdom of *Rasselas,* it must be Nekayah's verdict on the arguments about marriage. "'Every hour,' answered the princess, 'confirms my prejudice in favour of the position so often uttered by the mouth of Imlac, "That nature sets her gifts on the right hand and on the left." Those conditions, which flatter hope and attract desire, are so constituted, that, as we approach one, we recede from another . . . Of the blessings set before you make your choice and be content . . . No man can, at the same time, fill his cup from the source

192

and from the mouth of the Nile'" (chap. 29)—or live both in the Happy Valley and in Cairo. This doctrine seems more cheerful than discouraging. With its emphasis on gifts and blessings, it offers much hope of contentment; so long as one shuns the futile effort to reconcile contradictions, one's cup can always be full.

Yet an undertone darkens the passage. Imlac's favorite saying recalls a graver image over which Johnson often brooded: "my Redeemer has said that he will set some on his right hand and some on his left."[44] The wrong choice of life might pave the way to damnation, and "the Being which made the soul, can destroy it" (chap. 48). Such final judgments do not govern *Rasselas*. By adopting Eastern characters and settings, Johnson deliberately keeps Christianity outside his secular thought experiment and allows the quest for happiness more prominence than the war between virtue and vice. Nevertheless, the closing chapters are shadowed by thoughts of guilt and death, the gloom of the catacombs. If most of the work attributes human discontent to a psychological principle—"Man has surely some latent sense for which this place affords no gratification, or he has some desires distinct from sense which must be satisfied before he can be happy" (chap. 2)—the last part implies a yearning of the soul, not merely the mind, and human beings cannot satisfy such yearnings by themselves. Celestial Wisdom keeps her distance here. In this respect contentment is not in our power. Nor does the book hold out much hope that minds can maintain their balance. However often the reader and writer may try to reclaim it, imagination prevails.

These shadows leave their mark on *Rasselas*. Is it really a work that young people ought to read? Since the beginning, critics have differed about its effects.[45] One case for the prosecution was made with characteristic gusto by William Hazlitt: "Dr. Johnson is also a complete balance-master in the topics of morality. He never encourages hope, but he counteracts it by fear; he never elicits a truth, but he suggests some objection in answer to it . . . 'He runs the great circle, and is still at home' . . . His Rasselas is the most melancholy and debilitating moral speculation that ever was put forth."[46] Unfair as this case may be, it does respond to the balance and circularity of the work itself, and assumes that they will debilitate any morally healthy and spirited young reader. Hazlitt puts his trust in imagination, a faculty he means to kindle, not hold in check.[47] Hence his quarrel with Johnson goes beyond matters of taste and touches the basic aim of education, its effort to set each student on the right path. He rejects the balance of hope and fear; he chooses another life.

Yet the full effect of *Rasselas* is far more complex than its critics acknowledge. If its flights of fancy plummet into a slough of embarrassing matters of fact, they also leave a trail of twinkling humor. Good nature distinguishes Johnson's warnings. The artist who tries to fly on Daedalian wings may end "half dead with terrour and vexation," but he does not drown: "His wings, which were of no use in the air, sustained him in the water" (chap. 6). Similar compensations occur throughout the book, cushioning its hard lessons with a bit of practical advice, an amusing twist, an interesting fact, a precept, a smile. Nor should one underestimate the pleasures of thinking.

A characteristic reflection occurs in chapter 4, after a former teacher of Rasselas has unwittingly inspired him to see the world by pointing out that only then will he know how to value his present state. "The old man went away sufficiently discontented to find that his reasonings had produced the only conclusion which they were intended to prevent." Most authors would stop on that sour note; the old man will play no more part in the story. But Johnson goes on. "But in the decline of life shame and grief are of short duration; whether it be that we bear easily what we have born long, or that, finding ourselves in age less regarded, we less regard others; or, that we look with slight regard upon afflictions, to which we know that the hand of death is about to put an end." What is the purpose of this pause for thought? Far from intensifying the irony of the old man's humiliation, it tends to dissipate its impact; in the long run he will not care, and neither will we. Nor do the three explanations for the indifference of the aged help at all to advance the action. Instead they deflate it, in one more example of Johnson's preemptive dejection, by keeping us from taking Rasselas' response too seriously: "This first beam of hope, that had been ever darted into his mind, rekindled youth in his cheeks." The reader already knows that such hopes will pass, along with youth itself. In case a reminder should be needed, another old man will appear in chapter 45, bearing no better comfort: "Nothing is now of much importance; for I cannot extend my interest beyond myself." Pausing for thought, the narrative places the hopes and dreams of its characters at a distance. The chill seems quite intentional. Once again all illusions are shattered; a single perspective comprehends both youth and age; we cannot identify with anyone or lose ourselves in this fiction. Only one solace remains: the pleasure of thinking, or seeing life as a whole. For Johnson, that will have to be enough.

At the same time, however, reflectiveness gives *Rasselas* a special sense of life: thinking becomes its doing. The tension of the narrative does not depend on where the plot might be going, but rather on the contrast between the uncertainty of its quest or thought experiment and the extreme assurance of its individual thoughts. Each scene is masterful; unerringly Johnson probes the weakness of every position. Hence the effect of the work, despite what its critics may say, is not to debilitate but to build one sort of confidence, a belief that life can be understood, if not overcome. Such understanding is heady. The pleasure of seeing through each phantom of hope, like blowing bubbles in order to watch them burst, may well addict the reader. In any case, it tends to subordinate action to observation. Perhaps a choice of life is implicit in *Rasselas* after all: the choice of a life that consists in observing choices of life.

In that event Johnson took his revenge on fiction. If reading romances did unsettle his mind and "prevented his ever fixing in any profession," then he might make a kind of profession from teaching others not to take romances to heart. Reclaiming imagination would be his mission—and he would begin with his own. Johnson's fiction obsessively reinforces that moral; it seems to have shaped his view of his own life story. Others might see him as a successful author, a master, a grown-up, a sage. That is not the way he sees himself in his fiftieth year. For all his differences from Rasselas and Imlac, he does identify with their drift, "designing to be some time or other both rich and wise," and yet somehow not ready. Few speeches in Shakespeare seem to have moved him more than the Duke's words in *Measure for Measure,* "Thou hast nor youth, nor age;/But as it were an after-dinner's sleep,/Dreaming on both" (III.i.32–34). "This is exquisitely imagined," Johnson comments. The young pass their time forming schemes for the future, the old recollecting the past; "so that our life, of which no part is filled with the business of the present time, resembles our dreams after dinner, when the events of the morning are mingled with the designs of the evening."[48] That limbo was the home where Johnson lived, and also the site of his fiction.

Yet finally the impulse to fiction melted away. Johnson did not have many stories to tell, and as he aged, like the old men in *Rasselas,* he preferred to puncture dreams and not to indulge them. Even his gift for metaphor, the keen imagination that finds a potential vignette or figure within each abstract idea, increasingly mocks itself, as in the series of half-fledged fables on Shakespeare's weakness for puns: "A quibble is to Shakespeare, what luminous vapours are to the traveller; he follows it at all adventures, it is sure to lead him out of his way, and sure to engulf him in the mire . . . A quibble is the golden apple for which he will always turn aside from his career, or stoop from his elevation . . . A quibble was to him the fatal Cleopatra for which he lost the world, and was content to lose it."[49] Each sentence concocts and travesties a tiny story, exemplifying the folly of indulging the fancy. Puns, like fictions, tempt writers to wander away from their goal; even Shakespeare wastes time. A similar charge would recur through Johnson's last major work, *The Lives of the Poets.* The famous indictment of "Lycidas"—"Where there is leisure for fiction there is little grief"—reproves not only Milton but fiction itself.[50] An old man has no time to waste.

And the author of *Rasselas* too is old at heart. Unlike his cast of characters, who can always rely on one another to keep themselves in tune, he lacks the one sure anchor of a life: companionship. Johnson's wife and mother had died, he was rooming at inns, and even Francis Barber had run away. He wrote Lucy Porter that she was "the only person now left in the world with whom I think myself connected."[51] Such isolation was perilous for writers as well as astronomers. The Johnson whom Boswell would meet in 1763, a figure who seems much older than fifty-three and who can be almost pathetically eager for company, has taken some lessons from his own fiction: to flee from solitude and also not to expect too much. Now he would try to stop dreaming. One writer at least had offered a cure for the "delirious extasies" of readers who had chased too many phantoms.[52] The time had come to go home to nature, and Shakespeare was waiting.

8

The Theater of Mind:
The Plays of William Shakespeare

> Robertson said one man had more judgment, an-
> other more imagination. JOHNSON. "No, sir; it is
> only one man has more mind than another."

IN THE MARRIAGE of minds between William Shakespeare and Samuel Johnson, one impediment often threatens to part them. David Garrick completes a triangle. When Johnson first proposed an edition of Shakespeare in 1745, eight years had passed since the two young men from Lichfield set out together for London to make their fortunes—Garrick, just twenty, the pupil, with three halfpence in his pocket (according to the story), and Johnson, at twenty-seven already a failed bookseller and schoolmaster, with twopence half-penny in his.[1] But eight years later Garrick had made his name as the greatest actor in England, perhaps the greatest of all time, and commanded at least £500 a year, while Johnson was still impoverished and unknown. Hack work for the *Gentleman's Magazine* had brought him a modest living, and the inner circle of the publishing world had recognized the talent of *London* and the *Life of Savage,* but his name had never yet appeared on a title page. He needed a project to prove what he could do.

Of course Shakespeare came to mind. As recent scholarship never lets us forget, the invention, commercialization, and imperial export of the national poet made a killing for eighteenth-century Britain, accounting for a massive positive balance of trade in real as well as cultural capital.[2] Cashing in on Shakespeare seemed an Englishman's birthright. A scholar who edited the works could count on good sales, the satisfaction of having done something for his country, and perhaps some reflected glory (not even Pope had been shy about standing in Shakespeare's light). Nor could Johnson have been unaware of the gold Garrick struck by presenting himself as champion of the authentic Shakespeare, a new improved Bard, organically home-grown. Money and fame awaited anyone who built a better canon.

Unfortunately the proposal fizzled. Shakespeare was big business, and those who ran it did not want competition. Jacob Tonson, who claimed to own the copyright, threatened to sue Johnson's sponsor, Edward Cave, and Cave quickly backed out.[3] The next edition of the plays would be entrusted to a far more famous critic, William Warburton, who having already condescended to edit Pope was willing to condescend to Shakespeare as well. More than ten years had to pass before the booksellers beat a path to Johnson's door, after the *Dictionary* had established his value as a literary property, and Johnson's *Shakespeare* did not come out until 1765. Meanwhile the spotlight stayed firmly on Garrick.

Even in 1745, however, a keen observer might have noticed some tension between two ways of reconstructing Shakespeare: put broadly, the difference between the player's and scholar's idea of a text; put narrowly, the rivalry between Garrick and Johnson. No contemporary production had created more of a sensation than Garrick's *Macbeth* in 1744, alleged to be "the Tragedy Reviv'd as Shakespeare Wrote It"—a faithful restoration of the original. Here at last the curtain went up on a pure and undefiled Bard. To be sure, the claim was preposterous. As every student of early music or performance knows, "authenticity" represents a particular style, a set of practices that vary from decade to decade as contemporary tastes keep changing the past. There is no authentic text of Shakespeare, critics now tell us, only a series of more or less plausible conglomerations and reconstructions. Garrick's "authentic" *Macbeth* included a pathetic death scene written by himself, in which "humanity triumphed over murder and barbarism."[4] Indeed, the naturalness for which the actor was famous consisted, at least in part, in replacing William Davenant's Restoration regicide with a Macbeth of quivering sensibilities, a man among (eighteenth-century) men.

One year later, when Johnson floated his proposal, it cannot be coincidence that he offered as a specimen *Miscellaneous Observations on the Tragedy of Macbeth.* He had aided Garrick in preparing a text for the stage;[5] now he would show what a scholar could do. More precisely, this little pamphlet displays Johnson's trademark up to that time, a combination of unassuming service with formidable learning. The name of the editor does not appear, and the main selling point of the proposal is that, while incorporating the readings of other editions, this set of books will be much cheaper. Yet at the same time the *Observations* is loaded with stores of knowledge, placing the language and attitudes of *Macbeth* firmly in Shakespeare's own time—an age when people still believed in witchcraft. Weight and dignity are the goods this editor has to sell. He treats the play less as a script for acting than as a classical text for readers to pore over, and he brings to bear the same skills and historical information that scholars applied to the ancients. And Shakespeare too is praised for his "judgment" and "knowledge"[6]—no mere player but a genuine man of learning.

The very first observation on the specimen sheet of proposals, in fact, belittles the learning of a player. When Macbeth complains that under Banquo "My Genius is rebuk'd; as it is said / Anthony's was by Caesar," Johnson is outraged. "I cannot but propose the rejection of this passage, which I believe was an insertion of some player, that having so much learning as to discover to what Shakespeare alluded, was not willing that his audience should be less knowing than himself, and has therefore weakened the author's sense by the intrusion of a remote and useless image into a speech bursting from a man wholly possess'd with his own present condition, and therefore not at leisure to explain his own allusions to himself" (*Works* 7: 24–25). The tone seems that of a schoolmaster rebuking a pupil. No other editor has accepted Johnson's excision, and indeed the reprimand would apply to Shakespeare himself as well as to some hypothetical actor.[7] Yet the superficial learning of players seems to have been very much on Johnson's mind. Shakespeare must be protected from that sort of person.

The question of how Johnson read Shakespeare, however, goes far beyond any petty envy he may have felt at Garrick's success. It raises some of the most basic issues about reading and writing literary works: what they are for, how we should judge them, how plays differ from other sorts of writing, what talents a writer most needs, and of course the issue that Johnson never stops raising, how reading can help us to live. Johnson's Shakespeare, like any great critic's creation, seems at once familiar and strange, a text we may know by heart but somehow have failed to recognize before. If we pay it attention, it forces us to see not only Shakespeare's works but other writings in a radically different way—perhaps alarming and disturbing, perhaps illuminating, but anyhow not what we have been used to for 200 years. We need to learn how to read all over again.

First of all, Johnson wants what he reads to be true. His literal-mindedness exceeds that of any other major critic. By far the longest observation on *Macbeth* casts a cold eye on the opening stage direction, *"Enter three Witches."* Witches are hard to swallow. A modern poet who made "the whole action of his tragedy depend upon enchantment . . . would be censured as transgressing the bounds of probability . . . and condemned to write fairy tales instead of tragedies." The play is founded on untruth, or "the darkness of ignorance." To be sure, Johnson raises the charge only to "prove that Shakespeare was in no danger of such censures, since he only turned the system that was then universally admitted to his advantage, and was far from overburthening the credulity of his audience" (7: 3). King James himself had established the doctrine of witchcraft, "and it became not only unpolite, but criminal, to doubt it." Yet Johnson, unlike many other critics, does not excuse the untruth on the grounds that it opens "new sources of terror, new creations of fancy"—a world of mystery and magic.[8] To cast such a spell would involve the artist in the very mystifications that he describes. Not even art has a license to bend the truth.

Nor is the stage exempted from the demand for an art without illusions or deceit. Johnson's standards for drama come through clearly in some words that he put in Garrick's mouth, the "Prologue Spoken by Mr. Garrick, at the Opening of the Theatre in Drury-Lane, 1747." The occasion called for a statement of policy as well as celebration. At the crest of his career, Garrick was taking over the management of Drury Lane, and the opening gave him a chance to announce a new direction. Naturally the theater would be a temple to Shakespeare, his idol and meal ticket. Hence the words that Johnson wrote to open the house affirm that everything begins with England's greatest playwright.

> WHEN Learning's Triumph o'er her barb'rous Foes
> First rear'd the Stage, immortal SHAKESPEAR rose;
> Each Change of many-colour'd Life he drew,
> Exhausted Worlds, and then imagin'd new:
> Existence saw him spurn her bounded Reign,
> And panting Time toil'd after him in vain:
> His pow'rful Strokes presiding Truth impress'd,
> And unresisted Passion storm'd the Breast.[9]

These sentiments were designed for Garrick. Johnson later confessed that he had changed a word or two at the actor's urging, not because the criticism was just but because "it was necessary he should be satisfied with what he was to utter."[10] Thus some of the praise for Shakespeare exceeds Johnson's usual respect for reality. Not content with life as it is, this Bard has imagined new worlds and spurned the bounded reign of Existence; and passion, rather than truth, is given the last word. Yet the lines still reflect a scholar's point of view. The triumph of learning not only made Shakespeare possible, by rearing the stage, but also includes him as an ally, as if great playwriting were the fulfillment of learning. Nor does his art have anything to do with catering to an audience. Instead, by drawing life, with powerful strokes, he presses truth home.[11] The scene of this theater is the mind of the writer, not the stage and its shows.

The rest of the prologue enforces that moral. Since the triumph of learning and Shakespeare, Johnson argues, drama has gone steadily downhill, from obscene Restoration wit to frigid declamation to song and dance and gaudy, empty stage effects, "the new-blown Bubbles of the Day." Garrick had not been backward in putting on a good show. But now, speaking with Johnson's voice, he asks the audience to reform its taste and call for a theater to nourish the mind. On this note the prologue concludes.

'Tis yours this Night to bid the Reign commence
Of rescu'd Nature, and reviving Sense;
To chase the Charms of Sound, the Pomp of Show,
For useful Mirth, and salutary Woe;
Bid scenic Virtue form the rising Age,
And Truth diffuse her Radiance from the Stage.[12]

Once again the moralist dominates the performer. The prologue seems to have been quite popular, and indeed is calculated to flatter the audience by bowing to its authority and attributing high-minded intentions to it. Just as Garrick's claim of authenticity had a cash value, so did the claim of a player to be above the theatrics that furnished his living. But history does not record the birth of a new age of scenic virtue and truth. Ironically, the charm of the prologue stems from the unreality with which it recommends reality to the patrons of the theater. Like Samson in the temple, Johnson stubbornly tries to bring down the props that surround him—or rather, Garrick. The show must not go on. Instead, good drama ought to appeal to the mind; most of all, to the literal mind.

It is often said that Johnson's literal-mindedness stems from a lack of imagination. I believe that in fact the opposite is true: a surplus of imagination drives him. The seeming paradox depends on two different senses of the word. For Johnson, as for most of his predecessors and contemporaries, "imagination" stands for "Fancy; the power of forming ideal pictures; the power of representing things absent to one's self or others"—in other words, the ability to see or hear things that are not there, and to see and report those illusions vividly and in full detail.[13] This was the foremost mark of a poet. Like the lunatic and the lover, as Shakespeare's Theseus had noted, the poet has an eye that "bodies forth / The form of things unknown"; though fortunately, unlike the others, the poet also has a pen that "gives to airy nothing / A local habitation and a name."[14] That ability to communicate visions to other people, to share imaginings with the reading public, offers some slight defense against the "dangerous prevalence of imagination" that threatens every solitary, dreaming human being with lunatic obsessions. No theme recurs more often in Johnson's work.

During the past few centuries, however, another meaning of imagination has prevailed. It represents the source of all creation, the faculty that produces new forms and worlds of mind and art. In the clearest moment of Coleridge's celebrated definition, the imagination "struggles to idealize and to unify. It is essentially *vital*"—indeed, the principle of life. No longer a danger, the word now stands for an ultimate blessing and privilege: the spirit that sees the one in the many and the many in the one, carrying everywhere relationship and love. To lack imagination would confine one to a world of unrelated objects, "essentially fixed and dead."[15] So the Romantics said— and in this respect almost all of us, including our lexicographers, are still Romantics. Johnson did not understand what we understand.

My object is not to force a choice between these two definitions. But certain consequences follow from taking one forking path rather than the other, and among such consequences is a divergence between two basic modes of reading and interpretation.[16] One mode, almost universally recommended since Johnson's time, insists on the role of imagination in bringing together part and whole. In Coleridge's terms, a good reader will struggle to unify the text. This is still a popular method in school. Presented with a poem or play by Shakespeare, for instance, the student tries to grasp the meaning of the whole, and adjusts each part to that whole. But reading is not so easy. Some of the parts do not seem to fit; to accommodate them, readers may have to modify their sense of the whole. And that new understanding, in turn, requires rethinking the parts; some come forward, some vanish into the background. So the process goes on forever. Each time one reads *Hamlet*—or even a sonnet—it turns into something else, a new set of relations between part and whole. Nor can the struggle to unify be escaped. Whether the act of interpretation is viewed as a logical impasse, in which hypotheses about the meaning of the work as a whole always precede a grasp of the particulars they are supposed to explain—the so-called hermeneutic circle—or more benignly as a progressive movement ever nearer to an ideal goal that might or might not be reached, to resist the attempt would be to refuse the effort of reading itself. The one approach that modern readers are warned *not* to take is picking and choosing: "'To be, or not to be' is wonderful, except for the bodkin and fardels, but the speech in which Hamlet spares Claudius because he thinks he is praying is horrible; Rosencrantz and Guildenstern belong in some other play, maybe a comedy; all the scenes about Fortinbras ought to be cut; Hamlet's treatment of Ophelia wrecks my sympathy for him; toward the end I got bored and skipped most of the duller passages." Such reading would show a fatal lack of imagination—not unlike Johnson's.[17]

Instead good readers look for the whole in the part and the part in the whole, a unified *Hamlet* held in the mind not mechanically but through leaps of imaginative sympathy. I know no better way to read or to teach others to read. In my more sanguine moments, indeed, I think of the circular movement of interpretation as one of the great modern inventions, perhaps the only indispensable gift of literary criticism to the progressive refinement of human understanding and its instruments of analysis. Earlier ages paid lip service to the goal of reading each work of art as a whole. Modern critics have shown how it can be accomplished.

Yet the process entails some costs. The most spectacular, harped on endlessly by poststructuralists, is the metaphysics needed to maintain each work of art as a world of its own, called forth by a single creator, organically unified, indivisibly One. Where does such unity exist? Only in the imagination. But in that regard the creative imagination seems trapped in illusion fully as much as the image-making fancy of earlier times. To speak of a work of art as a living thing, a world of its own, or a perfect whole is to perpetuate a metaphysical fiction, and to forget that works of art are social constructions, made not born, fitted together piece by piece, and tied to the things of this world. The reason that *Hamlet* changes with every reading is that there is no one *Hamlet,* but only a series of words and impressions, like a deck of cards that every new reader and age must shuffle, arranging whatever combinations come down.

Moreover, the stress on unity costs us other ways of reading. One example might be the more worldly reading of Johnson, fond of variety, concerned with the truth, and never for one moment

205

forgetting that works of art belong to this world as well as their own. But the first recorded encounter of Johnson with Shakespeare exemplifies something much simpler. "When he was about nine years old, having got the play of Hamlet in his hand, and reading it quietly in his father's kitchen, he kept on steadily enough, till coming to the Ghost scene, he suddenly hurried up stairs to the street door that he might see people about him."[18] Here is imagination with a vengeance—conjuring ghosts out of nothing, confusing illusion with reality, and letting a part of the work interrupt the whole. Nor did Johnson ever unlearn this way of reading. In the *Observations on Macbeth,* commenting on the "dreadful soliloquy" in which Macbeth imagines "wither'd Murder," who "tow'rds his design / Moves like a ghost," the critic feels the same fear: "He that peruses Shakespeare, looks round alarmed, and starts to find himself alone" (7: 20).

Once again a surplus of imagination swells out the response. Quietly reading, Johnson sees the Ghost or Murder materialize in the room; naturally he is startled. One might call this reaction foolishly literal-minded, taking the letter for the spirit or absence for presence. Yet I suspect that many readers will also envy the intensity of Johnson's reading. This is one critic who is not ashamed to confess that sometimes texts can carry him away, boring or moving him until he looks round for relief. Half a century after he first read *Hamlet,* he still felt that the Ghost "chills the blood with horror." And the same intensity marks the edition of Shakespeare, as Johnson unaffectedly notes that "I was many years ago so shocked by Cordelia's death, that I know not whether I ever endured to read again the last scenes of the play till I undertook to revise them as an editor," or after the murder of Desdemona that "I am glad that I have ended my revisal of this dreadful scene. It is not to be endured."[19]

One reason for the strength of Johnson's responses may be his own temperament. The crucial word "endured," from a critic who held that "the only end of writing is to enable the readers better to enjoy life, or better to endure it," implies that the pain of life as well as writing can often seem unendurable to someone who feels it.[20] Johnson's black dog of melancholy always pursues him; and as Burton and other authorities had warned, the melancholy man is especially susceptible to suicidal fantasies. Moreover, even in his own time Johnson was famous as a passionate reader who tore the heart out of books. If reading served to keep the black dog at bay, it also expressed the violence with which he brought the written word to life.

Yet Johnson's way of reading was not eccentric. Most eighteenth-century readers were trained to visualize what they read, to "see" the pictures that the text projected.[21] To some extent that skill has atrophied, as modern imagination has replaced the older methods of imagining. Nothing is more difficult, in teaching eighteenth-century poetry, than opening eyes to the visions that poets once thought they were painting. Modern readers tend to be blind to those pictures. The crucial figure is personification. When Johnson told his audience, at the end of the "Drury-Lane Prologue," to "Bid scenic Virtue form the rising Age, / And Truth diffuse her Radiance from the Stage," he would have expected them to visualize two female forms, Virtue and Truth, one winged and the other holding a torch, just as the following year, in "The Vision of Theodore," he would picture *Innocence* as "a modest virgin in a white robe" and *Education* as "a nymph more severe in her aspect."[22] Abundant evidence suggests that audiences did respond as he expected, filling in the details of expression and dress and, when requested, able to sketch them with pencil or brush. Today such personifications lie dead on the page. Ironically, the very ability of eighteenth-century readers to draw pictures from the slightest verbal hint has worked to leave later readers in the dark, not knowing what they are missing. To read such poetry well, these days, requires a good deal of imagination—the sort of imagination that is not in our vocabularies, let alone our inner eyes.

Consider Johnson's reading of another "dreadful soliloquy" in *Macbeth,* Lady Macbeth's apostrophe to night.

> Come, thick night!
> And pall thee in the dunnest smoke of hell,
> That my keen knife see not the wound it makes;

> Nor heav'n peep through the blanket of the dark,
> To cry, hold, hold!

"In this passage is exerted all the force of poetry, that force which calls new powers into being, which embodies sentiment, and animates matter."[23] Christopher Ricks, in *The Force of Poetry,* identifies that force with powers of language—in Johnson's case, finding the living metaphor inside the dead cliché.[24] But Johnson has something more than language in mind. His analysis specifically opposes ideas (or "mental images") to words, and argues that the feeble vulgarity of the diction—"dun," "knife," "peep," "blanket"—counteracts the power of the personifications, Night and Heaven. Of course he cares about these lapses in language, if only because they divert him from the force of poetry. "While I endeavour to impress on my reader the energy of the sentiment, I can scarce check my risibility, when the expression forces itself on my mind; for who, without some relaxation of his gravity, can hear of the avengers of guilt 'peeping through a blanket'?"[25] If modern readers do not find the expression so funny, one reason may be that they never bother to picture the image at all. Who but a cartoonist would actually visualize heaven peeping through a blanket? Yet Johnson pays attention to these pictures. They represent the force of poetry for him, that eye of the mind "which calls new powers into being, which embodies sentiment, and animates matter." Here his own language strains against the limits of language, as if poetry could break through the barrier of words and bring things to life, or call Night and Heaven into personified being. These are no mere rhetorical figures but real ideas, a part of the mental world that every reader inhabits.

The vividness of such images can also distract the reader, however. Johnson's suppressed laughter, even amidst a scene of overwhelming terror, shows the potential of the eye of his mind to eclipse the play. When figures multiply, the sense often disappears behind them. Some readers rebelled against Johnson's own teeming or labored personifications, as in the image from the "Drury-Lane Prologue," "And panting Time toil'd after him in vain," which Garrick did not think "the happiest line in the praise of Shakespeare." Johnson took this criticism with a smile: "Prosaical rogues! next time I write, I'll make both time and space pant."[26] But Garrick was not the only one who would have preferred more prose and fewer pictures. Too much imagination can be a burden.

Moreover, an eye absorbed by images may fail to notice what is happening in front of it. Johnson's alertness to the force of poetry induces a sort of double vision, in which Lady Macbeth competes against Night and Heaven for his attention. The theater that matters to him occurs in his mind. Like many other critics of Shakespeare, he looks at the plays as texts to be read, not as scripts to be performed, and is moved as one who "starts to find himself alone," not as one who shares his emotions with a crowd. Under the circumstances, it is difficult not to be disappointed by playgoing, where flesh-and-blood actors often mangle the text and imagination finds itself enchained by the here and now of somebody else's reading. The mind can easily wander at such events.

Famously, Johnson did not have much respect for the theater and theater people. Boswell attributes this "prejudice against players" to "the imperfection of his organs" (eyes and ears), "the cold rejection of his tragedy" *(Irene),* and his envy of Garrick's success; and more recently Jonas Barish has taken the same line in citing Johnson as a notorious example of "the antitheatrical prejudice."[27] But this ignores the issue of what Johnson *did* see. A theater of mind can condescend to the life of a play on the stage, just as a literary critic may condescend to actors. Yet it also offers one way of appreciating dramatic art—through the *idea* of a theater.[28]

One reason that Johnson responds so strongly to Shakespeare's images, of course, is that Shakespeare himself created so many pictures for the mind. The double vision that I have noted affects not only Johnson but every playgoer, to some extent, who listens closely to the poetry while simultaneously following the action ("DRA'MA. A poem accommodated to action"—Johnson's *Dictionary*). Our attention is often divided. Modern theories of imagination tend to ignore this experience, which contradicts the illusion of unity in which action and poetry, the guilt of Lady Macbeth and the personifications of Night and Heaven, are supposed to be one and the same. In prac-

209

tice, however, most audiences are torn, and sacrifice some images to the flow of spectacle and feeling (if the director has not already cut a good deal of Shakespeare's language). Even the most faithful Shakespeareans sometimes admit to double vision, regarding a text as one thing when closely read in the study and quite another when performed on a stage. "A play read," according to Johnson, "affects the mind like a play acted" (7: 79). But that depends on how energetically the mind has grasped it.

In Johnson's mind the images spring to life. Nor does he want the actors to get in the way. On more than one occasion he entertained himself by asking some player like Garrick to recite a speech, and then demonstrating that the emphasis had been put on the wrong word. Though Garrick had studied his art and Shakespeare's texts more carefully than other performers, and though he excelled in character and expression, he "was no declaimer; there was not one of his own scene-shifters who could not have spoken *To be, or not to be,* better than he did."[29] Perhaps Johnson even preferred declamation to acting. The spectators come to the playhouse, he wrote in the "Preface to Shakespeare," "to hear a certain number of lines recited with just gesture and elegant modulation" (7: 77). In that case naturalistic acting like Garrick's, exciting the crowd to laugh and cry and empathize, could only interfere with the recitation. Ideally Shakespeare, not the player, would storm the breast with passion or impress the mind with truth; and the most effective performer would know how much ought to be left to imagination.

Indeed, the best drama always takes place in the mind, according to Johnson. The scenes that move him work on the inner eye, the private darkness where fears and wishes put on phantom forms. Poetry and ghosts, for him, have much in common. A remarkable instance of this conjunction is what he once called "the finest poetical passage he had ever read," the description of the temple in Congreve's *Mourning Bride;* "he recollected none in Shakspeare equal to it." As one might have predicted, Johnson was talking to Garrick at the time, and seems to have enjoyed the alarm of the actor at hearing the "God of his idolatry" compared unfavorably with a mere mortal. "Sir, this is not comparing Congreve on the whole, with Shakspeare on the whole; but only maintaining that Congreve has one finer passage than any that can be found in Shakspeare."[30] This did not relieve Garrick's pain. But Johnson's opinion was genuine, not only a way to "teize" his old student.[31] He repeated it in print, years later, in his "Life of Congreve," when quoting "the most poetical paragraph" in "the whole mass of English poetry":

> *Almeria.* It was a fancy'd noise, for all is hush'd.
> *Leonora.* It bore the accent of a human voice.
> *Almeria.* It was thy fear, or else some transient wind
> Whistling thro' hollows of this vaulted aisle;
> We'll listen—
> *Leonora.* Hark!
> *Almeria.* No, all is hush'd and still as death,—'Tis dreadful!
> How reverend is the face of this tall pile,
> Whose ancient pillars rear their marble heads,
> To bear aloft its arch'd and ponderous roof,
> By its own weight made stedfast and immoveable,
> Looking tranquillity! It strikes an awe
> And terror on my aching sight; the tombs
> And monumental caves of death look cold,
> And shoot a chillness to my trembling heart.
> Give me thy hand, and let me hear thy voice;
> Nay, quickly speak to me, and let me hear
> Thy voice—my own affrights me with its echoes.[32]

Why did Johnson put such a high value on this passage? A part of the answer must be that he reverberated to the tone of emptiness and vacancy as well as to the fear of death. Whether or not Mrs. Thrale was right in saying that "the general Tenor of his reasonings commonly ended" in "the vacuity of Life," there is no doubt that it fascinated him, and the void in Congreve's temple echoes the void from which God made the world and to which the world might always return.[33] Technically, Johnson also admired the poetic economy of means: "you can shew me no passage where there is simply a description of material objects, without any intermixture of moral notions, which produces such an effect." By comparison, the description of Dover Cliff in *Lear* filled its vacuum with too many details, thus failing to "impress the mind at once with the horrible idea

211

of immense height," and other descriptions put people or "moral no-tions" into the scene.[34] In this one inspiration, at least, Congreve "en-joyed the confidence of nature."[35]

Johnson's most characteristic praise of the passage, however, dwells on the reader. "He who reads these lines enjoys for a moment the powers of a poet: he feels what he remembers to have felt be-fore, but he feels it with great increase of sensibility; he recognises a familiar image, but meets it again amplified and expanded, embell-ished with beauty, and enlarged with majesty."[36] Above all the image seems *familiar;* everyone recognizes it, everyone feels it. Not all of us have visited the Alhambra or stood within such a temple, but all of us sense what the poet sensed.

The reason, I think, is that the locus of the description is the reader's mind, and that what it describes is an allegory of mind. If the play were staged, it would be a great mistake to build high scenery with marble heads; that would only deter the audience from cooperating with Almeria's awestruck imagination as it brings the vacant places home. Much of the force of the passage depends on its subtle merger of the inhuman with the human, until nothing fright-ens the speaker more than her own voice. Thus the noise of the wind, which fear at first gives "the accent of a human voice," eventu-ally yields to a stillness in which the human voice itself causes fear by echoing the place. At the same time, each feature of the temple takes on a ghastly animation, like the reverend "face" of the tall pile. The sequence of active verbs—"rear," "bear," "looking," "strikes," "look," "shoot"—suggests a supernatural agency, as if the tombs and caves were livelier than the passive heroine. One fine touch is the ambiguity of "Looking tranquillity" (so different from looking tran-quil). Perhaps "looking" means "appearing," and tranquillity is all in the eye of the beholder; but a grammatically correct reading would give the roof its own power of "communicating" or "expressing." Similarly, the parallelism of "look cold" and "shoot a chillness" im-plies that the caves of death have taken command and look at the one who is looking at them. That is the truth of the scene—not a truth about ghosts but a truth about the mind, which transforms inanimate objects into semblances of living death. Describing what she sees, Almeria simultaneously describes the impression it makes upon her, and colors the world with her fears. Moreover, each reader recognizes the place she describes, that solitary, shadowy place where life is spent. Johnson heard its echoes at once, and thought it the beginning and end of poetry.

If poetry and drama rely so much on the mind and its fantasies, however, how can Johnson ever expect what he reads to be true? The classic reply of poets is that poetry does tell the truth—the truth about illusions. Congreve shows us the real state of Almeria's mind, and *The Vanity of Human Wishes* exposes the "fancied Ills" and "airy Good" that lead humanity astray. In this respect the poet serves as diagnostician, tracking phantoms in order to root them out. Bad writers sometimes succumb to their own fantasies; good writers see through them, and help other people to heal themselves as well.[37]

This line of thought arrives at a crescendo in Johnson's "Preface to Shakespeare." "This therefore is the praise of Shakespeare, that his drama is the mirrour of life; that he who has mazed his imagination, in following the phantoms which other writers raise up before him, may here be cured of his delirious extasies, by reading human sentiments in human language; by scenes from which a hermit may estimate the transactions of the world, and a confessor predict the progress of the passions" (7: 65). The cloistered lives of hermits and confessors lay them open to the dangerous prevalence of imagination, but Shakespeare can teach them exactly how the world goes.

Nevertheless, some uneasiness slips through the praise. The reader whom Shakespeare cures has been infected previously by *other* writers, the carriers of psychic fever; nor is Shakespeare himself, as Johnson tells us elsewhere, completely immune. Every poet, still more every dramatist, builds a house of illusion, and truth is often concealed among the shadows. The stage seems especially prey to fabrications. In the theater of mind, Almeria's speech endows the reader "with great increase of sensibility," but the audience in a playhouse might easily wallow in superstitious dread like children around a campfire, egging each other on. People go to the theater to be beguiled. Hence Johnson never quite trusts the in-

tegrity of drama. The medium itself invites corruption, both artistic
and moral, and forces truth to run a gauntlet of lies.

In a curious way, in fact, Johnson finds truth in the theater only
when theater resists itself, through a deliberate defiance of acting
and shows and spectators. Like Hamlet, he boasts "I know not
seems." The attack on seeming is a well-attested theatrical strategy,
to be sure, in which the unmasking of illusion provides a deeper illusion of reality. But Johnson takes it seriously. We have already seen
him implore the Drury Lane audience to sacrifice entertainment for
virtue and truth; and a year and a half later, when his own *Irene*
opened at Drury Lane, he challenged the audience with a prologue
that many might have considered insulting:

> YE glitt'ring Train! whom Lace and Velvet bless,
> Suspend the soft Sollicitudes of Dress;
> From grov'ling Business and superfluous Care,
> Ye Sons of Avarice! a Moment spare:
> Vot'ries of Fame and Worshippers of Pow'r!
> Dismiss the pleasing Phantoms for an Hour.
> Our daring Bard with Spirit unconfin'd,
> Spreads wide the mighty Moral for Mankind . . .
> Learn here that Peace from Innocence must flow;
> All else is empty Sound, and idle Show.[38]

Defensive pride inspires this aggressive assault. The way that
Johnson imagines the patrons of the theater, as monsters of vanity
and self-satisfaction, anticipates his later resentment of Lord
Chesterfield. In the "Drury-Lane Prologue," speaking on Garrick's behalf, he had already implied a complaint against patronage: "The
Stage but echoes back the publick Voice. / The Drama's Laws the
Drama's Patrons give, / For we that live to please, must please to
live."[39] Now, speaking for *Irene* in his own voice, he presents himself
as a hero of honesty and independence, someone who can never be
bought and dares the "lords of the drama" to oppose him.[40]

> He scorns the meek Address, the suppliant Strain,
> With Merit needless, and without it vain.

In Reason, Nature, Truth he dares to trust:
Ye Fops be silent! and ye Wits be just![41]

In fact the dare was successful. Though nothing could ever make *Irene* popular, it received a respectful hearing, ran for nine nights, and earned the playwright almost £300. For the most part it also achieved what Johnson regarded as the only tribute that modern tragedies could expect, "that they avoid gross faults, and that if they cannot often move terror or pity, they are always careful not to provoke laughter."[42] Significantly, the one exception to this rule, strangling Irene on the stage with a Turkish bowstring, may well have been Garrick's idea; the first-nighters cried "Murder! Murder!" until the actress was taken away to die out of sight. Otherwise no one found anything at all to laugh at. Propriety mattered to the playgoers of London, and Johnson gave them that, as well as the sort of declaration of independence that always appealed to true-born Englishmen. What he did not give them was any kind of show.

Perhaps that was his ultimate source of pride. The defensiveness of the prologue, which was probably written just before *Irene* opened, reflects an encounter with reality, as Johnson brooded over what would happen when his lifeless closet drama, begun in his schoolteaching days, actually faced a living London audience. He could not have felt optimistic. Garrick, who certainly knew the stage, kept trying to enliven the production, not only with colorful costumes and scenery but also with cuts in dialogue and faster-moving action, including a mad scene. Johnson resisted. The words with which he spurns the gallery at Drury Lane—"Be this at least his Praise; be this his Pride; / To force Applause no modern Arts are try'd"—doubtless were rehearsed on Garrick himself.[43] *Irene* would remain an actor-proof play, if only because it gave no opportunities for acting.

That resistance composes the very heart of the play. The theme of *Irene* is apostasy. From the moment that a beautiful Christian captive is tempted to give up her religion for the glory of becoming Empress of Turkey, everything goes wrong for her; she loses first her principles and then her life. Selling one's soul does not profit, even in this world, and Johnson takes care not to make the downward path seem too alluring. In this work the color of guilt is gray. But Johnson himself was not indifferent to dreams of glory. Insofar as the story interested him, the reason must have been its appeal to his sense of heroism. *He* would not give in to temptation, not even the author's temptation to please. Rereading the play after many years, he must have been satisfied—and worried as well—to observe how little he had sold out. No sermon could be less sexy. Instead the characters lecture the audience and each other, in terms quite often similar to Johnson's prologues:

> If yet this shining Pomp, these sudden Honours,
> Swell not thy Soul . . .
> Or tune thine Ear to soothing Adulation,
> Suspend awhile the Privilege of Pow'r
> To hear the Voice of Truth; dismiss thy Train. . . .[44]

The spectators as well as the heroine need to be daunted, lest a false sense of well-being should snare their souls. Hence Johnson puts them through a saving ordeal of boredom. The resistance to stage illusions will prove he is no apostate.

At the same time, he turns the theater against itself in the interests of truth. To guarantee honesty, the actor should never fall into the cant of believing himself the character he plays; "Punch has no feelings."[45] Nor should the playwright lose himself in the images he has created. Even Shakespeare had committed one very grave fault, a fault from which the author of *Irene* was free. According to the "Preface to Shakespeare," "his first defect is that to which may be imputed most of the evil in books or in men. He sacrifices virtue to convenience, and is so much more careful to please than to instruct, that he seems to write without any moral purpose" (7: 71). The urge to please is the great pitfall of theater, the fatal Cleopatra for which it loses the world. To counteract it, Johnson sometimes seems to recommend a sort of alienation effect, in which the play is deliberately stripped of fantasies until illusion yields the stage to naked precepts. Truth, like love, is found to be a native of the rocks. More often, however, one stage illusion struggles against another, and truth emerges from the clarity with which spectators perceive that dreams dissolve into light and revels have ended. Prospero and Shakespeare understand the limitations of theater. Their highest art consists in driving vicious phantoms from the mind with the white magic of virtuous phantoms or mirrors of life. At its best the imagination can cure itself.

Johnson's defensiveness about the theater eventually eased. The illusion that he was a playwright did not last long, and soon he found his calling as a writer of moral essays and criticism. One might even argue that his excursion into drama changed his career for the better by provoking a new self-dramatizing strain in his writing, the proud independence and defiance of fashion that so struck readers of the *Rambler* and the Preface to the *Dictionary*. Playwriting, like patronage, had taught him what he was not, and if he could not submerge himself in other characters, at least he could rise to the challenge of being himself. As a reward, his refusal to be too pleasing turned out to be popular. Let Garrick enjoy his shows. Johnson's success would be made of more solid stuff.

Yet still he had a rendezvous with Shakespeare. As several scholars have pointed out, the *Dictionary* served as ideal preparation for an editor who had to know the precise meaning and quality of words no longer in use.[46] Moreover, Shakespeare was to some extent its hero. Not only was he the writer most frequently quoted and commented on; he also provided a standard of elegant usage, above all for "the diction of common life." In the preface to his edition, Johnson pays tribute to Shakespeare as "one of the original masters of our language." This poet represents the eternal spirit of English. "If there be, what I believe there is, in every nation, a stile which never becomes obsolete, a certain mode of phraseology so consonant and congenial to the analogy and principles of its respective language as to remain settled and unaltered; this stile is probably to be sought in the common intercourse of life . . . There is a conversation above grossness and below refinement, where propriety resides, and where this poet seems to have gathered his comick dialogue" (7: 70). Every speaker of English owed him thanks. Nor could the nation overlook another claim of the *Dictionary,* that "the chief glory of every people arises from its authours"—a reputation to which the lexicographer hoped to add. England had a right to expect a Shakespeare whom Johnson would help make more glorious yet.

"Proposals for Printing, by Subscription, the Dramatick Works of William Shakespeare, Corrected and Illustrated by Samuel Johnson," were issued in June 1756, and a good deal of money was raised.[47] Then much time passed. Publication, first set for the end of 1757, was delayed for some months, then a year, then more years. In September 1762 Charles Churchill wrote what many people were thinking: "He for *Subscribers* baits his hook, / And takes their cash—but where's the Book?"[48] Finally Johnson heaved into action. The edition came out in October 1765.

Why so long a delay? No one quite knows. The task itself was intimidating, of course, and during those years the black dog hounded Johnson. Perhaps his "genuine sentiments," however, were those he offered Sir John Hawkins, who one morning "congratulated him on his being now engaged in a work that suited his genius, and that, requiring none of that severe application which his *Dictionary* had condemned him to, I doubted not would be executed *con amore.*—His answer was, 'I look upon this as I did upon the *Dictionary:* it is all work, and my inducement to it is not love or desire of fame, but the want of money, which is the only motive to writing that I know of.'"[49] In that case the subscribers had made a bad mistake by paying him in advance. But his lack of enthusiasm for working on Shakespeare must have been equally significant. The nation might regard the thoughts of its best critic on its best poet as destiny, not to say duty, but idol worship was not Johnson's business. Once again he fell back on resistance.

Nor does he seem to have agreed with Hawkins that the work suited his genius. Although Johnson's proposals demonstrate how well he understood what an editor ought to do, they hardly demonstrate zeal. Some editors identify with their heroic authors. Johnson aligns himself with other editors, and counsels modesty. "The editor, though he may less delight his own vanity, will probably please his reader more, by supposing him equally able with himself to judge of beauties and faults." More useful tasks include correcting the text and explaining obscure passages, and these require consulting the opinions of other

218

people, since no one has exclusive rights to knowledge or good sense. Johnson consciously merges his talents with the community of scholars past and present. "The former editors have affected to slight their predecessors: but in this edition all that is valuable will be adopted from every commentator, that posterity may consider it as including all the rest, and exhibiting whatever is hitherto known of the great father of the English drama."[50] This generosity bore good fruit. Whatever the shortcomings of Johnson's edition, its inclusiveness made it a good place to start; and more than luck is involved in the process by which this edition, improved by such associates as George Steevens and Edmond Malone, eventually turned into the standard text of Shakespeare. Yet that text was not *Johnson's* Shakespeare. Critics and annotators could never be more than "satellites of their authours," and all their work was doomed to be confuted and rejected. "How canst thou beg for life, says Homer's hero to his captive, when thou knowest that thou art now to suffer only what must another day be suffered by Achilles?" (7: 99). An editor had better not dream about being a hero.

As soon as Johnson started, therefore, he was struck by preemptive dejection. No glory would come from this work. Moreover, he tended to question glory itself. Fame had not made him happy, and he did not write out of love. But more important, he seems to have felt uncomfortable about what the nation was expecting. No edition could ever be definitive; he knew that as well as any modern editor does, and was not inclined to waste his labor on something impossible. As a short-term project stretched into a decade, however, the stakes became higher. The pension awarded him in 1762 might well raise expectations that, in exalting Shakespeare, the pensioner would give something back to his country. But Johnson's pride, we have seen, did not hang on being pleasing. The more he was expected to speak for England, the more he determined to speak for truth and himself.

Nor did he relish the thought of collaborating with the patriotic glorification of Shakespeare that Garrick and others had done so much to encourage. He had played a part, to be sure, in that glorification. The "Drury-Lane Prologue" exhorts the playgoers of Britain to be worthy of their immortal Bard, and Gallophobia helps drive the praise for English Shakespeare in the *Dictionary*. Many readers would have been pleased to see the defense of national honor pressed much further. During the Seven Years' War or Great War for the Empire (1756–1763), when *Henry V* was mounted every year and Garrick mobilized Shakespearean hearts of oak against French harlequins, flags waved over the theater.[51] These were the years when Johnson worked, or did not work, on his edition. But he detested the war. Imperialism had always outraged him, but now his scorn repeatedly flashed out—"The *Europeans* have scarcely visited any coast, but to gratify avarice, and extend corruption; to arrogate dominion without right, and practise cruelty without incentive"—and turned upon his countrymen as well.[52] Blood lust against the French was his particular abomination.[53] In *Idler* 22, a family of vultures puzzles over the strange propensity of herds of men to slaughter each other, and concludes that wars are arranged to benefit vultures.[54] Only a friend to vultures, in Johnson's view, would fan the anti-French hysteria of patriots, or try to muster Shakespeare in the cause.[55]

Thus a specter of patriotism forewarns the edition against an insular Bard. No idols will be suffered by this critic. Whenever Garrick flies toward heaven on Shakespeare's and the nation's wings, Johnson reaches quickly for his bow. It is no coincidence that his teasing of his old pupil would be sharpest right after the Stratford Jubilee of 1769, which Garrick had organized to apotheosize the "blest genius of the isle" and "god of our idolatry" once and for all.[56] In the same year, Elizabeth Montagu's *Essay on the Writings and Genius of Shakespear* would draw similar fire. That book, by a woman whom Johnson esteemed, was in many ways the defense of the national poet that had been expected from Johnson himself. Montagu mounts a point-by-point reply to Voltaire, who not only had presumed to question the merits of Shakespeare but also had attributed "barbarism and ignorance . . . to the nation by which he is admired." The great French wit may laugh at the ghosts in *Macbeth,* but "he either had not learnt English, or had forgot his Latin," since comparable spirits appear in the *Aeneid* as well as Euripides, and if "the laurel crown must be adjudged to the poet who throws most of the sublime and the marvellous into the supernatural agent," then "there surely can be no dispute of the superiority of our countryman."[57] Most English readers, including Garrick, thought she had won her case. But Johnson found "not one sentence of true criticism": "none shewing the beauty of thought, as formed on the workings of the human heart."[58] To some extent he must have been objecting to her emphasis on the *marvels* of Shakespeare rather than on "general nature." Yet he also doubted that a defense on patriotic grounds was worth the effort. If Voltaire's critique of Shakespeare had been provincial, a cosmopolitan English critic would refute him best by appealing directly to nature, the home of all humanity. Perhaps Johnson believed that the "Preface to Shakespeare" had already done just that.

Indeed, the main point of the "Preface to Shakespeare" may be what is not there. Johnson goes out of his way not to notice England. Instead he addresses Shakespeare as an ancient, a poet to be measured not on a national standard but against "the general and collective ability of man." Typically Shakespeare's genius had been compared with Ben Jonson's art, as in the "Drury-Lane Prologue," or with the formal correctness of French classical drama.[59] Johnson compares him rather with Homer, as a poet whose supreme powers of invention seem "to transcend the common limits of human intelligence" (7: 60). The "Preface" approaches its subject from a great distance, as if eternity supplied the point of view. Four paragraphs roll by without so much as a mention of Shakespeare, and even the fifth refers to him only as "the poet, of whose works I have undertaken the revision." All inessentials, including names, must be stripped away. When the name does finally appear, at the end of the sixth paragraph, it comes as a sort of concession. Since even the test of time is not infallible, "it is proper to inquire, by what peculiarities of excellence Shakespeare has gained and kept the favour of his countrymen" (7: 61). Johnson does not say "*our* favour" or "*this* country." Rather, he stands apart, willing to test the favorite poet of one particular nation against principles that apply to every place and time. England's partiality will be judged.

The passage that follows contains Johnson's own most enduring critical statement: "Nothing can please many, and please long, but

221

just representations of general nature" (7: 61). Dozens of critics have combed through these words, and schools have been founded upon them.[60] But a few observations about the context might still be useful. The first is that Johnson drastically shifts his focus, from "peculiarities of excellence" and "the favour of his countrymen" to all-embracing excellence and everyone's favor. Shakespeare's "characters are not modified by the customs of particular places, unpractised by the rest of the world . . . they are the genuine progeny of common humanity, such as the world will always supply, and observation will always find" (7: 62). The world takes over from England. Hence the favor the poet has gained and kept slides into his more global power of pleasing many and long. Already a classic, soon he will mingle with other ancients; Euripides, Hierocles, and Petronius make appearances in the next few paragraphs. As Shakespeare's mirror of life omits the "particular manners" of times and countries, so his own allegiances are erased by the critic. "Just representations" imitate no particular country.

Second, "general nature" seems to mean mostly "human nature," and above all the workings of the mind. Again and again Johnson comes back to the reciprocal relations between the nature outside and inside the reader's head. "The pleasures of sudden wonder are soon exhausted, and the mind can only repose on the stability of truth." Thus truth involves a characteristic self-recognition, in which the mind is quieted by coming home, from "that novelty of which the common satiety of life sends us all in quest," to its own familiar furniture. Shakespeare reminds each reader of something already known. "His persons act and speak by the influence of those general passions and principles by which all minds are agitated, and the whole system of life is continued in motion" (7: 61–62). The reason that a poet can represent general nature, therefore, is that *all* minds are agitated by the same passions and principles; to be true to any one mind will entail the whole system of life.

Johnson's absorption in the mind draws his critical judgments together. Each of the four traditional elements of criticism—the writer, the reader, the form of the work, the world—is defined in terms of the same preoccupation. Thus form, for Johnson, depends on no rule but the state of mind through which the work passes. Does

Shakespeare mix comedy with tragedy and history? Of course, says Johnson, and no matter: "Through all these denominations of the drama, Shakespeare's mode of composition is the same; an interchange of seriousness and merriment, by which the mind is softened at one time and exhilarated at another" (7: 68). Does Shakespeare fail to observe the unities? Of course, says Johnson, but "a play read, affects the mind like a play acted," and "no more account of space or duration is to be taken by the auditor of a drama, than by the reader of a narrative, before whom may pass in an hour the life of a hero, or the revolutions of an empire" (7: 79). The mind can make whatever form it chooses. Similarly, the world an artist imitates is always mental in the last resort, a portion of reality adapted to the understanding. Both form and world derive from a compact between the writer and reader. If the theoretical foundations of Johnson's criticism finally rest on what the writer communicates to the reader, as W. R. Keast has persuasively argued,[61] that is because the subject of the communication—passions and principles, the system of life—always already consists of things shaped to the mind.

Hence Johnson tries, as a critic, to read not only Shakespeare's works but his mind. Nor are the two quite the same. Every work, Johnson knows, is imperfect, disfigured by the standards of its age, by circumstances out of the author's control or (especially in drama) by what the audience wants. Shakespeare is no exception. "He has scenes of undoubted and perpetual excellence, but perhaps not one play, which, if it were now exhibited as the work of a contemporary writer, would be heard to the conclusion" (7: 91). Johnson's relentless catalogue of Shakespeare's faults, an exercise that upset Garrick and other contemporaries as well as later critics, enforces the moral: this writer may differ from others in degree, but not in kind; he is all too human. Hence the works show obvious signs of haste and carelessness. But for that very reason, what Shakespeare wrote must be distinguished from his powers of mind, his capability of writing works still greater. Remarkably, Johnson even suggests that Shakespeare agreed with him, because the sorry state of the texts, uncorrected by the author, implies a "superiority of mind, which despised its own performances, when it compared them with its powers, and judged those works unworthy to be preserved, which the criticks of following ages were to contend for the fame of restoring and explaining" (7: 112). Here Shakespeare's "negligence of fame" serves as evidence of his superior state of mind. Only a very great writer would hold those plays in such contempt.

How does a critic estimate a mind? Everything in Johnson's "Preface" fixes on that point. The powers of a mind cannot be known until we know what materials it had to work with;

> and though to the reader a book be not worse or better for the circumstances of the authour, yet as there is always a silent reference of human works to human abilities, and as the enquiry, how far man may extend his designs, or how high he may rate his native force, is of far greater dignity than in what rank we shall place any particular performance, c`uriosity is always busy to discover the instruments, as well as to survey the workmanship, to know how much is to be ascribed to original powers, and how much to casual and adventitious help.   (7: 81)

"Original powers" are the residue left when everything else has been cleared away: the facts of history, biography, philology, and (not least) national bias. Hence the critic who wants to know Shakespeare must study his life and times, not to preserve them but to factor them out. English Shakespeare, Renaissance Shakespeare, man-of-the-theater Shakespeare, even Shakespeare the poet yield to Shakespeare alone.

The ultimate object of Johnson's search is not Shakespeare, however, but *man:* the native force or abilities of human beings at their best. Glimpsing the mind of Shakespeare, we learn what men and women can achieve. In this respect, the individual matters less than the example, the scale of excellence set for those who come after. One of Johnson's strongest points in Shakespeare's favor is that, unlike the individuals in other writings, a character in his works "is commonly a species." Much the same might be said about Shakespeare himself; he belongs to the species. His mind, at its height, encompasses all of life and stretches the definition of human nature. Nor are his powers only those of a poet. Johnson did not believe in

any "peculiar genius, or mental constitution, framed for the reception of some ideas, and the exclusion of others."[62] Instead, "the true
Genius is a mind of large general powers, accidentally determined to
some particular direction." To be sure, "one man has more mind
than another," but mind can adapt to any sort of study. "I am persuaded that, had Sir Isaac Newton applied to poetry, he would have
made a very fine epick poem."[63] And Shakespeare, presumably,
might have discovered the optics. Whether or not we agree with
Johnson's thesis, it lends his critical method a special interest. The
issue of how to rank Shakespeare's works becomes a question that
takes in the human race, its history, its powers, its potential: nothing
less than "the general and collective ability of man, as it is discovered in a long succession of endeavours" (7: 60) from China to Peru.
Every reader has a stake in this question. However deflating, comparing our minds with Shakespeare's gives each of us an ideal after
which to aspire.

Johnson's respect for the mind and its powers inspires almost all
his praise. Like Dryden, whose tribute to Shakespeare as "the man,
who, of all modern and perhaps ancient poets, had the largest and
most comprehensive soul" is saved for the end of the "Preface," he
especially values how much that mind could take in.[64] Others select
a part of life, but Shakespeare includes it all in a single vision; he
"has united the powers of exciting laughter and sorrow not only in
one mind but in one composition" (7: 67). No specialty, not even the
world of the stage, is ample enough to contain him.

At the same time, however, the focus on mind reminds Johnson of
the weakness that Shakespeare shares with the rest of his species.
"No man will be found in whose mind airy notions do not sometimes
tyrannize,"[65] and writers people the air with imagination; no wonder
that their minds are never in their right state. Moreover, no other
writer, except for Homer, invented as much as Shakespeare. Whole
worlds spring to life in his wonderful fancy, as airy notions inhabit
and charm him. When Johnson considers the faults of "this great
poet," he too is carried away. The brilliant passage on Shakespeare's
love of a pun—"It has some malignant power over his mind, and its
fascinations are irresistible"—runs on and on, in a cascade of images, until it conjures up a fatal, and preposterous, Cleopatra (7: 74).

Clearly, Johnson enjoys his own invention, and the parody of imagery sprouting out of control includes himself. Yet the danger he sketches is all too present to him. Perhaps we really are such stuff as dreams are made on; the largest mind has room for many dreams.

Moreover, it reaches too high. Of all Johnson's doubts about Shakespeare, none causes him more concern than the dreams of greatness that run through the plays. Shakespeare's heroes seem larger than life and are asked to endure much more than a human being can. This makes Johnson nervous. To some extent, the blame falls on Shakespeare's "gross and dark" public, which preferred "strange events and fabulous transactions" to the reality of general nature. Every writer needs to satisfy the audience of the time, and "the mind, which has feasted on the luxurious wonders of fiction, has no taste of the insipidity of truth" (7: 82). But overindulgence is bad for the health of the mind. Johnson would rather praise the writer who cures his readers of fantasies than the writer who feeds them. Hence even his praise for the "restless and unquenchable curiosity" that Shakespeare excites may hint at ambiguous feelings. "Such is the power of the marvellous even over those who despise it, that every man finds his mind more strongly seized by the tragedies of Shakespeare than of any other writer" (7: 83). Seizing the mind is surely a feat that any tragic playwright might envy. Yet Johnson, if he does not despise the marvelous, does not approve it either. Shakespeare, using the weapons of his age, exerted a power that might well work against the better interests of the minds he captured. Transported to superhuman heights, readers forget that they are creatures of earth.

Johnson's discomfort at such high-mindedness may help explain why he prefers the comic to the tragic Shakespeare. Bombast as well as marvels warps the tragedies; the author "strains his faculties" in striving to be great. Nor do the heroes avoid the same fault. Even the magnanimity of Othello, "boundless in his confidence, ardent in his affection, inflexible in his resolution, and obdurate in his revenge" (8: 1047), contributes to his destruction. No speech in Shakespeare makes a greater impression on Johnson than the few words with which Macbeth replies to his wife's attempt to spur his ambition:

> I dare do all that may become a man,
> Who dares do more, is none.

Of this line and a half, in Johnson's view, "it may almost be said, that they ought to bestow immortality on the author, though all his other productions had been lost." Macbeth instructs the audience "by distinguishing true from false fortitude"; like a fragment from some ancient text, his wisdom seems eternal.[66] Yet not many readers keep the line and a half in mind. Lady Macbeth soon overwhelms her husband's scruples, persuading him that his lack of daring has been unmanly, and what sticks in the memory tends to be the amazing heartlessness with which she imagines dashing out the brains of her baby.[67] Johnson cannot bear to contemplate such images. At best they serve the same purpose as the savage and shocking cruelty of *Lear,* whose multiplication of perfidy impresses "this important moral, that villany is never at a stop, that crimes lead to crimes, and at last terminate in ruin" (8: 704). Even so, neither moral nor tragic necessity can reconcile the critic to the suffering of the innocent. Shakespeare's tragedies are painful to read. At the end of *Hamlet,* "the gratification which would arise from the destruction of an usurper and a murderer, is abated by the untimely death of Ophelia, the young, the beautiful, the harmless, and the pious" (8: 1011). There is something inhuman in Shakespeare's indifference to justice. His greatness violates the codes of decent daily life.

Johnson's heart goes out instead to unexceptional people, the harmless and pious; Ophelia, Cordelia, and Desdemona apparently move him more than Hamlet, Lear, and Othello. Women have a prominent place in Johnson's commentary, less as objects of desire than as touchstones of value. To some extent this feminized Shakespeare may result from the editor's unusual attention to his female readers. In *As You Like It,* "I know not how the ladies will approve the facility with which both Rosalind and Celia give away their hearts. To Celia much may be forgiven for the heroism of her friendship" (7: 264). The moral delicacy and high standards of conduct are typical of eighteenth-century writings aimed at women, which keep a daunting watch on proper behavior. But Johnson also feels sympathetic to women.[68] In many ways his heroines—for instance, Aspasia (in *Irene*) or Floretta—seem closer to him than his heroes, if only because the courage of being true to oneself means more to him than martial bravery. With fewer opportunities to shine in public affairs, women avoid some temptations to fantasize about greatness. Hence, more than men, they heed what Johnson considers really important: unselfishness and prudence and virtue and faith.

Such a woman prevails in his favorite passage in Shakespeare. In *Henry the Eighth*, "the meek sorrows and virtuous distress of Catharine have furnished some scenes which may be justly numbered among the greatest efforts of tragedy" (8: 657). When the dowager gently submits to death, forgiving her enemy Wolsey, imploring good treatment for her servants, envisioning heaven, and blessing her husband, she mounts above any hero:

> I thank you, honest lord. Remember me
> In all humility unto his highness.
> Say his long trouble now is passing
> Out of this world. Tell him in death I blessed him,
> For so I will. Mine eyes grow dim. Farewell,
> My lord. Griffith, farewell. Nay, Patience,
> You must not leave me yet. I must to bed,
> Call in more women. When I am dead, good wench,
> Let me be used with honour. Strew me over
> With maiden flowers, that all the world may know
> I was a chaste wife to my grave. Embalm me,
> Then lay me forth. Although unqueened, yet like
> A queen and daughter to a king inter me.
> I can no more.[69]

Johnson can hardly restrain his admiration. "This scene is above any other part of Shakespeare's tragedies, and perhaps above any scene of any other poet, tender and pathetick, without gods, or furies, or poisons, or precipices, without the help of romantick circumstances, without improbable sallies of poetical lamentation, and without any throes of tumultuous misery" (8: 653). The critic's impressive list of everything the scene is *not* conveys his misgivings about more showy effects. If Katherine is not great, she is surely a

Christian, and one who has taught other Christians the right way to die. The moral could not be less ambiguous. As this heroine rises, however, other, more famous scenes of Shakespeare descend. What would *Lear* or *Hamlet* be without "tumultuous misery"? Evidently Johnson feels no need for such greatness. General nature, the nature of simple people, can please him quite enough.

Moreover, the reader can also find a place in this scene. In *Rambler* 60, Johnson had already spelled out the principles that make a story interesting:

> All joy or sorrow for the happiness or calamities of others is produced by an act of imagination, that realises the event however fictitious, or approximates it however remote, by placing us, for a time, in the condition of him whose fortune we contemplate . . . Our passions are therefore more strongly moved, in proportion as we can more readily adopt the pains or pleasures proposed to our minds, by recognising them as once our own, or considering them as naturally incident to our state of life.

Since few of us know what it means to be great, few of us care very much about the tribulations of kings. "Histories of the downfal of kingdoms, and revolutions of empires, are read with great tranquillity."[70] Nor do most of us want to read about extraordinary anguish. The putting out of Gloucester's eyes, according to Johnson, "seems an act too horrid to be endured in dramatick exhibition, and such as must always compel the mind to relieve its distress by incredulity" (8: 703). Johnson never forgets the most basic stroke of criticism, snapping a book decisively shut. The shock of Cordelia's death kept him from looking again at *Lear,* and hardly anyone returns to *Titus Andronicus.* What cannot be endured will not be read.

Works that abound in touches of humanity, by contrast, hold their readers. *The Merry Wives of Windsor* has any number of flaws, as Johnson notes; "but its general power, that power by which all works of genius shall finally be tried, is such, that perhaps it never yet had reader or spectator, who did not think it too soon at an end" (7: 341). The same might be said about the two parts of *Henry the Fourth.* "Perhaps no authour has ever in two plays afforded so much

delight," and "none of Shakespeare's plays are more read" (7: 522).
Johnson concurs with the reader. One challenge faced by any critic
of Shakespeare was and is the character of Falstaff—a challenge not
only because so many critics have clapped so loudly for him, but
also because the pleasure he gives seems to suspend any possibility
of judgment and to make vice lovable. Could a moralist like Johnson
do justice to such a rogue? In practice he solves the problem not by
avoiding it but by facing it squarely.

> But Falstaff unimitated, unimitable Falstaff, how shall I describe
> thee? Thou compound of sense and vice; of sense which may be ad-
> mired but not esteemed, of vice which may be despised, but hardly
> detested. Falstaff is a character loaded with faults, and with those
> faults which naturally produce contempt . . . Yet the man thus cor-
> rupt, thus despicable, makes himself necessary to the prince that
> despises him, by the most pleasing of all qualities, perpetual gaiety,
> by an unfailing power of exciting laughter . . .
>
> The moral to be drawn from this representation is, that no man
> is more dangerous than he that with a will to corrupt, hath the
> power to please; and that neither wit nor honesty ought to think
> themselves safe with such a companion when they see Henry se-
> duced by Falstaff.   (7: 523)

Morals like this exasperate modern critics and account for Johnson's reputation as a sort of Polonius, plucking chestnuts out of the
embers of sin.[71] But the tone of this set piece is anything but superior, in relation either to Falstaff, addressed with an intimate "thee"
and "thou," or to the implied reader of wit and honesty, whose pleasure is shared despite the vulnerability it fosters. A fine-tuned moral
vocabulary enables Johnson to perceive some essential distinctions—admired / esteemed, despised / detested—for which later
ages would hardly have words. Still more, however, it invites the
reader to take part in the process of judging. By starting with his
own difficulty in describing a character so full of surprises, Johnson
appeals to everyone's perplexed affection for Falstaff. By ending
with an explicit warning about this seduction, he returns us to the
theater of our own minds, where most of us, like Henry, have been

taken in. This moral turn is generous; it includes the characters, the reader, and the critic within a single party of human nature.

Nor does Johnson believe that he has anything unique to say. As a reader of Shakespeare, he is no hero, no more conclusive than anyone else. The test of time counts more than any critic's opinions, and Falstaff as well as his author is everyone's kin. A few months before his death, Johnson told William Windham that "the merit of Shakspeare was such as the ignorant could take in, and the learned add nothing to."[72] Such praise did not leave much for scholarship to hope for. A certain gloom pervades the final pages of the "Preface to Shakespeare." Remembering other editors, Johnson foresees his fate: "To dread the shore which he sees spread with wrecks, is natural to the sailor" (7: 109). He has not settled the texts of the plays, and his notes are "necessary evils" at best, since Shakespeare kindles the attention of readers and "the mind is refrigerated by interruption" (7: 111). No one ought to expect too much from this edition. As the work draws near its end, the editor seems to feel not a glow but a chill.

Perhaps such gloom was no more than Johnson's conditioned response. The lack of solicitude he professes to feel about the reception of his work, so similar to the "frigid tranquillity" with which he had dismissed the *Dictionary,* cannot be quite the whole truth. The edition of Shakespeare marked a period of his life. Just as the *Dictionary* brought him not only fame but an Oxford degree, so the new publication coincided with an LL.D. from Trinity College, Dublin; henceforth he would have to cope with being a Doctor. More significantly, the project he closed had been in his thoughts for more than twenty years, before the *Dictionary* began, and to finish it left him not only high but dry. For the first time in two decades, the public had no claim on him.[73] This meant that he was free. It also caused more than a little anxiety. What would he do now?

One key to Johnson's mood may be his last comment on Shakespeare in the "Preface," remarking "that superiority of mind, which despised its own performances, when it compared them with its powers." Whether or not this insight applies to the playwright, it certainly fits his critic. Seven years later, after revising and correcting not only the *Dictionary* but the edition of Shakespeare,[74] Johnson took stock of his career in a poem, and did not like what he saw; in relation to Scaliger's scholarship, his work had been puny.[75] The self-deflation repeats (and may have been prompted by) a droll aside toward the end of the "Preface to Shakespeare" where, after citing Scaliger's dissatisfaction with his own editorial conjectures, Johnson adds that "the emendations of Scaliger and Lipsius, notwithstanding their wonderful sagacity and erudition, are often vague and disputable, like mine or Theobald's" (7: 110)—associating himself with Pope's prime Dunce. Here modesty itself seems like a form of heroism. Despising his own performances, Johnson reveals his sense of powers that have never been tapped.

Nevertheless, he had made his choice long ago. When Johnson took the mind of humanity for his province, he also ensured that no greatness, not even Shakespeare's, would ever be enough to satisfy him. A superior mind would best use its powers in service to others, helping them to enjoy life or endure it. The rest was vanity. In this respect even Garrick, who had made such good use of his talents, served as a better example than those who dreamt forever of future glory. Johnson's last words on Garrick—his death "has eclipsed the gaiety of nations, and impoverished the publick stock of harmless pleasure"—accept the real value of the stage.[76] Like Falstaff, who had "the most pleasing of all qualities, perpetual gaiety," Garrick had won universal affection, and, unlike Falstaff, what he gave the public was *harmless*. This is by no means faint praise. Bringing Shakespeare to life, the actor drives away the phantoms that afflict most people in private. Johnson honors his gift.

Yet a greater drama also fills Johnson's pages on Shakespeare: the drama of a mind that, however much it comprehended, could still have done more. Shakespeare tests the bounds of human nature, but we can always imagine another Shakespeare, one who never fell below his best. Some kinds of genius aim higher. Johnson's most moving instance of this genius is Pope, who whatever his deficiencies had "a mind active, ambitious, and adventurous, always investigating, always aspiring; in its widest searches still longing to go forward, in its highest flights still wishing to be higher; always imagining something greater than it knows, always endeavouring

232

more than it can do."[77] A mind of such genius will never be content. Perhaps Johnson's Shakespeare is too complacent about his power of pleasing. But no one can ever say that Johnson was too contented. In his theater of mind, the fear of greatness and hunger for greatness strive with each other forever.

9

Journeying Westward:
Political Writings; A Journey
to the Western Islands of Scotland

How small, of all that human hearts endure,
That part which laws or kings can cause or cure.

I N FEBRUARY 1767, during the famous conversation between
George III and the monarch of letters, "His Majesty enquired if he
was then writing any thing. He answered, he was not, for he had
pretty well told the world what he knew, and must now read to
acquire more knowledge . . . he thought he had already done his part
as a writer." The king would not be put off, and by the end of the
interview, when he proposed that Johnson undertake "the literary
biography of this country," the loyal subject "signified his readiness
to comply."[1] But nothing came of that pledge for more than a
decade. Johnson had spoken frankly to the king, and when he
thought about writing he was oppressed by feelings of emptiness.
The time of great projects—the dictionary, the moral essays, the
Shakespeare edition—had passed. Now, for the first time in twenty
years, the author was free to do as he wished, without a sense of
aversion or duty or guilt. Yet freedom brought no happiness, because it brought no spark of a new idea. Perhaps, it occurred to him,
he had nothing to say?

A long psychological crisis lies behind this pit of emptiness.
Throughout his fifties Johnson had struggled against a current of las-
situde and morbid fears that often threatened to overwhelm him.

234

"My indolence," he confided to his journal on the day before Easter 1764, "has sunk into grosser sluggishness, and my dissipation spread into wilder negligence . . . A kind of strange oblivion has overspread me, so that I know not what has become of the last year, and perceive that incidents and intelligence pass over me without leaving any impression." He was also terrified of going mad.[2] By the time he spoke to the king, a gradual recovery, or at least remission, had begun. In the summer of 1766 the Thrales gave him shelter at Streatham, their country house, and there he would feel at home and sometimes at peace for the next sixteen years. Yet mortification about the vice that kept him in thrall—his idleness, his vacancy of mind—remained among his prevailing private emotions. The inability to write confirmed his worst anxiety, that he might be unworthy of grace.

Such problems of writing may well have provoked as well as exemplified the crisis of late middle age. Johnson had forged an identity as an author, and an author who did not write would decline into nothing. This was a situation he could not endure. Had he in fact made the wrong choice of life? At times he preferred to think of himself as drifting, not quite committed to any profession, as if in the miraculously prolonged adolescence of Rasselas (and Imlac), always delaying the choice to some indefinite future when he might hope to realize his potential at last. No one knew how to tell that story better than he did. But it was no longer a plausible personal story. In 1764 a biographical sketch referred to Johnson as "This excellent Writer, who is no less the Glory of the present Age and Nation, than he will be the Admiration of all succeeding ones."[3] Like it or not, he now had a long reputation (with a doctorate to match), and all the world accepted him as an author. So he *had* made his choice of life. The question, therefore, was not whether what he had done amounted to something, but whether he had anything left to give. He would have to find a new story to tell, a story that took account of what happens to someone whose wish has been granted, whose talent is spent. At last he would have to think about a conclusion.

Any author who lives long enough will face a similar trial.[4] But not many authors have been as unwilling as Johnson to look back at their choices, or have taken less satisfaction from reflecting on their careers. "Frigid tranquillity" expresses what he feels, or says he feels, when he lets his work go.[5] One obvious reason for this urge to distance himself must be the "secret comparison" he habitually draws between the end of life and of any of its parts, most memorably in *The Idler* of April 5, 1760:

> The Idler, with all his chilness of tranquillity, is not wholly unaffected by the thought that his last essay is now before him.
> This secret horrour of the last is inseparable from a thinking being whose life is limited, and to whom death is dreadful.[6]

Some writers savor the finishing stroke of the pen; it stands for accomplishment and hope about the future. For Johnson the end is always a kind of dying. Against his will and his own advice, he takes the occasion to note how far short he has fallen. "We can conceive so much more than we can accomplish, that whoever tries his own actions by his imagination, may appear despicable in his own eyes."[7] He cannot help succumbing to that mistake. All the palliatives of preemptive dejection, his lifelong effort to avoid disappointment by smothering expectation, prove useless when he weighs himself and his work in the balance. Each final period brings him nearer the end.

Johnson's classic statement about the feelings of an author when a long work comes to an end—one of the classic statements in any language—is the Latin poem subtitled "Post Lexicon Anglicanum Auctum et Emendatum" (After Enlarging and Correcting the English Dictionary), which he headed with the Greek maxim ΓΝΩΘΙ ΣΕΑΥ–ΤΟΝ (*Gnōthi seauton,* "Be acquainted with thyself").[8] When he wrote the verses, in December 1772, he had spent a year and a half revising the *Dictionary* for its fourth edition (published in March 1773), and now it was done.[9] Clearly, the labor had brought back his past, the time of anonymity and drudgery. Beating the track of the alphabet once more, he was walking a treadmill, haunted by *déjà vu.* But this time the boredom was still more bitter. When young, he could blame his situation on other people, but now the treadmill seems to express his soul. In *London,* Juvenal's famous phrase for straitened circumstances, *res angusta domi,* was rendered as "Poverty," depressing Worth. But when Johnson quotes the same phrase in "*Gnōthi Seauton,*" he attaches it to poverty of *mind:*

> Quicquid agam, quocunque ferar, conatibus obstat
> Res angusta domi, et macrae penuria mentis.[10]

> (Whatever I do, wherever I am borne, scarce resources
> And mean impoverishment of mind frustrate my efforts.)

There is no way out of the circle, this time; he has made it himself.

At the same time, however, the poem exposes "a critical and dangerous time" of life, the grand climacteric.[11] Johnson takes stock of himself at sixty-three and finds the storehouse empty—out of material, as he had told the king. In a remarkable image, he personifies his "Animus," or soul, as the lord of a high fortress who cannot employ or admire his own treasures of mind, nor count his past works and honors as rewards of a well-spent life, but shudders instead at the sight of his gloomy kingdom, "where empty images, and fleeting shades,/and wispy shapes of things flutter through the void."[12] The figure works in several ways at once. To some extent it draws on ancient conventions for representing the body as a hierarchy of faculties, in which the Animus (the seat of feeling and the will), with Reason as its minister, rules over the various provinces that it keeps in good order and that sustain it in turn. In these terms a threat of physical and mental decay haunts the poem. Parts of Johnson's body have begun to desert him, and he cannot regulate his mind. When he tries to survey what he is and what he has done, the watcher in the tower peers into a silent landscape shrouded by night.

Yet Johnson's kingdom includes other people as well. What gives the passage its peculiar force is the divided or alienated outlook of the author as he reflects on his career. From one point of view, he seems to envision himself as others might, the Cham or commander of the literary world, gazing down from his heights on heaps of treasure and on subjects who pay respect to his authority. Johnson has reached a stage of life when he can expect to accumulate credit and honors. Like a general reviewing his troops, he counts the orderly rows of his works and his years ("operum serie, seriem dum computat aevi"; line 46). The *Dictionary* itself is a fortress. Yet all this show seems mock-heroic. The truth is that he takes no pride or joy in the past, and that his present standing brings no satisfaction. Thus his fortress is also a prison. Whatever his reputation may be, at home he lives among phantoms, the idle thoughts that will never take form or fill his vacancy. The great author feels like a pretender. Even the adulation that he receives from devotees such as Boswell only increases the sense of distance between the master seen by the world and the cipher within. Once again he has finished a work; once again it means nothing. This is indeed a critical time of life.

The poem as a whole is built on the same division. A *discordia concors,* or "harmonious discord," structures it:[13] the resemblance and contrast between Johnson and Joseph Scaliger, another great lexicographer. Despite the title he gives his poem, Johnson spends almost half the space (the first twenty-three of fifty-four lines) on his opposite number; to know yourself depends on knowing who you are not. Moreover, the comparison proves to be devastating, since Scaliger cannot be equaled. Johnson was not indulging in false modesty. From his early years he had reverenced the younger Scaliger (1540–1609), whom many considered the greatest scholar of all time (a claim that still has life), and who Johnson himself had agreed was "a godlike man, indeed Nature's greatest work."[14] When Scaliger complained that a lexicon was unworthy of his talents, therefore, "he was certainly right, that lofty, learned, penetrating one" ("Ille quidem recte, sublimis, doctus, et acer"; line 6).[15] The passage concludes with a lovely conceit in which Johnson imagines all languages applauding the master, whose scholarship has made it possible for voices around the earth to converse in a new *discordia concors.* But then the poet turns to himself, from *"Te"* to *"Me,"* and scorns his own complaints. Scaliger's voyage on the wide sea of words had reached its port in well-deserved applause; now Johnson's will be greeted with silence.

Nevertheless, it seems that something sticks from the comparison. To be inferior to Scaliger is no disgrace; implicitly it pleads their common cause. When Johnson measures himself, he uses the highest standard and puts his whole life on the scale. Even the title, in retrospect, might be equivocal. As a sign of humility, it suggests that the author accepts his own limitations; knowing himself, he knows that he will never be fit for heroic tasks. Yet it also hints at a quiet, furtive pride. Walking in Scaliger's footsteps, Johnson converts his own life story into an allegorical journey, like *The Choice of Hercules* or *The Pilgrim's Progress*. Thus he gains an immense perspective on his own problems. It is true that Scaliger had arrived at a destination, the ether where he was welcomed by celestial Wisdom herself ("Sapientia dia/Excipit aethereis"; 20–21), while his disciple still wanders and struggles to find a path (32–33). Yet the pilgrimage itself, not only the destination, gives meaning to life. Even the darkest moment of Johnson's journey provides a glint of striking self-knowledge (35–36):

> Notior ipse mihi fieri, incultumque fateri
> Pectus, et ingenium vano se robore jactans.
>
> (I am forced to become acquainted with myself, and confess an
>   uncultivated
> Breast, and the hollow hardwood of a talent for bravado.)

Ruthlessly viewing himself from outside, he reduces his character to a familiar, eternal type; and though he does not like what he sees, it does make sense.

The poem ends not with answers, however, but with a series of questions—all versions of the one great riddle, "What shall I do?" Should he wait for the darkness? arm himself boldly for weightier trials of strength? or meekly request new dictionaries? The treadmill starts again. But a saving touch of self-deprecating humor redeems the last words from despair or self-pity. Johnson reserves the right to draft alternative endings for the story of his life, and the final droll anticlimax only points up the natural climax that had preceded it, a possible ambitious project on the horizon. In this conclusion, nothing is yet concluded. But one moral, at least, is clear: the author needs to lay in new materials, new reserves of learning. Not even Phidias can create unless he has enough marble (38–39), and Johnson does not trust his own powers of creation. To acquire more knowledge would have to be his aim. Then, perhaps, he could think of a destination.

In fact his storehouse had never really been empty. At the very moment he told George III that he had stopped writing, he was in the midst of a massive collaboration with Robert Chambers, *A Course of Lectures on the English Law;* Johnson may well have been working on this project, in the library at Buckingham House, when the king interrupted him.[16] We cannot know specifically how much of the lectures Johnson wrote,[17] but his research and reflections on the history of English law would stamp everything he published for years to come. Nor would he lack other plans for long. Before revising the *Dictionary,* he had already thrown himself into the political pamphleteering that dominated his early sixties, and later in 1773 he would go off to Scotland with Boswell, gathering grist to grind and write about. From this point of view his later years belied his sense that he had dried up as a writer. All he had really wanted was good occasions.

That is not the whole truth, nonetheless. For an author's career cannot be reckoned in terms of the number of pages filled and chores carried out. Even aside from the fallow years of the 1760s, when only a trickle flowed from Johnson's pen, much of his later writing did not meet his own standards of accomplishment. The work to which he turned his hand did not seem work that he was born to do. As the end of his life approached, the question "What shall I do?" took on new urgency. In the past he had thought he knew, or knew what he hoped. The dreams of the young Enthusiast in *The Vanity of Human Wishes* may be doomed, yet they had been Johnson's own. The Rambler, as he looks back at his serious essays in his last number, feels "pleasure, which no blame or praise of man shall diminish or augment," and hopes to "be numbered among the writers who have given ardour to virtue, and confidence to truth."[18] The author of the *Dictionary* sets a goal that could hardly be more lofty: "The chief glory of every people arises from its authors: whether I shall add any thing by my own writings to the reputation of English literature must be left to time." Now time was running out. Would a work like *The False Alarm* come up to such standards?

In one respect, perhaps, it could. Johnson's pride as an author had never depended on the prestige of the challenge or genre he chose. So far as we know, he did not dream of writing an epic poem.[19] Instead he had reinvented authorship itself, by proving that the humblest commercial task—a catalogue, a lexicon, a preface, a review—could rise to the dignity of a calling. The grubstreet Odysseus had spent his whole life repairing the split between the hack and the master. Hence even the most occasional work or political pamphlet allowed a true author the scope to show how far he could see. In fact *The False Alarm* is a perfect example. No work could be more clearly tied to its moment or cause célèbre—an "alarming crisis," to use the call to arms that Johnson's title sets out to cancel.[20] He wrote the piece in just twenty-eight hours, "between eight o'clock on Wednesday night and twelve o'clock on Thursday night,"[21] and it was published less than a week later, January 17, 1770. The campaign to seat John Wilkes in the House of Commons was the general provocation; the immediate stimulus was the opening of Parliament, when the king himself had snubbed the Wilkites, the day before Johnson entered the fray.[22] Undoubtedly a zest for controversy whips the piece on, and Wilkes himself, dismissed with contempt, may be forgiven for describing it as an "effusion of servility and bombast" of which Johnson was "the spitter forth."[23] Yet *The False Alarm* goes out of its way to claim the high ground. It begins by setting the whole affair at a distance, diminishing it to a remnant of the bad old days of illiteracy and superstition, before the advent of knowledge and civilization. "One of the chief advantages derived by the present generation from the improvement and diffusion of philosophy, is deliverance from unnecessary terrours, and exemption from false alarms" (*Works* 10: 317–318). Wilkes is the sort of meteor that warlocks use to scare ignorant people, and "the advancement of political knowledge" will someday dispel such fears. Hence the author presents himself as above the battle, serenely distributing wisdom from his high tower.

Predictably, nothing annoyed the opposition more than that stance. Johnson's vituperation was bad enough, but his pretense of magnanimity was truly outrageous. One strong reply, which Boswell inferred, "both from his silence and his looks," had much impressed

Johnson, was written by Joseph Towers, who professes himself most offended just *because* he has so much admired "the writer of so moral, so elegant, and so valuable a work" as *The Rambler,* as well as other literary works "in which you had displayed great force of genius, extensive knowledge, and uncommon powers of language."[24] Now Johnson has degraded his better self with "party violence and rancour" and compromised his own authority. This is a very effective line of attack. Nevertheless, it also is double-edged. By conceding the continuity between the great man of letters and the haughty political hireling, Towers leaves room for another interpretation of Johnson's career, in which the Rambler's principles now turn to the public weal. It is not the occasion that makes the author, on this reading, but the author who makes the occasion. After all, even Johnson's enemies had recognized his authentic hand in the anonymous *False Alarm.* Had his wisdom now failed, or was it they whom party rancor blinded?

The issue is far from settled. To a large extent it remains at the center of recent debates about Johnson. One party of modern scholarship, represented especially by Donald J. Greene, regards his political views as deeply rational and levelheaded, if occasionally overexuberant, and esteems him as the spokesman for a "skeptical conservatism" that retains its power today. Another party, represented especially by J. C. D. Clark, regards his political views as consciously partisan, in every way molded by the conflicts of his time, and rather old-fashioned even then. According to Greene no set of labels—least of all the label Tory—can do justice to "Johnson's rigorously empirical approach to the facts of political power as it actually exists."[25] According to Clark three labels—Tory, Nonjuror, Jacobite—place Johnson firmly within "the spectrum of possibilities presented by his age."[26] Each scholar selects a different kind of evidence to support his position. For Greene, the coherence of Johnson's own thought is what matters, and the scholar must concentrate on the writings themselves and not on other people's interpretations. For Clark, reactions to Johnson are vital clues in defining where he stands, and the author's own works often seem to count less than the accusations of critics. No truce can be declared between these clashes of parties.

Perhaps the schism has lasted so long because it reflects a tension in Johnson himself. In almost all his major political writings, two voices collide. The first is that of the sage whose farseeing vision brings wisdom to bear on some squabble that petty minds have blown out of proportion. The second is that of a man who is very angry. The pamphlets tend to begin on a note of composure, as mild and detached as the philosophy they recommend, and rhetorically under control. Sweet reason furnishes a guide to analyze the fundamental truth of some proposition. Then gradually the temperature begins to rise; there are villains abroad. Most of Johnson's memorable sallies—"how is it that we hear the loudest yelps for liberty among the drivers of negroes?" (10: 454)—spring up near the end of his pamphlets. The voice of the partisan swells, and, in place of our impartial guide, what we hear is "contemptuous censure."[27] Nor can one justify this shift through some requirement of structure, as if the sequence had built deliberately to a climax; often the anger works quite the opposite way, overextending the argument until it breaks. Before *Taxation No Tyranny* was published, in March 1775, the government ordered some conciliatory revisions, particularly at the end, which Johnson himself admitted had originally been "indeed rather contemptuous."[28] But such diplomacy was not to his liking. His party spirit needed to find a vent.

The double register of Johnson's political voice is especially striking in what is often judged his most successful political pamphlet, *Thoughts on the Late Transactions Respecting Falkland's Islands* (1771). Here if anywhere he draws upon the skills he had acquired as a historical scholar as well as a journalist. With elegant precision, and not a little dry irony, the first half of the piece tells the story of how these distant and barren islands were discovered and became disputed by England and Spain. Then Johnson turns to the horrors of war and its futility in cases like these: "As war is the extremity of evil, it is surely the duty of those whose station intrusts them with the care of nations, to avert it from their charge" (10: 370). This argument serves North's ministry, which had indeed averted war against the clamor of the opposition. But it also contrives to rise above the battle, by keeping not only the Falklands but also the quarrel about them in proportion.

Thus far the work seems a model of statesmanship, as fresh in Thatcher's era as in North's. But then the argument comes home and turns upon the "bellowers of sedition" who thirst for blood. These "patriots" secretly want their country to fail; "Their hope is malevolence, and their good is evil" (10: 375). As the Falklands vanish, for several pages, the specter of Junius rises and fans the prose into a blaze of imagery: "what folly has taken for a comet that from its flaming hair shook pestilence and war, enquiry will find to be only a meteor formed by the vapours of putrefying democracy, and kindled into flame by the effervescence of interest struggling with conviction; which after having plunged its followers in a bog, will leave us enquiring why we regarded it" (10: 378). Johnson is evidently carried away. According to eighteenth-century theory, such visions reflect the writer's pitch of excitement, when he begins to *see* what his imagination has called forth.[29] Yet here the effect is somewhat contradictory. What Folly views as a comet with flaming hair is viewed by Enquiry, a cooler spirit, as no more than marsh gas or a will-o'-the-wisp, which will disappear as soon as readers stop paying attention. Hence imagination tries to cancel itself, reducing Junius to a symptom of rot. Nevertheless, strong images of "putrefying democracy" retain their stink, and it is hard to credit Johnson's indifference.[30]

The close of the pamphlet sinks still further into the language of gutters. "To fancy that our government can be subverted by the rabble, whom its lenity has pampered into impudence, is to fear that a city may be drowned by the overflowing of its kennels."[31] The body politic may be infested by lice, Johnson continues, but that is a shame, not a danger. Let patriots fade in peace. "To be harmless though by impotence obtains some degree of kindness; no man hates a worm as he hates a viper; they were once dreaded enough to be detested, as serpents that could bite; they have now shewn that they can only hiss, and may therefore quietly slink into holes, and change their slough unmolested and forgotten" (10: 386). Again the imagery belies the calm that it is supposed to portray. Protesting that there is nothing to fear, Johnson seems haunted by enemies who lurk in the sewers or under the ground and feed on his own sickly fancies. Each patriot harbors a serpent; in this passage, as in

244

the description of Junius and elsewhere throughout the pamphlets, the real antagonist seems to be Milton's Satan. We have come a long way from the Falklands.

What motivates this furious change of course? Each party of readers will vote for a different answer. A good many scholars think Johnson essentially justified, in this case, and for them the conclusion may sound like no more than righteous and appropriate indignation. But others might hear, in the jeer at the rabble, a desperate effort to turn back the tide, and for them the conclusion will show the underside of Johnson's argument, a rage that he has vainly tried to mask. Even his soundness of mind might come into question. The immediate spur to Johnson's renewed attention to politics was not a matter of theory, nor even of repaying the government for his pension, but something much more personal: his role in the parliamentary career of Henry Thrale.[32] Campaigning and writing for Thrale, he helped to preserve the family order that kept him in balance. John Wilkes was a threat to that order, and so was the rabble, which never took kindly to Thrale ("if Jesus Christ and St Paul were to stand candidate next election," according to one Southwark voter, "our folks would raise an opposition in favour of Barrabas").[33] Hence political issues could menace Johnson's hard-won equilibrium. It is not surprising that his response might sometimes be savage.

More broadly, however, the double voice of Johnson's pamphlets seems to reflect a doubt that he had seldom faced before, a doubt about his audience. Above all other political issues, this one strikes an author where he lives. For whom was he writing? The question had not troubled him through most of his career. He wrote, of course, for the public, or for some part of the public with which he was well acquainted: the readership of the *Gentleman's Magazine* and later the *Literary Magazine;* the apprentices who needed *The Preceptor;* the young people who drew so much of their sense of life from fiction; the London theatergoers whom he addressed at Drury Lane; and those who could appreciate a little Latin. To be sure, his relations with his audience were not always smooth. When he spoke to the fops and wits at Drury Lane, he was more prepared to defy than to please them; and though the Rambler seems quite familiar with the sort of people who look at periodical essays, he usually sticks at giving them the entertainment they want. He also knows exactly what is *not* the right audience for him: the *beau monde* that picks up *The World;* Lord Chesterfield; Horace Walpole. Such people are too polite, and think themselves the owners and patrons of English. Hence the *Dictionary* deliberately leaves out their favorite words. But otherwise Johnson aims at the whole British public, or at least the literate public of common readers. Whether they like him or not, he knows who they are.

The political pamphlets aim at a different public. Johnson speaks to those who agree with his party, or to those who would with a bit of encouragement; converting the heathen—or the American—is not what he undertakes. The interests of party dictate to him.[34] But his doubts about the audience go much deeper. During Johnson's own time the literate public had rapidly grown, and so had the press that fed its appetite for information and power.[35] Now the stakes of writing and reading had changed, in a volatile market. "Junius burst into notice with a blaze of impudence which has rarely glared upon the world before, and drew the rabble after him as a monster makes a show" (10: 376–377). This rabble could *read.* No British public had ever been so well informed or so quick to take up a cause. Johnson had played his own part in creating this public, but he was not certain that he could still communicate with it. Surely the reader, like everything else in the world, would thrive best under restraint. But those who were most attuned to the new reading public had learned a more reckless way of catching its interest. "Novelty captivates the superficial and thoughtless; vehemence delights the discontented and turbulent. He that contradicts acknowledged truth will always have an audience; he that vilifies established authority will always find abettors" (10: 376). Hereafter that rebel audience could never be Johnson's. His choice was to change his tone or to change his readers.

This problem preoccupies Johnson during his sixties. Even revising the *Dictionary* becomes an opportunity for shaping those who will read it, drawing them into a community of words in which established creeds of the church and state provide the ultimate authority.[36] The first edition had been more confident about the English reader, if not about the fate of England itself; despite its conservative principles, it

246

welcomes a future when many more people will have the resources for independent writing and reading. The fourth edition looks to the past and focuses more upon doctrine. Johnson adds relatively few new words; "literary," for instance, is still excluded, despite his past involvement with the *Literary Magazine*. Yet he does take the chance to insert many new illustrations, especially from Anglican divines. Not many readers could have been in doubt about the meaning of the adjective "one." But when the fourth edition introduces a sense previously ignored, "Not many; the same," it also expounds the creed of John Pearson: "The church is therefore *one*, though the members may be many; because they all agree in *one* faith. There is *one* Lord and *one* faith, and that truth once delivered to the saints, which whosoever shall receive, embrace, and profess, must necessarily be accounted *one* in reference to that profession: for if a company of believers become a church by believing, they must also become *one* church by believing *one* truth."[37] A dictionary hardly needs such pounding repetition, but the lexicographer apparently wants to drill the point into his readers. One congregation still survives in England—at least between the covers of this book.

Two words that Johnson uses often in the 1770s express his ambivalent attitude toward the newly literate masses. In happier moments he likes to refer to the *people*. The word seems particularly reassuring because it combines the sense of a particular class of persons (the "vulgar" or "commonalty") and the sense of "Men, or persons in general" with the sense of a multitude unified into *one:* "A nation; those who compose a community."[38] Johnson's most extended statement about the people, in a sermon he wrote for his friend John Taylor, considers how their happiness may be best promoted and concludes (as any sermon might) that politics is far less effective than faith. "The first duty therefore of a governour is to diffuse through the community a spirit of religion, to endeavour that a sense of the divine authority should prevail in all orders of men." For their part, the people must avoid envy, confusion, and strife, "and every man ought to incite in himself, and in his neighbour, that obedience to the laws, and that respect to the chief magistrate, which may secure and promote concord and quiet." In this peaceable kingdom, based on subordination, writers like Junius will have no place: "he that encourages irreverence, in himself, or others, to publick institutions, weakens all the human securities of peace, and all the corroborations of virtue."[39] Instead good readers should choose more respectable matter. Johnson imagines an ideal reading public: a nation; a group with a common purpose; the people.

Another word, however, crops up still more insistently in his writing: the impudent *rabble*.[40] Some of the people are clearly much better than others. "The people," Johnson explains in *The Patriot*, "is a very heterogeneous and confused mass of the wealthy and the poor, the wise and the foolish, the good and the bad. Before we confer on a man, who caresses the people, the title of Patriot, we must examine to what part of the people he directs his notice." If such a man appeals to the indigent, the weak, the ignorant, the profligate, "let his love of the people be no longer boasted."[41] Thus the rabble, as Johnson defines it ("A tumultuous croud; an assembly of low people"), comprises a living paradox: at once a part of the people and its opposite. Again faith furnishes a key. Johnson associates "the rabble, of whose religion little now remains but hatred of establishments," not only with Dissenters but with atheists.[42] Robert South had done the same a century before, in a sermon quoted by the *Dictionary*: "That profane, atheistical, epicurean *rabble*, whom the whole nation so rings of, are not the wisest men in the world." The church door shuts them out. Like the people, the rabble exist only as a collective, a crowd or assembly, but unlike the people they cannot sustain any common purpose: "who can guess the caprice of the rabble?"[43] They come to life only when *roused*, and decompose just as quickly. Hence such persons betray the people's latent weakness, a volatility that separatists can always exploit.

The rabble also make a great deal of noise. The word itself, etymologically related to both "babble" and "rap," suggests a constant stream of sound and a short attention span.[44] In his "Prologue to Goldsmith's *The Good Natur'd Man*" (1768), premiered just before a general election, Johnson compares the audience at the playhouse to a gang of electors: "loud rabbles vent their rage,/As mongrels bay the lion in a cage."[45] Such an audience will never be silent long enough to take the measure of a full Johnsonian period. Nor can he easily conceive them as his readers, now or in the future. Whether or not it is true that

"Johnson's pamphlets are declarations on behalf of a system threatened by forces perceived by him as seditious and rabble-rousing, whose nature he manifestly doesn't fully understand,"[46] he certainly understands that a world in thrall to such forces will have no time for him. The canceled proofs at the end of his last political pamphlet, *Taxation No Tyranny,* foretell (as in a nightmare) that the American population, a century and a quarter hence, will more than equal that of Europe.[47] "When the Whigs of America are thus multiplied, let the princes of the earth tremble in their palaces. If they should then continue to double and to double, their own hemisphere will not long contain them. But let not our boldest oppugners of authority look forward with delight to this futurity of . . ."[48] As the catchword at the bottom of the page informs us, the next page, had one been printed, would have begun with "whiggism." But in its absence, a reader would not be far wrong who substituted "The End." Futurity could hardly hold a greater terror than a world overrun by Whigs and the rabble.

Yet Johnson was not ready to write *finis* yet. A restless mind is still at work in the political pamphlets, nor has it lost faith in the people. In his happier moments, Johnson liked to assert that diffusion of knowledge had made the mass of the English people more civilized than any nation had ever been; by comparison, the ancient Greeks and Romans were no more than *barbarians.*[49] Even England, in his own youth, had been much inferior to what it had now become. "That general knowledge which now circulates in common talk was in [Addison's] time rarely to be found. Men not professing learning were not ashamed of ignorance; and in the female world any acquaintance with books was distinguished only to be censured . . . His attempt succeeded; enquiry was awakened, and comprehension expanded. An emulation of intellectual elegance was excited, and from his time our own life has been gradually exalted, and conversation purified and enlarged."[50] Johnson accepted that mission as his own; he would be Addison, and more than Addison, for the people of the new expanding Britain. If every great writer helps to create the set of tastes by which he will be read, as the Romantics would preach, then nothing could be more important for an author than to mold a readership that valued what he valued. That would be labor enough for Johnson's old age.

Meanwhile, the Whigs and rabble still seemed to be winning. Much as Johnson approves the dispersion of knowledge and the prosperity it fosters, he also reckons their cost. "Subordination is sadly broken down in this age. No man, now, has the same authority which his father had,—except a gaoler."[51] This is an old man's complaint, which Johnson resisted—most of the time. But politics brought it on strongly, locking him into the language of masters and rebels, of jailers and jailed. His distinctive gift as an author had always been his genius for taking long views, no matter how petty the topic; to the Rambler, the past and the future would watch forever over the same human nature. Now the present absorbed him, and one group of persons looked more like vermin or brutes. Perhaps he needed to look somewhere else to regain his perspective. The time had come for some travel, not only to renew his supply of knowledge but also to recall the principles of human life, the happiness and pain that governments could neither cause nor cure and that he shared with everyone else. If the road ahead was unclear, he might settle for one long restoring step backward: a journey to remind him how far he had come.

In the autumn of 1773, when Johnson visited the Hebrides, he traveled light but brought along the baggage of an author. Boswell later suggested "that a great part of what was in his *Journey to the Western Islands of Scotland* had been in his mind before he left London," and Johnson replied "Why yes, Sir, the topicks were; and books of travels will be good in proportion to what a man has previously in his mind; his knowing what to observe; his power of contrasting one mode of life with another . . . A man must carry knowledge with him, if he would bring home knowledge."[52] The *Journey* is a summary and test of what its last sentence calls "my thoughts on national manners," the thoughts he had been mulling for six years at least. Virtually every "topick" rehearses some theme from *A Course of Lectures on the English Law* or the political pamphlets: the differences between an oral and a literate culture, an economy of scarcity and a prosperous commercial economy, a feudal society based on subordination and force and a modern society regulated by religion and law, a country resistant to change and a country enfeebled by emigration, a people engrossed by local or special interests and a people unified by the sovereign power of Great Britain. All these issues Johnson had weighed or turned into a cause. But now he met them face to face, embodied in particular men and women. At every stage he found new images of life to test his thoughts.

Scotland was also a test for his theory of travel writing. "Few books disappoint their readers more than the narrations of travellers," he had observed in *Idler* 97, and now he would be put to the proof. "He only is a useful traveller who brings home something by which his country may be benefited; who procures some supply of want or some mitigation of evil, which may enable his readers to compare their condition with that of others, to improve it whenever it is worse, and whenever it is better to enjoy it."[53] What could make a trip to the Hebrides useful? Only a keen concern for the minds of readers—above all *English* readers—who might want to know how others live in order to gain another perspective on their own lives.[54] Two different vistas inform almost all the *Journey*. Since travel writing can serve no purpose unless it reports the truth, Johnson keeps one eye on what is immediately before him, and he interrogates the islanders to verify their (usually untrustworthy) stories and explanations. Yet he also keeps an eye on the reader at home—specifically on Hester Thrale, to whom he wrote long letters that formed the basis for much of the *Journey,* and whose attention to him made her an ideal audience.[55] Almost as much as Boswell, she is his companion. In a book of travels that appeared not long before the *Journey,* Giuseppe Baretti credited Johnson with suggesting his method: "I have spared no pains to carry my reader in some measure along with me; to make him see what I saw, hear what I heard, feel what I felt, and even think and fancy whatever I thought and fancied myself."[56] Johnson returned the compliment with extravagant praise of Baretti: "I know not whether the world has ever seen such travels before."[57] The best gauge of a journey would be the ideas it stirred in those who stayed at home.

That principle has always escaped some critics—especially the Scots. Though English reviewers tended to like the *Journey,* the Scottish reaction was fierce. Yet most of it misses the point. Johnson's reputation preceded him and made many readers defensive; assuming that he means to sit in judgment on Scotland, they bridle at his unconcern for Edinburgh or enlightenment.[58] But in fact he heads for the Western Islands just because they provide a contrast with the familiar, enlightened Scotland as well as with England. This will be no place like home. Johnson wants to journey into the past, into a primitive state of life and mind that may be vanishing moment by moment. Nor does he prejudge what he will find. To say that he is free of prejudice would be too much; there is no mistaking, for instance, his disdain for "epidemical enthusiasm, compounded of sullen scrupulousness and warlike ferocity" (*Journey,* p. 3), when the sight of a ruined cathedral reminds him of Knox. Yet most of the *Journey* stays remarkably balanced. Some conversations recorded by Boswell, as well as a few cancelled leafs in the *Journey* itself, show how opinionated the book might have been.[59] But that is a book that Johnson deliberately chose not to write. Changing his mind as occasion offers, he travels through history as well as through the landscape.[60] Nor does he miss the forest for the trees.

A similar balance marks his political views. For those who are certain that they understand what Johnson thinks, and who confidently decode his silences, the reticence of the *Journey* as it visits the lair of Jacobitism must signal his fear of exposing his real allegiances; since Charles Edward Stuart is never mentioned, "Johnson's book is *Hamlet* without the Prince."[61] But the *Journey* provides no evidence that Johnson regarded the Forty-five and its aftermath as tragedy. Whatever affection he may have felt for the Good Old Cause, the book confines itself to weighing the effects, both good and bad, of the laws passed after the Pretender's defeat, especially the Disarming Act of 1746.[62] Clearly the author is not a Whig, and he does pause briefly to honor Flora Macdonald (*Journey,* p. 54). Nor is he afraid to express some unfashionable regret for what has been lost, the old "blind veneration" for both religion and rulers. "If the remembrance of papal superstition is obliterated, the monuments of papal piety are likewise effaced" (p. 53). Such independence was too much for George III; on reading the book, he said (according to Horace Walpole), "I protest, Johnson seems to be a Papist and a Jacobite!"[63] But this reaction comes from someone unused to having to ponder both sides of an issue. The *Journey* is by no means a lament over yester-

day's battles and beautiful losers; Johnson would leave such sentiments to James Macpherson.[64] Nor did he go two miles out of
his way to visit Culloden. Instead he took two days to make a pilgrimage to the "illustrious island" of Iona, an ancient, neglected seat
of learning, precisely to distance himself from the world of false
alarms and daily news. "Whatever withdraws us from the power of
our senses; whatever makes the past, the distant, or the future pre-
dominate over the present, advances us in the dignity of thinking beings" (pp. 123–124). In the outposts of the Hebrides, political parties
seem very far away; and that is one good reason why Johnson went
there.

A retreat into thought also inspires the narrative as a whole. Just
as the travelers finally enter the Highlands, a long, self-conscious,
poetic passage sketches the time and place of the book's conception. "I sat down on a bank, such as a writer of Romance might have
delighted to feign. I had indeed no trees to whisper over my head,
but a clear rivulet streamed at my feet. The day was calm, the air
soft, and all was rudeness, silence, and solitude. Before me, and on
either side, were high hills, which by hindering the eye from ranging,
forced the mind to find entertainment for itself. Whether I spent the
hour well I know not; for here I first conceived the thought of this
narration" (*Journey,* p. 31). This self-centered paragraph is unusual
in Johnson's work, not least for the number of "I"s. The *Journey* ordinarily speaks of "we," including Boswell and the guides, but here the
author seems quite alone. Boswell's own *Journal* hardly notices
the spot, in fact, except for a long note that endorses the opinion of
the *"Critical Reviewers,"* who "are fully persuaded that the hour in
which the entertaining traveller conceived this narrative will be considered, by every reader of taste, as a fortunate event in the annals
of literature."[65] The tribute reinforces the special quality or *literari-
ness* of the description, a set piece that places writing and thought
above mere journeying. In this valley, as in a romance, imagination
is king. Johnson conceives his book in an hour of seclusion, when
the mind predominates over the senses and the author comes into
his own.

The following paragraph sets out the idea of the book as a whole.
What was Johnson thinking about as he sat on the bank? He was

wondering whether he could survive by himself. The trip to the Hebrides had required a good deal of courage; a man well into his sixties, and not in the best of health, would have to manage without his usual comforts, to dine at need on oats, to sleep sometimes on hay for want of a bed, to scale a cliff or be tossed about in a boat. Johnson's pride in his own uncomplaining fortitude supplies a constant undercurrent of pleasure in the *Journey,* as well as a more explicit drama in Boswell's *Journal.* But the danger also makes him sensitive to his surroundings. "The imaginations excited by the view of an unknown and untravelled wilderness are not such as arise in the artificial solitude of parks and gardens, a flattering notion of self-sufficiency . . . The phantoms which haunt a desert are want, and misery, and danger; the evils of dereliction rush upon the thoughts; man is made unwillingly acquainted with his own weakness, and meditation shews him only how little he can sustain, and how little he can perform." In such a place a solitary wanderer might starve or freeze to death. "Yet what are these hillocks to the ridges of Taurus, or these spots of wildness to the desarts of America?" (*Journey,* pp. 31–32). Traveling down a road that takes him away from civilization, Johnson pursues his train of thought to the furthest frontiers, barely able, if at all, to sustain human life. Survival itself is at issue.

This early reverie might lead in two different directions. One would be to deplore the lack of comforts and even necessities, contrasting the rude and barren Hebrides invidiously with the refinements of England (as Johnson's Scottish critics accused him of doing). But another would be to admire the resourcefulness and tenacity of a rural society, even under the least promising circumstances, and perhaps to imagine ways in which its life might be better. The latter seems what Johnson has in mind. He is interested in the process of civilizing, not as an abstract noun (the *Dictionary* does not include the modern sense of "civilization")[66] but as a verb that points to the various arts by which "savageness and brutality" can be reclaimed. The Western Islands do not lack civility, in his account. But more important, their arrangements of life stir thoughts about the interdependence of people, the social covenants all too easily forgotten by the pampered *beau monde,* with its "placid indulgence of voluntary delusions" (p. 32). The *Journey* explores a society that cannot afford such delusions, a society plain enough to reveal the history and common efforts that hold it together.

Yet the social fabric that he finds is also quite frail. When Johnson wonders about his own survival in the wilderness, he must be thinking about the local population as well; a good many islanders had already embarked for "the desarts of America." One starting place for the *Journey* might be the concluding lines that Johnson had furnished for Goldsmith's *Deserted Village* (1770):

> That trade's proud empire hastes to swift decay,
> As ocean sweeps the laboured mole away;
> While self-dependent power can time defy,
> As rocks resist the billows and the sky.[67]

A vision of "self-dependent power," like "self-sufficiency," offers some hope to those who fear that Whiggish ideas and luxury will inundate Britain. Yet the image balances between an economic and a moral principle. Johnson had never stopped preaching that "virtue only is in our power," and the thought of an indomitable island-nation, immune to change and self-contained as a rock, draws much of its strength from its association with the ideal of an incorruptible soul. If such was the virtue of Britain, at least in potential, so much more did it apply to the Hebrides, where rocks were anything but metaphorical and the natives had no choice but to rely on their own efforts. Here a traveler could hope to encounter the life of a former time, more simple and stable than the soft conveniences of the mainland. But manners were changing fast. Johnson perceives the signs of a break with the past wherever he goes. The Highlanders, whose rocks once "secluded them from the rest of mankind, and kept them an unaltered and discriminated race . . . are now losing their distinction, and hastening to mingle with the general community" (*Journey*, p. 38). Worse yet, subordination itself begins to decay. "There seems now, whatever be the cause, to be through a great part of the Highlands a general discontent . . . He that cannot live as he desires at home, listens to the tale of fortunate islands, and happy regions, where every man may have land of his own, and eat the product of

255

his labour without a superior" (p. 78). Soon enough the Hebrides may become like every place else—except more poor.

Johnson's response is not at all sentimental. Unlike Goldsmith, he does not believe that luxury hurts any nation,[68] nor can he forget the wretchedness of some old ways of life. The islanders dwell in a cold hard climate, not in sweet Auburn, and "if to the daily burden of distress any additional weight be added, nothing remains but to despair and die" (p. 115). Even the threat of depopulation fails to torment him. "If they are dissatisfied with that part of the globe, which their birth has allotted them, and resolve not to live without the pleasures of happier climates . . . I know not by what eloquence they can be persuaded, or by what offers they can be hired to stay" (p. 80). All he can do is suggest a few means of quieting their resentments, or "inquire, whether something may not be done to give nature a more cheerful face" (p. 116). Once again a long view removes the sting of local grievances. Johnson cares about particular people, but people can make their own choices of how to endure and survive. Thus he remains an observer, not a reformer, and peruses the Hebrides as if they were a collection of interesting practical knowledge. The suffering of the people of Mull does not affect him personally, except through a comparison with England. "All travel has its advantages. If the passenger visits better countries, he may learn to improve his own, and if fortune carries him to worse, he may learn to enjoy it" (p. 115). Some readers might call this hard-hearted. But Johnson stays true to his own portrait of the useful traveler, whose duty is to bring something home for his country.

What he brings home, finally, is a sense of invigoration. A tour of the Western Islands might have proved quite dangerous for Johnson, not only physically but spiritually. Journeying westward, into a region of chronic privation, he could easily have succumbed to acedia. In such a place, "the evils of dereliction rush upon the thoughts," and dereliction ("an utter forsaking or leaving; an abandoning") is the earthly equivalent, Hooker had said, of God's withdrawing of grace.[69] The elegiac tone of much of the *Journey* reminds us that time can run out for authors as well as for places. It also especially haunts one letter to Hester Thrale, when Johnson fears that bad weather may trap him on Skye for months. "You remember the

Doge of Genoa who being asked what struck him most at the French Court, answered, 'Myself.' I can not think many things here more likely to affect the fancy, than to see Johnson ending his Sixty fourth year in the wilderness of the Hebrides." But he quickly resolves not to return "without seeing or doing my best to see what these places afford."[70] The prescription for melancholy is not to be idle, and Johnson fills his days with curiosity and action. His confinement on Skye resulted, in fact, in an extended series of historical and anthropological investigations, querying everything from the uses of tacksmen to the authenticity of second sight and the poems of Ossian (*Journey,* pp. 63–99). Whether or not his conclusions are right, they are certainly not elegiac. A questing mind informs the *Journey,* and it is in search of the future as well as the past.

As Johnson approaches the end of his travels, his health and good humor seem to grow stronger. The journey has been successful, not least in taking the author out of himself. "We had amplified our thoughts with new scenes of nature, and new modes of life" (p. 130). But the surest sign of how far he has come is the place where he chooses to finish. Such a book, by its vagabond nature, might close almost anywhere: pushing away from the shore of the islands, or arriving at Inveraray or back home in London. Instead it concludes at a school for the deaf and dumb, a "subject of philosophical curiosity to be found in *Edinburgh,* which no other city has to shew" (p. 135). Johnson had read about the teaching of the deaf before, but here "the improvement of Mr. *Braidwood*'s pupils is wonderful" and obviously intrigues him. When he poses an arithmetic question, one young lady, "quivering her fingers in a manner which I thought very pretty, but of which I know not whether it was art or play," solves it with ease (p. 136). To some extent this is a test of Johnson as well; historically, acknowledging the ability of the deaf to communicate in ways other than speech has meant accepting them into the human family.[71] He passes that test, and uses it to draw a moral for the *Journey* as a whole. "It was pleasing to see one of the most desperate of human calamities capable of so much help: whatever enlarges hope, will exalt courage; after having seen the deaf taught arithmetick, who would be afraid to cultivate the *Hebrides?*" (pp. 136–137). Here many threads of the book are wound together: not only the satisfaction of curiosity and the hope to help people in need, but the over-coming of *fear*. If the *Journey* has balanced between the strains of elegy and hope for progress, a tension also in Johnson's mind as he thinks of his own past and future, it ends with a bold look forward. The author is happy; he still has questions to ask.

One final paragraph carries the lesson further. Instead of review-ing his journey, Johnson turns back to himself and stresses his own limitations. As a city dweller, "I may have been surprised by modes of life and appearances of nature, that are familiar to men of wider survey and more varied conversation. Novelty and ignorance must always be reciprocal, and I cannot but be conscious that my thoughts on national manners, are the thoughts of one who has seen but little" (p. 137). This show of humility disappointed Boswell: "Is not your concluding paragraph rather too modest?"[72] But Johnson's diffidence, so contrary to the assertive anger that ends each of his political pamphlets, restores his youthful ambition and sense of duty. No longer a master imprisoned in his high tower, no longer asking "What shall I do?", he now remembers how he began, by serv-ing his public and nation. Johnson is not afraid to confess his own weakness or how much he has to learn. Nearing the end of his jour-ney, he turns his eyes again toward new modes of life.

10

Touching the Shore:
The Lives of the English Poets

What land and people are this, what men live here?

THE WORK THAT CLIMAXED Johnson's career was sparked by a booksellers' war. Early in 1777 John Bell, an enterprising young publisher, began to advertise his forthcoming series of *The Poets of Great Britain Complete from Chaucer to Churchill,* intended "to furnish the public with the most beautiful, the correctest, the cheapest, and the only complete uniform edition of the British Poets."[1] The project aroused anxiety among London's leading booksellers, "the trade." Just three years earlier, in *Donaldson v. Becket,* the case for perpetual copyright had finally been quashed by the House of Lords; now rival publishers felt free to print their own editions of standard works. Bell had to be taken seriously. His twenty-one-volume edition of *British Theatre* (1776–1781) had already begun to compete successfully with the London trade's twelve-volume *New English Theatre* (1776–77); an excellent Edinburgh firm, the Apollo Press, was printing his *Poets;* and there was no doubting his entrepreneurial skills.[2] Thirty-six booksellers joined forces to parry this "invasion of what we call our Literary Property."[3]

Quickly they turned to Johnson. On March 29 a delegation called on him to solicit "a concise account of the life of each authour" for a new standard edition of *The English Poets,* and a bargain was struck at once. This was good publishing practice. In a fiercely competitive market, a name linked to the English language and Shakespeare would provide insurance against any edition that came less highly recommended; whether or not a purchaser dipped into the poets, he

259

or she could learn what the greatest living critic thought about them. Furthermore, Johnson gave excellent value. Though commissioned to write what he called "little Lives, and little Prefaces, to a little edition,"[4] and paid only 200 guineas, he cranked out copy that when first published, from 1779 to 1781, amounted to ten volumes (the booksellers rewarded him with another 100 guineas, and paid him 100 pounds more for revising a second edition).

What exactly had Johnson written, however? Its title, as well as its nature, remains in doubt. The first edition calls it *Prefaces, Biographical and Critical, to the Works of the English Poets,* and in the beginning these volumes could not be purchased separately from the poems. But almost at once the connection began to break down. Some readers rebelled against having to buy "a perfect litter of poets in fillagree"—sixty-eight volumes in small print—in order to get hold of Johnson.[5] As soon as the "prefaces" appeared, a Dublin edition pirated them in three volumes as *The Lives of the English Poets, and a criticism of their works, by Samuel Johnson* (1779–1781). And the London trade then issued a four-volume set, which Johnson suggested calling either *An Account of the Lives and Works of some of the most eminent English Poets* or *The English Poets biographically and critically considered,* but which the printer, John Nichols, less modestly titled *The Lives of the Most Eminent English Poets; with Critical Observations on their Works* (1781).[6] Soon enough the *Lives of the Poets* parted company from its parent, *The English Poets.* Today almost no one thinks of them as a set.

More than a proper title is at stake in these skirmishes. They bear on important changes in publishing, authorship, and the reading public. In earlier times, the want of an authoritative, uniform edition of British poets seems not to have troubled anyone or even to have been noticed. To some lovers of poetry, the very idea of such a series—in Bell's edition, 109 small volumes—might call up a nightmare vision of the age of print, as bad and good verse in identical packages covers the walls of libraries like so many bricks, inspiring collectors but straining the eyes and sinking the hearts of readers. Yet suddenly, in the 1770s, an urge for English poets in bulk swept over the public; these editions turned a good profit. The reasons for this new market are very complex. They surely include the rise of nationalism and the diffusion not only of literacy but also of widespread public interest in the arts. "The chief glory of every people arises from its authours," the Preface to the *Dictionary* had claimed, and within a few decades a great many English people desired to bask in and identify with that glory. At the same time, the peculiar notion that poets had expressed some essential national spirit invited a sorting out of past accomplishments, in a surge of literary criticism, biography, and history that classified poems into schools and orders of merit.[7] Such discriminations had once been the preserve of a few literati, whose wealth or expertise gave them access to great collections. Now stores of taste were available to any number of common readers—at least to those who could afford a sum of eight or nine pounds.

Yet what did they think they were buying? *The Works of the English Poets* did not speak for themselves. In the first place, someone had to decide which works and poets to choose or leave out, as well as some principles and contexts supporting the choice. To call this activity "canon-making" might overstate the editor's function, both because such editions aim to be comprehensive, not exclusive, and because copyright and the market, not critical fastidiousness, largely determine who will be in or out. Famously, Johnson agreed "to furnish a Preface and Life to any poet the booksellers pleased," including a few he despised, and he added only a handful.[8] To comment on a poem was not to approve it. Yet presence in the edition did imply a sort of worthiness, as if these poets, and only these, belonged to the main line of English verse. Moreover, the purchaser bought something more than poetry; *lives* were a selling point. As Johnson was well aware, many readers prefer information about the poet to poems: "There are few books on which more time is spent by young students, than on treatises which deliver the characters of authors."[9] Human interest might motivate that sort of reader to buy the edition. And others might buy from motives of patriotism, or social prestige, or in order to furnish a room.

The booksellers knew that poems alone would not sell their editions. Bell's *Poets of Great Britain* works hard to persuade its customers that they are buying the "English classics," a native equivalent to the traditional eminences of Greece and Rome. The copy texts derive from standard editions, and prefaces were lifted or patched together from the best-known biographical and critical sources (including Johnson's own *Life of Savage* and, as they became available, other *Lives of the Poets*).[10] Bell's *Poets* was also adorned by engravings, among them portraits copied from the famous collection in Chesterfield's Library.[11] All this conspires to wrap an air of authority around the series. In addition, Bell claimed that his edition would be "complete." The boast could hardly be sustained; despite the inclusion of Chaucer, Spenser, Donne, and Churchill, who were not among the rival *English Poets,* the set comprised only fifty authors and concentrated on the period when verse had become "correct," beginning with the Restoration. Yet not many purchasers seem to have felt deprived. Assured that they now possessed the whole tradition of British poetry, or at least as much as any reasonable person required, they owned an accredited stock of collectible treasures.

The readers of the other edition received a different kind of assurance: they were in Johnson's hands. Though he had not started or chosen the *English Poets,* he lent the project a consistent point of view. *Bell's Edition* was a proprietary affair, with the bookseller's name on the title page and the editorial work performed anonymously and under his supervision. *Johnson's Poets,* so called on the spines of the volumes though not on their title pages, were linked by one specific author. To be sure, that author indignantly disowned the attribution. "It is great impudence to put *Johnson's Poets* on the back of books which Johnson neither recommended nor revised. He recommended only Blackmore on the Creation, and Watts. How then are they Johnson's? This is indecent."[12] In the revised edition of *The Lives of the most eminent English Poets,* he distanced himself still more from the *Works* by referring to "the late collection," as if he had nothing to do with it. Yet readers who bought the set for its brand name had not been misled. Accompanied by its prefaces, the *Works of the English Poets* provides an occasion for Johnson to coach the public in his way of reading. Cowley's poems, by themselves, might seem out of date, but the critic puts them in a historical context: they grow out of the race of metaphysical poets and leave "such specimens of excellence" in versification "as enabled succeeding poets to improve it" (*Lives* 1: 65).

Hence the preface complements and justifies the collection. In order for readers to assimilate the tradition of English poetry, a good guide had first to invent it.[13]

This responsibility to the public drives Johnson's writing. In the "Advertisement" of 1779, explaining the length of the *Prefaces,* he remarks that "I have been led beyond my intention, I hope, by the honest desire of giving useful pleasure" (*Lives* 1: xxvi). That may not be the whole truth; opinions on poets and poetry had been ripening in Johnson over a lifetime, and once they began to come out they could not be resisted. But his sense of himself as an author still stands on an ideal of service. Just as the *Dictionary* had balanced between two views of its maker, one an anonymous drudge and the other a heroic guardian of England's heritage, so the *Prefaces* feature a servant of booksellers, poets, and readers who is also defiantly independent. In both cases, moreover, the author defines himself through an alliance with the public. By distilling the great English writers into a language or a poetic tradition that everyone can use, Johnson becomes the surrogate for a literate nation. The end of the *Prefaces* makes this alliance especially conspicuous. When first published, in 1781, the sequence closed with Gray, so that the memorable final paragraph—"In the character of his *Elegy* I rejoice to concur with the common reader; for by the common sense of readers uncorrupted with literary prejudices, after all the refinements of subtilty and the dogmatism of learning, must be finally decided all claim to poetical honours" (3: 441)—takes leave of all lives together.[14] The critic resigns his authority—and also asserts it, by merging the public judgment into his own. Johnson's whole career as an author had led to this moment.

Yet self-effacement was no longer his personal style. The writer of *Prefaces* and the author of *Lives* coexist at the price of some tension. Even before their separation from the *Works,* the *Prefaces* betray an unease with the subordinate genre to which they are supposed to belong. Ordinarily, such prefaces strain to place their subjects in a good light. Like letters of recommendation, they make the best possible case for the candidate's qualities and, without necessarily lying, leave the rest unsaid. *Bell's Poets* follows that pattern; so far as possible, a leading advocate introduces each poet, presumably whetting the reader's appetite. Johnson's procedure is different; he says what he thinks.[15]

The art of the anti-preface reaches a comic height with Edmund ("Rag") Smith, who is undermined right from the start. "Edmund Smith is one of those lucky writers who have without much labour attained high reputation, and who are mentioned with reverence rather for the possession than the exertion of uncommon abilities" (*Lives* 2: 1). There follows the preface supplied to Smith's *Works* by his friend William Oldisworth, who arranges a remarkably fulsome bouquet; for example, "Every subject that passed under his pen had all the life, proportion, and embellishments bestowed on it which an exquisite skill, a warm imagination, and a cool judgement could possibly bestow on it. The epique, lyrick, elegiack, every sort of poetry he touched upon (and he touched upon a great variety), was raised to its proper height . . ." (2: 7). Then Johnson's voice returns. "Such is the declamation of Oldisworth, written while his admiration was yet fresh, and his kindness warm; and therefore such as, without any criminal purpose of deceiving, shews a strong desire to make the most of all favourable truth. I cannot much commend the performance" (2: 11). Under some withering scrutiny, Smith's high reputation dissolves. Addison, for instance, had called the neglect of *Phaedra and Hippolytus* a national disgrace (an opinion seconded by Dick Minim).[16] "The authority of Addison is great," Johnson concedes, "yet the voice of the people, when to please the people is the purpose, deserves regard. In this question, I cannot but think the people in the right . . . What I cannot for a moment believe, I cannot for a moment behold with interest or anxiety" (2: 16). Nor is the reader encouraged to look further into Smith's work. The final pages of the anti-preface turn from the poet to Johnson's own past: to Gilbert Walmsley, a link between generations, who in his youth had known Smith and who in late middle age had befriended Johnson; and finally to a eulogy for David Garrick, another link with old times. No reader would begrudge these interpolations. Like Milton's references to himself in *Paradise Lost*, they might be considered the most moving part of the work. Yet their attraction has little to do with the *Works of the English Poets*. Instead they provoke the reader to think about life.[17]

Hence the *Lives of the Poets,* far more than their works, turned out to be what the public wanted to buy and what still lives in print. Very few readers care about Smith's or Savage's poems, but Johnson's way of judging the poets holds its interest. He had been reflecting on these matters from boyhood; half a century after meeting Walmsley, "it may be doubted whether a day now passes in which I have not some advantage from his friendship" (2: 21). Reminiscences color much of the *Lives,* which recreates the small London circle of writers and booksellers largely from memory rather than from documentation. A majority of the poets included had still been living in Johnson's time, and several of the later ones—Collins, Shenstone, Akenside, Gray—were actually younger than he. Thus the survey of poets and poetry has more than a hint of autobiography. The *Lives* was Johnson's summing up, a book he owed himself as well as the public. In pronouncing on the works of the English poets, he was also retracing, for one last time, the hopes and vanities of an author's career.

The life of an author poses a special challenge. Though Johnson had written many himself, "talking of biography," in 1773, "he said he did not know any literary man's life in England well-written." The context throws some light on this remark. Earlier the talk had been about lives of Swift; "MacLeod asked if it was not wrong in Orrery to expose the defects of a man with whom he lived in intimacy," and Johnson replied, "Why no, sir, after the man is dead, and it is done historically." But the reply was probably aimed at Boswell too. In Scotland Johnson could hardly forget that his traveling companion was eagerly gathering bits of his life. If the threat or promise of being a future biographical subject made him sometimes uneasy and caustic, it also prodded him to give instructions about what a proper literary biography should do: "It should tell us his studies, his manner of life, the means by which he attained to excellence, his opinion of his own works, and such particulars."[18] Information like this can help a reader understand that writing is a vocation; the work comes first. Hence the biographer ought to take us into the workshop and focus on how the writer produced his work. Other details, like those personal quirks and obiter dicta for which Boswell rummaged, have little to do with what matters most. Authorship should be the heart of the life of an author.

In practice, however, Johnson was not so proper. His biographical turn of mind, most fully exposed in *Rambler* 60, put weight on searching out "invisible circumstances," the small revelations of "a man's real character" that servants or close acquaintances were best equipped to notice. "The business of the biographer is often to pass slightly over those performances and incidents, which produce vulgar greatness, to lead the thoughts into domestick privacies, and display the minute details of daily life, where exterior appendages are cast aside."[19] The public record was seldom useful, and authors' writings could not be trusted as clues to their lives.[20] From this point of view, the challenge of writing an author's life might be the distance, or even the contradiction, between the work and the person who made it. Authors were skilled at creating fictions, but readers had to be warned against believing them. "Very few can boast of hearts which they dare lay open to themselves, and of which, by whatever accident exposed, they do not shun a distinct and continued view" (*Lives* 3: 207).

Thus the best biographer had to keep watch on whatever might rise to the surface, in hope of extracting an inner life that the subject might want to conceal. If Johnson sometimes seems to feel that Boswell is spying on him, his own advice may be responsible. A year before the trip to the Hebrides, he argued that "nobody can write the life of a man, but those who have eat and drunk and lived in social intercourse with him," and Boswell quickly said "that if it was not troublesome and presuming too much, I would request him to tell me all the little circumstances of his life; what schools he attended, when he came to Oxford, when he came to London, &c. &c. He did not disapprove of my curiosity as to these particulars; but said, 'They'll come out by degrees as we talk together.'"[21] The example is especially interesting because Boswell, despite persevering in his curiosity, never learned that Johnson had stayed at Oxford only a little more than a year (not three)—a circumstance that may have had a major influence on his life. Even an intimate friend can miss such details, through not knowing the right questions to ask or through putting a false construction on the answers. Parts of Johnson's history and soul were closed to Boswell. Yet later biographers could never recover the opportune moment to pry into inner recesses.

By his own standards, therefore, Johnson was not equipped to remedy the faults of previous lives. Except for the rare case like Savage, he had little access to the "volatile and evanescent" incidents, soon lost to memory, "which give excellence to biography."[22] Yet he did work out a practical equivalent, a sort of posthumous spying. From each biographical record, the *Lives* selects a limited number of anecdotes or "minute details of daily life" and interrogates them for evidence of character. Thus comments from servants often receive more attention than major public events. In the "Life of Pope," for instance, much of the central section inspects his "petty peculiarities," reported by "a female domestick of the Earl of Oxford" (3: 197). Similarly, the reader learns relatively little about Swift's actual dealings with national leaders, but two extended passages examine his "affectation of familiarity with the Great" (3: 61) and conclude that "no man, however, can pay a more servile tribute to the Great, than by suffering his liberty in their presence to aggrandize him in his own esteem" (3: 21). The harshness of this moral betrays some animus in Johnson; he disapproves of Swift's "general habits of thinking"—"the rage of neglected pride and the languishment of unsatisfied desire" (3: 61)—as well as his politics. Yet the method itself, sketching outlines of character from small, often fugitive signs of ulterior motives, is typical of the *Lives*. The poet most reveals himself when he is off-guard.

This method of writing a life attracted Johnson for two compelling reasons. The first was formal. Without access to many primary materials, and without the time or inclination to do much research, he was forced to rely not only on memory but also on standard biographical accounts, whether full lives of individual poets or collections such as Anthony à Wood's *Athenae Oxonienses* (1691–92), the *Biographia Britannica* (1747–1766), and "Cibber's" *Lives of the Poets* (1753).[23] The recital of facts in the *Lives* tends to stay close to sources, condensing and sometimes paraphrasing their information.[24] But Johnson's use of his predecessors is hardly mechanical. Converting a problem to an advantage, he casts a skeptical eye on the sources themselves, and makes his analysis of their plausibility or doubtfulness a center of interest. The first paragraph of the *Lives* criticizes Sprat's *Life of Cowley,* postponing the poet's birth to the second paragraph, and the following paragraphs seem less concerned with Cowley's youth than with Sprat's distortions. This divided attention persists through the *Lives.* It is as if Johnson looks at each poet over the shoulders of other writers or considers those writers as screens that challenge his powers of penetration. To find the life he must search and see through the sources.

Such sleuthing and probing were deeply ingrained in Johnson. He may have learned the technique from the great Pierre Bayle, whose "perpetual commentary"—an effort to sift out truth by reviewing and correcting the texts that had transmitted errors through generations—provided a method for the *Biographia Britannica* (as well as for enlightenment in general). "Bayle's Dictionary," Johnson told Boswell, "is a very useful work for those to consult who love the biographical part of literature, which is what I love most."[25] But classical scholars had always followed a similar chain of commentary on commentaries, a plan approved by Johnson in his edition of Shakespeare; and another favorite book, Sir Thomas Browne's *Vulgar Errours* (1646), could also have furnished a model.[26] What is new in the *Lives* is the prominence of the reflections, which assume that the poet's life and biography are valuable as examples of conduct for anyone's life. The moral asides do not interrupt the work; they carry its weight. The biographical narrative seldom contrives much suspense. Instead the reader becomes engaged in the process of excavating the truth, as both the poet's concealments and the dubiousness of the sources enter into a plot that Johnson patiently helps to uncover. In this way the method instills a lesson in how to read as well as write a life.

A second reason for Johnson's procedure may well have been still more important: it suited his sense of how life is best defined. The grand sweep of a public calling, the triumphal march to a certain goal, the hero's rendezvous with destiny were not the stories that he felt comfortable telling. When Johnson pictures life as a journey, it almost never arrives at a destination. Despite his fondness for *The*

Pilgrim's Progress, he ends his allegories still at sea or climbing the mountain, if not with a fall; only God knows how the story will end. Preemptive dejection shadows Johnson's images of other careers as well as his own. On the rare occasions when he does grant a happy ending to a life, like Scaliger's ascension in "Post Lexicon Anglicanum" or Robert Levet's sudden freedom, the victory clinches a contrast with the dismal existence of those who survive: the lexicographer going round in circles, or the rest of us who continue to toil from day to day. More typically death functions as an ironist, arriving just in time to show the vanity of a wish. Other writers might aim at a satisfying close, as Thomas Gibbons, in a passage quoted by Johnson, exalted Isaac Watts: "his days were numbered and finished, and, like a shock of corn in its season, he ascended into the regions of perfect and immortal life and joy" (*Lives* 3: 306). But the true Johnsonian note is sounded for Ambrose Philips, the next poet in line: "Having purchased an annuity of four hundred pounds, he now certainly hoped to pass some years of life in plenty and tranquillity; but his hope deceived him: he was struck with a palsy, and died June 18, 1749, in his seventy-eighth year" (3: 323).[27] Even the aged do not rest in peace in the *Lives.*

What characterizes the stories that Johnson tells about life, however, is less the pessimistic way in which he shapes the whole than his unwillingness to shape a whole at all. In prospect or retrospect, biographers usually want to view the various incidents of the subject's résumé as somehow fated, an inescapable pattern that draws all threads together. Most earlier biographies had traced such patterns, epitomizing legends of the saints. Poets especially seemed to follow a well-established course, or even to plan their lives along the lines of a Virgilian wheel or *cursus honorum:* a pastoral youth, a georgic maturity, an epic old age.[28] Johnson is not at home in that tradition. His own career had proceeded by fits and starts, or by whatever projects some entrepreneur had commissioned, and he seldom took pride in recalling his old achievements. If not for the chance of the booksellers' war, if no one had offered to pay him, the work that capped his last years would never have happened.

Hence *accidents* play a leading role in the *Lives.* The word occurs twice as early as the third paragraph, which explains how chancing upon *The Faerie Queene* made Cowley a poet. "Such are the accidents, which, sometimes remembered, and perhaps sometimes forgotten, produce that particular designation of mind and propensity for some certain science or employment, which is commonly called Genius. The true Genius is a mind of large general powers, accidentally determined to some particular direction" (1: 2). Johnson rehearses one of his favorite themes, the notion that genius, vulgarly misunderstood as a gift for one particular vocation, is actually "good sense applied with diligence to what was at first a mere accident."[29] To believe in the cant of genius would be pernicious, reducing human accomplishments to an effect of predestination and discouraging any but the elect from trying to reach the heights. The test of a life is not what is given, Johnson insists, but what one makes from opportunities that chance throws in the way.

Therefore there is nothing inevitable about Johnson's *Lives*. Rag Smith may have been born with talents second to none, but his life story fritters away in unkept promises. If such a story has a finishing stroke, it can only be some touch of poetic justice. When Smith prepared at last to write his masterpiece, he ate and drank until he felt the need for a violent purge, which an apothecary warned him against. "Smith, not pleased with the contradiction of a shopman, and boastful of his own knowledge, treated the notice with rude contempt, and swallowed his own medicine, which, in July 1710, brought him to the grave" (2: 18). Abrupt as it is, the catastrophe certainly seems appropriate and even satisfying—a matter of just deserts. Self-indulgence always doomed this poet. Yet both the moral and the life are treated casually; as narrative, Smith's whole existence is haphazard. When Johnson was young, he felt indignant at the *lie* made public by Gay's Epitaph, that *"Life is a jest."*[30] The sentiment would not have pleased the older Johnson either, and he never mentions the epitaph in the "Life of Gay." But if life seems far from a comedy, in the *Lives,* it also tends to lack a tragic dimension. Contingencies and accidents can always meddle with the best-shaped life, and death arrives at very inopportune moments.

Even a life that disappoints as a story, however, will offer a wealth of occasions for valuable lessons in prudence and virtue. The meaning of life, for Johnson, depends on countless small decisions, the turpitude and decency that everyone must cope with every day. From this point of view, a thorough study of just a few hours of behavior might yield more insight than a long survey of biographical facts.

The *Lives* is poised between diverging paths, the long and short prospects of life. Two brief Greek allegories deeply influenced eighteenth-century narratives: the "Table of Cebes," or "Picture of Human Life," which envisions life as a climb up the steep hill of Virtue, past many temptations, to the Abode of True Learning; and "The Choice of Hercules, between Virtue and Pleasure."[31] Johnson embraced them both. The allegories complement each other, and together they conclude *The Preceptor* (1748), to which Johnson added his own "Vision of Theodore," converting their morals to Christian faith.[32] Yet the two fables also represent artistic alternatives. "Cebes" views life across a vast expanse, as a panorama stretching from birth to death and beyond; "Hercules" focuses on one crossroads at one crucial moment of choice. One allegory lends itself to pageantry, the other to portraiture. The *Lives of the Poets* borrows freely from each.

Nevertheless, it was to a picture of life as a choice that Johnson usually turned.[33] Even his sweeping panorama, "The Vision of Theodore," departs from similar visions in its emphasis on *Habit,* which constantly threatens to lure *Reason's* followers off the right path, as if the long march of existence amounted to a series of tiny steps, interminable and frequently fatal. Nor is the visionary Theodore vouchsafed a sight of his life as a whole; he wakes midway up the mountain, besieged by *Habit* still. Johnson will not pretend that he knows how the story comes out. As a moralist and a God-fearing Christian, he shrinks from putting himself in the place of a final judge. The first edition of the *Lives* described Gilbert West as "one of the few poets to whom the grave needed not to be terrible," but the sentence later became conditional, "to whom the grave might be without its terrors" (3: 331); the pious West might deserve the names of "Poet and Saint" (3: 329), but the biographer has no license to jump to conclusions. All Johnson can show is a model of

271

daily virtue: "Perhaps it may not be without effect to tell that he read the prayers of the publick liturgy every morning to his family, and that on Sunday evening he called his servants into the parlour, and read to them first a sermon and then prayers" (3: 329). Here habit triumphs, securing the poet a good choice of life.

As a poet, however, West made rather poor choices; he lavished his skill on imitations of Spenser, a genre that "can be only pretty, the plaything of fashion and the amusement of a day" (3: 333). The life of a poet cannot omit such verdicts. Indeed, the short title *Lives of the Poets* misnames its contents by slighting the criticism that follows close on and completes each life. In the long run, as interest in most of those lives faded and much of the information about them needed correction, the poets turned into instructive occasions for Johnson's pronouncements; his criticism would survive a good deal of the verse it assessed. Nor did any one life, or any body of poems, compare in interest with the value placed on English poetry as a whole. What readers wanted and received from the *Lives* was a special sort of collective sequence, a panorama that took in Parnassus as well as Existence.[34]

What are the qualities of an ideal critic?

> The first I shall name is Mr. Johnson, a gentleman that owes to Nature excellent faculties and an elevated genius, and to industry and application many acquired accomplishments. His taste is distinguishing, just, and delicate; his judgement clear and his reason strong, accompanied with an imagination full of spirit, of great compass, and stored with refined ideas. He is a critick of the first rank; and, what is his peculiar ornament, he is delivered from the ostentation, malevolence, and supercilious temper that so often blemish men of that character. His remarks result from the nature and reason of things, and are formed by a judgement free, and unbiassed by the authority of those who have lazily followed each other in the same beaten track of thinking.　(*Lives* 2: 244–245)

Mr. Johnson, the perfect critic, never existed. He was invented by Richard Blackmore for *The Lay Monk* (1713–14), a periodical that needed a hero.[35] But Samuel Johnson enjoyed the fiction enough to

272

quote it at length in his "Life of Blackmore"; "the gigantick Johnson" was "such a constellation of excellence that his character shall not be suppressed."[36] With a playful wink to the reader, the two Johnsons merge into one, impartial, wise, and generous—a model of what the English critic should be.

That model critic stands behind the *Lives of the Poets.* One function of the work is distributing justice, not only by sorting out the achievements of English poetry but also by exemplifying a criticism that has risen above the pettiness of times and places and parties. Johnson added Blackmore to the roster of poets specifically to right an old wrong. Though scorned by the wits and remembered mostly as "a byeword of contempt" (2: 252), he had surpassed himself in one poem, *Creation,* which, "if he had written nothing else, would have transmitted him to posterity among the first favourites of the English Muse" (2: 244) and from which his implacable enemy Pope might well have learned the art of reasoning in verse. "Contempt is a kind of gangrene" (2: 250), yet magnanimity like Blackmore's deserves to live on.[37] Johnson, like Mr. Johnson, will think for himself, but he also considers the good of the common reader.

At the same time he tempts the reader to think about him. Without the coincidence of name and critical character, would Johnson have spent so much space on Mr. Johnson? Probably not. A sly self-reference, not boastful but mischievous, peeps through the lines. Much of the *Lives* invites us to wear the same bifocals, adjusted to watch the critic's reactions as well as the work he judges. This personal note surpasses anything in Johnson's earlier writings; he had never revealed so much of himself to the public, not even in the first-person narrative of the *Journey to the Western Islands of Scotland.* The critic has now come home. One reason must be his sense of a particular friendly audience, the Thrales, in whose house at Streatham some of the *Lives* was composed, and whom he entertained by reading selections at breakfast.[38] Their responses—especially Mrs. Thrale's—spurred him on and encouraged him to find ways to hold their attention. Yet another reason must be that opinions on writers had pervaded his conversation for most of his life. Never before had his writing been so in accord with his voice. The *Lives of the Poets* represents its author's own world.

In sharing that world with his readers, he founds the act of criticism on mutual interests. Johnson had always ranked criticism among "the subordinate and instrumental arts."[39] Since "the end of poetry is to instruct by pleasing," and the final test of poetry is whether it "can please many, and please long,"[40] in the long run "the voice of the people" must be decisive. The *Lives* is faithful to this principle. However low John Pomfret's critical standing might be, Johnson added his poems to the *English Poets* on the grounds that he "has always been the favourite of that class of readers, who without vanity or criticism seek only their own amusement," and "he who pleases many must have some species of merit" (1: 302). The critic humbly defers to a higher authority, the enjoyment of those who know only that they are pleased. Nor is Johnson's humility false. The tensions so keen a few years earlier in his political pamphlets, the fear that the *rabble* might drown out the *people,* play almost no role in the *Lives.* He seems to trust his readers now, "and the publick, which is never corrupted, nor often deceived, is to pass the last sentence upon literary claims."[41]

One clause, however, does leave some room for the critic: "nor often deceived." Apparently the public sometimes needs expert help. In his last *Adventurer,* Johnson had pointed out that books do not always fall into the right hands. "If mankind were left to judge for themselves, it is reasonable to imagine, that . . . a just opinion would be formed"; but "a few, a very few, commonly constitute the taste of the time" and thus have power to pervert the public judgment.[42] Critics can be potentially useful, therefore, if only by voiding the partiality of other critics and restoring mankind's freedom of choice. Johnson welcomes that mission. Identifying himself with the public interest, he tries to mold a reader in his image. In this respect, the famous tribute to the common sense of common readers, "uncorrupted with literary prejudices, after all the refinements of subtilty and the dogmatism of learning" (*Lives* 3: 441), is far from disinterested, since Johnson has spent the earlier part of his critique attacking prejudices, refinements, and dogmatism—not only Gray's but also his devotees'. Now that the fog of prejudice has been lifted, the reader can be relied on to see things clearly. Common readers are not only born; they are made by good critics.

Hence Johnson gives lessons in reading throughout the *Lives.* Assuming the role of a teacher, he constantly calls the class to attention and directs its eyes to the text. This purpose accounts for much of what has been called, and often condemned as, his literal-mindedness. In the "Prospect of Eton College," for instance, Gray's "supplication to father Thames, to tell him who drives the hoop or tosses the ball, is useless and puerile. Father Thames has no better means of knowing than himself" (3: 345). Many critics have taken this comment as a sign of hostility to metaphor as well as to Gray, or even of Johnson's insensitivity to figurative language (a charge that seems peculiar in light of the thicket of metaphors in his own writing).[43] But what Johnson remarks is the imprecision of the metaphor: father Thames, like the poet himself, can observe the scene, but cannot be supposed to know the boys' names. A careless reader, lulled by the encompassing air of pathos, will easily overlook the slack detail, and a modern critic might argue that the futility of putting questions to father Thames contributes to the disillusionment that the whole poem expresses. Johnson is less forgiving of lapses, nor will he excuse a faulty part for the sake of the whole. Both poets and readers must be trained in vigilance. Not even Pope, who "examined lines and words with minute and punctilious observation, and retouched every part with indefatigable diligence, till he had left nothing to be forgiven" (3: 221), can be pardoned "a line in which the 'Zephyrs' are made 'to lament in silence'" (3: 224).

Such lessons in reading are bound to be controversial. A critic who keeps a close watch on faults may be in danger of cutting texts to pieces, like a harsh schoolmaster, while forgetting to enter their spirit. More appreciative readers will always find ways to justify poems that they love. Nor can one deny that what provokes readers depends on personal taste and the tastes of the age. The poetic effects that distract Johnson most—the useless supplication of father Thames, the silent lament of the zephyrs—consistently verge on what some later critics would call the highest pleasure of art, the sublime: a mode of baffling the mind by reaching beyond what the senses can comprehend. A zephyr one hears without hearing transcends the realm of perception and forces readers to imagine the unrealizable. But readers may well develop a taste for what they

275

cannot conceive. Since Johnson's own time, many critical theories have used the sublime as their standard of art at its best.[44]

Moreover, such critics often demand that readers be very uncommon. In an unconditional challenge to Johnson, Thomas De Quincey bitterly scorns his appeal to the common reader: "To the great majority of readers [*Paradise Lost*] is wearisome through mere vulgarity and helpless imbecility of mind; not from overstrained excitement, but from pure defect in the *capacity* for excitement . . . What is *ideally* grand lies beyond the region of ordinary human sympathies; which must, by a mere instinct of good sense, seek out objects more congenial and upon their own level."[45] What right had readers to measure Milton against their own paltry selves?

Perhaps no passage in English criticism offended Romantic critics more than Johnson's comments on "the want of human interest" in *Paradise Lost*.[46] "The man and woman who act and suffer are in a state which no other man or woman can ever know. The reader finds no transaction in which he can be engaged, beholds no condition in which he can by any effort of imagination place himself; he has, therefore, little natural curiosity or sympathy . . . *Paradise Lost* is one of the books which the reader admires and lays down, and forgets to take up again. None ever wished it longer than it is" (*Lives* 1: 181, 183). The final sentence, a particular favorite of common readers, speaks the kind of truth for which Johnson is famous: refreshing and down to earth. Yet it also dares the reader to disagree. A single opponent could refute it by wishing sincerely that the poem *were* longer (surprisingly few have taken up the dare). How could Johnson possibly know that no one had an experience different from his own? Evidently he finds the common reader within, or else deliberately adjusts his responses to those that anyone might have—a process that De Quincey would call "levelling."[47] Johnson does not deny the poet extraordinary powers; the comments on human interest frame a tribute to Milton's amazing genius and vigor of mind, "fermented by study and exalted by imagination" (1: 183). But the *Lives* is written for men and women who cannot live up to that shining example, and who cannot make one with the uniqueness of Adam and Eve and Milton. Johnson will not look down on his read-

276

ers. Through stubborn acts of imagination, he wills himself into their lives.[48]

The common thus becomes his critical standard. Courage was needed to put so much weight on such an equivocal word. If the *Dictionary* acknowledges the positive nuance of *common* prayer— "4. Publick; general, serving the use of all"—it also defines the lowness of *common* men—"3. Vulgar, mean; not distinguished by any excellence; often seen; easy to be had; of little value; not rare; not scarce . . . 5. Of no rank; mean; without birth or descent . . . 7. Prostitute." In eighteenth-century society (and perhaps in later times as well), associating oneself with the common, as well as rejoicing in it, can seem like a sort of penance—or even defiance.

Johnson refuses to back away from those implications. A belligerent repetition of "common" tops off his censure of the Eton ode. "Gray thought his language more poetical as it was more remote from common use: finding in Dryden 'honey redolent of Spring,' an expression that reaches the utmost limits of our language, Gray drove it a little more beyond common apprehension, by making 'gales' to be 'redolent of joy and youth'" (*Lives* 3: 435). This is a shrewd analysis, so far as it goes. Gray did strive "to widen the space of separation" between poetry and the everyday language of prose,[49] and a reader who knows that "redolent" means "sweet of scent" *(Dictionary)* will try in vain to sniff that fragrance in the gales. Nor does the image reflect originality of thought; decoded, it "suggests nothing to Gray which every beholder does not equally think and feel" (3: 434). Thus mannerisms of diction are out of place in this poem; they contradict its common humanity (as does the uncommon language of the *Elegy* itself). To be sure, not every reader would want to limit poetic language to "common use" and "common apprehension." But poets and connoisseurs must remember that they are the custodians of language, not its owners. Johnson's aggressive championing of hoi polloi against what he regards as Gray's elite scholastic affectations sets up a little drama, to be resolved only when the common reader triumphs at the end. The *English Poets* will not be allowed to belong to a few; the people alone have the right to decide who best represents them.

Hence the *Lives* is possessed by the people, in every respect. Even when reading exceptional poems, Johnson locates their appeal in common concerns. The sparkle of *The Rape of the Lock,* for instance, is often considered to reflect its pictures of high society, a courtly showcase in which even the gods are enlisted as servants of glamour. Johnson sees Pope's world in a different light. He begins by noting the praises heaped on the poem "by readers of every class, from the critick to the waiting maid," and tries to explain its universal attraction in terms of general principles: "new things are made familiar, and familiar things are made new" (3: 232–233). The charms most likely to be appreciated by educated or fashionable readers— the epic allusions, the pleasures of London and gossip—are never mentioned at all. This critic does not observe any class distinctions. "The subject of the poem is an event below the common incidents of common life," where every reader can feel socially adequate, even when rubbing elbows with a spirit. "A race of aerial people never heard of before is presented to us in a manner so clear and easy, that the reader seeks for no further information, but immediately mingles with his new acquaintance, adopts their interests and attends their pursuits, loves a sylph and detests a gnome" (3: 234). Similarly, the poetic moral is brought home to the daily lives of ordinary people: "The freaks, and humours, and spleen, and vanity of women, as they embroil families in discord and fill houses with disquiet, do more to obstruct the happiness of life in a year than the ambition of the clergy in many centuries" (3: 234). Johnson ignores the mystique of *The Rape of the Lock,* its glorification of beauty and art and the things of this world. Instead he tracks its sources in human nature.

Nor does the *Lives* underestimate the depth of the people. "About things on which the public thinks long it commonly attains to think right" (2: 132), precisely because it cannot be fooled about things that touch its own humanity. An onus is put on the critic to match that depth, by helping the public to trust its best instincts and understand why they are just. The common reader's love for *The Rape of the Lock* may be explained but not set aside. Moreover, the weight of opinion and passage of time will try the critic himself. Mr. Johnson, Blackmore's ideal critic, had been the leader of a club, in an age before "an emulation of intellectual elegance" had been excited among a large public (2: 146). By the late eighteenth century, the club of poetry readers included much of the nation. Even the elegant Addison had come to seem superficial, since readers had outgrown "the blandishments of gentleness and facility" (2: 147) through which he had polished their tastes. The *Lives* sets out to build on Addison's most lasting criticism, "in which he founds art on the base of nature, and draws the principles of invention from dispositions inherent in the mind of man" (2: 148). At last English poetry finds its place, in the mind of the English reader.

The human nature of poets also must be put to the test. If part of Johnson honors the common reader, another part glories in the genius of authors. Ultimately he sees no contradiction between them, since the greatest poets express what everyone thinks and feels— "just representations of general nature"—and, in those kindred thoughts and feelings, readers will recognize their own best selves, or what a human being can achieve. The reader, the poet, the critic ideally share the same humanity. In practice, however, as Rasselas grumbles, "no human being can ever be a poet"—that is, no single person can know everything and stand for everyone. The lives of poets show how peculiar these very flawed creatures may be. Furthermore, a poetic vocation puts strains upon human nature. When Imlac feels "the enthusiastic fit" and proceeds "to aggrandize his own profession," he succumbs to the hazards of all his tribe, who feed on wishes and dreams.[50] Poets aspire to be immortal, to shape the world according to their fancies. No wonder their lives and dreams so often are at odds.

The form of each of the *Lives* embodies the separation of human being and poet. The first section describes the life, the last judges the poems, while a brief middle section typically offers a character sketch that may or may not connect them. Implicit tensions run from part to part. In the biographical section on Waller, for instance, Johnson does not conceal his "contempt and indignation" for "the laxity of his political principles and the weakness of his resolution" (1: 271, 281), and the sycophantic "Panegyrick" on Cromwell is called "judicious" only because it manages not to mention "the rebel or the regicide" (1: 269). Yet the later critical comment remarks that the poem, despite "its great fault" in "the choice of its hero," "has obtained from the publick a very liberal dividend of praise, which however cannot be said to have been unjustly lavished; for such a series of verses had rarely appeared before in the English language. Of the lines some are grand, some are graceful, and all are musical" (1: 289). However much Waller's character may be scorned, the poet Waller must be given his due. Johnson draws a careful line between them.

Nevertheless, the line often seems frayed. From the beginning, some readers have always suspected that Johnson's attitude toward a life story—especially the poet's political leanings—slants his critical judgments of the poems. Defenders of Milton were quick to charge that the "strictures on Milton's poetry . . . are tainted throughout with the effects of an inveterate hatred to Milton's politics, with which, as the Biographer of a Poet the author of *Paradise Lost,* the Critic had very little to do."[51] To some extent this accusation mirrors the fault it condemns: a liking for Milton's politics, and loathing for Johnson's, makes the angry critic assume that only Tory prejudice could explain why anyone might yawn over *Paradise Lost* (such critics conveniently overlook Johnson's *praise*). Yet even impartial readers hear echoes of biography in the critical section. The relations of art and life still fascinate critics, a fascination that started with Johnson himself, as author and subject.[52] In the Romantic period, the collective biographies that followed the pattern of *Lives of the Poets* often tended to erase the distinction between biography and criticism, as if the central character sketch absorbed the life as a whole.[53] The effort continues today, when many biographers hope that an accumulation of details about the writer will somehow cast light on the writing. No matter how often the effort may fail, it remains an attractive ideal. This book itself defers to that ideal.

In many ways, however, Johnson's example resists the association of lives with works. Readers, he knows, perpetually want to meet authors whose writings they love, but readers whose wish is granted "have indeed had frequent reason to repent their curiosity; the bubble that sparkled before them has become common water at the touch."[54] Such warnings abound in Johnson's writing; he never stops pricking the bubble. "The biographer of Thomson has remarked that an author's life is best read in his works: his observation was not well-timed. Savage, who lived much with Thomson, once told me how he heard a lady remarking that she could gather from his works three parts of his character, that he was 'a great lover, a great swimmer, and rigorously abstinent'; but, said Savage, he knows not any love but that of the sex; he was perhaps never in cold water in his life; and he indulges himself in all the luxury that comes within his reach" (*Lives* 3: 297–298). In this case the lady's error may have been harmless, but other confusions of life and work lead readers astray. The petty failings of Bacon leave his great wisdom intact in his works, nor should Savage's failure to practice what he preached be allowed to diminish respect for the virtue his poems display.[55] The test of the work is not where it comes from but what it does for the reader.

Nor does Johnson believe that the works of each poet express a unique and autonomous spirit. All literate people can be taught to write verse, but some write better than others. Poems are performances, not inspirations, in this view, and the powers they exhibit must be compared with mental powers in general. Hence the final interest in writing the life of a poet will not be to find the secret source of his poems but to judge his powers, how well they have been used, and what might be learned from them.[56] In the next generation, the genius of Chatterton would become the type of the poet—self-created and self-destroyed. Johnson, too, was absorbed by young people's feats of remarkable learning and talent. One of his early lives commemorates John Philip Barretier (Baratier), who before his death at nineteen had distinguished himself in every field with "such a proficiency as no one has yet reached at the same age,"[57] and the *Lives of the Poets* pays special attention to early signs of promise such as "the learned puerilities of Cowley" (1: 3). But Johnson concentrates most on what these prodigies reveal about the human possibilities that can be shared—for instance, the scheme of education that produced a Barretier—not on their differences from all other mortals. Exceptional talent is uninteresting if, like Rag Smith's, it seldom is used. Nor can the greatest poetry, like Milton's, excuse the selfish failings of a life. Encouraging readers to follow Milton's "sullen desire of independence" in order to write like him would be the worst conceivable lesson; "like other heroes he is to be admired rather than imitated" (1: 194). To some extent the critic guards the poems against the poet's self-absorption.

What *does* connect the life and work, then? The right answer must be a poetic career, a part of the life that bears directly on what the poet has done. When Johnson complained that "he did not know any literary man's life in England well-written," he was thinking about the writer's routines and resources: "his studies, his manner of life, the means by which he attained to excellence, his opinion of his own works, and such particulars."[58] The life of a poet should concentrate on a lifework, and much of the *Lives* delves into the tricks of the trade. The biographical section on Pope's *Iliad,* for instance, gives a good deal of space to how the subscription was managed, then offers several pages of manuscript revisions: "To those who have skill to estimate the excellence and difficulty of this great work, it must be very desirable to know how it was performed, and by what gradations it advanced to correctness" (3: 119). By contrast, details about Pope's private life are minimal; among the women closest to his heart, Martha Blount hardly puts in an appearance, and Teresa Blount goes unmentioned. It is the poet whom Johnson cares about most, and the traits of the man seem less important unless they bear on his work.

As a moralist and student of human nature, however, Johnson keeps his eye on poetic malpractice. The private life does come into play when it hints at faults that also weaken the poems. The "Life of Cowley" sets the tone immediately. "The basis of all excellence is truth: he that professes love ought to feel its power." Although Cowley wrote love poems, he was not a real lover. "This consideration cannot but abate in some measure the reader's esteem for the work and the author . . . No man needs to be so burthened with life as to squander it in voluntary dreams of fictitious occurrences" (1: 6–7). When Johnson comes back to the love poems in the critical section, he presses the same point home. "Considered as the verses of a lover, no man that has ever loved will much commend them . . . they turn the mind only on the writer, whom, without thinking on a woman but as the subject for his talk, we sometimes esteem as learned and sometimes despise as trifling, always admire as ingenious, and always condemn as unnatural" (1: 40, 42). The criticism extends beyond Cowley to the whole race of metaphysical poets, whose self-conscious learning departs from nature in order to impress—but not delight—the audience. Here Cowley's choice of life and choice of poetry seem of a piece; he is a poet's poet, not a reader's. Despite Johnson's admiration for learning, and his inclination to think of poetry as a kind of learning, he shrinks from writers whose lucubrations on love can take the place of knowing what love is.[59] Such poets disregard "that uniformity of sentiment, which enables us to conceive and to excite the pains and pleasures of other minds"; they write "rather as beholders than partakers of human nature" (1: 20). One can hardly believe that this critical comment does not also impugn a poet's whole way of life.

Poetic poses constantly suffer this fate in the *Lives*. The juxtaposition of life and art reveals how often poems dress up a sordid truth, how close they come to lies. Moreover, most biographies collaborate in this process by exalting the poet or constructing a fiction in which the poet merges into his poems. Johnson dismantles the fiction. Skeptically analyzing not only the poet's representations of life but also the biographical traditions that accumulate around them, he teases out the ordinary likelihood behind the implausible ideal. This critic does not credit miracles, at least when human beings are supposed to have brought them about. According to one popular eighteenth-century view, aggressively argued by John Dennis, "the great Design of Arts is to restore the Decays that happen'd to human Nature by the Fall, by restoring Order"; each poem should strive to recreate the perfection of Eden. "As Man is the more perfect, the more he resembles his Creator; the Works of Man must needs be more perfect, the more they resemble his Maker's."[60] But Johnson will not allow that poets and poems can nullify original sin. When he contemplates the state of innocence in *Paradise Lost* (Dennis' prime example), he doubts "if indeed in our present misery it be possible to conceive it" (1: 180); that is one reason why the poem lacks human interest. The *Lives* finds few saints and martyrs among its

283

poets. Hence the chief result of connecting lives and works may be to implicate poetry in the same human frailties that its art temporarily masks.

Yet the pattern of the *Lives* as a whole suggests a more positive view. Most readers would have felt that the work was progressive, in two decisive respects. The first is the story it tells about English poetry, a sequence of gradual, solid improvement. Other critics in Johnson's own time perceived a decline, or even a crushing descent from the heights of Spenser and Shakespeare and Milton. Thomas Warton's ground-breaking *History of English Poetry*, whose third volume was published in 1781, the same year as the last of the *Lives*, laments the passing of an age of "original and true poetry," succeeded by mere prose in modern times,[61] and Collins and Gray had expressed in anti-progress poems their sense of having come too late. Johnson does not agree. Despite his lack of sympathy with much of the verse that appeared after his own taste had been formed, during the heyday of Pope,[62] he often approves of modern refinements in culture and art. One reason he dislikes the modish experiments of younger poets is that he finds them preciously archaic—"All is strange, yet nothing new."[63] There is little or no nostalgia in the *Lives*. Beginning with Cowley foretokens a clear line of progress: "if he left versification yet improvable, he left likewise from time to time such specimens of excellence as enabled succeeding poets to improve it" (1: 65). Later English verse had kept that promise. If the booksellers had been able to include the poems of Goldsmith (still covered by copyright) among the *English Poets*, Johnson would surely have praised them in the highest terms (not only because he himself had written some of the lines),[64] and as late as 1783 he read Crabbe's *Village* with great delight.[65] In any case, the collection itself implied that English poetry had reached its harvest season.

The structure of each individual life, moreover, offers a second, still more decisive token of progress: it moves from human faults to poetic achievements. The biographical section rarely ends well. When death does not follow a long decline, in the *Lives of the Poets*, it tends to interrupt some futile hope. Nor does the irony cease at death, which often sets off fresh squabbles among the survivors, as in the horrendous if spurious tale of Dryden's funeral.[66] Yet the critical section repairs the damage by turning to what will last. If life reveals the fictions of art, then art can display the fruits of a life devoted to it, and in the *Lives* it is art that has the last word. Even a writer imperfect as Young is blessed by a final sentence: "But, with all his defects, he was a man of genius and a poet" (3: 399). The major poets receive extended tributes, as conclusive as anything Johnson ever wrote. In the end, apparently, great poetry vindicates life and sometimes may even redeem it. After all reservations and enmities have been put in the ledger, Johnson converts his account of Milton's intransigence into a reason for praise: "His great works were performed under discountenance and in blindness, but difficulties vanished at his touch; he was born for whatever is arduous; and his work is not the greatest of heroick poems, only because it is not the first" (1: 194). The regicide fades; the poet rises to glory.

His glory also sheds luster upon the nation. Collectively, the final paragraphs of major lives compose a sanguine history of English poetic refinement. Cowley showed the way to rival the ancients. Milton surpassed all epic poets but Homer. Dryden disclosed the innate potential of English: "Perhaps no nation ever produced a writer that enriched his language with such variety of models . . . he found [English poetry] brick, and he left it marble" (1: 469). Pope, in the last of the *Lives* to be written, perfected English versification—"Art and diligence have now done their best"—and left a model of poetry for the ages: "If Pope be not a poet, where is poetry to be found?" (3: 251). And progress continues, if not with Gray, then with the improved and unprejudiced common reader. The *Lives of the Poets* records an achievement far greater than that of any individual poet, an achievement in which every British reader might feel some involvement. Even the stringent gatekeeping, which leaves so many poems and poets in limbo, validates the high standards that other poets have met. From the *Lives* as a whole, the reader can gather a sense of what poets and readers have built together, the national genius.[67]

That genius can take in both life and art. Of all the poems by his contemporaries, Johnson seems to have been most moved by "the character of the British nation" in Goldsmith's *Traveller,* at once a celebration of independence—"Pride in their port, defiance in their eye,/I see the lords of human kind pass by"—and a warning against its excesses—"That independence Britons prize too high,/Keeps man from man and breaks the social tie."[68] When each person pursues self-interest, Goldsmith cautions, both kings and poets will die unhonored; the national memory depends on holding interests in common. The *Lives* adopts that cause. Without denying the problematic consequences of British freedom—not only eccentricity like Swift's but rebellion like Milton's—it shows how singular gifts can be made to combine in a unified poetic commonwealth. Memory is the ultimate social tie. Just as the self-interest of any life exemplifies some principles of human nature, so the course of any career flows into the stream of English poetry. In the end, the *Lives of the Poets* remembers, the lives and works alike belong to one people.

Yet Johnson was also reviewing his own career. The dream of authorship that had been with him from his earliest years, a dream compounded equally of heroism and self-effacement, had been brought down to earth at last, in the reality of the lives he was sizing up and the life he had lived. Looking back at poetry, he also looked into himself. On the whole, the experience turned out to be less painful than he might have expected as a young author, fifty years before. Despite his usual discontent with his work—not only preemptive dejection but also frigid withdrawal—he knew that he was giving pleasure as well as doing his duty. An eager audience awaited the "little lives" that kept growing bigger; there was always something else he wanted to say. Moreover, as his seventies came on he thought that he was writing "with all my usual vigour."[69] Attacks of ill health and depression did not eclipse his good fortune in retaining his powers, his public, and friends. The easy and confident style of the *Lives* marks a writer commanding his subject.

In retrospect, it is as a critic that Johnson defines himself. A reader of the *Lives of the Poets* would be hard pressed to infer that its author had ever published a poem. If the lady who read Thomson's character from his work had tried her art on Johnson, she would have been justified in concluding that, whatever else he might have done, he had scorned to write imitations like *London;* "such imitations cannot give pleasure to common readers" (3: 247). Most poet-critics use their own verse as a model; this one does not. Though a gift for poetry stayed with him to the end of his life—the poems of his last few years are among his best—Johnson reserves it mainly for private occasions such as mourning or prayer. So far from claiming a role in English poetry, like one of the heroes of the *Lives,* he was quite content to contribute lines to Goldsmith and Crabbe (among others) without taking credit. He never seems to have labored at writing verse; it came to him precipitately, as something ready to hand and unearned. Perhaps that is why he prided himself so little on it. He had not devoted his life to augmenting that God-given talent.

Johnson the critic, however, pervades the *Lives.* The booksellers' choices had cut the range of English poetry short, as the author of the *Dictionary* and editor of Shakespeare could hardly forget.[70] English criticism is more inclusively treated. The *Lives* supplies its reader not only with principles and models of criticism but also with its history, from Dryden, who "may be properly considered as the father of English criticism" (1: 410),[71] through Addison, who popularized general critical knowledge "in the most alluring form, not lofty and austere, but accessible and familiar" (2: 146), to current, more solid standards of judgment, implicitly represented by Johnson himself. At times this emphasis puts poetry in the shade. Johnson considered the "Life of Cowley" "as the best of the whole," according to Boswell, "on account of the dissertation which it contains on the *Metaphysical Poets.*"[72] If so, he must have been especially pleased by his brilliant review of critical traditions, in which imitative and rhetorical theories sanctioned by Aristotle, Dryden, and Pope are trumped with a definition of Wit "more rigorously and philosophically considered as a kind of *discordia concors;* a combination of dissimilar images, or discovery of occult resemblances in things apparently unlike" (1: 20).[73] The critic presents his credentials, not so much those of a reader of poems as those of an expert accustomed to looking deeply into "general precepts, which depend upon the nature of things and the structure of the human mind" (1: 413).

One way of characterizing the *Lives,* in fact, might feature its anthology of criticism. In addition to specimens of his own (including a reprinted "Dissertation on the Epitaphs written by Pope"), Johnson spends many pages transcribing Dryden's and Settle's niggling attacks on each other, Dryden's comments on Rymer's views of tragedy, Collier's quarrel with Congreve, Dennis' lengthy strictures on *Cato* and *An Essay on Criticism,* and even Blackmore's muddled thoughts about wit. "Those who delight in critical controversy will not think [Dennis] tedious" (2: 136), and evidently one of those is Johnson himself. A good deal of the *Lives* engages in spirited running battles with other critics. Although the antagonists are seldom named, their sophistries provoke the most extreme critical passions. Had it not been the case that "one of the poems on which much praise has been bestowed is *Lycidas*" (1: 163), Johnson might never have tried to bring it so low; and his final tribute to Pope owes everything to Joseph Warton's pedantic question, "Whether Pope was a poet?" (3: 251).[74] The many critics who took offense at the *Lives* helped continue its project by joining the conversation. And the revolutionary elite of the next generation defined their aims by opposing everything Johnson had stood for. No English critic had loomed so large before.

Hence the *Lives* provides a critical context for Johnson's life as an author. In retrospect it weaves a thread through much of his earlier writing, now seen as contributing to the rise of a major critic and man of letters, the capstone of an era in "English literature" (as it would henceforth be called). Nor was he a critic of literature alone. Through biographies and character sketches as well as moral reflections on poems, the *Lives* passes judgment on ways of life. Johnson the critic reviews the efforts of dozens of poets to cope with changing political circumstances as well as poetic fashions, and thus reviews the state of the nation through the preceding hundred years.

He also finds many traces of his own state. The interest of studying other lives, he had always maintained, was its efficacy in "placing us, for a time, in the condition of him whose fortune we contemplate," so that we feel the pains or pleasures of others "by recognising them as once our own."[75] To refuse such sympathy, for instance by assuming a superiority to Savage, would be to deny a part of one's human nature. The *Lives* is true to the principles of its author. Despite its unsparing appraisals of moral and poetic weakness, it does not expect poets to be better than anyone else. Nobody soars above common concerns, no matter how much an artist like Pope may feign "insensibility to censure and criticism" (3: 209). Johnson always pursues the motive that ordinary people might share. Nor does he keep his distance from such motives. From the beginning, readers have sensed that Johnson's sketches often contain some hint of self-portraiture. Thomson's anxiety at the first night of *Agamemnon,* when (Johnson remembers) he recited the lines along with the actors, stirs thoughts of *Irene*'s ordeal. Still more, however, the characters of the great English poets, as well as their faults, touch chords in the critic: what has he done, what might he have done, with his gifts? The pride of Milton, the abounding knowledge of Dryden, the good sense of Pope seem familiar to Johnson because he finds them within.[76] Thus the *Lives of the Poets* recalls his own journey through life.

Perhaps in the end it is Dryden who touches him most. Milton's superhuman self-reliance, Addison's elegant manners, and Pope's perfectionism inspire admiration without leaving much room for the foibles of lesser mortals. Dryden, by contrast, is certainly all too human. Courting applause, he sinks into vices of writing that threaten to corrupt the reader's mind as well as his own: "Such degradation of the dignity of genius, such abuse of superlative abilities, cannot be contemplated but with grief and indignation" (*Lives* 1: 398–399). Nor does this poet respect the demands of art. "His faults of negligence are beyond recital. Such is the unevenness of his compositions that ten lines are seldom found together without something of which the reader is ashamed" (1: 464). Johnson takes these faults personally, with shame, as if responding to the weakness of an old friend. Yet reproaches of Dryden do not conceal an underlying affection or even indulgence. When the "Life of Pope" compares his poetic character with Dryden's, in a brilliant set piece that recalls both poets' own comparisons of Homer and Virgil, Dryden's superior genius is favored by being coupled with Homer's: "If the flights of Dryden therefore are higher, Pope continues longer on the wing. If of Dryden's fire the blaze is brighter, of Pope's the heat is more regular and constant. Dryden often surpasses expectation, and Pope never falls below it. Dryden is read with frequent astonishment, and Pope with perpetual delight."[77] Then Johnson confesses his bias: "if the reader should suspect me, as I suspect myself, of some partial fondness for the memory of Dryden, let him not too hastily condemn me" (3: 223). He had felt such fondness from youth, when he first wanted to write a Life of Dryden, and now he liked the poet the more because he remembered a lifetime attachment to him.

"In drawing Dryden's character," Boswell ventures, "Johnson has given, though I suppose unintentionally, some touches of his own."[78] Boswell is thinking about the love of argument that had turned so often against him, and that Johnson projects on Dryden: "The power that predominated in his intellectual operations was rather strong reason than quick sensibility . . . He is therefore, with all his variety of excellence, not often pathetick; and had so little sensibility of the power of effusions purely natural that he did not esteem them in others" (*Lives* 1: 457–458). Here like calls to like. Both authors might have argued their way to success in the law, some critics have maintained, and if "Dryden's was not one of the 'gentle bosoms'" (1: 458), neither was Johnson's. Whether or not one accepts this emphasis on ratiocination as characteristic of both, however, other affinities cannot be overlooked. When Johnson suggests that Dryden, despite his fluency as a critic, did not enjoy the process of writing, and wrote only for money—"when occasion or necessity called upon him, he poured out what the present moment happened to supply" (3: 220)—he seems to be speaking from personal knowledge. Unlike Pope, moreover, both writers "knew more of man in his general nature" than "in his local manners" (3: 222). Johnson responds to Dryden's intellectual range, his questing, fallible, generous powers of mind.

Still more, "the father of English criticism" gives Johnson a way of reflecting filially on his own generation. In the "Postscript to the Reader" appended to his *Aeneis* (1697), an aging Dryden had weighed his achievement as posterity might judge it, a credit "to my Native Country; whose Language and Poetry wou'd be more esteem'd abroad, if they were better understood. Somewhat (give me leave to say) I have added to both of them in the choice of Words, and Harmony of Numbers which were wanting, especially the last, in all our Poets."[79] This passage seems to have been in Johnson's ear at the end of *The Rambler,* when he summed up his efforts to refine English prose: "Something, perhaps, I have added to the elegance of its construction, and something to the harmony of its cadence."[80] The deliberate echo pays homage to Dryden's project and offers to take it further. Now, in the *Lives,* a long perspective implies that the project has reached its fulfillment. "To him we owe the improvement, perhaps the completion of our metre, the refinement of our language, and much of the correctness of our sentiments" (1: 469). The majestic first-person plurals convert a singular genius into the measure of a whole people. All Dryden's imperfections have now been smoothed over. The evidence is the high standard of judgment that common readers bring to their national poets—the standard embodied by the *Lives* itself. As teacher and spokesman for those readers, Johnson inherits the critical mantle. His life as an author has not, after all, been in vain; he has carried on Dryden's work.

The common reader, however, has the last word. In spite of its willingness to match wits with some of the giant figures of English poetry, the *Lives* does not advance an agenda of its own or look to the future. No bookseller paid Johnson to select a personal canon. In the *Lives* as a whole (as opposed to the handful devoted to famous poets), the great achievements sparkle against a shadowy background of trifles and lost opportunities, if only because mediocre verses so outnumber the others. Moreover, Johnson's progressive view of verse cannot keep the collection from running downhill, since he considers so few of the later poets worth reading. Even his old friend Collins "gives little pleasure"; Dyer "repels the reader"; Shenstone is negligible; Mallet, already forgotten; Akenside's odes are spared review, "for to what use can the work be criticised that will not be read" (3: 420); and Lyttelton's poems have "little to be admired." On the positive side, one might say that Johnson, like Pope, confirms a high ideal of poetry; on the negative, that poets very rarely meet it. But the sum of the *Lives* is more than one man's opinions. Critics, like poets, draw breath from a community that always has the power of paying them no regard. "Had Gray written often thus it had been vain to blame, and useless to praise him" (3: 442).

When readers join ranks in judgment, even the best of critics must fall in line. Johnson leaves his work to the nation and disappears into the crowd.

There would be no more major projects. A month after Johnson completed the *Lives,* he watched his friend Henry Thrale die, on April 4, 1781, "and with him were buried many of my hopes and pleasures."[81] Never again would he feel himself part of a family circle, the intimate audience that comforted him and awaited and trusted his writing. Soon Hester Thrale would begin to distance herself. The widening of that rift, over the next three years, into a total breakdown of communication was to have been the subject of Samuel Beckett's *Human Wishes.*[82] The breach became irrevocable in 1784 when she married Gabriel Piozzi. By that time Johnson had only months to live, and he had long since stopped looking forward. Increasingly he dwells on the past or on eternity. Nor does he seem to care much about his legacy as an author, some future edition to keep his works alive. In his own mind he is anything but a hero, and although he fears death, he does not fear ending as he began, an anonymous private person.

The depth of this authorial humility comes through especially strongly in the verses "On the Death of Dr Robert Levet."[83] Great authors, it has been noted, seldom waste praise on anyone as lowly as the member of Johnson's household who "used to bleed one, & blister another, & be very useful, tho' I believe disagreeable to all."[84] But Johnson centers the poem on Levet and refers to himself only as part of the mass of humanity, in the first person plural.

> Condemn'd to hope's delusive mine,
>   As on we toil from day to day,
> By sudden blasts, or slow decline,
>   Our social comforts drop away.   (Lines 1–4)

Hope seems at once the enslaving owner of the mine and the ore to be dug out. But all are prisoners here, and any gain will turn into fool's gold. The poem absorbs personal grief within a general human condition, as all the achievements of any life's work—the difference between one toiler and another—are viewed as equally vain. Probably the loss of a greater social comfort, Thrale, weighs upon Johnson's mind. Yet he does not allow his own complaints to block Levet's example of ceaselessly doing good.

> His virtues walk'd their narrow round
>> Nor made a pause, nor left a void;
> And sure th' Eternal Master found
>> The single talent well employ'd.   (25–28)

Such diligence implicitly reproaches the author himself, who has squandered multiple talents.[85] Success in the eyes of the world is no excuse. Johnson's elegy, like Gray's, preemptively chides any snob who might look down on this subject: "Nor, letter'd arrogance, deny /Thy praise to merit unrefin'd."[86] But Johnson's fate is not, like Gray's, the covert subject of the poem, nor will he submerge "th' unhonour'd Dead" in common anonymous heaps. LEVET stands out in capitals from the crowd. "Of ev'ry friendless name the friend" (as if, in the end, a name were all that any poor soul amounted to), he is given the one reward a friend can bestow, a name that survives in print.

Meanwhile the author withdraws. Johnson's last poems repeat the timeless rhythms of water flowing and the passing of seasons and years. When, in nostalgic Latin verses, he visits the stream where he learned to swim as a boy, its persistence reminds him of duty and friendship, not of how far he has come.[87] The stream will still be there when he is gone. Nor does he cling to the hope of being remembered. Many authors have left some version of Horace's "Exegi monumentum" ("I wrought a monument more lasting than bronze"; *Odes* 3.30), one last reminder of what they have made. Johnson picked a different ode of Horace, "Diffugere nives" (*Odes* 4.7), to speak through in his final English poem, a month before his death. "The snow dissolv'd no more is seen," and the freshness of spring only mocks irretrievable human losses. In the face of mortality, even the greatest name of hero or poet resigns its power, for "wretched Man, when once he lies/Where Priam and his Sons are laid/Is nought but Ashes and a Shade."[88] The egalitarianism of death ex-

293

tends to Johnson's choice of an example. Horace mentions "pius Aeneas," Tullus, and Ancus, but "Priam and his Sons" deletes the founder of Rome in favor of a family group at once more sweeping (Priam had fifty sons) and more pathetic (since Troy itself died along with Priam and Hector).[89] Aeneas himself, like everyone else, in the long run is no one at all.

Johnson's long journey was over. He had made his choices and shaped his career until everyone called him an author, and he had redefined the terms of authorship itself; but a name on the title page or the spine of a book did not, in the end, give much comfort. He would soon be alone with his God, where public renown meant nothing and only one Author knew the true sum of a life. In the beginning, obscure and unvalued, Johnson sought refuge in giving himself to his readers, whom he might help to endure. Now, at the last, he retreated into the language that everyone shares, the prayers and fears that erase all distinctions between one self and another, the great and the small. The private person had done what he could and would go to the grave with his secrets. But the life of Johnson, the life of an author, was far from over, of course. Henceforth the author would always belong to his readers.

11

The Life to Come:
Johnson's Endings

CLOV: Do you believe in the life to come?
HAMM: Mine was always that.

A S JOHNSON LAY DYING, in December 1784, people took an unusual interest in how he would meet his end. "The death of Dr. Johnson," according to Arthur Murphy, "kept the public mind in agitation beyond all former example," and many years later a certain Miss Berry remembered "how the world of literature was perplexed and distressed—as a swarm of bees that have lost their queen—when Dr. Johnson died."[1] Several reasons may be offered for this keen and perhaps morbid state of excitement. Celebrity ought to come first: there was a market for stories about this author. While the great man arranged his affairs and destroyed private papers, inquisitive writers prowled around the house in Bolt Court, hoping to get their hands on something newsworthy. Meanwhile a coven of more respectable biographers—Boswell, Hawkins, Mrs. Piozzi—gathered their notes and waited for their time. Like Johnson's life, his death would soon belong to literature.

Moreover, death scenes fascinated eighteenth-century readers. Many biographers—though not Johnson himself[2]—climaxed their narratives with the last words that might reveal the state of the soul at its moment of passing. A great man was supposed to die well; according to Addison, "the end of a Man's Life is often compared to the winding up of a well-written Play."[3] Naturally many of the great or would-be great rehearsed their deaths carefully. The ever-prudent

Addison called in a loose-living young nobleman to listen to these words: "I have sent for you that you may see how a Christian can die"[4] (the point was especially sharp because Addison's *Cato* had shown how well a noble pagan could die). Such stories raise expectations or create an atmosphere that encourages competitive dying.[5] Boswell, for instance, kept score. Anxious that Johnson should end at least as well as David Hume, who on his deathbed cheerfully maintained his disbelief in any afterlife, he came back to the topic again and again, despite Johnson's reluctance.[6] An atheist could not be allowed to overmatch a Christian. Hence a good death would involve much more than Johnson's personal comfort. In the eyes of his followers, it was his public duty.

Yet another reason for curiosity was that the dying man had spoken and written so powerfully about death.[7] Characteristically, Johnson's writings aim to show the *usefulness* of keeping mortality always in mind: "Nothing confers so much ability to resist the temptations that perpetually surround us, as an habitual consideration of the shortness of life."[8] Death reminds us that life is precious and not to be wasted. Nor does Johnson, like Boswell, dream about playing the hero and conquering fear. Pious Christians put their hopes in the consolations of revelation and divine mercy, not in their own deserts.[9] But wisdom and piety go only so far; those who knew the man knew his terror of death. Boswell, who shared that terror and even exacerbated it to draw Johnson out, organized much of the *Life* around the suspense of whether his hero could master it in the end. The scenes he composed are almost unbearably vivid.

> JOHNSON. "I am afraid I may be one of those who shall be damned."
>   (looking dismally.)
> DR. ADAMS. "What do you mean by damned?"
> JOHNSON. (passionately and loudly) "Sent to Hell, Sir, and punished
>   everlastingly."[10]

Nor was Boswell alone in brooding over Johnson's ordeal. Six months before the end, Hannah More "was grieved to find that his mind is still a prey to melancholy, and that the fear of death operates on him to the destruction of his peace. It is grievous—it is unaccountable!"[11] Johnson's last days would provide the finishing stroke for this drama. Would visions of hell pursue him to the grave, or would he tranquilly resign his soul to the life to come?

The answer depends on who is telling the story. However well authors plan their last words, they cannot review their own deaths. The final moment enfolds an intensely private experience, and what the central character really is thinking remains his secret. "Enquiries into the heart are not for man," Johnson wrote of Dryden; "we must now leave him to his Judge."[12] Hence the survivors must make what they will of the dead, piecing together ambiguous signs, confirming what they believe or wish to believe. As no one knew better than Johnson himself, biographers partly create the lives they sum up; a skeptic can always point out some holes in the story.

The facts support more than one reading of Johnson's last words.[13] Many people attended the great man on his deathbed, and the anecdotes they brought back varied according to what they wanted to hear, what he wanted to tell them, and what others expected to hear. Thus Hannah More, "perplexed, and longing to be comforted,"[14] was relieved to learn (at third hand) that Johnson had spent his final hours trying to convert his physician to the one true faith: "My dear doctor, believe a dying man, there is no salvation but in the sacrifice of the Lamb of God." Miss More draws a pious conclusion: "No action of his life became him like the leaving it . . . It is delightful to see him set, as it were, his dying seal to the professions of his life, and to the truth of Christianity."[15]

Others found similar morals. One version of Johnson's "official" last words was staged for edification: a young lady entered the room to ask his blessing; he turned in bed and said, "God bless you, my dear!"[16] We do not know what train of thought she may have interrupted. But Boswell preferred that version. Though he handles the deathbed scene with restraint, he flanks it with two other documents. One is a prayer, composed by Johnson eight days before he died: "Support me, by thy Holy Spirit, in the days of weakness, and at the hour of death; and receive me, at my death, to everlasting happiness, for the sake of JESUS CHRIST. Amen."[17] The other suggests that the prayer was answered. A letter reports the impressions of a

297

servant who sat with Johnson on his last morning and said "that no man could appear more collected, more devout, or less terrified at the thoughts of the approaching minute." This "agreeable" account "has given us the satisfaction of thinking that that great man died as he lived, full of resignation, strengthened in faith, and joyful in hope."[18] *Q.E.D.* Boswell proceeds to the tributes and character sketch. Johnson had died with the dignity he deserved—a hero to the last, triumphant over fear and himself.

That was not, however, the sort of story found in the *Lives of the Poets.* A writer whose whole career had preached and expressed preemptive dejection, the vanity of human wishes, and the deflation of overblown expectations would hardly have approved such a rosy, well-rounded conclusion. Readers in tune with Johnson's own way of looking at lives might well prefer an inconclusive, ruthlessly honest end. And their wish also was granted. In one of the earliest Lives, slapped together by William Cooke and published two weeks after Johnson's death, the last coherent words pop out of a delirious fit: "seeing a friend at the bedside, he exclaimed, 'What, will that fellow never have done talking poetry to me?'"[19] Here literature has its comeuppance; at some point the chatter must stop.

Yet a far darker version is given by Hawkins, who did not idolize his old friend or offer much comfort. Like others at the deathbed, he witnessed the end of a Christian, but one who "strictly fulfilled the injunction of the apostle, to work out his salvation with fear and trembling." Fear dominates this account. Johnson's last words, *"Iam moriturus"* (I who am about to die), suggest the doomed gladiator, as if imaginary beasts assailed him to the final stroke.[20] But "the particulars of his last moments" conclude with a still more terrible scene. Bloated with dropsy, Johnson tries to discharge the water by stabbing his legs with a lancet and scissors until the bedclothes are covered with blood. He even reproaches his surgeon for not daring to delve far enough. "Deeper, deeper;—I will abide the consequence: you are afraid of your reputation, but that is nothing to me." Then Hawkins records one more sentence, perhaps the most aggressive parting shot in the canon: "To those about him, he said,—'You all pretend to love me, but you do not love me so well as I myself do.'"[21]

These words are unconventional as well as unpleasant, and are most unlikely to have been staged or rehearsed. Dying people are not supposed to say such things. Yet they suit one aspect of Johnson superlatively: a man who clings to life with such ferocity that all about him pale; a man who speaks the truth to those who would rather not hear it; a skeptic; and one who resists any threat to his own free will.

Nevertheless, no author has the last word. The struggle over what Johnson represents, a tug of war already strenuous as he lay dying, intensified in the major biographies of the following years; it continues to rage today. One reason must be the investment of so many readers in his life story. No one worries about the last words of Shakespeare or Milton, but something seems to be at stake in remembering Johnson. For good or ill, the life has encroached on the work, and modern authorship has never quite disentangled the writer from what has been made of the writings. Boswell remains a key figure. In the advertisement to his second edition (1793), he boasted that "*I have* Johnsonised *the land; and I trust they will not only* talk, *but* think, *Johnson*"[22] ("talk" and "think" but not necessarily "read"); and, as Leo Braudy contends, Boswell had satisfied his own hunger for fame by authoring as well as capitalizing on a personalized and very peculiar image: Johnson as the immortal uncommon man.[23]

That image would take on a sometimes monstrous life of its own in years to come. Macaulay's notorious review of Boswell's *Life* (1831) exaggerated the portrait into a freakish, Falstaffian Johnson—"We see the eyes and mouth moving with convulsive twitches; we see the heavy form rolling; we hear it puffing; and then comes the 'Why, sir!' and the 'What then, sir?' and the 'No, sir!' and the 'You don't see your way through the question, sir!'"—and along with Macaulay's later *Essay on Johnson* (1856), this gross cartoon became a standard school text, far more familiar than Johnson's own writings, which Macaulay assured the reader were "every day fading."[24] The wonder was that such great powers could coexist with such low prejudices. A century later, Clive Bell strikes the same superior note when he caps the pleasures of civilization—"the champagne and caviare of the spiritual life"—with the cultivation "to understand why Dr. Johnson is a credit to the race and a ridiculous old donkey to boot."[25] The praise may be even more embarrassing than the insult. But the influence of Macaulay's cartoon survives, not only in those who embrace the petrified, prejudiced image of Johnson as a conservative icon but also in the many scholars who still devote their work to proving Macaulay wrong (like Boswell before him, not to mention Clive Bell). Perhaps they have made their case by now, for Johnson's writings show few signs of fading.

Yet even without the popular image, readers of Johnson would differ about what he represents as an author. He planted the seeds of conflict right at the start, when he conceived himself as both nameless public servant and timeless hero, and the hybrid identity followed him to the end. Even the contrasting versions of Johnson's last words might be seen as posing a question about what an author should be: should he allow himself to be translated into whatever his readers want, or should he insist on dying a death of his own? Humble submission and fierce resistance contend. When the "retired and uncourtly Scholar" erupts, in the letter to Chesterfield, he spurns "the Great" but also augurs a new kind of greatness, drawn from the mighty, anonymous public. The gambit turned out to be potent; the public responded. From then on, Johnson would always be known as somehow both unique and one of the people. His last major work, the *Lives of the Poets,* confirms the reputation of the author. It is one man's history of English poetry, strong-minded, candid, decisive; yet this uncommon critic is not ashamed to close with a more reliable judge, the common reader's simple common sense, as if he spoke with the common voice of the nation. Not many authors have the confidence to speak that way. Johnson drew it from his whole life as an author.

Of course the claim could be challenged. No one can speak for all of a nation, and Britain itself was divided by politics, class, and religion, and soon to be riven much more by stirrings of revolution. Miss Pinkerton's school, which opens *Vanity Fair,* owes its reputation to a visit from "the late revered Doctor Samuel Johnson," but when the standard parting gift of the "Dixonary" is handed to Becky Sharp, she flings it from her coach back into the garden.[26] Her ingratitude was not unprecedented. Some readers did not like Johnson, and some objected to almost everything he stood for as an author (whatever that was). For those who subscribed to the cult of the author as genius, a refusal to idolize genius could not be forgiven. In modern times Johnson's role as a canon-maker, bringing order to language as well as literature, has often typed him as a "literary dictator" (as Leslie Stephen put it).[27] To some contemporaries and Romantic successors, however, he was not canonical *enough;* he had found fault with Shakespeare and Milton, and regarded their works as a series of uneven performances, not as emanations from a singular higher spirit. On the other hand, readers who valued the journeyman author, a source of polite opinions that everyone shared, could not help noticing how often Johnson thought for himself. Perhaps this author had too much genius for comfort. When Boswell Johnsonized the land, evidently he left a few patches uncovered.

The sharpest debates about what Johnson represents as an author, however, concern his authority. Becky Sharp was not willing to play by the book, and many modern critics take her side. Nor is their questioning of authority unwarranted. No dictionary or set of critical judgments lasts forever, and even Johnson's partisans do not think he is always right about a word or poem. But the problem goes deeper. What is the source of Johnson's power? Why should one take his word? From one point of view, his authority looks like a mystery or mystification; no academy stands behind him, no law or police force. When he appeals to the common reader, moreover, he calls a witness that he himself has invented. Does anything solid back this imposing façade? Only a text, retreating into more texts.[28] Yet, from another perspective, the questions themselves seem peculiar. They presuppose a sinister interpretation of authorship, as if the reader were not free to differ (as Johnson himself did so often), or as if some epistemological conspiracy could fetter an unwilling mind. Not everyone bought the *Dictionary,* but those who did knew the source of its power; it gave them something they wanted. In this respect, a suspicion of Johnson's authority seems to amount to a distrust of readers who find him interesting or useful.

Authority is always dispersed in Johnson's own writings. The early anonymous hackwork represents the *Gentleman's Magazine,* not anyone's byline. The Rambler keeps his identity secret, absorbed into a voice of traditional, impersonal wisdom. The *Dictionary* builds on its illustrations, more than 100,000 examples from the best and most trustworthy writers of English. The Shakespeare edition concedes its dependence on other editions. The *Lives of the Poets* defers to booksellers as well as to common readers. And even Johnson's most ambitious poems tag after Juvenal. He took so little credit for much of his work that the canon is full of holes and needs constant revision.[29] This diffusion of responsibility for particular texts—though not for their moral standards—seems to mark an era in the history of authorship. In Britain that era is called the Age of Johnson, not only in honor of one particular writer, but also in acknowledgment that he represents, by a sort of popular vote, a large community of writers and readers, if not print culture or the nation itself.

That kind of authority casts a spell. Though Matthew Arnold, for instance, views Johnson's criticism of poetry as tainted by an age of prose, he cannot help envying the power of his historical moment. "We have not Johnson's interest and Johnson's force; we are not the power in letters for our century which he was for his."[30] Even the ambiguous first-person pronoun reeks of nostalgia; is Arnold speaking for anyone but himself? At any rate, many others have shared his longing. When Virginia Woolf titled two collections of essays *The Common Reader,* with the end of the "Life of Gray" for epigraph, she was consciously reaching out for "the sanction of the great man's approval."[31] Despite her mixed reactions to Johnson, Woolf strongly identified with both sides of his self-portrait as author: the anonymous aid to the public, the aspirant to literary glory. Moreover, she also knew that each had its own authority. Much of *The Common Reader* first appeared anonymously in the *Times Literary Supplement,* whose reviewers spoke from behind a veil like oracles, and that concealment conferred a good deal of power. At the same time, there was no doubt that Woolf was uncommon, with insights unlike anyone else's; that too conferred power. The Second Series of *The Common Reader* concludes with a gesture much like Johnson's, as Woolf allies herself with ordinary lovers of reading. The great critics—Coleridge, Dryden, Johnson—"can do nothing for us if we herd ourselves under their authority and lie down like sheep in the shade of a hedge. We can only understand their ruling when it comes in conflict with our own and vanquishes it."[32] Once again the first person seems awkward, the sacrifice of a rebellious "I" to some ideal of the normal. If part of Woolf wants to shrink to nothing or to vanquish the self, another part clearly wants to match wits with the fathers. The spell of Johnson's authority oppresses and fascinates her.[33]

It also promises conflicts in the future. What Johnson represents as an author is not a closed book but a continuing struggle. Looking over a manuscript that attacked the *Lives of the Poets,* shortly before he died, he noted "that authors would differ in opinion, and that good performances could not be too much criticized," and volunteered to aid its publication with a biography of the writer, the late John Scott.[34] Books stayed alive when they were talked about, not shelved in reverent dust, and so did authors. Quarrels about authority still freshen Johnson's name. To those who view him as a patriarch or monarch of letters, he stands as an inviting target to knock down. To those who remember his long climb upward, as well as the helping hand he offered men and women below, his defiance of lords and masters will always be precious. The pious believer, the withering skeptic equally join in his writing. Such authors do not rest in peace.

Nor can they be caught in a phrase or a story. No single masterpiece contains the essential Johnson, the irreducible core of his work as a whole. Lesser authors have sometimes written better poems, better fiction, and certainly better plays. If Johnson had never lived, others would have produced their versions of the *English Dictionary,* editions of Shakespeare, biographies of anthologized worthies; and though his periodical essays and literary criticism have not been surpassed, very few readers work their way through the whole of *The Rambler* and the *Lives of the Poets*. Yet the author survives in the principles that inform almost all his writing: the freedom from cant, and the care for the trials—above all the troubles of mind—that everyone faces. In the "Preface to Shakespeare," Johnson imagined an author whose powers far surpassed the wonderful but imperfect works he performed, a possible Shakespeare who might have felt contempt for the merely actual Shakespeare. Similarly, throughout Johnson's life, the author he might have been reproached the struggling writer he was, whose great expectations rarely arrived at a moment for looking back in contentment. Yet the struggle itself turned out to be his bequest as an author. The last word on Johnson has yet to be written; he still has a life to come.

ABBREVIATIONS

NOTES

INDEX

ABBREVIATIONS

BLJ James Boswell, *The Life of Samuel Johnson,* ed. G. B. Hill, rev. L. F. Powell, 2d ed., 6 vols. (Oxford: Clarendon Press, 1934–1964)

Boulton James T. Boulton, ed., *Johnson: The Critical Heritage* (London: Routledge & Kegan Paul, 1971)

Correspondence Marshall Waingrow, ed., *The Correspondence and Other Papers of James Boswell Relating to the Making of the "Life of Johnson"* (New York: McGraw-Hill, 1969)

Hawkins Sir John Hawkins, *The Life of Samuel Johnson, LL.D.*, ed. Bertram H. Davis (New York: Macmillan, 1961)

JM G. B. Hill, ed., *Johnsonian Miscellanies,* 2 vols. (Oxford: Clarendon Press, 1897)

Letters Bruce Redford, ed., *The Letters of Samuel Johnson,* 5 vols. (Princeton: Princeton University Press, 1992–1994)

Lives Samuel Johnson, *The Lives of the English Poets,* 3 vols., ed. G. B. Hill (Oxford: Clarendon Press, 1905)

Poems David Nichol Smith and E. L. McAdam Jr., eds., *The Poems of Samuel Johnson,* 2d ed. (Oxford: Clarendon Press, 1974)

Works *The Yale Edition of the Works of Samuel Johnson* (New Haven: Yale University Press). Vol. 1: *Diaries, Prayers, and Annals,* ed. E. L. McAdam Jr. with Donald and Mary Hyde (1958); vol. 2: *The Idler* and *The Adventurer,* ed. W. J. Bate, John M. Bullitt, and L. F. Powell (1963); vols. 3–5: *The Rambler*, ed. W. J. Bate and Albrecht B. Strauss (1969);

vol 6: *Poems,* ed. E. L. McAdam Jr. with George Milne (1964); vols. 7–8: *Johnson on Shakespeare,* ed. Arthur Sherbo (1968); vol. 9: *A Journey to the Western Islands of Scotland,* ed. Mary Lascelles (1971); vol. 10: *Political Writings,* ed. Donald J. Greene (1977); vol. 14: *Sermons,* ed. Jean H. Hagstrum and James Gray (1978); vol. 15: *A Voyage to Abyssinia,* ed. Joel J. Gold (1985); vol. 16: *Rasselas and Other Tales,* ed. Gwin J. Kolb (1990). This edition is planned to be complete in 24 vols.

NOTES

Introduction

The epigraph is from Edward Young, *Two Epistles to Mr. Pope, Concerning the Authors of the Age* (London, 1730), p. 26.

1. Bertrand H. Bronson, "The Double Tradition of Dr. Johnson" (1951), reprinted in *Johnson Agonistes and Other Essays* (Berkeley: University of California Press, 1965), p. 176.

2. Mona Wilson, *Johnson: Prose and Poetry* (Cambridge, Mass.: Harvard University Press, 1951), p. 9.

3. *BLJ* 1:25.

4. Roland Barthes, "The Death of the Author" (1968), in *Image—Music—Text,* trans. Stephen Heath (New York: Hill and Wang, 1977), pp. 142–148; see also "Authors and Writers" (1960), in Barthes' *Critical Essays,* trans. Richard Howard (Evanston: Northwestern University Press, 1972), pp. 143–150. Michel Foucault, "What Is an Author?" (1969), in *Language, Counter-Memory, Practice,* trans. D. F. Bouchard and Sherry Simon (Ithaca: Cornell University Press, 1977), pp. 113–138.

5. Seán Burke, *The Death and Return of the Author: Criticism and Subjectivity in Barthes, Foucault and Derrida* (Edinburgh: Edinburgh University Press, 1992), thoughtfully examines the issues; see also H. L. Hix, *Morte d'Author: An Autopsy* (Philadelphia: Temple University Press, 1990). I have noted some implications for literary history in "Life, Death, and Other Theories," in *Historical Studies and Literary Criticism,* ed. Jerome J. McGann (Madison: University of Wisconsin Press, 1984), pp. 180–198.

6. See Fredric V. Bogel, *The Dream of My Brother: An Essay on Johnson's Authority* (Victoria, B.C.: University of Victoria, 1990). Despite its interesting insights, this essay projects its own misgivings about "authority" anachronistically on Johnson and his age. The "search for a new authority" among writers on painting from 1670 to 1790 is the topic of a chapter in Lawrence Lipking, *The Ordering of the Arts in Eighteenth-Century England* (Princeton: Princeton University Press, 1970).

7. *Lives* 1: 194.

8. "For myn entent is, or I fro you fare,/The naked text in English to declare/Of many a story, or elles of many a geste,/As autours seyn; leveth hem if yow leste!" Prologue to *The Legend of Good Women,* Text G, ll. 85–88;

The Poetical Works of Chaucer, ed. F. N. Robinson (Cambridge, Mass: Riverside Press, 1933), p. 570.

9. See Mark Rose, *Authors and Owners: The Invention of Copyright* (Cambridge, Mass.: Harvard University Press, 1993), p. 1.

10. "By the general consent of cricticks the first praise of genius is due to the writer of an epick poem, as it requires an assemblage of all the powers which are singly sufficient for other compositions"; *Lives* 1: 170.

11. *The Letters of John Keats,* ed. H. E. Rollins (Cambridge, Mass.: Harvard University Press, 1958), 1: 374. I have expatiated on the statement in *The Life of the Poet: Beginning and Ending Poetic Careers* (Chicago: University of Chicago Press, 1981), pp. 3–11.

12. Raymond Williams, *The Long Revolution* (London: Chatto & Windus, 1961).

13. *Adventurer* 99, *Works* 2: 431.

14. *Rambler* 60, *Works* 3: 320.

1. The Birth of the Author

The epigraph is from Jacques Lacan, "Seminar on 'The Purloined Letter,'" trans. Jeffrey Mehlman, in *The Purloined Poe,* ed. J. P. Muller and W. J. Richardson (Baltimore: Johns Hopkins University Press, 1988), p. 53.

1. *The World,* no. 100, in the collected volumes (London, 1755), 3: 264, 266–269, 270. The hints on ladylike language appeared the following week, Thursday, December 5, in issue no. 101.

2. According to its editor, Edward Moore ("Adam Fitz-Adam"), *The World* was "the only fashionable vehicle, in which men of rank and genius chose to convey their sentiments to the public." This boast appears in the dedication of volume 5 (1757) to Soame Jenyns, the man of the world who in that same year would become the target of Johnson's devastating "Review of *A Free Inquiry into the Nature and Origin of Evil*" (*Literary Magazine,* nos. 13–15). Volume 1 of *The World* was dedicated to Chesterfield, volume 2 to Horace Walpole. Though Johnson often wrote for Dodsley, he did not contribute to *The World.*

3. *The World,* no. 101, 3: 270, 275.

4. *Letters* 1: 94–97. I have replaced the abbreviation, S. J., with Johnson's full signature.

5. *The celebrated Letter from Samuel Johnson, LL.D., to Philip Dormer Stanhope, Earl of Chesterfield; Now first published with Notes, by James Boswell, Esq.* (London, 1790). Boswell was probably less interested in sales than in protecting his copyright.

6. "Entertaind" is the word of William Adams. "It was indeed an Entertainment being written in a lofty style that became the Spirit of it, and full of keen well pointed Satyr"; *Correspondence,* p. 61.

7. "Dr. Adams mentioned to Dodsley that he was sorry Dr. Johnson had

written his letter to Lord Chesterfield. Dodsley said he was very sorry too; for that he had a property in the *Dictionary* to which Lord Chesterfield's patronage might be of consequence"; *Correspondence,* p. 24.

8. *BLJ* 1: 265.

9. "Boswell's Life of Johnson" (1832), in Carlyle's *Works* (New York: Funk and Wagnalls, 1905), 6: 296.

10. Alvin Kernan, *Printing Technology, Letters, and Samuel Johnson* (Princeton: Princeton University Press, 1987), pp. 20, 105.

11. The conventional view of a drastic decline of patronage in midcentury England, set forth by A. S. Collins, *Authorship in the Days of Johnson* (London: R. Holden, 1927) and *The Profession of Letters* (London: Routledge, 1928), and Michael Foss, *The Age of Patronage: The Arts in England, 1660–1750* (Ithaca: Cornell University Press, 1972), has been challenged by Dustin Griffin, *Literary Patronage in England, 1650–1800* (Cambridge: Cambridge University Press, 1996), who argues that a variety of kinds of patronage—not exclusively aristocratic—continued to dominate literary production, both economically and politically. Paul Korshin had previously stressed the complexity of the patronage system in "Types of Eighteenth-Century Literary Patronage," *Eighteenth-Century Studies* 7 (1974): 453–473.

12. *Adventurer* 115 (December 11, 1753), *Works* 2: 458.

13. "It is clear that the (ideal) relationship between patron and writer is for Johnson a complex moral calculus of claim, desert, right, debt, tribute, and gift that he did not fully articulate in a single essay"; Griffin, *Literary Patronage,* p. 235.

14. William Warburton's compliment to Johnson, conveyed by William Adams; *Correspondence,* p. 61.

15. "Dr. Douglas told [Boswell] that he was confident from memory that Johnson's letter to Lord Chesterfield was more pointed than in the copy which he dictated many years after it was written"; ibid., p. 61n.

16. *BLJ* 1: 260.

17. *Rambler* 152, *Works* 5: 43.

18. Preface to *The Preceptor* (1748), in *Samuel Johnson's Prefaces & Dedications,* ed. Allen T. Hazen (New Haven: Yale University Press, 1937), p. 180.

19. Bruce Redford discusses the theory and practice of letter writing in *The Converse of the Pen: Acts of Intimacy in the Eighteenth-Century Familar Letter* (Chicago: University of Chicago Press, 1987). However, the letter to Chesterfield might be considered the antithesis of a familar letter, not only because of its formality but because of its denial of intimacy or acquaintance.

20. *Lives* 3: 207.

21. The repeated misspelling of "adress," spelled correctly in the *Dictionary,* may indicate that the letter is aping a French mode of address (the spelling mistake is common among those whose first language is French). It

is also possible, of course, that Baretti erred in his transcription and Johnson failed to correct it.

22. "Dr. Johnson's knowledge and esteem of what we call low or coarse life was indeed prodigious; and he did not like that the upper ranks should be dignified with the name of *the world*"; Mrs. Piozzi, *JM* 1: 53.

23. *Rambler* 152, *Works* 5: 7.

24. Definition 7 of "period" in the *Dictionary*. Johnson's emphasis on full stops shows his attention to the rhythm as well as the structure of the sentence.

25. *BLJ* 1: 447–448. When Johnson asked Catherine Macauley to let her footman dine with them, he may have been doubting the humility of her condescension.

26. The resemblance of the dispute to a formal duel is especially striking in Sir John Hawkins' account of the delegation Chesterfield sent to Johnson. Intending to appease him, Sir Thomas Robinson insulted him again by expressing a wish to give him money. "'Sir,' replied Johnson, 'if the first peer of the realm were to make me such an offer, I would show him the way downstairs'"; Hawkins, p. 82.

27. *The World,* no. 101, 3: 270.

28. *Correspondence,* p. 234n.

29. Ibid., p. 235. "With all this haughty contempt of gentility, no praise was more welcome to Dr. Johnson than that which [said he] had the notions or manners of a gentleman"; Mrs. Piozzi, *JM* 1: 253–254.

30. John Henry Newman, *The Idea of a University,* ed. I. T. Ker (Oxford: Clarendon Press, 1976), p. 179.

31. W. K. Wimsatt, *The Prose Style of Samuel Johnson* (New Haven: Yale University Press, 1941), p. 156.

32. *Poems,* p. 76, line 177. *London* came out anonymously. According to a well-known anecdote, Pope inquired after the author and, after learning that he was some obscure man named Johnson, said, "he will soon be *déterré*" (*BLJ* 1: 128–129). This was hardly prophetic, however; a year later, Johnson was still unknown and trying "to emancipate himself from the drudgery of authorship" (*BLJ* 1: 134). In 1742, at the back of miscellanies published by Edward Cave and James Roberts, "S. Johnson" was finally named as the author of *London;* James L. Clifford, *Young Sam Johnson* (New York: Oxford University Press, 1961), p. 354.

33. For a scrupulous examination of Johnson's labors and earnings in the years before he began work on the *Dictionary,* see Thomas Kaminski, *The Early Career of Samuel Johnson* (New York: Oxford University Press, 1987).

34. Though some of Johnson's contributions to the *Gentleman's Magazine* were initialed "S. J.," only a few intimates knew what the initials stood for, and before 1747 none of his works but *London* had been acknowledged.

35. On Johnson's gradual disengagement from Chesterfield's views about

language, see Howard Weinbrot, "Samuel Johnson's *Plan* and the Preface to the *Dictionary:* The Growth of a Lexicographer's Mind," in *New Aspects of Lexicography* (Carbondale: Southern Illinois University Press, 1972), pp. 61–72.

36. *The World,* no. 100, 3: 264.

37. Lines 159–160. "Garret," the word in 1749, changed to "Patron" when the poem was printed in Dodsley's *Collection* (1755), a month after the letter to Chesterfield.

38. According to Dustin Griffin, "Johnson is ultimately concerned with the patronage system not as an economic or political arrangement, but as an occasion for moral reflection"; *Literary Patronage,* p. 238.

39. Paul Fussell, *Samuel Johnson and the Life of Writing* (New York: Harcourt Brace Jovanovich, 1971), p. 122.

40. "Septimus octavo propior iam fugerit annus/ex quo Maecenas me coepit habere suorum/in numero"; Horace, *Satires* 2.6.40–42. The allusion was noticed by Niall Rudd (Fussell, *Johnson and the Life of Writing,* p. 122).

41. Johnson himself notes the connection in *Adventurer* 92, *Works* 2: 420.

42. Virgil, *Eclogues* 8.43–45. The Latin is quoted by Johnson in *Rambler* 37, *Works* 3: 203, which also includes a free translation by Dryden—"I know thee, love, in desarts thou wert bred,/And at the dugs of savage tygers fed:/Alien of birth, usurper of the plains"—and a version from Pope's *Pastorals,* "Autumn," ll. 89–92.

43. *Rambler* 37, *Works* 3: 204. Johnson's criticism includes Dryden and Pope as well as Virgil.

44. "Preface to Shakespeare," *Works* 7: 63.

45. Boswell reports a story that Johnson declined to read the letter to another nobleman, "saying, with a smile, 'No, Sir; I have hurt the dog too much already'"; *BLJ* 1: 260n.

46. *BLJ* 1: 261n. Presumably this was a reward for the dedication of the *Plan* (1747), and thus not technically part of the seven years of neglect.

47. Preface to the *Dictionary,* par. 92.

48. The difficulty of Johnson's effort "to translate literary freedom into the trappings of formal professionalism" is remarked by Penelope J. Corfield, *Power and the Professions in Britain, 1700–1850* (London: Routledge, 1995), p. 185.

49. According to one story, "Johnson wrote his letter only after he knew that Chesterfield was ready to give him £100 on the assumption that the *Dictionary* would be dedicated to him"; James L. Clifford, *Dictionary Johnson* (New York: McGraw-Hill, 1979), p. 135.

50. *Coriolanus,* V.iii.35–37, illustrating the first definition of "author": "The first beginner or mover of any thing; he to whom any thing owes its original."

51. *Works* 8: 823.

52. John Cannon puts the *Dictionary* in the context of nationalism in *Samuel Johnson and the Politics of Hanoverian England* (Oxford: Clarendon Press, 1994), pp. 237–239.

53. In "The Johnson-Chesterfield Relationship: A New Hypothesis," *PMLA* 85 (1970): 247–259, Paul Korshin suggests that political animosities between the two can be traced back to the 1730s.

54. *The World,* no. 100, 3: 267–268.

55. Preface to the *Dictionary,* par. 86.

56. *The World,* no. 100, 3: 275, 278.

57. Since debates could not be reported verbatim, journalists imitated or invented putative versions of the speeches. The standard study is Benjamin B. Hoover, *Samuel Johnson's Parliamentary Reporting* (Berkeley: University of California Press, 1953); on Chesterfield, see pp. 43–44, 112–113, 119–120.

58. Preface to the *Dictionary,* pars. 62–63.

59. "The Bravery of the English Common Soldiers" (1760?), *Works* 10: 283.

2. First Flowers

The epigraph is from Ben Jonson, "To the Immortall Memorie, and Friendship of That Noble Paire, Sir Lucius Cary, and Sir H. Morison," in *The Complete Poetry of Ben Jonson,* ed. W. B. Hunter (Garden City, N.Y.: Doubleday/Anchor, 1963), pp. 223–224.

1. James L. Clifford, *Young Sam Johnson* (New York: Oxford University Press, 1961), pp. 76–78. Robert DeMaria Jr., *The Life of Samuel Johnson* (Oxford: Blackwell, 1993), pp. 12–13, points to the influence of the metaphysical tradition.

2. *Poems,* p. 3. The verses were sent to Boswell by Johnson's old school friend Edmund Hector in 1785 and again in 1791, but Boswell did not publish them.

3. Donald Greene supplies this translation, along with the Latin text, in his edition of selected writings, *Samuel Johnson* (Oxford: Oxford University Press, 1984), p. 39. As Greene points out (p. 799), the text for the exercise is Juvenal, *Satires* 10.141–142: "Quis enim virtutem amplectitur ipsam,/praemia si tollas?" (Who indeed would embrace virtue herself,/If you took away her rewards?). *The Vanity of Human Wishes,* Johnson's later imitation of the same satire, does not translate these cynical lines.

4. "There is a tradition, that the study of friar [Roger] Bacon, built in an arch over the bridge, will fall, when a man greater than Bacon shall pass under it." This note, in Dodsley's *Collection* (London, 1755), explains "And *Bacon's* Mansion trembles o'er his Head," line 140 of *The Vanity of Human Wishes.*

5. Hector to Boswell (1785), *Correspondence,* p. 48.

6. W. Jackson Bate, *Samuel Johnson* (New York: Harcourt Brace Jovanovich, 1977), p. 111.

7. "He seems to conclude . . . that felicity is a thing ever in prospect, but never attainable. This conclusion, instead of exciting men to laudable pursuits, which should be the aim of every moral publication, tends to discourage them from all pursuits whatever"; Owen Ruffhead's review of *Rasselas* (1759), in Boulton, p. 142.

8. One rare exception to this rule is John Sitter, "To *The Vanity of Human Wishes* through the 1740s," *Studies in Philology* 74 (1977): 445–464, which puts the poem in the context of contemporary trends in verse.

9. A. E. Housman, "Epitaph on an Army of Mercenaries" (1917).

10. Hawkins, p. 46.

11. *Lives* 2: 80. After Lichfield, Addison went to Pembroke College, Oxford, like Johnson after him.

12. *Lives* 1: 235.

13. See, for instance, Leopold Damrosch, *Samuel Johnson and the Tragic Sense* (Princeton: Princeton University Press, 1972), pp. 109–138.

14. Allen Reddick, *The Making of Johnson's Dictionary, 1746–1773* (Cambridge: Cambridge University Press, 1990), pp. 14–16. Cf. *Lives* 2: 113.

15. *Lives* 2: 148.

16. Johnson's own phrase, according to Arthur Murphy, *JM* 1: 467. "Raphael" may refer equally to the painter or to Milton's archangel, whose "angelick counsel," Johnson wrote, "every man of letters should always have before him" (*Works* 5: 183).

17. In an ingenious chapter, "(Mis)Reading *The Spectator: The Rambler* in Bloom," in *Samuel Johnson after Deconstruction: Rhetoric and The Rambler* (Carbondale: Southern Illinois University Press, 1992), pp. 21–64, Steven Lynn adopts Harold Bloom's vision of the anxiety of influence in order to argue that Johnson deliberately misreads and suppresses Addison's example. Most of the time, however, Johnson openly acknowledges his subordination to Addison (as well as to Sir Francis Bacon's *Essays*). For instance, the *Rambler* essays on the versification of *Paradise Lost,* following Addison's famous series on that poem, are supposed by Lynn to expose a serious error: "Johnson, arriving late on the scene, after Addison has harvested whatever he wishes, finds his predecessor has ignored the primary, quintessential concern—and thus again inserts himself beforehand, momentarily silencing his dead precursor" (pp. 47–48). But Johnson himself comments that Addison, as the first major critic of Milton, "had many objects at once before him, and passed willingly over those which were most barren of ideas, and required labour, rather than genius" (*Works* 4: 88–89). This statement clearly implies that Johnson follows in Addison's steps, as a laborer follows a genius, culling some leftover critical scraps.

18. *Lives* 2: 83.

19. *JM* 1: 283.

20. *Rambler* 208, *Works* 5: 319.

21. W. K. Wimsatt, *Philosophic Words* (New Haven: Yale University Press, 1948).

22. *Rambler* 208, *Works* 5: 319.

23. See Joseph Brodsky, "Nadezhda Mandelstam (1899–1980): An Obituary," in *Less than One* (New York: Farrar Straus Giroux, 1986), pp. 145–156.

24. Robert Burrowes (1786), in Boulton, p. 334.

25. Samuel Taylor Coleridge (1818), in Boulton, p. 355.

26. *BLJ* 3: 174.

27. *Lives* 3: 52.

28. Nathan Drake (1809), in Boulton, pp. 347–348. "Bow-wow" was Lord Pembroke's term for Johnson's manner (*BLJ* 2: 326n.); Coleridge picked up the term in *Table Talk*.

29. *Lives* 2: 149.

30. *JM* 1: 233.

31. *Rambler* 208, *Works* 5: 320.

32. Lawrence Lipking, *The Life of the Poet* (Chicago: University of Chicago Press, 1981), pp. 13–64.

33. *Rambler* 1–5, *Works* 3: 3, 12, 15, 24, 29–30.

34. *Spectator* 303 (February 16, 1712), in *The Spectator,* ed. Donald F. Bond (Oxford: Clarendon Press, 1965), 3: 84.

35. *Works* 5: 80.

36. *Lives* 1: 190.

37. *Works* 3: 6, 7.

38. *Works* 3: 334; 4: 93.

39. Isobel Grundy provides a fine description of this process in "Samuel Johnson: Man of Maxims?" in *Samuel Johnson: New Critical Essays,* ed. Grundy (London: Vision Press, 1984), pp. 13–30.

40. Horace, *Epistles* 1.1.14–15; the translation, by James Elphinston, was added to the collected edition of *The Rambler* in 1756. Steven Lynn's analysis of the motto in *Samuel Johnson after Deconstruction,* pp. 160–161, borrows the translation of Robert C. Olson: "Not obligated to swear by any master's orders,/I turn in for refuge wherever the tempest drives me"—*Motto, Context, Essay* (Lanham, Md.: University Press of America, 1984), p. xxv—to suggest that Johnson hints at the "refuge" of religious faith. But "refuge" does not appear in the Latin, whose point is that Horace has become a rambler, temporarily a guest wherever the storm drives him.

41. A classic statement of the need to humble intellectual pride is Sermon 8, on the text "Be not wise in your own conceits" (*Works* 14: 85–95).

42. "It is, indeed, always dangerous to be placed in a state of unavoidable comparison with excellence . . . He that succeeds a celebrated writer, has the same difficulties to encounter; he stands under the shade of exalted merit, and is hindered from rising to his natural height, by the interception

of those beams which should invigorate and quicken him" (*Rambler* 86, *Works* 4: 87). This quotation provides a starting point for W. Jackson Bate's classic study, *The Burden of the Past and the English Poet* (Cambridge, Mass.: Harvard University Press, 1970).

3. Becoming an Author

The epigraph is from "A Project for the Employment of Authors," *Universal Visiter,* April 1756, in *The Works of Samuel Johnson, LL.D.* (Oxford, 1825), 5: 358.

1. *BLJ* 5: 35; 1: 134.

2. Aleyn Lyell Reade, *Johnsonian Gleanings* (London: Lund, Humphries, 1909–1952), 6: 96–114.

3. *Life of Savage,* ed. Clarence Tracy (Oxford: Clarendon Press, 1971), p. 12.

4. Hawkins, p. 15.

5. Johnson's first book was *A Voyage to Abyssinia* (1735), an abridged translation of a French version of a Portuguese manuscript by Jerónimo Lobo. The project, for which Johnson was paid five guineas, was fostered by his friend Edmund Hector and by Thomas Warren, a Birmingham bookseller in whose house Johnson lived for six months in 1732–33. The *Voyage* has been edited by Joel J. Gold, *Works* 15.

6. *Chair' Ithakē met' aethla, met' algea pikra,/Aspasiōs teon oudas hikanomai; Greek Anthology* 9, no. 458, "What Odysseus would say on landing in Ithaca." Johnson crops the last word of the first line, *thalasses* (at sea).

7. *BLJ* 1: 296n. Edward A. Bloom, *Samuel Johnson in Grub Street* (Providence: Brown University Press, 1957), surveys Johnson's career as journalist and "Grub Street historian."

8. Johnson To Thomas Warton, February 1, 1755, *Letters* 1: 92.

9. "For we have neither Grammar nor Dictionary, neither chart nor Compass, to guide us through this wide sea of words" (1747). Johnson quotes the phrase as "this vast Sea of words," *Letters* 1: 92.

10. *Poems,* p. 33.

11. *BLJ* 1: 348.

12. Various essays on "Intellectual Property and the Construction of Authorship" are collected in *Cardozo Arts & Entertainment Law Journal* 10, no. 2 (1992).

13. Thomas Carlyle, *On Heroes, Hero-Worship, and the Heroic in History* (1840), ed. Michael Goldberg (Berkeley: University of California Press, 1993), pp. 152–158.

14. Annette Wheeler Cafarelli, *Prose in the Age of Poets: Romanticism and*

Biographical Narrative from Johnson to De Quincy (Philadelphia: University of Pennsylvania Press, 1990), pp. 30–69, discusses Johnson's "indelible stamp" on the genre of collective biography.

15. Alvin Kernan, *Printing Technology, Letters, and Samuel Johnson* (Princeton: Princeton University Press, 1987), pp. 91–94.

16. William H. Epstein discusses these changes in "Patronizing the Biographical Subject: Johnson's *Savage* and Pastoral Power," in *Johnson after Two Hundred Years,* ed. Paul Korshin (Philadelphia: University of Pennsylvania Press, 1986), pp. 141–157.

17. Brean Hammond, *Professional Imaginative Writing in England, 1670–1740* (Oxford: Clarendon Press, 1997), p. 36. Mark Rose makes the case for the legal construction of modern authorship in *Authors and Owners: The Invention of Copyright* (Cambridge, Mass.: Harvard University Press, 1993); on Johnson's role, see pp. 85–86, 105–108.

18. See Linda Joan Zionkowski, "The Value of Words: Writing and the Eighteenth-Century Commerce in Letters" (Ph.D. diss., Northwestern University, 1988). As Dustin Griffin argues in *Literary Patronage in England, 1650–1800* (Cambridge: Cambridge University Press, 1996), the patronage system may not have *declined,* but it was increasingly *resisted.*

19. Pat Rogers compares the myth and realities of authorship in *Grub Street: Studies in a Subculture* (London: Methuen, 1972).

20. See Bertrand A. Goldgar, *Walpole and the Wits: The Relation of Politics to Literature, 1722–42* (Lincoln: University of Nebraska Press, 1976); and Christine Gerrard, *The Patriot Opposition to Walpole: Politics, Poetry, and National Myth, 1725–1742* (Oxford: Clarendon Press, 1994).

21. Hammond, *Professional Imaginative Writing in England,* argues that Pope "refashioned himself into an honorary aristocrat" who spread an antiprofessional animus among the public (p. 195).

22. Pope's versions of the *Iliad* and *Odyssey,* the basis of his fortune, appeared from 1715 to 1726; his edition of Shakespeare was published in 1725. His entrepreneurial mastery is documented by David Foxon, *Pope and the Early Eighteenth-Century Book Trade,* rev. and ed. James McLaverty (Oxford: Clarendon Press, 1991).

23. *The Twickenham Edition of the Poems of Alexander Pope* (London, 1961), 1: 6.

24. *Lives* 3: 241–242.

25. *Lives* 3: 251.

26. See Robert J. Griffin, *Wordsworth's Pope: A Study in Literary Historiography* (Cambridge: Cambridge University Press, 1995).

27. W. H. Auden, *The Dyer's Hand* (New York: Random House, 1962), p. 38.

28. *Lives* 3: 394.

29. See Allen Reddick, *The Making of Johnson's Dictionary, 1746–1773* (Cambridge: Cambridge University Press, 1990), pp. 130–131.

30. *Lives* 3: 399, 394.

31. *Correspondence,* p. 49n.

32. Edward Young, *Two Epistles to Mr. Pope, Concerning the Authors of the Age* (London, 1730), pp. 13–14.

33. *BLJ* 1: 54–55. This is an early version preserved by Edmund Hector. The version revised for print in 1743 is given in *Poems,* pp. 33–34.

34. *Lives* 1: 375. Settle had been a prominent butt of *The Dunciad Variorum,* just before "The Young Author" was written, and Johnson may also have been recalling Pope's jeer at John Ogilby (1600–1676): "Here swells the shelf with Ogilby the great"; *Dunciad* 1.121.

35. Edward Young, "On Lyric Poetry" (1728), in *Eighteenth-Century Critical Essays,* ed. Scott Elledge (Ithaca: Cornell University Press, 1961), 1: 410.

36. Young, *Two Epistles to Mr. Pope,* p. 23.

37. In 1731 John Husbands published Johnson's Latin translation of Pope's "Messiah" in his *Miscellany,* without permission; Johnson is said to have been "very angry" (*Poems,* pp. 43–44). But he could hardly have been "panting for a name" on this occasion. The first version of "The Young Author" most likely dates from 1730.

38. Thomas Kaminski, *The Early Career of Samuel Johnson* (New York: Oxford University Press, 1987), pp. 24–40, surveys the world of the *Gentleman's Magazine* and Johnson's involvement in it. The *Grub-street Journal* was a rival; inspired by Pope, it specialized in satire; see Rogers, *Grub Street,* pp. 353–363.

39. *Rambler* 106, *Works* 4: 200, 204.

40. *Gentleman's Magazine* 9 (1739): 3.

41. Francis Bacon provided a standard source for the claim that poetry is a part of learning ("feigned history") in *The Advancement of Learning* (1605), ed. G. W. Kitchin (London: J. M. Dent, 1915), pp. 82–85.

42. Sermon 8, *Works* 14: 88; *Rasselas, Works* 16: 38–45.

43. *JM* 1: 180.

44. *Adventurer* 115 (1753), *Works* 2: 457, 458.

45. Isobel Grundy, "Samuel Johnson as Patron of Women," *Age of Johnson* 1 (1987): 59–77, details his services to women writers. As James Basker points out in "Johnson, Gender, and the Misogyny Question," *Age of Johnson* 8 (1997): 175–187, Johnson is cited more often than any other writer in Janet Todd's *Dictionary of British and American Women Writers, 1660–1800* (1987).

46. *Adventurer* 115, *Works* 2: 460.

47. Johnson's role in the rising status of the book trade is emphasized by John Cannon, *Samuel Johnson and the Politics of Hanoverian England* (Oxford: Clarendon Press, 1994), pp. 200–214.

48. J. W. Saunders, *The Profession of English Letters* (London: Routledge and Kegan Paul, 1964), pp. 141–145, concludes that the profession was established through the example of Johnson's career.

49. *Letters* 1: 6.

50. On Cave's attentiveness to readers, see C. Lennart Carlson, *The First Magazine* (Providence: Brown University Press, 1938).

51. *Works* 6: 40–41. The ode appeared in March 1738, p. 156, followed in May, p. 268, by the English "imitation" reproduced here.

52. *JM* 1: 377. For further discussion of the poem, see Kaminski, *Early Career,* pp. 16–18. Mathiae Casimiri Sarbievii, *Lyricorum Libri IV* (Cambridge, 1684), Ode 3, p. 10.

53. *London Magazine,* April 1738, p. 196; reprinted in *Works* 6: 42.

54. *Gentleman's Magazine* 8 (1738): 268.

55. *London, Poems,* pp. 60–81.

56. See Thomas Kaminski, "Was Savage 'Thales'?: Johnson's *London* and Biographical Speculation," *Bulletin of Research in the Humanities* 85 (1982): 322–335. A. L. Reade laid out the facts of the case in *Johnsonian Gleanings,* 6: 77–84. The crucial piece of evidence is the Rev. John Hussey's note that "Johnson told me that London was written many years before he was acquainted with Savage, and that it was even published before he knew him" (*Correspondence,* p. 234n.). Richard Holmes, who renews the speculation with a biographer's artistry in *Dr Johnson & Mr Savage* (London: Hodder & Stoughton, 1993), is forced to accuse Johnson himself of "prevarications about the poem's links with Savage" (p. 184). John Cannon's claim that Hussey's statement is "clearly impossible, since Savage left for Wales in 1739" (*Samuel Johnson and the Politics of Hanoverian England,* p. 45), is poorly reasoned; Johnson may well have written much of *London* many years before 1739. Most recent arguments on the question are interested in finding Jacobite allusions in the poem. But these arguments tend to be circular: e.g., "It is hard to believe that Johnson did not know of Savage's Jacobite sympathies. His complete silence on the subject and his rapid dismissal of Savage's early pamphlets in the *Life of Savage* might be as revealing as his feigned ignorance over the Stage Licensing Act" (Gerrard, *The Patriot Opposition to Walpole,* p. 234).

57. On the "Jacobite innuendo" of "*true Briton,*" see Howard Erskine-Hill, "The Political Character of Samuel Johnson," in *Samuel Johnson: New Critical Essays,* ed. Isobel Grundy (London: Vision Press, 1984), pp. 126–127.

58. T. S. Eliot, "Johnson as Critic and Poet" (1944), in *On Poetry and Poets* (New York: Farrar, Straus and Cudahy, 1957), p. 205. See also Geoffrey Finch, "Johnson's 'Sincerity' in *London,*" *Papers on Language and Literature* 17 (1981): 353–362.

59. Links between the two poems have been studied in three articles by Edward A. and Lillian D. Bloom: "Johnson's *London* and its Juvenalian Texts" and "Johnson's *London* and the Tools of Scholarship," *Huntington Library Quarterly* 34 (1970–71): 1–23, 115–139; and "Johnson's 'Mournful Narrative':

The Rhetoric of 'London,'" in *Eighteenth-Century Studies in Honor of Donald F. Hyde,* ed. W. H. Bond (New York: Grolier Club, 1970), pp. 107–144. Niall Rudd, *Johnson's Juvenal* (Bristol: Bristol Classical Press, 1981), includes Latin texts and translations of Juvenal's *Satires* 3 and 10 along with Johnson's imitations.

60. Definition 3 in the *Dictionary;* Dryden is given as the authority.

61. *Letters* 1: 16.

62. Wallace Stevens, "The Pleasures of Merely Circulating," in *The Palm at the End of the Mind,* ed. Holly Stevens (New York: Alfred A. Knopf, 1971), p. 97.

63. A classic statement is *Rambler* 121, on the "Echoes" of Spenser (*Works* 4: 280–286). Joel Weinsheimer, *Imitation* (London: Routledge & Kegan Paul, 1984), argues that Johnson, despite his reservations about such echoes, nonetheless agrees with Gadamer that imitation supplies the "fusion of horizons" on which all interpretation, if not all reading and writing, depends. See also his essay "'London' and the Fundamental Problem of Hermeneutics," *Critical Inquiry* 9 (1982): 303–322.

64. *Rambler* 154, *Works* 5: 59.

65. *Lives* 3: 246–247. Pope's *Imitations of Horace* supply the immediate object of criticism.

66. "Augusto recitantes mense poetas"; Juvenal, *Satires* 3.9.

67. *An Essay on Criticism,* ll. 624–625; in *Poems of Alexander Pope* 1: 310.

68. Edward Young, Satire VI, "On Women," in *Love of Fame, the Universal Passion* (London, 1728), p. 146.

69. *England's Doom; as debated in a junto of infernal spirits: detected and opposed by Michael and the holy angels. A poem. Wherein the notorious increase of atheism, immorality, and profaneness . . . is boasted of by the evil, and lamented by the good spirits* (London, 1736).

70. *BLJ* 1: 463.

71. See W. Jackson Bate, *Samuel Johnson* (New York: Harcourt Brace Jovanovich, 1977), pp. 59–60.

72. Stephen Hobhouse sketches Drummond's career in *William Law and Eighteenth Century Quakerism* (London: Allen & Unwin, 1927), pp. 73–75. The feminist implications of Drummond's preaching are spelled out in a poem suspiciously attributed to "a young Lady" in *Gentleman's Magazine* 5 (1735): 555. "That woman had no soul, was their pretence,/And womans spelling, past for woman sense./'Till you most generous heroine stood forth,/And shew'd your sex's aptitude and worth."

73. Another source may have been satires of Methodist preaching; see Albert M. Lyles, *Methodism Mocked: The Satiric Reaction to Methodism in the Eighteenth Century* (London: Epworth, 1960), pp. 62–81.

74. In his epilogue to Delarivière Manley's *Lucius* (1717), for instance, Matthew Prior puts these words into the mouth of an actress speaking of fe-

male authors: "As long as We have Eyes, or Hands, or Breath,/We'll Look, or Write, or Talk You All to Death"; *The Literary Works of Matthew Prior,* ed. H. B. Wright and M. K. Spears (Oxford: Clarendon Press, 1971), 1: 438.

75. "Que George vive ici, puisque George y sait vivre"; Boileau, *Satires* 1.34. The allusion was noticed by Fred Springer-Miller, "Johnson and Boileau," *Notes & Queries* 196 (November 10, 1951): 497.

76. Robert Dodsley, ed., *A Collection of Poems* (London, 1748), 1: 101.

77. Isaac Kramnick emphasizes the "nostalgia" of the literary opposition in *Bolingbroke and His Circle: The Politics of Nostalgia in the Age of Walpole* (Cambridge, Mass.: Harvard University Press, 1968), pp. 205–235.

78. *Lives* 1: 447.

79. Robert DeMaria Jr., *The Life of Samuel Johnson* (Oxford: Blackwell, 1993), pp. 49–50, emphasizes Thales' reputation for piety and moral wisdom as well as his resistance to tyrants, which had been chronicled by Thomas Stanley's *History of Philosophy* (1655–1660).

80. *Gentleman's Magazine* 1 (1731): 54. Thales "refuted this error" by cornering the market in olives. Stanley's version of the story, which vindicates Thales' skill in astrology, seems less likely to have been a source for *London.*

81. The first two definitions in the *Dictionary;* the third is "importance; valuable quality."

82. In *The Stylistic Life of Samuel Johnson* (New Brunswick, N.J.: Rutgers University Press, 1977), William Vesterman argues that "slidings of the meaning of 'worth' into purely economic senses" exemplify a confusion or contradiction about money (pp. 108–113), but that "confusion" seems exactly what the poem condemns in its society.

83. See Kramnick, *Bolingbroke and His Circle,* pp. 39–55, 121–124. It is questionable, however, whether Walpole's political use of patronage was different in kind from that of other ministers or the opposition.

84. *Works* 10: 19–51.

85. These are the years when Johnson is known to have written the *Debates;* he also played some part in editing or writing them during 1738–1741. See Benjamin B. Hoover, *Samuel Johnson's Parliamentary Reporting* (Berkeley: University of California Press, 1953).

86. *JM* 1: 378–379.

87. According to Adam Potkay, *The Fate of Eloquence in the Age of Hume* (Ithaca: Cornell University Press, 1994), pp. 30–40, the "Demosthenic moment" that looks back to ancient traditions of liberty and eloquence was a central motif of the opposition to Walpole.

88. *Gentleman's Magazine* 13 (1743): 181.

89. Donald Greene, *The Politics of Samuel Johnson,* 2d ed. (Athens: University of Georgia Press, 1990), p. 128. See also Robert Giddings, "The Fall of Orgilio: Samuel Johnson as Parliamentary Reporter," in Grundy, *Samuel*

Johnson: New Critical Essays, pp. 98–100. A version of the speech by William Coxe, Walpole's biographer, differs completely from Johnson's.

90. *Life of Savage,* p. 45.

91. *An Author To be Lett* (London, 1729), pp. 2, 3, 12. James Sutherland has edited the text for the Augustan Reprint Society, no. 84 (Los Angeles: Clark Library, 1960).

92. *Life of Savage,* p. 8.

93. Ibid., p. 104.

94. *Lives* 1: 173.

95. *Life of Savage,* p. 45. See Clarence Tracy, *The Artificial Bastard: A Biography of Richard Savage* (Cambridge, Mass.: Harvard University Press, 1953), pp. 60–65.

96. "To the modern reader he appears to have been skating on thin ice, for was he not himself in exactly the position of the men he was attacking?"; Tracy, *The Artificial Bastard,* p. 115.

97. *An Author To be Lett,* p. 8.

98. *Life of Savage,* p. 103.

99. Pat Rogers credits, or blames, the book for much of "the rise of the Grub Street myth" in *Grub Street,* pp. 363–369.

100. *Life of Savage,* pp. 4, 97, 46, 51.

101. See George Irwin, *Samuel Johnson: A Personality in Conflict* (Auckland: Auckland University Press, 1971), pp. 16–17; Gloria Sybil Gross, *The Invisible Riot of the Mind: Samuel Johnson's Psychological Theory* (Philadelphia: University of Pennsylvania Press, 1992), pp. 48–54; and Toni O'Shaughnessy Bowers, "Critical Complicities: *Savage* Mothers, Johnson's Mother, and the Containment of Maternal Difference," *Age of Johnson* 5 (1992): 115–146.

102. Clarence Tracy concludes that "whatever the truth may have been, Savage believed what he said" (*The Artificial Bastard,* p. 27), a view also adopted recently by Richard Holmes, *Dr Johnson & Mr Savage,* pp. 233–235.

103. Holmes makes a case both for "something unique and unprecedented" in Savage's work and for Johnson's appreciation of it; *Dr Johnson & Mr Savage,* pp. 146–155.

104. *Life of Savage,* pp. 139, 101.

105. Ibid., p. 3.

106. An alternative view, put forward by J. C. D. Clark in *Samuel Johnson* (Cambridge: Cambridge University Press, 1994), would attribute "the strange emotional intensity" of the *Life of Savage* to another model, "the tragedy of the House of Stuart" (p. 58). On the parallel between Savage's story and that of the Stuarts, see Lawrence Lipking, "The Jacobite Plot," *ELH* 64 (1997): 843–855. Johnson's *Life* does not mention Savage's subversive Jacobite writings of 1715–1717.

107. *Life of Savage,* p. 97.

108. Robert Folkenflik, *Samuel Johnson, Biographer* (Ithaca: Cornell University Press, 1978), interprets Johnson's Savage as "a tragic hero *manqué*" (p. 203).

109. "The Ant," *Poems*, p. 154.

110. *Life of Savage*, p. 74.

111. Ibid., pp. 57–58, 79.

112. Ibid., p. 137.

113. *BLJ* 1: 124.

114. *Life of Savage*, p. 140.

115. Dustin Griffin analyzes the fallacies of Savage's sense of *entitlement* to patronage in *Literary Patronage*, pp. 169–188.

116. *Life of Savage*, p. 138.

117. See Benjamin Boyce, "Johnson's *Life of Savage* and Its Literary Background," *Studies in Philology* 53 (1956): 576–598.

118. *Life of Savage*, pp. 83, 139.

119. Ibid., pp. 135, 4.

120. Ibid., p. 140.

121. J. D. Fleeman, "The Making of Johnson's *Life of Savage*, 1744," *The Library* 22 (1967): 346–352.

122. *Life of Savage*, pp. 114, 135. Helen Deutsch analyzes the balance of sympathy and judgment in "'The Name of an Author': Moral Economics in Johnson's *Life of Savage*," *Modern Philology* 92 (1995): 328–345.

123. James L. Clifford, *Young Sam Johnson* (New York: Oxford University Press, 1961), pp. 270–272. There are good accounts of Johnson's work on the Harleian catalogue in Kaminski, *Early Career*, pp. 174–184; and DeMaria, *Life of Samuel Johnson*, pp. 94–109.

4. Preferment's Gate

The epigraph is from *The Vanity of Human Wishes*, ll. 73–76; *Poems*, pp. 110–133.

1. Alan St. H. Brock, *A History of Fireworks* (London: George G. Harrap, 1949), pp. 48–52. A fire inside the building curtailed the display and protracted the show till midnight.

2. *Gentleman's Magazine* 19 (January 1749): 8. Johnson is said to have written a Latin poem, many years later, on the fireworks of Torré (*JM* 2: 377). If so, it probably mocked another wet squib, since the show misfired the night he attended (*BLJ* 4: 324–325).

3. See Howard Erskine-Hill, "The Political Character of Samuel Johnson," in *Samuel Johnson: New Critical Essays*, ed. Isobel Grundy (London: Vision Press, 1984), pp. 107–136. Whether or not one finds a trace of Jacobite sympathies in Johnson's poem, however, only an ideologue could find Jacobitism the key to the poem.

4. James L. Clifford compares the political and poetic stagnation of the time with Johnson's melancholy frame of mind, *Young Sam Johnson* (New York: Oxford University Press, 1961), pp. 310–322.

5. "The Drury-Lane Prologue," ll. 47–50; *Poems,* p. 109.

6. *Works* 16: 179–212. I have studied relations between the "Vision" and the *Vanity* in "Learning to Read Johnson: *The Vision of Theodore* and *The Vanity of Human Wishes,*" *ELH* 43 (1976): 517–537. James E. Tierney surveys Dodsley's life and career in the introduction to his edition of *The Correspondence of Robert Dodsley, 1733–1764* (Cambridge: Cambridge University Press, 1988), pp. 3–50; and Dodsley's role as Johnson's mentor is stressed by Harry M. Solomon, *The Rise of Robert Dodsley* (Carbondale: Southern Illinois University Press, 1996). Barbara M. Benedict, *Making the Modern Reader* (Princeton: Princeton University Press, 1996), discusses Dodsley's role in shaping literary culture, pp. 157–160.

7. *Dictionary.* The full definition distinguishes three kinds of enthusiasm: (1) "A vain belief of private revelation; a vain confidence of divine favour or communication"; (2) "Heat of imagination; violence of passion; confidence of opinion"; (3) "Elevation of fancy; exaltation of ideas."

8. "To Doctor *D—l—Y* [Delany], on the Libels Writ against him," ll. 93–94, in *The Poems of Jonathan Swift,* ed. Harold Williams (Oxford: Clarendon Press, 1958), 2: 503. The allusion was noticed by Christopher Ricks, *Review of English Studies* 11 (1960): 413.

9. As Leopold Damrosch points out in *Samuel Johnson and the Tragic Sense* (Princeton: Princeton University Press, 1972), Swift had composed a satiric elegy on Marlborough, so Johnson's lines ironically compel "Swift and the man he hated to share the closed unity of a couplet, just as they have had to share the fate of man" (p. 144). See also Colin Horne, "The Roles of Swift and Marlborough in *The Vanity of Human Wishes,*" *Modern Philology* 73 (1976): 280–283.

10. "The Choice of Hercules, between Virtue and Pleasure," ascribed to Prodicus and preserved in Xenophon's *Memorabilia,* was a standard school text; Robert Lowth's translation follows "The Vision of Theodore" in *The Preceptor.* In a review of George Graham's *Telemachus,* Johnson would claim that the choice of Hercules encompassed all other subjects, "for by this conflict of opposite principles, modified and determined by innumerable diversities of external circumstances, are produced all the varieties of human life; nor can history or poetry exhibit more than pleasure triumphing over virtue, and virtue subjugating pleasure"; *Critical Review* 15 (1763): 314.

11. *JM* 1: 180.

12. *BLJ* 1: 194.

13. J. G. Lockhart, *Memoirs of the Life of Sir Walter Scott* (Edinburgh, 1837), 2: 307.

14. "His fate was destined to a foreign strand,/A petty fortress and an

'humble' hand;/He left the name at which the world grew pale,/To paint a moral, or adorn a TALE." The changes are adapted to the premature death of Richard Coeur-de-Lion.

15. T. S. Eliot, "Introduction" to *London: A Poem and The Vanity of Human Wishes* (1930). Eliot's introduction is reprinted by Phyllis M. Jones, *English Critical Essays: Twentieth Century* (London: Oxford University Press, 1933), pp. 301–310. He remembers being struck by the quotation "about thirty years ago," when he would have been eleven or twelve, but thinks that it comes from one of Scott's chapter headings. In his tribute to the lines on Charles, Eliot may be recalling Johnson's own tribute to Pope: "If Pope be not a poet, where is poetry to be found?" (*Lives* 3: 251).

16. Eliot, "Introduction" (Jones, *English Critical Essays*), p. 309; Ezra Pound, *Guide to Kulchur* (1938; reprint, New York: New Directions, 1952), p. 179.

17. Allen Reddick describes this process comprehensively in *The Making of Johnson's Dictionary, 1746–1773* (Cambridge: Cambridge University Press, 1990), pp. 37–45.

18. Donald Davie, *Purity of Diction in English Verse* (London: Routledge & Kegan Paul, 1967), pp. 101–104. The postscript to this edition notes that the book, first published in 1952, had been a manifesto for the group of poets called The Movement. Davie, himself a poet-critic, aimed at recruiting Johnson to "help some practising poet to a poetry of urbane and momentous statement" (p. 107).

19. Preface to the *Dictionary*, par. 17.

20. T. S. Eliot, "Johnson as Critic and Poet" (1944), in *On Poetry and Poets* (New York: Farrar, Straus and Cudahy, 1957), p. 206; Pound, *Guide to Kulchur*, p. 180.

21. T. S. Eliot, "The Metaphysical Poets" (1921), in *Selected Essays* (London: Faber and Faber, 1951), p. 283; "Introduction," p. 302; "Johnson as Critic and Poet," p. 207. In the first instance, Eliot follows Scott in replacing "fall" with "fate" (forging a tautological "destined fate"). In the final instance, "pretty fortress" must be a printer's error.

22. Mrs. Piozzi, as reported to J. W. Croker (1831); *Poems*, p. 127n.

23. On "the accommodation of the sound to the sense," see especially the series of essays on Milton's versification, *Rambler* 86, 88, 90, 92, 94 (*Works* 4: 87–143). Even when Johnson ridicules the search for such "hidden beauties," in his sketch of Dick Minim the critic (*Idler* 60–61, *Works* 2: 184–193), his mock examples are very alert.

24. "Purple" is euphemistic; sense 2 in the *Dictionary* is "in poetry, red," and both illustrations refer to blood. It is possible, though not very probable, that Johnson also meant to suggest a mass, in which wine and wafer (or Host) stand in for blood and body. In that case, the tyrant's misplaced sense of dread would further expose the wastefulness of military sacrifice.

25. Hugh Blair, *Lectures on Rhetoric and Belles Lettres* (1783), 2: 371. I discuss such effects in Chapter 8.

26. Supplication of Heaven and celestial Wisdom, in Johnson's final lines, explicitly contradicts Juvenal's final reliance on human will: "nos te,/nos facimus, Fortuna, deam caeloque locamus" (It is we, we who make you, Fortune, a goddess and put you in the sky).

27. *Poems,* p. 140. In 1738 Johnson had advised Elizabeth Carter to translate Boethius (*BLJ* 1: 139). In the mid-1760s, to prepare for his own projected version of the *Consolations,* according to Mrs. Piozzi, he collaborated with her on a series of verse translations (*Poems,* pp. 169–177).

28. *Lives* 1: 21.

29. *Rasselas,* chap. 10; *Works* 16: 43.

30. Fine accounts of these changes in verse, with specific attention to Johnson, include John Sitter, "To *The Vanity of Human Wishes* through the 1740s," *Studies in Philology* 74 (1977): 445–464; and Eric Rothstein, *Restoration and Eighteenth-Century Poetry 1660–1780* (Boston: Routledge & Kegan Paul, 1981), chap. 4. I have written about the innovations of the 1740s in "The Genie in the Lamp: M. H. Abrams and the Motives of Literary History," in *High Romantic Argument: Essays for M. H. Abrams* (Ithaca: Cornell University Press, 1981), pp. 136–138.

31. This version of literary history is summarized and questioned by Robert J. Griffin, *Wordsworth's Pope: A Study in Literary Historiography* (Cambridge: Cambridge University Press, 1995).

32. Rothstein, *Restoration and Eighteenth-Century Poetry,* p. 120. John Sitter associates the *Vanity* with five shifts in poetry during the 1740s: (1) Epistle to Ode, (2) Persona to Personification, (3) Clarity to Obscurity, (4) Conversationalist to Solitary, and (5) Aggression to Solace; "To *The Vanity of Human Wishes,*" pp. 453–454.

33. Joseph Warton, *Essay on Pope* (London, 1806), 2: 401–402. Warton's principles are discussed in Lawrence Lipking, *The Ordering of the Arts in Eighteenth-Century England* (Princeton: Princeton University Press, 1970), pp. 362–369.

34. See W. R. Keast, "The Theoretical Foundations of Johnson's Criticism," in *Critics and Criticism,* ed. R. S. Crane (Chicago: University of Chicago Press, 1952), pp. 400–402.

35. *Lives* 3: 251n.

36. *Rambler* 121 ("The Echoes of Spenser"), *Works* 4: 286.

37. "Proposals for an Edition of Shakespeare" (1756), *Works* 7: 53.

38. These clichés about Johnson's later reputation are rehearsed by J. C. D. Clark, *Samuel Johnson* (Cambridge: Cambridge University Press, 1994), pp. 238–255.

39. *Lives* 3: 248.

40. *Lives* 1: 170. The context is Milton's effort "to teach the most impor-

tant truths," and "of his moral sentiments it is hardly praise to affirm that they excel those of all other poets; for this superiority he was indebted to his acquaintance with the sacred writings" (p. 179).

41. *Lives* 3: 242–243.

42. Johnson's most extended attack on doctrines like those of the *Essay* is his brilliant review (*Literary Magazine*, April–July 1757) of Soame Jenyns' *Free Inquiry into the Nature and Origin and Evil*. Jean Pierre de Crousaz, a Swiss theologian and logician and a well-known enemy of deism, exposed the contradictions in Pope's system, which was then defended by William Warburton; Johnson puts himself forward as a moderator between these overwrought antagonists.

43. "Buried Merit" refers specifically to Milton, whose bust had been placed in Westminster Abbey in 1737, as well as generally to unrewarded abilities. Johnson comments on "the peculiarity of Juvenal" in *Lives* 1: 447.

44. *Rambler* 29, *Works* 3: 158.

45. "Dedication to Mrs. Lennox's *Shakespear Illustrated*" (1753), *Works* 7: 47–48.

46. *Lives* 2: 218.

47. *Lives* 3: 418.

48. *Lives* 1: 291–292 (my italics).

49. Deirdre Bair, *Samuel Beckett* (New York: Harcourt Brace Jovanovich, 1978), p. 257. Johnson himself was to have been the central character of *Human Wishes* (1937). Ten manuscript pages survive; Samuel Beckett, *Disjecta*, ed. Ruby Cohn (New York: Grove Press, 1984), pp. 155–166.

50. David McCracken examines Johnson's presence in "The Wishing-Gate" (1828) in "Wordsworth on Human Wishes and Poetic Borrowing," *Modern Philology* 79 (1982): 386–399.

51. *Idler* 59, *Works* 2: 183–184. Johnson's commitment to poetic truth is analyzed by Rachel Trickett, *The Honest Muse* (Oxford: Clarendon Press, 1967).

52. Edwin Arlington Robinson, "George Crabbe" (1897), in *The Children of the Night* (New York: Scribner's, 1919), p. 64.

53. Pound, *Guide to Kulchur*, p. 178.

54. Hawkins, p. 238.

5. Man of Letters

The epigraph is from Thomas Carlyle, "The Hero as Man of Letters," in *On Heroes, Hero-Worship, and the Heroic in History* (1841), ed. Michael K. Goldberg (Berkeley: University of California Press, 1993), p. 134.

1. *Works* 10: 55, 51.

2. *Life of Savage*, ed. Clarence Tracy (Oxford: Clarendon Press, 1971), p. 140.

3. "A Short Scheme for compiling a new Dictionary of the English Lan-

guage," in *The R. B. Adam Library Relating to Dr. Samuel Johnson and His Era,* vol. 2 (London: Oxford University Press, 1929).

4. The relation of the "Scheme" to the *Plan* is discussed by James H. Sledd and Gwin J. Kolb, *Dr. Johnson's Dictionary: Essays in the Biography of a Book* (Chicago: University of Chicago Press, 1955), pp. 46–100.

5. *The Plan of a Dictionary of the English Language,* in *Johnson: Prose and Poetry,* ed. Mona Wilson (Cambridge, Mass.: Harvard University Press, 1951), pp. 136–137.

6. Allen Reddick describes the circumstances and reception of the *Plan* in *The Making of Johnson's Dictionary, 1746–1773* (Cambridge: Cambridge University Press, 1990), pp. 12–24.

7. *Plan,* p. 122.

8. The standard account of this period in Johnson's life is James Clifford, *Dictionary Johnson* (New York: McGraw-Hill, 1979).

9. *Plan,* p. 121.

10. See, for instance, Paul Fussell, *Samuel Johnson and the Life of Writing* (New York: Harcourt Brace Jovanovich, 1971), pp. 182–192.

11. Scott Elledge describes "their basic disagreement about language" in "The Naked Science of Language, 1747–1786," in *Studies in Criticism and Aesthetics, 1660–1800,* ed. Howard Anderson and John S. Shea (Minneapolis: University of Minnesota Press, 1967), pp. 266–277.

12. *Plan,* p. 138.

13. Johnson's involvement with the traditions of European humanism is a central theme of Robert DeMaria Jr., *The Life of Samuel Johnson* (Oxford: Blackwell, 1993); and, to a lesser extent, of J. C. D. Clark, *Samuel Johnson* (Cambridge: Cambridge University Press, 1994).

14. I analyze this poem in Chapter 9.

15. *Plan,* p. 122.

16. The standard intellectual biography is Anthony Grafton, *Joseph Scaliger: A Study in the History of Classical Scholarship,* 2 vols. (Oxford: Clarendon Press, 1983, 1993). Mark Pattison's *Essays,* vol. 1, ed. H. Nettleship (Oxford, 1889), provide a lively account of Scaliger's scholarly quarrels. Johnson owned a copy of Scaliger's "table talk," *Scaligerana* (1740).

17. Preface to *A Dictionary of the English Language* (London, 1755), par. 93. All paragraph numbers in the text refer to the Preface in this edition, the first. The *Gentleman's Magazine* 18 (1748): 8 had reprinted Scaliger's epigram.

18. The standard study is J. D. Fleeman, "The Revenue of a Writer: Samuel Johnson's Literary Earnings," in *Studies in the Book Trade in Honour of Graham Pollard* (Oxford: Oxford Bibliographical Society, 1975), pp. 211–230.

19. *BLJ* 1: 287n.

20. Clifford, *Dictionary Johnson,* p. 149.

21. This follows Johnson's definition of "lexicographer" as "a writer of dictionaries."

22. *Correspondence,* p. 159.

23. Reddick, *The Making of Johnson's Dictionary,* pp. 25–54, provides a thorough account of this crisis.

24. The fullest account of Johnson's indebtedness to lexicographical tradition remains that of Sledd and Kolb, *Dr. Johnson's Dictionary,* pp. 1–45. De Witt Starnes and Gertrude Noyes, *The English Dictionary from Cawdrey to Johnson, 1604–1755* (Chapel Hill: University of North Carolina Press, 1946), is still dependable. Allen Walker Read, "The History of Lexicography," in *Lexicography: An Emerging International Profession,* ed. Robert Ilson (Manchester: Manchester University Press, 1986), pp. 28–50, supplies a useful summary; and much information is added by Reddick and by Robert DeMaria Jr., *Johnson's Dictionary and the Language of Learning* (Chapel Hill: University of North Carolina Press, 1986).

25. Johnson once considered revising the *Cyclopaedia,* and he told Boswell that he had formed his style partly on Chambers; *BLJ* 1: 218–219.

26. Seán Burke, *The Death and Return of the Author* (Edinburgh: Edinburgh University Press, 1992), provides a good analysis of recent theories of authorship. For a sympathetic view of Foucault's influence on eighteenth-century scholarship, see John Bender, "A New History of the Enlightenment?" in *The Profession of Eighteenth-Century Literature,* ed. Leo Damrosch (Madison: University of Wisconsin Press, 1992), pp. 62–83.

27. DeMaria, *Johnson's Dictionary,* pp. 4–8, begins with Chambers' influence on Johnson in characterizing the lexicographer.

28. E. Chambers, *Cyclopaedia,* 5th ed. (London, 1741), 1: xxiii.

29. Ibid., p. xviii.

30. Rousseau's writings on music are collected in *Oeuvres complètes,* vol. 5 (Paris: Gallimard, 1995). His most influential polemic on behalf of (Italian) melody is *Lettre sur la musique française* (1753).

31. Robert Darnton, "Readers Respond to Rousseau: The Fabrication of Romantic Sensitivity," in *The Great Cat Massacre and Other Episodes in French Cultural History* (New York: Random House, 1985), pp. 215–256.

32. I examine Johnson's place in the history of reading in "Inventing the Common Reader: Samuel Johnson and the Canon," in *Interpretation and Cultural History,* ed. Joan. H. Pittock and Andrew Wear (New York: St. Martin's, 1991), pp. 153–174. Robert DeMaria Jr., *Samuel Johnson and the Life of Reading* (Baltimore: Johns Hopkins University Press, 1997), shows the variety of models of reading that Johnson provides.

33. Alberto Manguel, *A History of Reading* (New York: Viking, 1996), pp. 170–173, plays with the metaphor of eating books. Johnson's activity as "master reader" is described by Alvin Kernan, *Printing Technology, Letters, and Samuel Johnson* (Princeton: Princeton University Press, 1987), pp. 207–218.

34. Carlyle, "The Hero as Man of Letters," p. 157.

35. *BLJ* 1: 297n. For Tooke's attack on Johnson, see Sledd and Kolb, *Dr. Johnson's Dictionary*, pp. 183–191; and Hans Aarsleff, *The Study of Language in England, 1780–1860* (Minneapolis: University of Minnesota Press, 1983), pp. 55–56, 249–252.

36. The last line of David Garrick's epigram "*On* JOHNSON'S DICTIONARY," *BLJ* 1: 301.

37. Clifford, *Dictionary Johnson*, pp. 125–126, 133–134.

38. A fine history of the war between Ancients and Moderns is Joseph M. Levine, *The Battle of the Books* (Ithaca: Cornell University Press, 1991).

39. Edward Lye edited the *Etymologicon Anglicanum* from manuscripts left by Junius at his death in 1677. I have discussed Junius' reverence for the ancients in *The Ordering of the Arts in Eighteenth-Century England* (Princeton: Princeton University Press, 1970), pp. 23–31.

40. Though Johnson was the first English lexicographer to use quotations systematically, there were many antecedents in other languages. A. W. Read provides a good survey in "The History of Lexicography," pp. 28–37.

41. See Johnson's "Life of Browne" (1756), in *The Works of Samuel Johnson*, ed. Arthur Murphy (New York: Harper, 1846), 2: 373.

42. In an interesting note contributed to A. D. Horgan, *Johnson on Language: An Introduction* (New York: St. Martin's, 1994), pp. 201–202, J. D. Fleeman comments on "the inevitable conflict between definition and illustration" when quotations are selected from creative writers.

43. On Johnson's francophobia see Gerald Newman, *The Rise of English Nationalism* (New York: St. Martin's, 1987), pp. 112–113, 150–153.

44. Christine Gerrard discusses this "cultural patriotism" in *The Patriot Opposition to Walpole: Politics, Poetry, and National Myth, 1725–1742* (Oxford: Clarendon Press, 1994), pp. 46–51.

45. Cf. Part V of Thomson's *Liberty* (1736): "Shall Britons, by their own joint wisdom ruled/ . . . shall they/To Gallia yield? yield to a land that bends, /Depressed and broke, beneath the will of one?" (ll. 441, 444–446).

46. These definitions were not revised after Johnson accepted a pension in 1762, though in 1773 he did add one quotation from Young: "Chremes, for airy *pensions* of renown,/Devotes his service to the state, and crown."

47. "The edicts of an English academy would probably be read by many, only that they might be sure to disobey them . . . The present manners of the nation would deride authority, and therefore nothing is left but that every writer should criticise himself"; *Lives* 1: 233.

48. Samuel Taylor Coleridge, *Biographia Literaria*, ed. James Engell and W. J. Bate (Princeton: Princeton University Press, 1983), 1: 237–238.

49. E.g., George Alfred Stringer, *Leisure Moments in Gough Square, or The Beauties and Quaint Conceits of Johnson's Dictionary* (Buffalo, 1886).

50. *BLJ* 3: 280.

51. W. K. Wimsatt, *Philosophic Words: A Study of Style and Meaning in the Rambler and Dictionary of Samuel Johnson* (New Haven: Yale University Press, 1948), remains a valuable study of Johnson's diction, which also figures prominently in Susie I. Tucker, *Protean Shape: A Study in Eighteenth-Century Vocabulary and Usage* (London: Athlone Press, 1967).

52. Aarsleff, *The Study of Language in England,* p. 248.

53. These distinctions are central to two books by Basil Willey: *The Seventeenth Century Background* (London: Chatto and Windus, 1934), which focuses on Truth; and *The Eighteenth Century Background* (London: Chatto & Windus, 1940), which focuses on Nature.

54. Reddick, *The Making of Johnson's Dictionary,* pp. 55–59.

55. *Plan,* p. 123.

56. Ibid., p. 129. According to Dennis Dean Kezar Jr., "Radical Letters and Male Genealogies in Johnson's *Dictionary,*" *SEL* 35 (1995), Johnson's emphasis on illegitimate spawn and on respect for the language of fathers "invokes a lexicographic patriarchy" (p. 502).

57. Levine, *The Battle of the Books,* pp. 39–40. On the prescriptive ambitions of Johnson's plan, see Horgan, *Johnson on Language,* pp. 97–112, and Fleeman's notes, ibid., pp. 198–200.

58. Reddick, *The Making of Johnson's Dictionary,* pp. 45–51.

59. Bayle's relation to Johnson is discussed in Lipking, *The Ordering of the Arts,* pp. 76–83.

60. See James A. H. Murray, *The Evolution of English Lexicography* (Oxford: Clarendon Press, 1900), p. 40. As Murray points out, this must have been an accident; Johnson elsewhere distinguished the Portuguese word *Coco* (the grimace suggested by the three holes in the coconut) from *Cocoa,* a Latinized form of the Aztec word *Cacao* (the shrub whose seeds produce cocoa and chocolate).

61. *Lives* 1: 94, 193; *BLJ* 2: 407. Two illustrations of "lapidary" as a noun— "One who deals in stones or gems"—may have tricked Johnson into forgetting that he had left the adjective out.

62. Preface to the *Dictionary,* par. 43. Cf. *Rambler* 125: "Definition is, indeed, not the province of man; every thing is set above or below our faculties" (*Works* 4: 300).

63. *BLJ* 3: 253.

64. "Taxonomy" was not introduced into English until 1828. Though Linnaeus was a contemporary of Johnson and had visited England, Johnson is not known to have owned any of his works.

65. The categories also include Ignorance; Truth; Mind; Education; Language; The Arts of Writing, Reading, and Speaking; Arts and Sciences; and Fundamentals. As DeMaria is well aware, this classification of "the language of learning" derives from his own reading of the *Dictionary* (not from any

computer), and another reader would surely make a different list; *Johnson's Dictionary*, p. 37.

66. Diderot calls the use of cross-references "the most important part of our encyclopedic scheme" in his article on "The Encyclopedia"; *Rameau's Nephew and Other Works*, trans. Jacques Barzun and Ralph H. Bowen (Indianapolis: Bobbs-Merrill, 1964), p. 295. The article was first published in 1755, the same year as Johnson's *Dictionary*.

67. For one effort to construct such a theory, see Rackstraw Downes, "Johnson's Theory of Language," *Review of English Literature* 3 (1962): 29–41, which emphasizes Johnson's reliance on poetic diction as "a balance between originality and uniformity" (p. 37).

68. According to Murray Cohen, *Sensible Words: Linguistic Practice in England, 1640–1785* (Baltimore: Johns Hopkins University Press, 1977), pp. 90–94, this "disillusioned idea of language" is Johnson's main contribution to linguistics.

69. Sharon Achinstein analyzes an earlier stage of this conjunction between language, theology, and politics in "The Politics of Babel in the English Revolution," *Prose Studies: History, Theory, Criticism* 14 (December 1991): 14–44.

70. Cf. Nathan Bailey's definition (1730): "that part of grammar that shews the original of words, for the better distinguishing and establishing of their true signification." In other places as well, Bailey identifies "the original of words" with their "true meaning."

71. See Sledd and Kolb, *Dr. Johnson's Dictionary*, pp. 180–181.

72. John Locke, *An Essay Concerning Human Understanding* (1690), book 3, chap. 1. The influence of this passage is emphasized by Aarsleff, *The Study of Language in England*, pp. 31–33.

73. James McLaverty, "From Definition to Explanation: Locke's Influence on Johnson's Dictionary," *Journal of the History of Ideas* 47 (1986): 377–394, argues that Locke himself authorizes the turn to a historical understanding of knowledge.

74. As Elizabeth Hedrick points out in "Locke's Theory of Language and Johnson's *Dictionary*," *Eighteenth-Century Studies* 20 (1987): 422–444, Johnson sometimes "presents etymons as more abstract than the meanings that evolve out of them" (p. 436).

75. "Nature, and Nature's Laws lay hid in Night / God said, *Let Newton be!* and All was *Light.*"

76. Wimsatt, *Philosophic Words*, pp. 104–113. Wimsatt presents his case more succinctly in "Johnson's Dictionary," in *New Light on Dr. Johnson*, ed. F. W. Hilles (New Haven: Yale University Press, 1959), pp. 65–90.

77. Matthew Prior. Johnson, like his contemporaries, thought of Descartes primarily as a scientist whose theories had been superseded by Newton's.

78. John Cannon, *Samuel Johnson and the Politics of Hanoverian England*

(Oxford: Clarendon Press, 1994), pp. 215–247, offers a balanced view of the evolution of Johnson's attitudes toward nationalism.

79. Murphy, *The Works of Samuel Johnson,* 2: 455.

80. According to Clark, *Samuel Johnson,* the *Dictionary* may be "intended to be the foundation stone of a newly-strengthened vernacular culture, to replace the old: English was now to be raised to the dignity of Latin and Greek as a medium for cultural expression" (p. 74).

81. Mrs. Sutherland Orr, *Life and Letters of Robert Browning* (Boston, 1891), 1: 75.

82. Horace, *Epistles* 2.2.110–118, "To Florus."

83. "Le Tombeau d'Edgar Poe," line 6. Both T. S. Eliot and Ezra Pound associated Johnson with Mallarmé's project (see Chapter 4).

84. D. G. Scragg, *A History of English Spelling* (Manchester: Manchester University Press, 1974), pp. 82, 99–102, discusses Johnson's role in standardizing spelling. Horgan, *Johnson on Language,* pp. 144–147, criticizes the effort to make pronunciation conform to the norms of spelling in an age of print.

85. An exception might be made for "dialect": "The subdivision of a language; as the Attic, Doric, Ionic, Aeolic dialects"; but significantly no illustration is given outside the Greek examples or the "corrupt dialect" exemplifying "cant." Nor does the *Dictionary* allow, in its definition of "accent," the possibility of foreign or regional accents.

86. *Lives* 3: 16. Swift's zeal was probably more political than linguistic; see Marilyn Francus, *The Converting Imagination: Linguistic Theory and Swift's Satiric Prose* (Carbondale: Southern Illinois University Press, 1994), pp. 118–140.

87. In *Swift and the English Language* (Philadelphia: University of Pennsylvania Press, 1988), Ann Cline Kelly argues that the *Proposal* contradicts some of Swift's own positions; ordinarily, he believed "that proper language was not the exclusive province of the literate" (p. 112).

88. "Our Sons their Fathers' *failing* Language see, /And such as *Chaucer* is, shall *Dryden* be"; Pope, *An Essay on Criticism,* ll. 482–483. Dryden had translated Chaucer into modern English in *Fables Ancient and Modern* (1700).

89. Jonathan Swift, *A Proposal for Correcting, Improving and Ascertaining the English Tongue* (London, 1712), pp. 42, 32.

90. Ibid., p. 28. Alan Chalmers emphasizes Swift's personal stake in preserving the language in *Jonathan Swift and the Burden of the Future* (London: Associated University Presses, 1995), pp. 40–45.

91. *The World,* no. 101, 3: 273–279. The *Dictionary* defines "flirtation" as "A quick sprightly motion. A cant word among women" (*not* "the first hints of approximation, which subsequent coquetry may reduce to those preliminary articles, that commonly end in a definitive treaty"; *The World,* p. 273);

"to fuzz" as "to fly out in small particles" (*not* "to make drunk or fuddle," as in fashionable usage); and "vastly" as "greatly; to a great degree."

92. Robert DeMaria Jr., "The Politics of Johnson's *Dictionary*," *PMLA* 104 (1989), concludes that "the *Dictionary*, by virtue of its range of selection and presentation, belongs to the liberal tradition and fosters democracy" (p. 72).

93. John Barrell, *English Literature in History 1730–80: An Equal, Wide Survey* (London: Hutchinson, 1983), p. 158. Note the insistent repetition of the indefinite "now." Barrell's analysis depends on stringing the Preface together with *The False Alarm* and *The Patriot*, as if they constituted a single text.

94. *The World*, no. 103 (December 19, 1754): 3: 288–289.

95. "Preface to Shakespeare," *Works* 7: 70. Cf. *Rambler* 194, where a young man's efforts to learn "the customs of the polite part of mankind" result in a dialect of "fashionable barbarism"; *Works* 5: 249–250.

96. *Lives* (Butler) 1: 214.

97. The ideological conflicts are analyzed by Michael McKeon, "Politics of Discourses and the Rise of the Aesthetic in Seventeenth-Century England," in *Politics of Discourse*, ed. Kevin Sharpe and Steven Zwicker (Berkeley: University of California Press, 1987), pp. 35–51.

98. Lois Potter, *Secret Rites and Secret Writing: Royalist literature, 1641–1660* (Cambridge: Cambridge University Press, 1989), points out that Charles I, in his final days, could be quoted only through the language of the Book of Common Prayer, which was banned to everyone else (pp. 168–169).

99. "When I published my Dictionary, I might have quoted *Hobbes* as an authority in language, as well as many other writers of his time: but I scorned, sir, to quote him at all; because I did not like his principles"; Johnson to Thomas Tyers, *The Early Biographies of Samuel Johnson*, ed. O. M. Brack and Robert E. Kelley (Iowa City: University of Iowa Press, 1974), p. 82.

100. In *The Politics of Language 1791–1819* (Oxford: Clarendon Press, 1984), Olivia Smith argues that Johnson, by emphasizing the distinction between refined and vulgar English, popularized hegemonic ideas of language for following generations (pp. 13–20).

101. *The Correspondence of Samuel Richardson*, ed. Anna Letitia Barbauld (London, 1804), 4: 282. This is the first use of the word recorded by the *OED*. W. R. Keast, "The Two *Clarissas* in Johnson's *Dictionary*," *Studies in Philology* 54 (1957): 429–439, shows that Johnson drew many quotations from the collection of "moral and instructive sentiments" appended to vol. 7 of the fourth edition of *Clarissa* (1751).

102. Reddick, *The Making of Johnson's Dictionary*, pp. 141–169, demonstrates that much of the new material responds to "contemporary politico-theological debate" (p. 122).

103. Ibid., pp. 132–140.

104. *Lives* 3: 52.

105. Johnson to Cave, November 25, 1734, *Letters* 1: 6.

106. E. Chambers, "Criticism," in *Cyclopaedia*. Though there are many kinds of criticism, Chambers claims that "the ordinary use of the word is restrained to Literary Criticism."

107. *Samuel Johnson's Prefaces & Dedications*, ed. Allen T. Hazen (New Haven: Yale University Press, 1937), pp. 128–131.

108. In his useful survey of "literature" in *Keywords* (New York: Oxford University Press, 1985), Raymond Williams suggests that the idea of *English Literature* "is implicit in Johnson" (p. 185); but the idea as well as the phrase is explicit in Johnson's Preface. Cf. Tucker, *Protean Shape*, pp. 198–199.

109. *BLJ* 3: 354.

110. Both Bacon and Addison were highly praised by Johnson for bringing their knowledge "home to men's business and bosoms"; see *Rambler* 106, *Works* 4: 204; and *Lives* 2: 146.

111. The claim might be disputed. Among many other candidates, note the claim of the *Critical Review* in 1775 that "every reader of taste" will consider the hour when Johnson conceived his *Journey* "as a fortunate event in the annals of literature" (*BLJ* 5: 141n.).

112. *Lives* 1: 1. A recent discussion of the embarrassing "arbitrariness of the definition of literature" chooses Sprat as its example of what is *not* literature: "Browne's *Religio Medici* has traditionally been taken to be a literary text, while Spratt's [*sic*] *History of the Royal Society* is accorded only 'background' status"; Lee Patterson, "Literary History," in *Critical Terms for Literary Study*, ed. Frank Lentricchia and Thomas McLaughlin (Chicago: University of Chicago Press, 1990), p. 256. This distinction between two authors he valued would have been unintelligible to Johnson.

6. The Living World

The epigraph is from *Rambler* 4, *Works* 3: 20.

1. Both Payne and Johnson belonged to the Ivy Lane Club, whose lively discussions seem to have provoked some of the *Rambler* essays. James L. Clifford, *Dictionary Johnson: Samuel Johnson's Middle Years* (New York: McGraw-Hill, 1979), pp. 71–85, gives a reliable account of how the essays were written and published.

2. *JM* 2: 414.

3. "I am willing to flatter myself with hopes, that, by collecting these papers. I am not preparing for my future life, either shame or repentance"; *Rambler* 208, *Works* 5: 318. This edition is the source of all references in the text.

4. John Dryden, "To the Earl of *Roscomon*, on his Excellent *Essay* on *Translated Verse*" (1684), ll. 30–31.

5. *Lives* 1: 236; *Rambler* 106, *Works* 4: 204.

6. As Boswell points out, Johnson had earlier jotted notes for many of the essays in a commonplace book; *BLJ* 1: 204–208.

7. Hawkins, p. 111.

8. Richardson's essay rebukes the Rambler for not taking notice, like the Spectator, "of the manners of the better half of the human species" (*Works* 2: 154), and goes on to praise the good old days of the *Spectator,* when men kept their reverence for women because they could hardly meet them except at church.

9. The classic study of diction in *The Rambler* remains W. K. Wimsatt, *Philosophic Words* (New Haven: Yale University Press, 1948), chaps. 3–5.

10. See Robert Mayo, *The English Novel in the Magazines, 1740–1815* (Evanston: Northwestern University Press, 1962), pp. 93–117.

11. *Lives* 2: 148.

12. "Preface to Shakespeare," *Works* 7: 67.

13. Robert DeMaria discusses the *Rambler's* "circle of literary reference" in *The Life of Samuel Johnson* (Oxford: Blackwell, 1993), pp. 155–159.

14. James Boyd White, *When Words Lose Their Meaning* (Chicago: University of Chicago Press, 1984), pp. 138–162, devotes a chapter to the ways in which the *Rambler* essays teach "a language of morality."

15. *Rasselas,* chap. 44; *Works* 16: 150.

16. *Adventurer* 138, *Works* 2: 493.

17. Edward Bloom discusses "Symbolic Names in Johnson's Periodical Essays," *Modern Language Quarterly* 13 (1952): 333–352.

18. See Clifford, *Dictionary Johnson,* pp. 149–164.

19. "A Project for the Employment of Authors," *Universal Visiter,* April 1756.

20. James Elphinston published an early Edinburgh edition of *The Rambler* (approved by Johnson); his translations of classical mottos were later adopted by the fourth edition (London, 1756), which Johnson himself revised. The original *Rambler* 1 includes only Juvenal's Latin: "Cur tamen hoc libeat potius decurrere campo,/Per quem magnus equos Auruncae flexit alumnus,/Si vacat, et placidi rationem admittitis, edam" (*Satires* 1.19–21). Robert C. Olson supplies translations and commentaries on the mottos in *Motto, Context, Essay: The Classical Background of Samuel Johnson's Rambler and Adventurer Essays* (Lanham, Md.: University Press of America, 1984).

21. *Works* 3: 7. "—Quid enim? Concurritur—horae/Momento cita mors venit, aut victoria laeta" (*Satires* 1.1.7–8); Dr. Philip Francis' translation. Clare H. Nunes, "Classical Allusion in the 'Rambler' Essays of Samuel Johnson" (Ph.D. diss., Princeton University, 1979), analyzes the effects of Johnson's quotations.

22. "Non fumum ex fulgore, sed ex fumo dare lucem/Cogitat, ut speciosa dehinc miracula promat"; *Ars poetica* 143–144 (Not smoke after a lightning flash, but after smoke light he intends/To give, so that henceforth he may illuminate splendid and wonderful things).

23. Cf. *Idler* 102: "The gradations of a hero's life are from battle to battle, and of an author's from book to book" (*Works* 2: 312).

24. Jacob Leed, "Patronage in the *Rambler*," *Studies in Burke and His Times* 14 (1972): 5.

25. The justification for Johnson's grievance has been debated by Jacob Leed, "Johnson and Chesterfield: 1746–47," *Studies in Burke and His Times* 12 (1970): 1677–90; Paul Korshin, "Johnson and Literary Patronage: A Comment on Jacob Leed's Article," ibid. (1970–71): 1804–11; and Leed, ibid., 13 (1971): 2011–15.

26. *Dictionary*. Three other senses are also given: "A guardian saint"; "Advocate; defender; vindicator"; "One who has donation of ecclesiastical preferment."

27. See Bertrand A. Goldgar, *Walpole and the Wits: The Relation of Politics to Literature, 1722–1742* (Lincoln: University of Nebraska Press, 1976); and J. A. Downie, "Walpole, 'the Poet's Foe,'" in *Britain in the Age of Walpole*, ed. Jeremy Black (New York: St. Martin's, 1984), pp. 171–188.

28. According to Dustin Griffin, *Literary Patronage in England, 1650–1800* (Cambridge: Cambridge University Press, 1996), in *The Rambler* "Johnson's real concern is not with patrons but with young writers, whose vain hopes need to be suppressed" (p. 224). This understates Johnson's resentment of patrons but not his concern for young writers.

29. E.g., "It forbids pride and ambition, and vain glory; and commands humility and modesty, and *condescension* to others" (Tillotson).

30. On Garrick, see *BLJ* 1: 216.

31. See especially "Competition," in Isobel Grundy, *Samuel Johnson and the Scale of Greatness* (Athens: University of Georgia Press, 1986), pp. 102–119.

32. Griffin analyzes "the cultural economics of literary patronage" in *Literary Patronage*, pp. 13–44.

33. *Poems*, p. 109; line 53.

34. Johnson's translation from *Greek Anthology* 7.128, quoted by Diogenes Laertius in his life of Heraclitus. Johnson later translated the same epigram into Latin.

35. *Works* 1: 43. Philip Davis, *In Mind of Johnson: A Study of Johnson The Rambler* (Athens: University of Georgia Press, 1989), pp. 172–242, discusses Johnson's endeavor to be "an Anglican saint."

36. *Works* 7: 72. "The Stability of Truth" is the title of Chapter 4 of W. Jackson Bate's *The Achievement of Samuel Johnson* (New York: Oxford University Press, 1955).

37. Ezra Pound, *ABC of Reading* (New Haven: Yale University Press, 1934), p. 15.

38. *Lives* 1: 59.

39. In a fine study of *Samuel Johnson and Eighteenth-Century Thought* (Ox-

ford: Clarendon Press, 1988), for instance, Nicholas Hudson argues that Johnson's sense of moral obligation places him with "a small group of ethical philosophers who came into prominence during the 1750s," who advocated the doctrine of "Christian epicureanism" (p. 66).

40. E.g., "far from believing that there is nothing really new under the sun, Johnson is keenly aware of the eternal flux in which all mankind is involved"; Paul Alkon, *Samuel Johnson and Moral Discipline* (Evanston: Northwestern University Press, 1967), p. 19.

41. Analyses of the polarities, indeterminacies, and even deconstructive tendencies of Johnson's rhetoric include Cyril Knoblauch, "Samuel Johnson and the Composing Process," *Eighteenth-Century Studies* 13 (1980): 243–262; and Steven Lynn, *Samuel Johnson after Deconstruction: Rhetoric and The Rambler* (Carbondale: Southern Illinois University Press, 1992), esp. 65–114.

42. *Works* 7: 59; *Lives* 1: 59.

43. Leopold Damrosch, "Johnson's Manner of Proceeding in the *Rambler*," *ELH* 40 (1973): 70–89, stresses the unsettling effect of this procedure.

44. *Rasselas,* chap. 8; *Works* 16: 33.

45. *The Correspondence of Samuel Richardson,* ed. Anna Letitia Barbauld (London, 1804), 1: 169.

46. Horace, *Satires* 1.3.18–19.

47. W. Jackson Bate, *Samuel Johnson* (New York: Harcourt Brace Jovanovich, 1977), p. 494.

48. William Mudford (1802), in Boulton, p. 76.

49. L. F. Powell gathers the evidence for Johnson's authorship in *Works* 2: 323–338.

50. *Works* 2: 487; Pythagoras, *Aurea carmina* 42.

51. *Works* 2: 489, 492.

7. Reclaiming Imagination

The epigraph is from William Wordsworth, "Hart-Leap Well," line 97.

1. Hawkins, p. 94. Compare the remark by a mercenary "Author" in Fielding's *Amelia* (1751): "In Truth, the Romance Writing is the only Branch of our Business now, that is worth following. Goods of that Sort have had so much Success lately in the Market, that a Bookseller scarce cares what he bids for them"; *Amelia,* ed. Martin C. Battestin (Middletown, Conn.: Wesleyan University Press, 1984), p. 320.

2. *BLJ* 2: 173. "Johnson was inclined, as being personally acquainted with Richardson, to favour . . . his writings, but he seemed not firm in it, and could at any time be talked into a disapprobation of all fictitious relations, of which he would frequently say they took no hold of the mind"; Hawkins, pp. 96–97.

3. *Rambler* 96, *Works* 4: 152.

4. Carey McIntosh describes Johnson's place in "the rise of the novel" in *The Choice of Life: Samuel Johnson and the World of Fiction* (New Haven: Yale University Press, 1973), pp. 23–29.

5. *Rambler* 3, *Works* 3: 16–19.

6. *Rambler* 4, *Works* 3: 19–24.

7. *Works* 3: 19n.

8. *BLJ* 1: 192, 537. Thomas Percy reported the comment in 1760.

9. *The Collected Works of Samuel Taylor Coleridge,* 12, *Marginalia,* ed. George Whalley (Princeton: Princeton University Press, 1984), 2: 693.

10. Sheldon Sacks, *Fiction and the Shape of Belief* (Chicago: University of Chicago Press, 1964), p. 1.

11. "We do not care what Blifil *does*—the deed, as separate from the agent, may be good or ill—but Blifil *is* a villain—and we feel him to be so"; Coleridge, *Marginalia,* 2: 693. I have explored these issues more fully in "Arguing with Shelly," *Critical Inquiry* 6 (1979): 193–208. Johnson's emphasis on deeds is a central theme of Robert Voitle, *Samuel Johnson the Moralist* (Cambridge, Mass.: Harvard University Press, 1961).

12. *BLJ* 1: 49. The influence of such romances on Johnson is the subject of a full-length study by Eithne Henson, *"The Fictions of Romantick Chivalry": Samuel Johnson and Romance* (Rutherford, N.J.: Fairleigh Dickinson University Press, 1992).

13. *BLJ* 3: 357.

14. *Works* 1: 71.

15. *Rasselas,* chap. 44; *Works* 16: 152.

16. Sacks, *Fiction and the Shape of Belief,* p. 26. Occasionally the Rambler also writes *satire,* "a work organized so that it ridicules objects external to the fictional world created in it" (p. 26), but never the sort of story that Sacks calls the "action" or "novel," in which "characters about whose fates we are made to care are introduced in unstable relationships" which first are complicated and then resolved (p. 15).

17. *Lives* 1: 185.

18. *Works* 4: 285.

19. *Dictionary.* Cf. the comments in *A Course of Lectures on the English Law,* by Sir Robert Chambers in "association" with Johnson, ed. Thomas M. Curley (Oxford: Clarendon Press, 1986): "Wealth is the only superiority that can be successively transmitted. The son of a rich man will be rich, but the son of a wise man will not always be wise. Wealth is therefore perhaps the only ground of hereditary greatness" (1: 249).

20. *Lives* 1: 185; 3: 233. Johnson's theory and practice of allegory have been discussed by Edwin C. Heinle, "The Eighteenth-Century Allegorical Essay" (Ph.D. diss., Columbia University, 1957); Bernard L. Einbond, *Samuel Johnson's Allegory* (The Hague: Mouton, 1971); and (very usefully) Carey McIntosh, *The Choice of Life,* pp. 102–116.

21. *Rambler* 96, *Works* 4: 149–152.

22. *Lives* 2: 149. The whole passage, on Addison as a teacher of wisdom, shows how closely Johnson associates his own allegorical mode, as exemplified by *Rambler* 96, with Addison's: "Truth is shewn sometimes as the phantom of a vision, sometimes appears half-veiled in an allegory, sometimes attracts regard in the robes of fancy, and sometimes steps forth in the confidence of reason. She wears a thousand dresses, and in all is pleasing."

23. *Rambler* 123, *Works* 4: 291, 295.

24. *Works* 16: 247. The partiality toward wit presumably represents not only Johnson's own choice but also his portrait of Hester Lynch Thrale, who thought herself the original Floretta; see Gwin J. Kolb, "Mrs. (Thrale) Piozzi and Dr. Johnson's 'The Fountains: A Fairy Tale,'" *Novel* 13 (1979): 68–81. Later, in 1789–90, she remade the tale into a three-act play, *The Two Fountains*. It was never produced, but the text has been edited by Stuart Sherman and Margaret Anne Doody (Philadelphia: The Johnsonians, 1994).

25. Quoted in *Works* 16: 228. Though Carter seems not to know that her friend Johnson wrote the tale, she observes that "This conclusion is liable to the same objection as Mr. Johnson's *Rasselas.*"

26. *Poems,* p. 174. Johnson's versions of Boethius were part of a collaborative project with Hester Thrale (the original "Floretta") and date from the same period as "The Fountains."

27. John Bunyan, *Grace Abounding to the Chief of Sinners and The Pilgrim's Progress,* ed. Roger Sharrock (London: Oxford University Press, 1966), p. 272.

28. "The Vision of Theodore," *Works* 16: 212.

29. *Rambler* 102, *Works* 4: 182, 184. I have commented more fully on *Rambler* 102 in "Johnson and the Meaning of Life," in *Johnson and His Age,* ed. James Engell (Cambridge, Mass.: Harvard University Press, 1984), pp. 1–27.

30. *BLJ* 1: 341.

31. Hawkins, p. 153. J. C. D. Clark surmises that Johnson was glossing over his true reason, his refusal to take the oath required by the Church of England; *Samuel Johnson* (Cambridge: Cambridge University Press, 1994), pp. 121–122.

32. *Letters* 1: 171.

33. Twenty months of "visionary bustle" (chap. 4); four months "resolving to lose no more time" (chap. 4); ten months of "fruitless searches" (chap. 5); one year waiting for wings (chap. 6); three months of rain (chaps. 7–13); an indeterminate period of tunneling (chaps. 13–14).

34. Hawkins claims that "Johnson had meditated a second part, in which he meant to marry his hero, and place him in a state of permanent felicity" (p. 157). Such a sequel was in fact written by Ellis Cornelia Knight: *Dinarbas; A Tale: Being a Continuation of Rasselas, Prince of Abissinia* (London, 1790).

35. *Rambler* 29, *Works* 3: 160; *Rasselas,* chap. 49. Gwin Kolb (*Works* 16: 176) notes the connection with *Rambler* 29.

36. For a consistent reading of *Rasselas* as a comic demystification of the Romanticism exposed by the oriental tale, see Paul Fussell, *Samuel Johnson and the Life of Writing* (New York: Harcourt Brace Jovanovich, 1971), pp. 216–245.

37. See Donald M. Lockhart, "'The Fourth Son of the Mighty Emperor': The Ethiopian Background of Johnson's *Rasselas*," *PMLA* 78 (1963): 516–528; Arthur J. Weitzman, "More Light on *Rasselas:* The Background of the Egyptian Episodes," *Philological Quarterly* 48 (1969): 42–58.

38. *Annual Register* (1759), in Boulton, p. 147.

39. M. M. Bakhtin, *The Dialogic Imagination,* trans. Caryl Emerson and Michael Holquist (Austin: University of Texas Press, 1981), pp. 262–263.

40. Cf. Johnson on Shakespeare, *Works* 7: 64.

41. *Rambler* 205, *Works* 5: 305.

42. *Letters* 1: 178.

43. Definitions 6 and 5 in the *Dictionary.* I have commented on the complexities of these definitions in "Johnson and the Meaning of Life."

44. *BLJ* 4: 300. The reference is Matthew 25: 31–46.

45. The history of *Rasselas* criticism is surveyed by Edward Tomarken, *Johnson, Rasselas, and the Choice of Criticism* (Lexington: University Press of Kentucky, 1989).

46. *Lectures on the English Comic Writers* (1819), in *The Complete Works of William Hazlitt,* ed. P. P. Howe (London: J. M. Dent, 1931), 6: 102. The (mis)quotation is from Cowper's *Task,* 4.119, where the subject of "runs" is appropriately "fancy."

47. For Hazlitt's faith in the "sagacity" of imagination, see James Engell, *The Creative Imagination* (Cambridge, Mass.: Harvard University Press, 1981), pp. 197–214.

48. *Works* 7: 193.

49. "Preface to Shakespeare," *Works* 7: 74.

50. *Lives* 1: 163.

51. January 23, 1759, *Letters* 1: 181–182. Francis Barber, the young freed slave whom Johnson took under his wing, went off to sea in July 1758. Unhappy as a sailor, he came back to Johnson's household in 1760.

52. "Preface to Shakespeare," *Works* 7: 65.

8. The Theater of Mind

The epigraph is from *Boswell's Journal of a Tour to the Hebrides,* ed. F. A. Pottle and C. H. Bennett (New York: McGraw-Hill, 1962), p. 19.

1. *BLJ* 1: 101n.

2. See especially Michael Dobson, *The Making of the National Poet: Shakespeare, Adaptation, and Authorship, 1660–1769* (Oxford: Clarendon Press, 1992); Gary Taylor, *Reinventing Shakespeare: A Cultural History, from the*

Restoration to the Present (New York: Weidenfeld & Nicolson, 1989); and Jonathan Bate, *Shakespearean Constitutions: Politics, Theatre, Criticism 1730–1830* (Oxford: Clarendon Press, 1989).

3. On Tonson's claims to ownership of the plays, see Taylor, *Reinventing Shakespeare,* pp. 69–74; and Margreta de Grazia, *Shakespeare Verbatim: The Reproduction of Authenticity and the 1790 Apparatus* (Oxford: Clarendon Press, 1991), pp. 191–202. Arthur Sherbo describes the genesis of Johnson's edition in *Samuel Johnson, Editor of Shakespeare* (Urbana: University of Illinois Press, 1956), pp. 1–14.

4. Jean Georges Noverre, quoted by George Winchester Stone Jr. and George M. Kahrl, *David Garrick: A Critical Biography* (Carbondale: Southern Illinois University Press, 1979), p. 558; Garrick's death scene is quoted on p. 250, and his performance is analyzed on pp. 549–559. On Garrick's claim of authenticity, see Stephen Orgel, "The Authentic Shakespeare," *Representations* 21 (1988): 14–20.

5. George Winchester Stone Jr., "Garrick's Handling of *Macbeth,*" *Studies in Philology* 38 (1941): 615–617.

6. *Johnson on Shakespeare, Works* 7: 35. This edition is the source of all references in the text.

7. Shirley White Johnston, "Samuel Johnson's *Macbeth:* 'Fair is Foul,'" *Age of Johnson* 3 (1990): 189–230, compares the notes of the *Observations* unfavorably with Johnson's later editing of Shakespeare.

8. Elizabeth Montagu, *An Essay on the Writings and Genius of Shakespear* (London, 1769), p. 173.

9. *Poems,* p. 107.

10. *JM* 2: 314.

11. According to the *Dictionary,* "impress" means "1. To print by pressure; to stamp. 2. To fix deep. 3. To force into service."

12. *Poems,* p. 109.

13. *Dictionary.* This is the first definition, illustrated especially by Bacon. The two other definitions are "Conception; image in the mind; idea," and "Contrivance; scheme." Cf. Chapter 4.

14. *Midsummer Night's Dream,* V.i.7–17.

15. Samuel Taylor Coleridge, *Biographia Literaria,* chap. 13.

16. A similar contrast between Johnson and Romantic criticism forms the center of G. F. Parker's fine study, *Johnson's Shakespeare* (Oxford: Clarendon Press, 1989), to which I am indebted, though I differ from his implicit assumption—conveyed in frequent references to *our* Shakespeare or the way *we* read—that modern readers share a superior, more accurate understanding of the plays.

17. Johnson does appreciate the importance of grasping the whole, as the "Preface to Shakespeare" demonstrates: "Parts are not to be examined till the whole has been surveyed; there is a kind of intellectual remoteness nec-

essary for the comprehension of any great work in its full design and its true proportions; a close approach shews the smaller niceties, but the beauty of the whole is discerned no longer" (*Works* 7: 111). As this passage indicates, however, he views whole and part as two distinct objects of attention, not as reciprocally interrelated.

18. *JM* 1: 158 (from Mrs. Piozzi's *Anecdotes*).

19. *Works* 8: 1011, 704, 1045.

20. "Review of a Free Inquiry into the Nature and Origin of Evil," in *Johnson: Prose and Poetry,* ed. Mona Wilson (Cambridge, Mass.: Harvard University Press, 1951), p. 366.

21. The classic study of this tradition is Jean H. Hagstrum, *The Sister Arts: The Tradition of Literary Pictorialism and English Poetry from Dryden to Gray* (Chicago: University of Chicago Press, 1958). Relevant applications to Johnson are drawn by Donald J. Greene, "'Pictures to the Mind': Johnson and Imagery," in *Johnson, Boswell and Their Circle,* ed. M. Lascelles et al. (Oxford: Clarendon Press, 1965), pp. 137–158; and Lawrence Lipking, "Quick Poetic Eyes: Another Look at Literary Pictorialism," in *Articulate Images,* ed. Richard Wendorf (Minneapolis: University of Minnesota Press, 1983), pp. 3–25.

22. *Works* 16: 199. In the *Dictionary,* the final definition of "Virtue," "One of the orders of the celestial hierarchy," is illustrated by Tickell: "A winged *virtue* through th' etherial sky,/From orb to orb unwearied dost thou fly."

23. *Rambler* 168, *Works* 5: 127. Johnson mistakenly assigns the speech (*Macbeth,* I.v.48–52) to Macbeth.

24. Christopher Ricks, *The Force of Poetry* (Oxford: Clarendon Press, 1984), pp. 80–88.

25. *Works* 5: 128. As Johnson emphasizes, "words become low by the occasions to which they are applied" (p. 126), so that historical context as well as associations with "unpleasing images" (like the association of a knife with "butchers and cooks") determines their effect on native speakers; Shakespeare's language has been debased by later usage. Here and elsewhere, the view of language is explicitly Lockean.

26. *BLJ* 4: 25.

27. *BLJ* 1: 167; Jonas Barish, *The Antitheatrical Prejudice* (Berkeley: University of California Press, 1981), pp. 280, 296.

28. On the theatricality of mid-century English poetry, see "The Theater of Mind," chap. 12 of Martin Price, *To the Palace of Wisdom* (Carbondale: Southern Illinois University Press, 1964).

29. *BLJ* 4: 243.

30. *BLJ* 2: 85–86.

31. See Mrs. Piozzi's anecdote, *JM* 1: 186.

32. *Lives* 2: 229–230.

33. *Thraliana: The Diary of Mrs. Hester Lynch Thrale,* ed. K. C. Balderston (Oxford: Clarendon Press, 1942), 1: 179. On the importance of vacuity in

Johnson's thought, see Arieh Sachs, *Passionate Intelligence* (Baltimore: Johns Hopkins Press, 1967), pp. 3–19; and Charles H. Hinnant, *Samuel Johnson: An Analysis* (New York: St. Martin's, 1988), pp. 1–26.

34. *BLJ* 2: 86–87.

35. *Lives* 2: 230. William Edinger, *Samuel Johnson and Poetic Style* (Chicago: University of Chicago Press, 1977), discusses the place of "nature" and other terms in forming Johnson's tastes in poetry.

36. *Lives* 2: 229–230.

37. This power of healing is a central concern of Walter Jackson Bate, *The Achievement of Samuel Johnson* (New York: Oxford University Press, 1955).

38. *Poems,* p. 280.

39. *Poems,* p. 109.

40. *BLJ* 1: 196n.

41. *Poems,* p. 281.

42. *Rambler* 125, *Works* 4: 305.

43. *Poems,* p. 280. James L. Clifford, *Dictionary Johnson: Samuel Johnson's Middle Years* (New York: McGraw-Hill, 1979), pp. 1–14, describes the preparation and reception of *Irene.*

44. Aspasia to Irene, III.viii.1–5; *Poems,* pp. 321–322. Bertrand Bronson provides a full analysis of the background and theme of *Irene* in *Johnson Agonistes & Other Essays* (Cambridge: Cambridge University Press, 1946).

45. *JM* 1: 457.

46. Marcus Walsh argues that the *Dictionary* "is itself, in its many thousands of citations and glosses of Shakespearean usages, a major work of Shakespearean exegetical scholarship"; *Shakespeare, Milton, and Eighteenth-Century Literary Editing* (Cambridge: Cambridge University Press, 1997), p. 169.

47. See J. D. Fleeman, "Johnson's *Shakespeare* (1765): The Progress of a Subscription," in *Writers, Books, and Trade,* ed. O. M. Brack Jr. (New York: AMS, 1994), pp. 355–365.

48. *The Ghost,* III.801–802; *The Poetical Works of Charles Churchill,* ed. Douglas Grant (Oxford: Clarendon Press, 1956), p. 126.

49. Hawkins, p. 151.

50. "Proposals," *Works* 7: 57–58. On Johnson's use of his predecessors, so extensive as to make his edition the first Shakespeare variorum, see Sherbo, *Samuel Johnson, Editor of Shakespeare,* pp. 28–45; and de Grazia, *Shakespeare Verbatim,* pp. 209–214. Shirley White Johnston stresses Johnson's fair treatment of other editors in "From Preface to Practice: Samuel Johnson's Editorship of Shakespeare," in *Greene Centennial Studies,* ed. Paul Korshin and Robert R. Allen (Charlottesville: University Press of Virginia, 1984), pp. 250–270.

51. Both Bate, *Shakespearean Constitutions,* pp. 27–28, and Dobson, *The Making of the National Poet,* pp. 202–204, discuss *Harlequin's Invasion* (1759),

in which Harlequin is beaten off the stage with Shakespeare's help, and for which Garrick wrote the words of the patriotic song "Heart of Oak."

52. Introduction to *The World Displayed* (1759); *Samuel Johnson's Prefaces & Dedications,* ed. Allen T. Hazen (New Haven: Yale University Press, 1937), p. 228.

53. See, for instance, the introduction that Johnson wrote in 1760 for a committee report on clothing French prisoners of war; *Works* 10: 285–289. Greene discusses Johnson's attitude toward the war in *The Politics of Samuel Johnson,* pp. 155–169, 268–270.

54. September 9, 1758; *Works* 2: 317. In the collected edition of *The Idler* (1761), this essay was suppressed.

55. Though Gary Taylor, Jonathan Bate, Michael Dobson, and Gerald Newman, *The Rise of English Nationalism* (New York: St. Martin's, 1987), are justified in associating Johnson's early references to Shakespeare with cultural nationalism, each of them overlooks the dramatic turn away from nationalism in the "Preface to Shakespeare," which does not fit their presuppositions. Newman blunders when he writes that Charles Churchill "elevated 'SHAKESPEARE and JOHNSON' in the 'patriot hope' to 'make England great in Letters as in Arms'" (p. 126). In context, it is clear that Churchill is referring to *Ben* Jonson (*The Rosciad,* ll. 223–230; *Poetical Works,* p. 9).

56. See Christian Deelman, *The Great Shakespeare Jubilee* (New York: Viking, 1964); and Dobson, *The Making of the National Poet,* pp. 214–232.

57. Montagu, *Essay on Shakespear,* pp. 2, 198–199.

58. *BLJ* 2: 88. These remarks are not inconsistent with the comment, reported by William Seward, that the *Essay* "was *ad hominem,* that it was conclusive against Voltaire; and that she had done what she intended to do" (*JM* 2: 307).

59. R. D. Stock, *Samuel Johnson and Neoclassical Dramatic Theory* (Lincoln: University of Nebraska Press, 1973), compares the principles of the "Preface to Shakespeare" with those of other mid-century critics of Shakespeare.

60. On "nature," Jean H. Hagstrum, *Samuel Johnson's Literary Criticism* (Chicago: University of Chicago Press, 1967), pp. 56–75, is still a useful place to start.

61. W. R. Keast, "The Theoretical Foundations of Johnson's Criticism," in *Critics and Criticism,* ed. R. S. Crane (Chicago: University of Chicago Press, 1952), pp. 389–407.

62. *Rambler* 25, *Works* 3: 139. "A genius, whatever it be, is like fire in the flint, only to be produced by collision with a proper subject."

63. *Lives* 1: 2; *BLJ* 5: 35.

64. In the "Life of Dryden," Johnson would argue that this "model of encomiastick criticism" had never been equaled by the editors and admirers of Shakespeare (*Lives* 1: 412). Jean Hagstrum uses the same passage to begin

his discussion of authors and genius in *Samuel Johnson's Literary Criticism*, pp. 38–55.

65. *Rasselas,* chap. 44; *Works* 16: 150.

66. *Works* 8: 767. G. F. Parker concludes *Johnson's Shakespeare* with an analysis of Johnson's response to these lines (pp. 195–198).

67. *Macbeth,* I.vii.46–59.

68. Mary Wollstonecraft, whose views on the condition of women often resemble Johnson's, included five of his pieces in her anthology, *The Female Reader* (1789). In a conversation not long before his death, he had "treated her with particular kindness and attention." See James G. Basker, "Radical Affinities: Mary Wollstonecraft and Samuel Johnson," in *Tradition in Transition: Women Writers, Marginal Texts, and the Eighteenth-Century Canon,* ed. Alvaro Ribeiro and Basker (Oxford: Clarendon Press, 1996), pp. 41–55.

69. *King Henry VIII (All Is True),* IV.ii.160–173.

70. *Rambler* 60, *Works* 3: 318–319.

71. In *Samuel Johnson on Shakespeare: The Discipline of Criticism* (Athens: University of Georgia Press, 1991), pp. 27–34, Edward Tomarken argues that, by confusing Johnson's morality with didacticism, most critics miss the point of his remarks on Falstaff.

72. *The Diary of William Windham,* in *Letters of Samuel Johnson, LL.D.,* ed. G. B. Hill (Oxford: Clarendon Press, 1892), 2: 440.

73. "To tell the truth, as I felt no solicitude about this work, I receive no great comfort from its conclusion, but yet am well enough pleased that the publick has no farther claim upon me"; letter to Joseph Warton, October 9, 1765, *Letters* 1: 255–256.

74. Sherbo, *Samuel Johnson, Editor of Shakespeare,* pp. 102–113.

75. I discuss this poem, "*Gnōthi Seauton,*" in the next chapter.

76. *Lives* 2: 21.

77. *Lives* 3: 217.

9. Journeying Westward

The epigraph is from *The Traveller, or A Prospect of Society* (1764), ll. 429–430; *The Poems of Gray, Collins, and Goldsmith,* ed. Roger Lonsdale (London: Longmans, 1969), p. 656. These are among the lines that Johnson acknowledged having contributed to Goldsmith's poem (*BLJ* 2: 5–6).

1. *BLJ* 2: 35, 40.

2. *Works* 1: 77–78. W. Jackson Bate provides a moving description of this incipient breakdown in *Samuel Johnson* (New York: Harcourt Brace Jovanovich, 1977), pp. 371–389; and more recently it has been put in a larger context by John Wiltshire, *Samuel Johnson in the Medical World* (Cambridge: Cambridge University Press, 1991), pp. 40–50, 165–194.

3. David Erskine Baker, "Mr. Samuel Johnson, M.A.," in *The Companion to*

the Play-House (London, 1764). Baker's sketch, which influenced several other memoirs of Johnson, is reprinted in *The Early Biographies of Samuel Johnson,* ed. O. M. Brack Jr. and Robert Kelley (Iowa City: University of Iowa Press, 1974), pp. 5–7.

4. I have written about the problems of ending poetic careers in "Harmonium," in *The Life of the Poet* (Chicago: University of Chicago Press, 1981), pp. 65–137.

5. The expression comes from the final sentence of the Preface to the *Dictionary:* "I therefore dismiss it with frigid tranquillity, having little to fear or hope from censure or from praise."

6. *Works* 2: 314–315.

7. *Adventurer* 128, *Works* 2: 480.

8. The translation is Johnson's own, in the two *Ramblers* (24 and 28) he wrote on the "dictate, which, in the whole extent of its meaning, may be said to comprise all the speculation requisite to a moral agent" (*Works* 3: 130). In "What Was It Like to Be Johnson?" *The Age of Johnson* 1 (1987): 37, I have noted that Johnson's translation "suggests a division between the two acquaintances, the self that acts and is and the self that watches."

9. For a thorough study of the revisions, see Allen Reddick, *The Making of Johnson's Dictionary, 1746–1773* (Cambridge: Cambridge University Press, 1990), pp. 89–169.

10. *"Gnōthi Seauton"* 40–41; *Poems,* p. 189.

11. The phrase is from the *Dictionary* under "Climacter," which Johnson prefers as the noun, reserving "Climacterick" and "Climacterical" for adjectives. In the "Life of Addison," however, he refers to 1713 (the year of *Cato*) as "the grand climacterick of Addison's reputation" (*Lives* 2: 98). For an extended discussion of the term, see Pat Rogers, *Johnson and Boswell: The Transit of Caledonia* (Oxford: Clarendon Press, 1995), pp. 11–20.

12. "Ubi vanae species, umbraeque fugaces,/Et rerum volitant rarae per inane figurae"; 50–51. These lines clearly draw on Virgil's description of the underworld (*Aeneid* 6.268–269), where Dis supplies a model for Johnson's lord or ruler ("dominator"). The image of the *mind* as lord probably alludes to Statius, *Silvae* 2.2.131. These and other classical allusions are noted by Susie I. Tucker and Henry Gifford, "Johnson's Latin Poetry," *Neophilologus* 41 (1957): 218–219.

13. Johnson later associated *discordia concors* (22), a phrase he might have known from Manilius or Horace, with metaphysical wit: "a combination of dissimilar images, or discovery of occult resemblances in things apparently alike"; *Lives* 1: 20.

14. This description, taken from Daniel Heinsius, appears in Johnson's contribution to the *Harleian Catalogue* (1743–1745) and is quoted by Robert DeMaria Jr., *The Life of Samuel Johnson* (Oxford: Blackwell, 1993), p. 101. On

Scaliger see Anthony Grafton, *Joseph Scaliger: A Study in the History of Classical Scholarship,* 2 vols. (Oxford: Clarendon Press, 1983, 1993).

15. Scaliger's Latin epigram on lexicographers, which Johnson also refers to in the Preface to the *Dictionary,* had been quoted in *Gentleman's Magazine* 18 (1748): 8. It is printed in *Poems,* p. 187.

16. See the introduction by Thomas M. Curley to his edition of *A Course of Lectures on the English Law* (Oxford: Clarendon Press, 1986), 1: 20–21.

17. E. L. McAdam Jr., who discovered the manuscript of the lectures, confidently assigns many passages to Johnson on stylistic grounds in *Dr. Johnson and the English Law* (Syracuse: Syracuse University Press, 1951), pp. 65–122, but Curley warns of the dangers of this procedure and shows that at least one of McAdam's attributions to Johnson is clearly mistaken (*A Course of Lectures,* pp. 7–8).

18. *Works* 5: 320.

19. Hawkins' *Life of Johnson* contains an impressive "catalogue of publications projected by him at different periods" (p. 46); among the poems are "Visions" of Sloth and Nonsense, but no epic (pp. 284–286).

20. On "alarming crisis," see Donald Greene's note in *Works* 10: 317. This edition is the source of references in the text.

21. *JM* 1: 173.

22. *Works* 10: 341n. Some of Johnson's argument follows the line of a speech in the House of Commons by Richard Rigby (10: 338n.). John Cannon, *Samuel Johnson and the Politics of Hanoverian England* (Oxford: Clarendon Press, 1994), pp. 71–78, offers a useful survey of the issues.

23. John Wilkes, in Boulton, p. 211.

24. *BLJ* 2: 316; Joseph Towers, in Boulton, pp. 225, 217. On Towers' own dissenting background, see J. C. D. Clark, *Samuel Johnson* (Cambridge: Cambridge University Press, 1994), pp. 226–228.

25. Donald J. Greene, *The Politics of Samuel Johnson,* 2d ed. (Athens: University of Georgia Press, 1990), p. 257.

26. Clark, *Samuel Johnson,* pp. 7–9.

27. *Works* 10: 343. Cf. Thomas Reinert, *Regulating Confusion: Samuel Johnson and the Crowd* (Durham: Duke University Press, 1996): "Johnson's political pamphlets begin complex and skeptical, but they end simple and authoritarian" (p. 161).

28. *Letters* 2: 185. The canceled paragraphs are printed in *Works* 10: 455.

29. Earl Wasserman, "The Inherent Values of Eighteenth-Century Personification," *PMLA* 65 (1950): 435–463, assembles many descriptions of this effect.

30. James T. Boulton reviews both the political and rhetorical issues at stake for Junius and Johnson in *The Language of Politics in the Age of Wilkes and Burke* (London: Routledge & Kegan Paul, 1963), pp. 16–51.

31. *Works* 10: 386. Unlike modern gutters, eighteenth-century kennels, or watercourses, were often in the middle of the street.

32. See J. D. Fleeman, "Dr. Johnson and Henry Thrale, M.P.," in *Johnson, Boswell, and Their Circle,* ed. M. Lascelles et al. (Oxford: Clarendon Press, 1965), pp. 170–189.

33. *Thraliana: The Diary of Mrs. Hester Lynch Thrale,* ed. K. C. Balderston (Oxford: Clarendon Press, 1942), 1: 115.

34. When the administration struck out a part of *Taxation No Tyranny,* Johnson told Boswell, "It was their business. If an architect says, I will build five stories, and the man who employs him says, I will have only three, the employer is to decide"; *BLJ* 2: 313.

35. *The Practice and Representation of Reading in England,* ed. James Raven, Helen Small, and Naomi Tadmor (Cambridge: Cambridge University Press, 1996), includes four essays on eighteenth-century practices of reading as well as a general introduction.

36. See Reddick, *The Making of Johnson's Dictionary,* pp. 141–169.

37. Reddick, pp. 159–160, provides a context for this quotation. Pearson's classic *Exposition of the Creed* (1659) was one of Johnson's favorite theological works.

38. This is the first sense in the *Dictionary,* illustrated from Revelations, Proverbs, and *Coriolanus.*

39. Sermon 24, the second of the two "political sermons"; *Works* 14: 256. 259. It cannot be dated with certainty, but we do know that some of Johnson's sermons were written in 1777 (*Works* 1: 276–279; 14: xxi–xxix).

40. Reinert analyzes Johnson's attack on the "rabble" in *Regulating Confusion,* pp. 153–159.

41. *Works* 10: 393–394. Christine Gerrard discusses Johnson's changing attitudes toward patriotism in *The Patriot Opposition to Walpole: Politics, Poetry, and National Myth, 1725–1742* (Oxford: Clarendon Press, 1994), pp. 230–247.

42. *Works* 10: 344.

43. To Hester Thrale, June 12, 1780; *Letters* 3: 273. The context is the Gordon riots, a time when Johnson frequently uses the word.

44. Johnson's association of rabblement and stridor is evinced in *A Journey to the Western Islands,* which describes a chieftain's retinue, "with their arms rattling," as "that animating rabble" (*Works* 9: 90). Though all editions agree on this reading, J. D. Fleeman, in his peerless edition of *A Journey to the Western Islands of Scotland* (Oxford: Clarendon Press, 1985), pp. 74, 145, accepts L. F. Powell's suggestion that "rabble" ought to be "rattle." Page references in the text subsequently refer to Fleeman's edition.

45. "Prologue to Goldsmith's *The Good Natur'd Man,*" *Poems,* p. 127.

46. Geoffrey Carnall, "A Conservative Mind under Stress: Aspects of John-

son's Political Writings," in *Re-Viewing Samuel Johnson,* ed. Nalini Jain (Bombay: Popular Prakashan, 1991), p. 39.

47. The calculation is based on Benjamin Franklin's *Observations Concerning the Increase of Mankind and the Peopling of Countries* (1751), which Johnson had also used earlier to gibe that Whigs "multiply with the fecundity of their own rattle-snakes" (*Works* 10: 414). Johnson takes these numbers to be a threat, not a firm computation.

48. *Taxation No Tyranny; Works* 10: 455. Boswell preserved five proof pages and transcribed them in *BLJ* 2: 313–315; see also Greene's note in *Works* 10: 409–411.

49. *BLJ* 2: 170–171 (March 31, 1772).

50. *Lives* 2: 146.

51. *BLJ* 3: 262. Johnson's defense of subordination against "an incipient breakdown of consensus" is analyzed by Leo Damrosch, *Fictions of Reality in the Age of Hume and Johnson* (Madison: University of Wisconsin Press, 1989), pp. 52–57.

52. *BLJ* 3: 301–302.

53. *Idler* 97, *Works* 2: 298, 300. On Johnson's relation to eighteenth-century views of travel, see Thomas M. Curley, *Samuel Johnson and the Age of Travel* (Athens: University of Georgia Press, 1976); and Charles L. Batten, *Pleasurable Instruction: Form and Convention in Eighteenth-Century Travel Literature* (Berkeley: University of California Press, 1978).

54. Thomas Jemielty examines this aim in "Dr. Johnson and the Uses of Travel," *Philological Quarterly* 51 (1972): 448–459.

55. According to J. D. Fleeman, "Johnson's documentary letters to Mrs Thrale" were probably "collateral descendants from the notebooks rather than intermediate sources for the eventual narrative manuscript of the *Journey.* Nevertheless there is presumptive evidence that the letters were consulted when the manuscript of the *Journey* was being written up" (*Journey,* p. 38). As Johnson himself points out, he thinks about the Thrales so often, in the Hebrides, that "I travel with my mind too much at home, and perhaps miss many things observable" (*Letters* 2: 95). Pat Rogers compares the letters with the *Journey* in *Johnson and Boswell,* pp. 108–138.

56. Joseph [Giuseppe] Baretti, *A Journey from London to Genoa, through England, Portugal, Spain and France* (London, 1770), 1: v–vi.

57. To Hester Thrale, July 20, 1770; *Letters* 1: 348.

58. E.g., "The Doctor hated Scotland; that was the *master-passion,* and it scorned all restraints;" Donald McNicol (1779), in Boulton, p. 243. Many recent studies also assume that "Johnson's real purpose in *A Journey* is to provide a critique of Scottish culture as a whole"; Karen O'Brien, "Johnson's View of the Scottish Enlightenment in *A Journey to the Western Islands of Scotland,*" *The Age of Johnson* 4 (1991): 60.

59. For example, see *Works* 9: 24.

60. John Radner describes "The Significance of Johnson's Changing Views of the Hebrides" in *The Unknown Samuel Johnson,* ed. John J. Burke and Donald Kay (Madison: University of Wisconsin Press, 1983), pp. 131–149.

61. Clark, *Samuel Johnson,* p. 223. Clark's explanation of the *Journey* as Johnson's expiation of his guilt for not supporting the Stuart cause more actively (p. 225) continues the flight of fancy.

62. The act proscribed both Highland dress and weapons; in each case Johnson perceives both benefits and costs (*Works* 9: 51–52, 90–92).

63. *BLJ* 2: 290.

64. For Johnson's attack on Macpherson's claim that poems he published were translations of Ossian, an ancient Gaelic bard, see *Letters* 2: 168–169, 170, 176–178, 180–181.

65. *BLJ* 5: 141.

66. "Civilisation," in the *Dictionary,* refers only to the law "which renders a criminal process civil." I have compared eighteenth-century French and English ideas of civilization in "M. Johnson and Mr. Rousseau," *Common Knowledge* 3 (Winter 1994): 109–126.

67. *The Deserted Village,* ll. 427–430; Lonsdale, *The Poems of Gray, Collins, and Goldsmith,* p. 694. Johnson marked these lines as his own in Boswell's copy (*BLJ* 2: 7).

68. *BLJ* 2: 217–219.

69. Quoted in the *Dictionary* as its one illustration of "dereliction."

70. September 30, 1773; *Letters* 2: 94.

71. See Harlan Lane, *When the Mind Hears: A History of the Deaf* (New York: Random House, 1984). As Lane points out, Johnson's notice of Braidwood "insured his reputation throughout the Continent" (p. 107).

72. Boswell's manuscript "Remarks" on Johnson's *Journey;* quoted by Fleeman, p. 247.

10. Touching the Shore

The epigraph is Odysseus to Athene, *Odyssey* 13.234.

1. *Morning Chronicle,* April 14, 1777; quoted by Thomas F. Bonnell, "John Bell's *Poets of Great Britain:* The 'Little Trifling Edition' Revisited," *Modern Philology* 85 (1987): 130.

2. On Bell's versatility, see Stanley Morison, *John Bell, 1745–1831: Bookseller, Printer, Publisher, Typefounder, Journalist, &c* (London: First Edition Club, 1930). As Bonnell points out, both in the article cited above and in "Bookselling and Canon-Making: The Trade Rivalry over the English Poets, 1776–1783," *Studies in Eighteenth-Century Culture* 19 (1989): 53–69, the booksellers managed to keep Bell's *Poets* from being sold in London bookshops but could not prevent its commercial success. An earlier Scottish edition of

The British Poets in 44 volumes (1773–1776) seems to have been effectively barred from wide distribution.

3. Letter from Edward Dilly to Boswell, September 26, 1777; *BLJ* 3: 110.

4. *Letters* 3: 20.

5. Frances Boscawen to Mary Delany, quoted by G. B. Hill in *Lives* 1: xxvi. Volume and page numbers in the text of this chapter refer to this edition.

6. *Letters* 3: 347.

7. I have discussed this process in *The Ordering of the Arts in Eighteenth-Century England* (Princeton: Princeton University Press, 1970). See also Douglas Lane Patey, "The Eighteenth Century Invents the Canon," *Modern Language Studies* 18 (1988): 17–37.

8. *BLJ* 3: 137.

9. *Rambler* 93, *Works* 4: 130.

10. Thomas F. Bonnell itemizes Bell's sources in "Patchwork and Piracy: John Bell's 'Connected System of Biography' and the Use of Johnson's *Prefaces*," *Studies in Bibliography* 48 (1995): 193–228.

11. David Piper gives a detailed description of this gallery in "The Chesterfield House Library Portraits," in *Evidence in Literary Scholarship,* ed. René Wellek and Alvaro Ribeiro (Oxford: Clarendon Press, 1979), pp. 179–195.

12. Johnson's note, February 19, 1783, on a receipt for payment from the booksellers; *BLJ* 4: 35n. In 1780 he had complained to John Nichols about "your Edition, which is very impudently called mine"; *Letters* 3: 226.

13. In "Copyright and the Invention of Tradition," *Eighteenth-Century Studies* 26 (Fall 1992): 1–27, Trevor Ross associates the emergence of both literary tradition and the modern author with debates on copyright.

14. Later in 1781, when the *Prefaces* were republished as the *Lives,* the sequence was altered and ended with Lyttelton. For parallel charts of the two sequences, see Annette Wheeler Cafarelli, *Prose in the Age of Poets: Romanticism and Biographical Narrative from Johnson to De Quincey* (Philadelphia: University of Pennsylvania Press, 1990), pp. 206–208.

15. When Boswell, disappointed that the booksellers had chosen the poets about whom Johnson would write, wondered "if he would do this to any dunce's works, if they should ask him," Johnson replied, "Yes, Sir; and *say* he was a dunce"; *BLJ* 3: 137.

16. *Idler* 60, *Works* 2: 187. Minim is Johnson's beau ideal of critical clichés.

17. Johnson's emphasis on *thinking about* (not merely evoking) the biographical subject is commented on by Catherine N. Parke, *Samuel Johnson and Biographical Thinking* (Columbia: University of Missouri Press, 1991), pp. 131–134.

18. *Boswell's Journal of a Tour to the Hebrides,* ed. F. A. Pottle and C. H. Bennett (New York: McGraw-Hill, 1962), pp. 202–204 (September 22, 1773).

19. *Rambler* 60, *Works* 3: 321.

20. "There has often been observed a manifest and striking contrariety between the life of an author and his writings"; *Rambler* 14; *Works* 3: 74.

21. *BLJ* 2: 166. John B. Radner, "'A Very Exact Picture of His Life': Johnson's Role in Writing the *Life of Johnson,*" *Age of Johnson* 7 (1996): 299–342, discusses the tension between biographer and subject.

22. *Rambler* 60, *Works* 3: 323.

23. These sources are surveyed by Pat Rogers, "Johnson's *Lives of the Poets* and the Biographic Dictionaries," *Review of English Studies,* n.s. 31 (1980): 149–171.

24. On Johnson's reliance on Ruffhead's *Life of Pope,* see Frederick W. Hilles, "The Making of *The Life of Pope,*" in *New Light on Dr. Johnson* (New Haven: Yale University Press, 1959), pp. 263–267.

25. *BLJ* 1: 425. I have discussed the relations of Bayle and perpetual commentary to Johnson in *The Ordering of the Arts,* pp. 76–83, 426–434. Cf. Martin Maner, *The Philosophical Biographer: Doubt and Dialectic in Johnson's Lives of the Poets* (Athens: University of Georgia Press, 1988), pp. 43–46; and Charles H. Hinnant, *"Steel for the Mind": Samuel Johnson and Critical Discourse* (Newark: University of Delaware Press, 1994), pp. 26–30.

26. In the life of Browne that he wrote for an edition of *Christian Morals* (1756), Johnson indicates his own interest in revising "Enquiries into vulgar and common Errours" (*Pseudodoxia Epidemica*): "It might now be proper . . . to reprint it with notes, partly supplemental, and partly emendatory, to subjoin those discoveries which the industry of the last age has made, and correct those mistakes which the author has committed not by idleness or negligence, but for want of Boyle's and Newton's philosophy"; *Works* (1846) 2: 373.

27. Actually Philips was seventy-four.

28. I have written about this pattern at length in *The Life of the Poet: Beginning and Ending Poetic Careers* (Chicago: University of Chicago Press, 1981).

29. *JM* 2: 287.

30. Pamphilus (Johnson) in *Gentleman's Magazine* 8 (1738): 537.

31. See Chapter 4 above. The artistic influence of "The Choice of Hercules" has been studied by Erwin Panofsky, *Hercules am Scheidewege* (Leipzig and Berlin, 1930). In "Johnson's *Rasselas:* Implicit Contexts," *Journal of English and Germanic Philology* 74 (1975): 1–25, Earl Wasserman contends that Cebes and Prodicus supply "implicit norms" for Johnson's narratives.

32. According to Johnson's preface to *The Preceptor,* both fables "are of the highest Authority, in the ancient *Pagan* World" (*Prefaces and Dedications,* p. 188). When Johnson recommended a curriculum to his cousin Samuel Ford in 1735, he headed the list with Cebes and also included Xenophon, whose *Memorabilia* preserved "The Choice" (*Letters* 1: 11–12).

33. Carey McIntosh notes that Johnson makes choice "the dominating

theme of both these fictions"; *The Choice of Life: Samuel Johnson and the World of Fiction* (New Haven: Yale University Press, 1973), p. 111.

34. "Collective sequence" is Annette Wheeler Cafarelli's term for the genre of the *Lives,* in *Prose in the Age of Poets,* pp. 30–69.

35. *The Lay Monk,* a collaboration between Blackmore and John Hughes, borrowed the idea of describing members of a club from *The Spectator,* to which it aimed to be a sequel; the character of Mr. Johnson may be based in part on Addison. The collected edition was called *The Lay-Monastery.*

36. *Lives* 2: 246, 244. Hill's notes point out that the words "constellation" and "gigantick" were elsewhere applied to Samuel Johnson himself.

37. Boswell maintains that "We trace Johnson's own character in his observations on Blackmore's 'magnanimity as an authour,'" and Mrs. Thrale wrote Johnson that he had rescued Blackmore "a little for love of his Christianity, a little for love of his physick, a little for love of his courage—and a little for love of contradiction"; *BLJ* 4: 55.

38. Frances d'Arblay, *Memoirs of Doctor Burney* (London, 1832), 2: 176–179.

39. *Rambler* 208, *Works* 5: 319.

40. "Preface to Shakespeare," *Works* 7: 67, 61.

41. *Rambler* 23, *Works* 3: 128.

42. *Adventurer* 138, *Works* 2: 496.

43. See Donald J. Greene, "'Pictures to the Mind': Johnson and Imagery," in *Johnson, Boswell and Their Circle,* ed. M. Lascelles et al. (Oxford: Clarendon Press, 1965), pp. 137–158. Johnson's understanding of metaphor is discussed by Jean Hagstrum, *Samuel Johnson's Literary Criticism* (Chicago: University of Chicago Press, 1967), pp. 114–122; Leopold Damrosch, *The Uses of Johnson's Criticism* (Charlottesville: University of Virginia Press, 1976), pp. 150–156; and Hinnant, *"Steel for the Mind,"* pp. 203–209. On the relation between "literal-mindedness" and "imagination," see Chapter 8, above.

44. Though Johnson praised Burke's *Essay on the Sublime and Beautiful* (1757) as "an example of true criticism," a work that shows "how terrour is impressed on the human heart" (*BLJ* 2: 90), in the *Dictionary* and elsewhere he defines the sublime as "The grand or lofty stile," associated with the general and not with the obscure. Thomas Weiskel, *The Romantic Sublime* (Baltimore: Johns Hopkins University Press, 1976), p. 108, points out that Johnson's dislike of obscurity made him unsympathetic to Collins' odes.

45. Thomas De Quincey, "Postscript respecting Johnson's Life of Milton" (1859), in Boulton, pp. 314–315.

46. See Stephen Fix, "Johnson and the 'Duty' of Reading *Paradise Lost,*" *ELH* 52 (1985): 649–671.

47. "The logic of [Johnson's] malignity is simply this: that he applies to Milton, as if separately and specially true of *him,* a rule abstracted from

human experience spread over the total field of civilisation. All nations are here on a level" (De Quincey, "Postscript," p. 314). De Quincey curiously echoes Hazlitt's well-known charge that Wordsworth's muse "is a levelling one. It proceeds on a principle of equality, and strives to reduce all things to the same standard"; *The Spirit of the Age* (1825), in *The Complete Works of William Hazlitt,* ed. P. P. Howe (London: J. M. Dent, 1931), 11: 87.

48. Clarence Tracy stresses Johnson's appeal to "the vulgar" or ungenteel in "Johnson and the Common Reader," *Dalhousie Review* 57 (1977): 405–423. In "Inventing the Common Reader: Samuel Johnson and the Canon," in *Interpretation and Cultural History,* ed. Joan H. Pittock and Andrew Wear (New York: St. Martin's, 1991), pp. 153–174, I discuss the historical place of Johnson's imagined reader in the organization of knowledge.

49. Wordsworth, "Preface to *Lyrical Ballads*" (1800). Johnson's view that Dryden reached "the utmost limits of our language" (which Gray exceeded) is consistent with his description of Dryden's wit: "He delighted to tread upon the brink of meaning, where light and darkness begin to mingle; to approach the precipice of absurdity, and hover over the abyss of unideal vacancy" (*Lives* 1: 460).

50. *Rasselas,* chap. 11; *Works* 16: 46.

51. Francis Blackburne (1780), in Boulton, p. 283.

52. Robert Folkenflik, *Samuel Johnson, Biographer* (Ithaca: Cornell University Press, 1978), p. 118–173, discusses the ways in which Johnson did and did not draw connections between art and life. James L. Battersby, "Life, Art, and the *Lives of the Poets,*" in *Domestick Privacies: Samuel Johnson and the Art of Biography,* ed. David Wheeler (Lexington: University Press of Kentucky, 1987), pp. 26–56, suggests that Johnson is most interested in the "career author," the author who has shaped the sequence of works as a whole, rather than in the "real," "dramatized," or "implied" author.

53. Cafarelli discusses Romantic departures from Johnson in *Prose in the Age of Poets,* pp. 70–112.

54. *Rambler* 14, *Works* 3: 74.

55. "These writings may improve mankind when his failings shall be forgotten" (*Lives* 2: 381). For Bacon, see *Adventurer* 131, *Works* 2: 482–483.

56. The debate "between noumenal and phenomenal interpretations of poetry" is summarized in Lipking, *The Ordering of the Arts,* pp. 466–472.

57. *Gentleman's Magazine* 10 (1740): 612. The information about "Barretier," who had died earlier in 1740, was supplemented in two later issues of the magazine, and all the accounts were gathered in *An Account of the Life of John Philip Barretier* (1744).

58. *Journal of a Tour to the Hebrides,* p. 204.

59. Hagstrum, *Samuel Johnson's Literary Criticism,* argues that Johnson's insistence on the canon of sincerity is grounded on his assumption that art

ought to communicate "simple universals that move all men everywhere" (p. 47), not fugitive or unnatural emotions.

60. "The Grounds of Criticism in Poetry" (1704), in *The Critical Works of John Dennis,* ed. E. N. Hooker (Baltimore: Johns Hopkins Press, 1939), 1: 335–336.

61. Thomas Warton, *The History of English Poetry* (1774–1781), 3: 501. Lipking, *The Ordering of the Arts,* pp. 352–462, discusses Warton's *History* and Johnson's *Lives* as complementary efforts to order English poetry.

62. See M. H. Abrams, "Dr. Johnson's Spectacles," in *New Light on Dr. Johnson,* ed. F. W. Hilles (New Haven: Yale University Press, 1959), pp. 177–187.

63. "Lines Written in Ridicule of Thomas Warton's Poems" (1777); *Poems,* p. 206. Cf. Chapter 4, above.

64. In a review of *The Traveller,* Johnson wrote that "since the death of Pope, it will not be easy to find anything equal" (*Critical Review,* December 1764, p. 462). According to J. C. D. Clark, *Samuel Johnson* (Cambridge: Cambridge University Press, 1994), the *Lives* defends an already fading Anglo-Latin tradition (Clark ignores the fact that Johnson's own additions, with the exception of Yalden, do not belong to that tradition), but the canon-making strategy was doomed to fail, since "within a decade, Wordsworth and Coleridge had begun the process which eventually sank a whole culture" (p. 32). For a corrective of this willfully anachronistic view of literary history, see Robert J. Griffin, *Wordsworth's Pope: A Study in Literary Historiography* (Cambridge: Cambridge University Press, 1995).

65. *Letters* 4: 116–117.

66. *Lives* 1: 389–392. Though Johnson distrusted this account, concocted by Elizabeth Thomas and later refuted by Malone, he prints it in full.

67. An unsigned review of the first volumes of the *Lives* begins by stressing the national interest: "As the general character of every polished nation depends in a great measure on its poetical productions, too much care cannot be taken, in works of this nature, to impress on foreigners a proper idea of their merit. This task was perhaps never so well executed as in the performance before us" (*Critical Review,* May 1779; in Boulton, p. 270).

68. *The Traveller, or A Prospect of Society* (1764), ll. 327–328, 339–340; *The Poems of Gray, Collins, and Goldsmith,* ed. Roger Lonsdale (London: Longmans, 1969), p. 650. According to Boswell, Johnson recited the passage "with such energy, that the tear started into his eye" (*BLJ* 5: 344).

69. Diary, April 20, 1778; *Works* 1: 292.

70. Walter B. C. Watkins, *Johnson and English Poetry before 1660* (Princeton: Princeton University Press, 1936), substantiates Johnson's familiarity with early poetry.

71. Johnson acknowledges the early critical "hints" given by Webbe,

Puttenham, Jonson, and Cowley but contends that "Dryden's *Essay on Dramatick Poetry* was the first regular and valuable treatise on the art of writing" (1: 411).

72. *BLJ* 4: 38.

73. Lipking, *The Ordering of the Arts*, pp. 430–433, suggests that Johnson is correcting the superficial critical views of Richard Hurd, whose *Select Works of Mr. A. Cowley* (1772) was still in print.

74. Comparing Johnson on Warton to Pope on Dennis, Mrs. Piozzi comments that "he could not bear to leave unoffended a cotemporary Scholar"; *Thraliana: The Diary of Mrs. Hester Lynch Thrale*, ed. K. C. Balderston (Oxford: Clarendon Press, 1942), 2: 621.

75. *Rambler* 60, *Works* 3: 319.

76. Several critics—among them Stephen Fix, "Distant Genius: Johnson and the Art of Milton's Life," *Modern Philology* 81 (1984): 244–264; Dustin Griffin, *Regaining Paradise: Milton and the Eighteenth Century* (Cambridge: Cambridge University Press, 1986), pp. 203–216; and Tim Fulford, *Landscape, Liberty and Authority* (Cambridge: Cambridge University Press, 1996), pp. 92–97—have made strong cases—in my opinion *too* strong—for Johnson's unwilling identification with Milton.

77. Dryden compared Homer and Virgil in the preface to *Fables Ancient and Modern* (1700), in *Essays of John Dryden*, ed. W. P. Ker (Oxford: Clarendon Press, 1900), 2: 251–254; Pope, in the Preface to *The Iliad* (1715), *Poems of Alexander Pope* (New Haven: Yale University Press, 1967), 7: 12. Johnson discusses Dryden's comparison in the "Life of Dryden" (1: 447–448). Since Dryden had translated Virgil, and Pope Homer, the parallel was inevitable, but not the association of Dryden with Homer and Pope with Virgil.

78. *BLJ* 4: 45.

79. *The Works of John Dryden* (Berkeley: University of California Press, 1987), 6: 807.

80. *Rambler* 208, *Works* 5: 319.

81. *Works* 1: 304.

82. Lionel Kelly, "Beckett's *Human Wishes*," in *The Ideal Core of the Onion: Reading Beckett Archives*, ed. John Pilling and Mary Bryden (Bristol: Beckett International Foundation, 1992), pp. 21–44, provides a thorough review of Johnson's importance to Beckett.

83. "On the Death of Dr Robert Levet," *Poems*, pp. 233–235.

84. *Thraliana* 1: 532; April 18, 1782. John Wiltshire, *Samuel Johnson in the Medical World* (Cambridge: Cambridge University Press, 1991), pp. 195–222, provides a thorough review of Levet's practice as an unlicensed physician.

85. The importance of the parable of the talents for Johnson is stressed by Paul Fussell, *Samuel Johnson and the Life of Writing* (New York: Harcourt Brace Jovanovich, 1971), pp. 95–97, 130.

86. *Poems,* p. 234. Cf. Gray's "Elegy," ll. 29 ff.: "Let not Ambition mock their useful toil.," etc. As Wiltshire points out, the title *Dr* Robert Levet, in the heading of Johnson's poem, suggests "an open defiance, it might seem, of professional protocol" (p. 206). In printings after Johnson's death, *Dr* was changed to *Mr.*

87. "In Rivum a Mola Stoana Lichfeldiæ diffluentem" (November 1784?), *Poems,* p. 261.

88. "Translation of Horace 'Odes,' Book IV.vii" (November 1784), *Poems,* p. 265. Samuel Beckett copied out all of this version in a manuscript book of *Human Wishes* (Kelly, "Beckett's *Human Wishes,*" p. 28).

89. Niall Rudd, *Lines of Enquiry* (Cambridge: Cambridge University Press, 1976), in an analysis of many translations of Horace's ode, considers Johnson's substitution "harmful," since it "diminishes the Roman element in the poem" (p. 197); but Johnson's verses are not about Rome.

11. The Life to Come

The epigraph is from Samuel Beckett, *Endgame* (New York: Grove Press, 1958), p. 49.

1. *JM* 1: 356.

2. See Isobel Grundy, "Samuel Johnson: A Writer of Lives Looks at Death," *Modern Language Review* 79 (1984): 257–265.

3. *The Spectator,* ed. Donald F. Bond (Oxford: Clarendon Press, 1965), 3: 299 (no. 349).

4. *Lives* 2: 117. "See in what peace a Christian can die" is Edward Young's reverential version; *Conjectures on Original Composition* (1759), ed. Edith Morley (Manchester: Manchester University Press, 1918), p. 45.

5. "Scarce any man dies in publick, but with apparent resolution; from that desire of praise which never quits us"; Johnson to Boswell, *BLJ* 3: 154. O. M. Brack Jr., "The Death of Samuel Johnson and the *Ars Moriendi* Tradition," *Cithera* 19 (1980): 3–15, shows the weight put on last words.

6. *BLJ* 2: 106; 3: 153. Ingeniously adapting Hume's own argument against belief in miracles, Johnson refused to believe in the sincerity of Hume's composure.

7. *The Oxford Book of Death,* ed. D. J. Enright (New York: Oxford University Press, 1983), quotes Johnson more often than anyone but Shakespeare.

8. *Adventurer* 120, *Works* 2: 470.

9. Johnson's fullest and most impassioned testament of faith in immortality is the funeral sermon he wrote for his wife in 1752; *Works* 14: 261–271.

10. *BLJ* 4: 299. Jean Hagstrum, "On Johnson's Fear of Death," *ELH* 14 (1947): 308–319, emphasizes the orthodoxy of such dread.

11. *JM* 2: 202.

12. *Lives* 1: 378.

13. See Paul J. Korshin, "Johnson's Last Days: Some Facts and Problems," in *Johnson after Two Hundred Years,* ed. Korshin (Philadelphia: University of Pennsylvania Press, 1986), pp. 55–76.

14. William Wordsworth, "Resolution and Independence," line 117 (1820).

15. *JM* 2: 206. Some evidence that Johnson himself, near the end, may have had a conversion experience is debated by Maurice Quinlan, "The Rumor of Dr. Johnson's Conversion," *Review of Religion* 12 (1948): 243–261; and Donald Greene, "Dr. Johnson's 'Late Conversion,'" in *Johnsonian Studies,* ed. Magdi Wahba (Cairo, 1962), pp. 61–92.

16. *BLJ* 4: 417–418. Cf. the narrative by John Hoole, *JM* 2: 159. As Korshin points out ("Johnson's Last Days," pp. 71–72), Boswell relied on the testimony of Johnson's black servant, Francis Barber, who was present at the time.

17. *BLJ* 4: 417.

18. *BLJ* 4: 419.

19. *The Early Biographies of Samuel Johnson,* ed. O. M. Brack Jr. and Robert E. Kelley (Iowa City: University of Iowa Press, 1974), p. 122.

20. Hawkins, p. 274. Francesco Sastres, to whom the words were addressed, was a good friend in Johnson's final years. On the image of the gladiator, cf. *BLJ* 2: 106.

21. Hawkins, p. 275.

22. *BLJ* 1: 13.

23. Leo Braudy, *The Frenzy of Renown: Fame and its History* (New York: Oxford University Press, 1986), pp. 380–389.

24. Thomas Babington Macaulay, *Critical and Historical Essays* (London: Longman, 1865), 1: 407. J. W. Croker's edition of Boswell's *Life of Johnson* provoked the review (*Edinburgh Review,* September 1831).

25. Clive Bell, *Civilization: An Essay* (New York: Harcourt, Brace, 1928), p. 177.

26. William Makepeace Thackeray, *Vanity Fair* (1847–48), chap. 1.

27. Leslie Stephen, *Samuel Johnson* (New York: Harper & Brothers, 1879), pp. 95 ff. As Stephen concedes, the "dictator" is largely Boswell's creation, not Johnson's (p. 142).

28. Deirdre Lynch, "'Beating the Track of the Alphabet': Samuel Johnson, Tourism, and the ABCs of Modern Authority," *ELH* 57 (1990): 357–405, views the ironies and contradictions she traces in Johnson's authority as a metaphysical dismantling of literary monuments.

29. See Donald J. Greene, "The Development of the Johnson Canon," in *Restoration and Eighteenth-Century Literature,* ed. Carroll Camden (Chicago: University of Chicago Press, 1963), pp. 407–427.

30. *Johnson's Chief Lives of the Poets* (New York: Henry Holt, 1889), p. v.

31. This phrase concludes the first paragraph of the title essay (1925) of *The Common Reader* (New York: Harcourt, Brace, 1948), p. 11.

32. Virginia Woolf, *The Common Reader,* Second Series, p. 294.

33. Beth Carole Rosenberg, *Virginia Woolf and Samuel Johnson: Common Readers* (New York: St. Martin's, 1995), associates both writers with a dialogic or conversational mode that leaves an opening for readers. I compare Woolf with Johnson in "Inventing the Common Reader: Samuel Johnson and the Canon," in *Interpretation and Cultural History,* ed. Joan H. Pittock and Andrew Wear (New York: St. Martin's, 1991), pp. 171–173.

34. John Scott, *Critical Essays on some of the Poems of several English Poets* (London, 1785), p. vi. See Herman W. Liebert, *Johnson's Last Literary Project* (New Haven: privately printed, 1948).